T0028865

"Through diligent research, brilliant insights, and clear, incisive writing, Streshinsky and Klaus have deepened our understanding of Robert Oppenheimer's emotional life and loves. To comprehend his fascinating complexity, readers interested in the 20th century's most intriguing American scientist must now supplement the many biographical Oppenheimer tomes with this marvelous concise and precise book. Anyone with the slightest interest in Oppenheimer's biography will not be able to put it down."

—Martin J. Sherwin, co-author of the 2006 Pulitzer Prize–winning
*American Prometheus: The Triumph and Tragedy of
J. Robert Oppenheimer*

"*An Atomic Love Story* is a story of many loves. A whole new range of Robert Oppenheimer's life emerges, a deeper and richer view of one of the pivotal figures of the 20th century."

—Richard Rhodes, Pulitzer Prize–winning author of
The Making of the Atomic Bomb

"It is impossible to see Robert Oppenheimer whole without understanding the three great loves of his life. A closed book to most of the world, he opened himself to these three women, showing them the depth and intensity of his longing for the intimacies of the spirit as well as those of the flesh. *An Atomic Love Story* gives us the missing piece of the man."

—Patricia O'Toole, author of *The Five of Hearts:
An Intimate Portrait of Henry Adams and His Friends* and
When Trumpets Call: Theodore Roosevelt after the White House

An Atomic Love Story

AN ATOMIC LOVE STORY

THE EXTRAORDINARY WOMEN IN
ROBERT OPPENHEIMER'S LIFE

SHIRLEY STRESHINSKY
AND PATRICIA KLAUS

TURNER
PUBLISHING COMPANY

Turner Publishing Company
4507 Charlotte Avenue, Suite 100
Nashville, TN 37209

www.turnerpublishing.com

An Atomic Love Story: The Extraordinary Women in Robert Oppenheimer's Life

Cover design: Gina Binkley
Book design: Kym Whitley

Library of Congress Cataloging-in-Publication Data

Streshinsky, Shirley.
 An atomic love story : the extraordinary women in Robert Oppenheimer's life / Shirley Streshinsky and Patricia Klaus.
 pages cm
 Includes bibliographical references and index.
 ISBN 978-1-61858-019-1 (hardback)
 ISBN 979-8-88798-005-8 (paperback)
 1. Oppenheimer, J. Robert, 1904–1967. 2. Oppenheimer, J. Robert, 1904–1967--Relations with women. 3. Oppenheimer, J. Robert, 1904–1967--Marriage. 4. Physicists--United States--Biography. 5. Women--United States--Biography. 6. Man-woman relationships--United States--History--20th century. 7. Sex role--United States--History--20th century. I. Klaus, Patricia. II. Title.
 QC16.O62S696 2013
 530.092--dc23
 [B]
 2013024440

Printed in the United States of America
13 14 15 16 17 18 0 9 8 7 6 5 4 3 2 1

For daughter Maria Streshinsky, who grew up listening to Oppenheimer stories, became a journalist and an editor, and deserves a place in the sun for her help in making *An Atomic Love Story* come true.

And for son Evan Klaus, who regularly called from 9,697 miles away in Africa to ask, "How's the book?" And for his inimitable PowerPoints, which have never failed to make me laugh at many times in my life.

Contents

CONTENTS

PROLOGUE:

JUNE 14, 1943

The light was fading by the time Robert Oppenheimer left Le Conte Hall.
He walked across campus at his usual fast clip, heading for the streetcar that would take him into San Francisco. He would have allowed his mind to skim over the consequences of what he was about to do. Not that he was weighing them; he had already made the decision to see Jean Tatlock. It would be more of an exercise to keep his mind occupied, to block the uncertainty of how he would find her. Radiant or remorseful. Perfect or flawed.

There would be hell to pay, that he knew. He would have stopped to light a cigarette, maybe taking the opportunity to glance around for the Army security agent he knew would be there. He was too important to the war effort to be allowed to go loose in the world. His slender, six-foot frame and his signature porkpie hat made him an easy target to tail. The security agents would inform Pash, and Pash would be delighted to inform General Groves, and the general would be livid.

Oppenheimer was the new scientific director of the Los Alamos section of the Manhattan Project, hidden on a mesa high in the Sangre de Cristo Mountains of New Mexico. It was possible that seeing Jean could cause him to be removed from the project altogether. The idea was so disturbing that it would have had to be put out of his mind, along with the wife and two-year-old son he had left behind in Los Alamos.

After one last deep drag of his cigarette, he would have flicked it away, then swung onto the Key System train that would carry him over the Oakland Bay Bridge and into the city. He was thirty-nine that June. Jean was twenty-nine. They had known each other, loved each other, for seven years. He would always want her; twice he had come close to marrying her.

Three months before, when he had been about to leave Berkeley for Los Alamos, Jean had asked to see him, but he had not gone to her then. Too much was happening, too fast. He wasn't allowed to tell her why he was leaving or where he was going, could not confide what he and a remarkable band of scientists were attempting to create. Probably he was glad for that; Jean would not have approved. She was one of the most principled people he had ever known; she believed above all else in the sanctity of life. She was a physician now, a resident in psychiatry at Mount Zion Hospital, working with troubled children. She did not know that ending World War II might depend on his group's ability to develop a weapon of mass destruction so horrific it would defeat America's enemies, unless the Germans got it first. That grim possibility played on his mind. The Germans were intent on conquering all of Europe, the world. Would Jean, with her kind and open heart, be able to grasp the enormity of such a catastrophe?

It was dark by the time the train rattled over the bridge. The FBI would have a file on Jean, on their relationship. What could they know about that relationship? All those years later, he would try to explain to strangers in a Washington, D.C., hearing room: "We had been very much involved with one another and there was still very deep feeling when we saw each other."

On that June evening in 1943, he knew that an agent would be lurking near her at the terminal in San Francisco where she would be waiting for him.

OPPENHEIMER ARRIVED AT 9:45 PWT, the FBI report reads. *He rushed to meet a young lady, whom he kissed and they walked away arm in arm. They entered a 1935 green Plymouth coupe and the young lady drove. The car is registered to Jean Tatlock. She is five foot seven, 128 [pounds], long dark hair, slim, attractive.*

SHE WAS SMILING, NOT HURTING, he could see that. The Jean he could not give up. He would have smiled as she raised her face to kiss him, would have studied her with that intensity that so unsettled others, the blue eyes riveted, as if he could record the synapses of her brain. Others wilted under this attention, Jean did not. She slipped her arm into his and led him to the roadster.

She drove east along the Embarcadero—the scene of much of the labor unrest she had reported in the *Western Worker*—then turned west on Broadway. She had decided where they would eat; not one of the posh restaurants he would have chosen, but a shabby place not far from her apartment on Telegraph Hill, good for the spicy food he favored and some proletarian privacy. An agent waited outside. He would report: *Drove to Xochiniloc Cafe, 787 Broadway, at 10 P.M. Cheap type bar, cafe, and dance hall operated by Mexicans. Had few drinks, something to eat, went to 1405 Montgomery where she lives on top floor ... Appears to be very affectionate and intimate ... At 11:30 lights went out.*

Within two weeks, Lieutenant Colonel Boris Pash, chief of counterintelligence for the Ninth Army Corps in San Francisco, would send a memo to the Pentagon recommending that Dr. Oppenheimer be denied a security clearance and be fired as scientific director of the Manhattan Project, citing among other things this overnight tryst with Jean Tatlock, identified as his mistress and a known Communist.

AN ATOMIC LOVE STORY

I

BLOODLINES REVEALED

The loves of his life:

JEAN AND RUTH AND KITTY

1

On bloodlines: 1620–1920

"Well, neither one of us came over on the Mayflower," Robert Oppenheimer offered, probably with a slightly sardonic smile

William Boyd, one of Robert's housemates at Harvard, would remember the remark. Boyd's own Scottish-German forebears would not have been on that iconic ship when it reached American shores in 1620 either, or on any of the other ships that followed soon after in the Winthrop Fleet, carrying English emigrants westward over the Atlantic at the beginning of what would come to be called the "Great Migration." The ancestors of two other Harvard friends—John Edsall and Jeffries Wyman—had arrived on Massachusetts shores in the 1630s, however.

These early settlers in the New World were not the huddled masses that would wash westward from Europe two hundred years later, but strong-minded, God-fearing, typically prosperous and well-educated people who had left their native England seeking freedom to worship. These were the Puritans, supremely confident in their own superiority, who helped to establish a distinctive American character: a kind of rock-ribbed perseverance, a determination that would not falter. The hellfire and damnation they preached would also linger long in the Puritan psyche, but would never be quite so deeply embedded as their belief in the spiritual value of good deeds and the ethics of hard work.

As the seventeenth century converged into the eighteenth, the English, some of them gentry, continued to make the long sea journey to the colonies in America, looking not so much to worship as they pleased as to make their fortunes. A social elite evolved around those who did not have a "dusky complexion," who were Protestant, who had married well or made money or, preferably, both. Harvard, established in 1636, was the college of choice for those families who "mattered." Their names became a litany—among them Adams and Cabot and Lodge, Saltonstall, Peabody, Forbes, and Lowell, and all of their many permutations. For another century and more, they merged and married each other as often as possible. In 1928, Robert Oppenheimer's Harvard friend Jeffries Wyman married Anne Cabot. (The Cabots had arrived in America in 1770, the Wymans 130 years earlier.) "It was a heritage that was old and rich in willpower, Puritan values and a strong sense of purpose," their daughter Anne Cabot Wyman would write. She describes her family as "entwined with grandparents, uncles and aunts and rafts of cousins. The generations met every year at big family parties and in old summer enclaves in Maine or on Cape Cod. In the winter, colonies of relatives clustered in the upscale Boston suburbs of Brookline or Dover or Milton. The men worked together in offices on State Street in downtown Boston or in labs at Harvard. Their wives belonged to 'Mothers' Clubs.' They were all considered—and considered themselves—'True Bostonians.'"[1]

IN 1922, ROBERT OPPENHEIMER'S FIRST year at Harvard, 21 percent of the student body was Jewish. The following year, Harvard's president—a Lowell—suggested a quota on Jews in the student body: no more than 15 percent.[2] It would have been impossible for anyone as smart and sensitive as Robert to be unaware of the prejudices that existed, or to believe they did not apply to him.[3]

Robert was at Harvard long enough to learn that bloodlines mattered; that while the gene pool would swirl and widen in the early decades of the twentieth century, New England, with its Great Migration core, would remain implacably white and Protestant. His German-Jewish roots would forever exclude him. And yet two of the women he would come to love in his lifetime had bloodlines that set them solidly inside the circle of those who belonged.

JEAN TATLOCK'S HERITAGE TRACED BACK TO important families of the 1636 Puritan colony in Connecticut. Her grandfather, William Tatlock D. D., arrived from England in 1853, and married Florence Perry, who in the course of time gave birth to a son, whom they named John S. P. Tatlock, the S for Strong and the P for Perry. Jean's grandfather would serve as rector and archdeacon of St. John's Episcopal Church in Stamford, Connecticut for thirty years.[4] His son John grew up to be a handsome young man, with a broad forehead, blue eyes, and a dignified demeanor and, in time, became a scholar of Chaucer and Dante. His first post was as a lecturer in the Department of English at the University of Michigan, where he was destined to meet a remarkable student named Marjorie Fenton.

The Fentons too had come early to America; they settled into the Hudson River Valley and played a lively role in the new colony's life. John Fenton served in the Revolutionary War as a drummer and worked his way to the rank of sergeant in the Commander-in-Chief's Guard.[5] Four score years later, another Fenton and another American war: fifteen-year-old Ernest left his New York home in 1860 to make his way to Washington, D.C., arriving just as Abraham Lincoln was about to become president and the Civil War loomed like a great dark cloud over the capitol.

In 1865, Virginian Mary Welsh Waters, just seventeen, was one of the hundreds of thousands of grieving wives left behind by the ravages of the Civil War. Ernest Fenton came safely through the carnage, moved back into a Washington boardinghouse, and returned to clerking, this time for the War Department. When the rather tall and dark-haired Ernest proposed, Mary accepted. In 1881, she gave birth to a girl they called Marjorie.

As the twentieth century opened, young Marjorie Fenton—showing the resilience of a Virginia-bred mother and the grit of a Yankee father—made her way west to Ann Arbor, where she enrolled at the University of Michigan, one of the land-grant colleges that accepted women and trained them to be teachers. It was 1901; she was to graduate Phi Beta Kappa with the class of 1905. Chance, Puritan predestination, or possibly simply a class assignment brought Professor John Tatlock face-to-face with Marjorie Fenton. They married in 1908. Three years later, Marjorie gave birth to Hugh, and in 1914, a year before the family was to leave for California and Stanford University, she had another child, a girl.

The spiraling threads of chromosomes that formed Jean Frances Tatlock's genome—not to be understood for another century—were provided by both parents from the far reaches of their families, then were selected into a template that would dictate the body she was to grow into: the color of her hair, the curve of her breasts, the lavish eyelashes and shining intellect. And something more, a disposition dark and troubling, hidden in those shards of inherited DNA.

RUTH SHERMAN WAS tall, elegant, and remarkably self-assured when she married Richard Tolman, whose family tree included some of the most positively principled, determined, wrong-righting women in New England history. Richard's grandmother was Elizabeth Buffum Chace, famous for confronting the ills of society head-on. Early in the 1800s, the storied Chace women—Quakers, abolitionists, suffragists—managed also to be exceptionally fecund.[6] Both Richard and his brother, Edward, had Chace as a middle name. They grew up in West Newton, an affluent suburb of Boston, and attended MIT, their father's college. Edward would go on to Harvard for a Ph.D. in the new field of psychology. Richard received his doctorate from MIT.

Ruth's own family was as inimitable as her husband's, but the Shearmans (as the English branch of the family had been known, being manufacturers of cloth—thus "shear men") had been prosperous, respected merchants who valued education. They sailed from Bristol in 1634 on the *Elizabeth and Ann,* bound for the Massachusetts Bay Colony, and then moved on to Connecticut. Down the line, other Shermans would make their way into the history books: the Honorable Roger Sherman, an unheralded Founding Father, was one of five men appointed by the new U.S. Congress to a committee to draft the Declaration of Independence, along with Thomas Jefferson, Benjamin Franklin, and John Adams.[7]

A generation or so later, Ruth's great-grandfather Walter Rowe Sherman would study to be a doctor, marry an Ohio girl, then push west again to Indiana, and the booming railroad town of Washington, not far from the Kentucky border. Walter settled his family into one of the big houses in the center of town, horse and buggy at the ready for country calls. On the eve of the outbreak of war, Walter's wife gave birth to twin sons. Then, not yet forty, he died, leaving little Walter and Warren to be reared by his wife's relatives. The war raged on without young Dr. Sherman of Washington, Indiana, but with a distant relative, William Tecumseh Sherman, a general in the Union Army. He would make the family name famous, or infamous, in the South, as his army burned everything in his path all the way to the sea.

In 1892, Warren was ordained a Presbyterian minister. The twins courted and married local girls; Warren chose Lillie Belle Graham from a prosperous Kentucky merchant family.[8] In 1886, Warren and Lillie Belle had a baby girl and named her Lillie Margaret; seven years later, in the last decade of the nineteenth century, another girl was born. She was called Ruth.

After the Civil War, the great, empty country beyond the Sierra Nevada Mountains beckoned, and another migration got under way. Sometime before 1883, Walter—now a doctor—and his wife and their children settled in Fresno, in California's Great Central Valley. Reverend Warren moved to Sacramento with his wife and two daughters; he became the pastor of one of the state capitol's largest Presbyterian churches. Lillie Margaret and Ruth were close friends with their cousin, Alma, all their lives.

HAD EITHER JEAN OR RUTH had any desire to trace her roots back through the litany of names of those Europeans who braved the Atlantic crossing in the 1600s, through all their convoluted permutations, they might well have found connections to one other. Both families—the Tatlocks and the Shermans—had been part of America's history since the earliest colonial days. Their innate belonging must have been important to Robert Oppenheimer, who, as the quintessential outsider, understood what it meant not to have come over on the *Mayflower*.[9]

Robert's father had come to America from Germany in the huge, late-nineteenth-century migration, when the holds of ships steaming across the Atlantic from Europe were packed. It was 1888 when seventeen-year-old Julius Oppenheimer arrived in New York; he had little or no English. Julius's story has been told as literally one of rags to riches, a tale beloved in the era: his father may have been an "untutored peasant and grain trader who had been raised in a hovel" but his uncles who had emigrated earlier were prosperous and well-connected in New York Jewish society by the time Julius arrived.[10] An ebullient, energetic young man, he quickly learned the language, taught himself to read, and devoured books on American history; he haunted museums and artists' galleries and learned how to dress tastefully—essentially, he invented himself. Everything worked; he would make a fortune supplying linings for men's suits.

By 1903, Julius could afford to court the lovely Ella Friedman, from a cultivated Baltimore family of Bavarian Jewish heritage,[11] and after marriage, move her into a Riverside Drive apartment. Ten years later, they had two much adored young sons who would have all their hearts' desires, if their father had his way. If he could not change their ancestry, he would do his best to deflect it by sending the boys to an innovative new school in New York City. As its name—Ethical Culture School—implied, it distanced itself from historic forms of Judaism, even as it emphasized an individual's responsibilities, social and moral—many of the same themes the Puritans had preached on the rocky New England shores almost three centuries earlier: duty and purpose and ethical living, without the immediate imperative of a relationship with God.

KATHERINE PUENING—KITTY—ARRIVED IN America in 1913 at the age of three, an only child, probably traveling in first class with her German parents, who were neither impoverished nor persecuted. Her grandfather had been a professor at the university in Munster and his son, Kitty's father Franz, reputedly had left-wing political views.[12] Franz became a chemical engineer working in metals, and he emigrated to America, in part, because he had invented a new model of blast furnace which he felt would be in demand in the Iron Belt of the United States. He was also, according to his daughter, eager to dwell in America, with its promise of equality.[13] His wife, Kaethe, was not so eager to shed her German social standing. She brought with her a cache of stories about her family's aristocratic connections, which would set the Puenings apart from the mainstream of German immigrants arriving in America in unprecedented numbers in that second decade of the twentieth century. Her daughter need not feel inferior to anyone in a country that called itself a melting pot.

Kitty would always insist that her father had asked her not to speak of his family's past, which she hinted was ever so much more regal than anyone could imagine. The King of Belgium, yes. Victoria of England, oh yes, Kitty might very well be a German princess.* And while her father wanted nothing to do with royal titles—he had supposedly renounced his position as a "princeling"—she said her mother had taken her to Europe every summer, to stay with various royal families.[14]

By the early 1920s, the Puenings had moved to Aspinwall, a wealthy suburb of Pittsburgh. Franz made an excellent living as an engineer; they had an impressive house. It didn't matter that Kitty went to public schools, which after all were very fine, or that her family didn't socialize with the Carnegies or the Mellons.

---

* Ulrich Vissering, Kitty's great-nephew, put to rest the question about any Vissering "royal" connections when he wrote that Kitty was "story telling" about the relationship between the Visserings and the "Belgian King or any other European kingdoms." He said that there may be "some little 'blue blood' in our veins, in its core . . . the Vissering family stands on civic, maybe sometimes a little bourgeois ground." July 30, 2013, note to Patricia Klaus

2

ROBERT WENT TO CAMP WITH
GEORGE ELIOT'S *MIDDLEMARCH* AND WROTE
HOME TO SAY THAT HE WAS GLAD HE HAD COME,
BECAUSE HE WAS GETTING AN EDUCATION
IN THE FACTS OF LIFE FROM THE OTHER BOYS.
IF HE THOUGHT HIS PARENTS WOULD FIND
THAT AMUSING, HE WAS WRONG.

Robert Oppenheimer's love story begins, as so many love stories do, with his mother, Ella Friedman. Her love story, in turn, was captured in breathless notes written in her flowing artist's hand near the end of the Victorian era, a decade before Proust published *In Search of Lost Time.*

Julius Oppenheimer was clear about what he wanted, and it required a wife with interests that mirrored his own—a woman with elegant taste, not so much his equal as his counterpoint. After Christmas of 1902, Ella used one of her special Florentine monogrammed note cards to write Julius a thank-you for the vase he had given her. The missives began to fly back and forth across New York City; if mailed in the morning, a letter could be delivered within a few hours. She confessed that she and her sister Clara had "talked a long while last night. Can you guess about whom, dear?" And she signed it, "Ever so much love to you from yours truly and only." He proposed, and she accepted. Some days later, her need for him spilled out with urgency: "My own dear fellow, I am so wide awake that I just must talk, and no one else will listen to me, so will you? Strange to say you are the only one to whom I feel like speaking at any and all times about everything."[15]

JULIUS WAS GREGARIOUS, SUCCESSFUL AND sentimental enough to save her letters for the rest of his life. She was "bright" and "clever"—*clever* being a euphemism for smart and ambitious—but that was only part of Ella Friedman's appeal. The intelligent eyes, the tenuous smile, the refined taste—what is known of her suggests that she was a woman not only willing to venture into uncharted territory, but to do so with a physical handicap. Her right hand was congenitally deformed; she wore a crude prosthetic device that included a spring between the artificial thumb and forefinger. Always, a chamois glove fit snugly over her mechanical hand, and she favored long-sleeved dresses as camouflage. Yet the damaged hand had not deterred her from embarking on a career as an artist and a teacher. With intense determination, she had taught herself not just to get by, but to draw and paint and maneuver in the world.

Although she had not married in her twenties, neither had she withdrawn into her well-to-do family, as some other daughters with a physical flaw might be inclined to do. She studied art in Paris and when she returned to the family apartment at 148 W. 94th Street, she arranged for a private rooftop studio, where she drew and painted, and took on a few students. And she taught in an art school, possibly at Barnard School for Girls.[16]

She was thirty-three when she married Julius, beyond the usual marriageable age yet still within childbearing years. Julius's interest in her had taken her by surprise. He was more than a year younger and, in her circles, considered rough around the edges. (The novelist Paul Horgan, one of the few of Robert's boyhood friends who spent time with the family, would offer this description: "Mr. Oppenheimer was a short, small man with high shoulders and an ant-like head which seemed to dominate his body because it was very small, funny, little. And desperately amiable, anxious to be agreeable, received with pleasure . . . and, I think, essentially a very kind man."[17]) Ella would have seen the possibilities: He was a shrewd businessman, even if he was entirely self-educated. And he had an insatiable appetite for learning, an instinctive artistic taste and an infectious delight in life itself. On the eve of their wedding, she wrote: "I do so want you to be able to enjoy life in its best and fullest sense, and you will help me take care of you? To take care of someone whom one really loves has an indescribable sweetness of which a whole lifetime cannot rob me. Good-night, dearest."[18]

Ella had the style and elegance Julius lacked. She possessed a serene demeanor that would compensate for his happy, outgoing—and at times overenthusiastic—nature. The word most often used to describe Ella Oppenheimer was *discreet.*

Although Julius was not, she would have appreciated his inquiring mind and his excitement about music and art.

Five months after their honeymoon, when Ella was at home in New York and he was out of town, she wrote, "It seemed so strange to go to bed alone . . . I did not sleep well. . . . Take care of yourself, dearest. The thought of you . . . is more sweet to me than I can tell."[19]

Their first child was born on April 22, 1904. The name they had selected was Robert, but—against the Jewish tradition that a child not be named for a living relative—the proud father could not resist adding his own name: Julius Robert Oppenheimer. The boy would be presented to the world as J. Robert Oppenheimer. In spite of a birth certificate that proved otherwise, Robert would always insist the J "stood for nothing."[20]

Soon after Robert's birth, the family moved into an entire floor of a building at 155 Riverside Drive, at West 88th Street. It was spacious enough for several servants and an Irish nanny. Automobiles were beginning to replace horse-drawn carriages, and the Oppenheimers had their own car and a uniformed chauffeur.

In the ideal Victorian marriage, the husband took care of his wife and their children. The wife's place was on a pedestal. Ella's art was now focused on making their home elegant; she supervised the staff and children, and lived very much within the cocoon of home and family. This Victorian ideal, enshrined in so many novels of the era, applied only to a small group of upper-middle-class women. Ella Oppenheimer was one of them.

FELIX ADLER'S CONCEPT OF "RIGHT LIVING" captivated Julius and he became an active participant in Adler's Ethical Culture Society, an outgrowth of American Reform Judaism dedicated to "social action and humanitarianism." It was an approach to living that suited secular upwardly mobile German Jews like the Oppenheimers, who wanted to be assimilated into American life and culture.[21]

When Robert first became interested in rocks and was studying formations in Central Park, he began a correspondence with local geologists of some note, plunking away on the family typewriter, not mentioning in any of his letters that he was only twelve years old. Robert's epistles must have been impressive, because one of the geologists put his name up for membership in the New York Mineralogical Club, and before long he was invited to deliver a paper to the membership. The boy begged not to go. Julius—thrilled by the prospect—would not hear of it. Both Ella and Julius watched as he climbed onto a box so he could see over the podium. The paper was read, Robert was roundly applauded, and the story was duly recorded as an early entry in what was to become the legend of J. Robert Oppenheimer. Much later, Robert would say that his mother would have preferred he be "like other boys."[22]

The legend of Robert grew while he was at the Ethical Culture School. The faculty was composed of carefully selected devotees of the progressive education movement, who were well aware of the exceptional mind in their midst, and the challenge it presented. Jane Didisheim, Robert's schoolmate and one of his few friends there, described Robert at fifteen as "still a little boy; he was frail, very pink cheeked, very shy, and very brilliant, of course. . . . he was physically rather, you can't say clumsy exactly; he was rather undeveloped." She went on, eager to get the description just right: "he wasn't childish, really. Just different."[23]

The summer he was fifteen, Robert was sent to summer camp. While the others went off sailing and swimming, he withdrew, read George Eliot's *Middlemarch,* and went on solitary rock-hunting expeditions. He wrote home that he was glad he had come, because he was getting an education in the facts of life from the other boys. If he thought his parents would find that amusing, he was wrong. Ella and Julius quickly appeared for an unscheduled visit. Soon after their departure, the camp director announced a ban on all salacious stories. Retribution was swift and cruel. After dark one night, a group spirited Robert off to the camp icehouse, where he was stripped naked. Even more humiliating, they painted his genitals green and locked him inside, where he spent a cold and miserable night.

Long after, a boy who had been there said, "I don't know how Robert stuck out those remaining weeks, not many boys would have—or could have—but Robert did. It must have been hell for him."[24] Robert Oppenheimer was, in fact, tougher and more resilient than anyone would have guessed.

PAUL HORGAN, CLOSE BOYHOOD FRIEND of Robert, also remembered that "Robert had bouts of melancholy, deep, deep depressions as a youngster. He would seem to be incommunicado emotionally for a day or two at a time. That happened while I was staying with him once or twice, and I was very distressed, had no idea what was causing it."[25]

There was a radical counter to these bouts of depression, one which began to reveal itself at the Oppenheimers' summer home on Long Island's Bay Shore, off the coast of which Robert and his brother learned to sail on small boats. On Robert's sixteenth birthday, his always generous father presented him with a twenty-eight-foot sloop. He quickly learned that summer storms were a challenge; he would race against the tides through the inlet at Fire Island and into the Atlantic. In high school and later when Robert was at Harvard, he would often invite friends to the beach. With Robert at the helm and his friend Horgan on board, the sloop got caught in a strong ebb tide and almost swept out to the enormous breakers at the mouth of the inlet, but Robert "tacked magnificently, back and forth, back and forth, and . . . finally got us back in the bay." Not long after their seventeenth birthdays, Robert took another friend, Francis Fergusson, for a sail. Fergusson would report: "It was a blowy day in spring—very chilly—and there was rain in the air. It was a little bit scary to me, because I didn't know whether he could do it or not. But he did; he was already a pretty skilled sailor. His mother was watching from the upstairs window and probably having palpitations of all kinds. But he had induced her to let him go. She worried, but she put up with it. We got thoroughly soaked, of course, with the wind and the waves. But I was very impressed."[26]

Sometimes his adoring younger brother, Frank, would tuck into the cockpit, while Robert would sail past the inlet, stand tall into the wind, pelted by rain, and eventually work the sloop into Great South Bay and home. When the waiting got too intense, Julius would take the motor launch out into the bay and shepherd the boys back, muttering "Roberty, Roberty,"[27] in an effort to rein his son in, to make him understand the risks he was taking. The admonitions went unheeded; Robert had discovered the excitement of sailing in demanding seas. At the tiller, on a roiling ocean, there was nothing of the shy young man prone to hiding in his room.

The Oppenheimers watched their elder son swing from painful withdrawal to wildly reckless, exhilarating behavior. They must have wondered about the source of this contradiction: a young man, a boy still, who could sit quietly at the easel and paint with his mother, who at times was awkward and withdrawn and yet could be charming and gracious, and who would challenge an angry ocean with a sense of his own invincibility. Robert's long and troubled adolescence was underway. He was going to have to cope on his own. At Harvard first, then on to England and Cambridge. It was not going to be an easy passage.

II
THE EXUBERANT YEARS

3

IN AMERICA, KITTY LEARNED TO BEHAVE
LIKE A GOOD LITTLE GERMAN GIRL: TO SIT
QUIETLY, HANDS FOLDED, NO FIDGETING; SHE
WOULD PLEDGE NEVER TO TURN INTO
"ONE OF THOSE STERN GERMAN OGRE-PARENTS
WHOSE CHILDREN ARE SO WELL TRAINED THAT
THEY SEEM MORE LIKE LITTLE MONSTERS
THAN LIKE CHILDREN."

World War I was one of the deadliest conflicts in history; Europe's losses were in the millions. A whole generation was shattered; too many young men died on the Western Front, too many women became widows or were destined to remain single. The U.S. entered the conflict late and took far fewer casualties than the other countries—some 300,000 compared with the British Empire's three million. Yet the Yanks had gone "over there," had helped turn the tide, had come home on the side of the victors. For those who had not lost someone dear, it was a heady experience. For others, like Richard Tolman, who had served, it would not only cause a delay in their lives, but inure them to the reality of war.

With the war over and the 1920s beginning, the country could turn its attention to other things besides death and deprivation. Inventions, innovations and experimentation flourished; the pulse of life quickened. American steel mills were blazing, the combustion engine made automobiles affordable and city streets were alive with Model T Fords. Tractors and fertilizers and hybrid corn increased production on farms. Prairies appeared, almost to the horizon, as great oceans of grain.

In New York City, Julius Oppenheimer, having added considerably to his fortune during the Great War, began filling the walls of the family's Riverside Drive apartment with canvases by Renoir and Vuillard, Picasso and Van Gogh. Julius, enchanted by Van Gogh's *Enclosed Field with Rising Sun,* which had been painted at Saint-Rémy in 1889, would urge visitors to sit in front of the painting long enough to observe its transformation in the changing New York light. Robert would leave the inner sanctum of Riverside Drive for Harvard and, in 1925, he was on to Cambridge in England. After an emotionally difficult year, which included a holiday in Corsica, he would reclaim his equilibrium and cross the English Channel to Göttingen in Germany.

At the beginning of the 1920s, at some of the most venerable centers of learning, including Cambridge and Göttingen, a small cadre of physicists and mathematicians were studying the universe on the smallest scale—molecules and atoms—and creating a theory called quantum mechanics that was poised to shake the world. Leading the effort were Denmark's Niels Bohr and Germany's Werner Heisenberg.

The century's first sexual revolution was also underway, especially on college campuses. Dating was the new rage, petting was permissible, and the taboo around sex before marriage was under siege. One report even claimed that in the 1920s, 51 percent of young unmarried women had lost their virginity.[28]

In the nineteenth century, women in the more urbane classes who developed strong emotional relationships with other women were referred to as "loving friends." Diaries and letters spill over with a romantic passion that today read like love letters. In the early twentieth century, a woman's increasing access to higher education came with a decreasing chance for marriage. Society demanded, however, that she sublimate her own desires, including career, in favor of husband and children. Some independent women chose career. The term *Boston marriage* was used to describe women who shared homes with one another—many were well educated, or independently wealthy. Some of these Boston marriages were simply practical, others romantic. In either arrangement, women were accepted as "loving friends."[29] If others whispered among themselves within these distinguished bastions of civility, and they did, seldom were there accusations that led to scandal.

However, psychologist Havelock Ellis, along with Richard von Krafft-Ebing, a neurologist known for his studies of sexual deviance, began to talk and write about sex between women. They decided that these relationships were not loving at all, but abnormal. Homosexuality was a congenital malady, they contended.

The women were labeled "inverted," a word that swept into the public vernacular, to be used with derision. In response, novelists began to write explicitly about sex and love between women, raising public awareness while at the same time alarming young women who suddenly found themselves troubled about their loving feelings for their girlfriends. They wondered if this meant that they, too, were "inverted."[30]

This immoderate decade would affect each of these three key women—Jean Tatlock, Kitty Puening and Ruth Tolman—as she moved in her own trajectory, until the time when she would encounter Robert Oppenheimer.

∽

RUTH AND HER OLDER SISTER, Lillie Margaret, grew up in the Protestant Church; their father ministered to one of the largest Presbyterian parishes in Sacramento, a state capital that remained a small western town. Both daughters and their cousin Alma would choose to go to college at the University of California, Berkeley, established only twenty-five years before Ruth was born. When Ruth graduated from Sacramento High, her father retired as an active pastor and the family moved seventy miles west to a big, comfortable house on tree-lined Ashby Avenue in Berkeley, in a neighborhood of established professors and professionals.

The Sherman girls came from a perfectly respectable family, but they hailed from the Midwest before they'd come to California's agricultural valley, so they were branded country girls on campus (their Founding Father ancestor notwithstanding). Lillie Margaret was said to have "a wonderful, friendly spirit, contagious sense of humor."[31] But it was cousin Alma—pretty, effervescent and talented—who set the pace for the cousins. She joined a sorority, was elected to honor societies, and both acted in and wrote plays.

Ruth entered college as a member of the class that would graduate in 1916; she threw herself into college life, signing on for classes in philosophy, Greek, German and Sanskrit. After all those Sundays of doing God's work, it was as if her energies had been set loose in this broader expanse of possibilities to explore. She followed her sister and cousin into the Kappa Kappa Gamma sorority, she sang with a choral group, volunteered at the YWCA where her older sister was now on staff, and played the piano with enthusiasm and skill.[32] While Lillie Margaret was friendly and funny, if plain, Ruth was open, eager and uncommonly pretty.

Without warning, in her third year, Ruth's energy ebbed; she was ill. Doctors were consulted. The diagnosis was tuberculosis. One of the leading causes of death in the country, tuberculosis was a scourge that paid little attention to social class or age. There was no cure, and no treatment other than fresh air, warmth and rest.

Ruth withdrew from the university in 1914 and left cool, foggy Berkeley. Perhaps she was sent inland to sunny Fresno, where her doctor uncle could look after her, or to one of the sanatoriums that had blossomed in the desert. Wherever it was she went, it took a year and a half for Ruth to regain her health and return to classes at Berkeley. By then, some of her optimism was gone, replaced with a more tempered outlook on life, and a solemn determination to make up for time lost.

In January of 1916—the year she was to have graduated—she reappeared for the spring semester with resilience restored, took a double load of classes, and graduated in May of 1917 with honors in philosophy. But the illness would forever change her, followed, as it was, by the country's entrance into the First World War. Some of the men on campus would leave to serve their country; Ruth kept up a spirited exchange of letters with at least one who had gone off to war.

For the next several years she stayed in Berkeley; at the YWCA with Lillie Margaret she helped female foreign students adjust to life on an American campus, and played the piano, including giving private lessons. She was thirty by the time she met Richard Tolman. He was forty-two, tall and handsome, a veteran. Richard came from a formidable New England family and there was much of the patrician about him. A Renaissance man, he was interested in everything: music, philosophy, politics. Richard ranked among the most important chemical physicists in the country, and was dean of the graduate school at the most prestigious scientific university on the West Coast—the California Institute of Technology in Pasadena. He was also, perhaps, more of a bachelor than Ruth might have wished, with at least one broken engagement in his past. But she had been confronting spinsterhood, so under the circumstances, he was the most distinguished husband she could have imagined, no matter his thinning hair.

They were married in the spring of 1924, and suddenly she had almost everything she had ever wanted: a husband of substance whom she adored, and an exciting new life. That summer Richard took his bride to an island off the New England coast to meet his family. His mother regularly rented a summer place where her large brood could gather. Richard's nieces would remember their arrival; Uncle Dickie was a family favorite, and everyone was interested in his new wife.[33]

Tall and slender, with warm brown eyes and glowing olive skin, Ruth favored uncluttered, beautifully made clothes, and wore her dark hair in a chic bob. She smiled often with a grace that was practiced, and exuded warmth that was not. Her lips were thin and bow-shaped, which gave her a charming quality, as if surprise might be lurking underneath her managed exterior.

In Pasadena, Ruth and Richard moved into a house in the Spanish Colonial style, with softly rounded colonnades, high-timbered ceilings—a house both historic and fashionable. Mrs. Tolman launched into her new role with verve; she ran their home with precision, hired help, developed appealing menus, befriended his friends. She was determined to be the best, most loving dean's wife she could be, which included providing Richard with children. That accomplished, she would have everything.

Ruth's childhood had been highly disciplined, structured around Sunday services, prayer meetings, Bible studies and music lessons. The Sherman girls had grown up to the cadences of the King James Bible, absorbing the "thou shalts" and "thou shalt nots" and the Corinthians' "though I's"—*Though I speak with the tongues of men and of angels, and have not charity, I am become as sounding brass, or a tinkling cymbal. And though I have the gift of prophecy, and understand all mysteries, and all knowledge; and though I have all faith, so that I could remove mountains, and have not charity, I am nothing.* Ruth would consider the meaning of charity all her life.

∽

STANFORD UNIVERSITY WAS SCARCELY THIRTY years old in 1920, and still trying to establish itself as the "Harvard of the West." Professor John S. P. Tatlock spent ten years as head of the English Department in this far-west upstart before moving his family back to Harvard in 1924.[34]

Jean Tatlock was ten years old when the family moved east. That summer, her mother, Marjorie, packed up jodhpurs and riding jackets and, with Jean and twelve-year-old Hugh, climbed aboard one of the great steam trains to Denver. There they met Marjorie's best friend, Winifred Smith, who had traveled west from Poughkeepsie, New York, with a nephew and a niece, Priscilla Smith. All the children were between the ages of ten and fourteen. Priscilla was the daughter of Winifred's brother, Preserved Smith (one in a long line of Preserveds; the first was born in one of the original ships to arrive on the New England shores, and his survival was regarded as so miraculous that he earned the name). When Priscilla was just four, her mother was felled by typhoid and died quickly. Winifred became a mother to Priscilla.

Marjorie and Winifred were such close friends that they "seldom let geography keep them very far apart."[35] Marjorie was angular and measured and had accepted the role of professor's wife; she did the requisite typing and proofing of manuscripts and earned praise on the acknowledgments page. But she also had her own passions. One was theater, the other a penchant for radical thinking; both explain her connection to the small and plainspoken Winifred, who already had a reputation as a rebel. She had earned a Ph.D. at Columbia, then taught English and drama at Vassar. (At one of the college's convocations, she addressed the students: "There are still many people who are afraid of letting girls go out into the world alone, afraid of their earning a living, of their getting ideas, of their being highbrows, of their looking or acting like thinking, grown-up individuals. It is your task to convince such people that experiments sincerely made, and new ideas actively held, do not hurt girls any more than they hurt boys, but on the contrary strengthen them; that you are human beings first and well brought up young women second.")[36]

From Denver, the two women and four children headed for one of the dude ranches in the Rawuneeche Valley, in the shadow of Colorado's Never Summer Mountains. Priscilla was four years older than Jean, yet she bowed to the younger girl's seeming invincibility. Mornings were given over to long trail rides. The valley floor was dry and strewn with tough grasses, but the wooded mountains were scattered with trails that climbed to the fittingly named Lake of the Clouds. There and back was a full day's ride. The women hired a guide to help keep the little troop—Jean especially—out of harm's way on the trip. The slender, intense little girl was in the habit of riding far ahead, at times pushing out of sight, and then wandering away from the trail. Marjorie understood that she needed to be cautious with her tightly wound daughter, so moved was she by the wild sky scape, the high-wheeling birds, the clouds that piled up over the Never Summer range. Eventually, unable to make Jean understand the risks inherent in the wilderness, she had to forbid her to leave the group. The horses reached the tree line and pushed on, their footing unsure as they climbed up and over a field of rocks and slippery talus. Finally the group reached the summit and the lake, well above 11,000 feet, its glacially cold waters shimmering in the cool midday sun. Jean was the only one to plead to go in for a swim.

Another morning the group rode across a hot, dry part of the valley floor, the horses lethargic in the heat. Their destination was a small village, with little but the remains of a deserted Catholic church. In an alcove, the children discovered an old trunk and pulled out the dusty remnants of priests' robes. Jean delivered a short sermon on her definite opposition to the ritual of religion, the "claptrap" of it. She announced that she was scrubbing her forehead every day, determined to wipe off the spot where she had been christened.[37]

Winifred Smith must have laughed out loud at the incident. Her own father, Henry Preserved Smith, was a leading Biblical scholar who had questioned the literal truth of the Bible, and had been convicted of heresy by his church. Winifred, thirteen at the time, was enraged at the church's proclamation; from then on, she introduced herself as "'the daughter of a heretic' and an atheist."[38]

No matter that the Tatlocks came from a long line of clerics. Young Jean became adamant: she was done with religion. And her mother's best friend agreed wholeheartedly. Yet Jean was not so much a contrary child as a passionate one, prodigiously bright. After mornings in the saddle, the small group spent after-noons reading aloud. Jean would be remembered for her rendition of Coleridge's "The Rime of the Ancient Mariner." Jean recited the sad tale of the old seaman who killed the magical albatross, condemning the ship and its crew to death. Her voice building dramatically, she read:

> Day after day, day after day,
> We stuck, nor breath nor motion;
> As idle as a painted ship
> Upon a painted ocean.
>
> Water, water, everywhere,
> And all the boards did shrink;
> Water, water, everywhere,
> Nor any drop to drink.

Jean, at ten, might have been considered little more than a bright and charm-ing child, except for the determination in the directness of her gaze, in her straight back, in the long pauses while she considered how to do what she wanted to do. Even Pris, two years older, sensed that there was something unique and unnerving about Jean.

At the end of summer, the friends packed up the children, left the mountains and headed east. With Winifred in Poughkeepsie and Marjorie in Cambridge, they would be 200 miles apart now rather than 3,000. John Tatlock was back in the place he felt he belonged, as head of the Harvard English Department. A medievalist, he was an authority on Chaucer, Dante, Middle English and Latin— a man perfectly at ease in the fourteenth century. Yet he could not comprehend a ten-year-old daughter with an ardent soul.

⌒

FOR THE OPPENHEIMER BROTHERS, SUMMERS in the high mountains of New Mexico became a yearly ritual beginning in 1922— the year Robert was to have enrolled at Harvard. Always seen as physically fragile, Robert had come down with a siege of trench dysentery in Europe early that summer. After that, he was diagnosed with chronic colitis, and tuberculosis was mentioned. What he needed, his parents decided, was warm, dry weather and a change of scenery. Julius quickly employed Herbert Smith, a popular young teacher at Ethical Culture School, recently out of Harvard, to take their delicate son west to a guest ranch called Los Pinos, near Cowles, New Mexico. The ranch, situated in the Sangre de Cristo Range, northeast of Santa Fe in the Pecos Valley, was owned by the Chaves family. Lineal descendants of a Spanish conquistador, they were the early aristocracy in the wild mountainous land of New Mexico. Don Amado was the current *patron;* his daughter, Katherine Chaves Page, was, at twenty-seven, tall, beautiful and as imperious as Smith's title for her—the "reigning princess of the House of Chaves." The year before, she had married a Chicago businessman old enough to be her father, and quickly regretted it. Having taught Spanish at the elite Finch School on New York's Upper East Side, Katherine had connections to many of the private schools, and a steady stream of young students—most from wealthy families— began making their way to Los Pinos, on the theory that horseback riding and fresh mountain air would invigorate them. Each season, Katherine had a swarm of adolescent boys competing for her favor. In 1922, she christened Robert her favorite, which put him squarely in the middle of the in crowd—a heady experience for a shy and spindly boy genius.[39]

The princess knew these mountains intimately, and spent many days leading her young charges on long trail rides; soon she was trusting Robert with the most challenging mounts. He could stay in the saddle all day and survive on graham crackers, and he was willing to risk trails that gave others pause. Smith would report that this was the first time in his life that Robert "found himself loved, admired, sought after."[40] By the end of the summer, those who knew the western Robert would no longer think of him as frail or delicate. And neither, it seemed, would Robert.

Robert returned to New York free of all signs of colitis or any other ailment. What he did have was a throbbing crush on Mrs. Page and an enduring love for the Pecos Valley and the Rio Grande, and the memory of the Sangre de Cristo Mountains rising around and above him in a kind of exultation. For many summers to come, the Oppenheimer family would go to Los Pinos. The parents would stay at the ranch keeping Mr. Page company, while Robert, Frank and Katherine would mount up to explore the slopes and valleys in all directions.

⤵

IN THE SUMMER OF 1924, fourteen-year-old Kitty Puening was preparing to enter high school in Aspinwall. Having arrived in the United States at age three, Kitty's first language was German. Although she spoke English without a trace of an accent, she also spoke perfect German. Kitty's mother had been taking her to Germany for the summers; their last trip was in 1913, a year before World War I erupted in Europe. The Puenings were whispered to have important, possibly royal, connections, but it seems likely that it was Kitty's mother, the handsome and imperious Kaethe, who originated the whispering. Over the next few years, though, Franz Puening would caution his wife not to speak of their family in Germany, especially after the sinking of the *Lusitania* and the American declaration of war on Germany in 1917.

Franz was determined to become an American citizen, so he did his work at the company and suffered the slurs sometimes spoken behind his back. Being labeled an "enemy alien" must have been especially grating to Kaethe, who was inordinately proud of her German heritage and had a brother and cousins fighting for the Kaiser. When the war was over, Kaethe would resume her summer holidays to Europe so young Kitty could grow up knowing her Vissering relatives, including Kaethe's aunt Apollinaire Keitel. In Germany, Kitty became acquainted with the world her mother loved, and perhaps she also met her mother's cousin, Wilhelm Keitel. As an officer attached to the Ministry of Defense, he was secretly working to triple the size of the German army.[41] And he would become a devoted follower of the man being proclaimed a new German messiah, Adolph Hitler.

Like other immigrants of the period, Kitty's father might have imagined America as a classless society without prejudice. The anti-German propaganda during the war would have disabused him of that notion. And even if the Puenings didn't socialize with the Carnegies, Fricks, or Mellons in Pittsburgh, Kaethe would see to it that her only child would know how to navigate in their world. Kitty learned to do all those things expected of a young woman from a well-to-do family. Typically, these girls learned to ride and jump, often competing at horse shows and riding to the hounds. It is no surprise that Kitty, small, lithe, and without fear, would become an excellent horsewoman.

In America, the lively Kitty learned to behave like a good little German girl: to sit quietly, hands folded, no fidgeting. To speak only when spoken to. To work hard and obey the rules. (In her twenties, a childless Kitty would write: "I often think that when the time comes I will turn into one of those stern German ogre-parents whose children are so well trained that they seem more like little monsters than like children. Only of course I won't.")[42]

4

1926: AFTER CORSICA, ROBERT WOULD WRITE HIS YOUNGER BROTHER, "I FEEL ABOUT AS MANLY AS A TADPOLE OR A CAULIFLOWER."

Along with the usual detritus accumulated by students on holiday, their packs were weighted with books— Dostoyevsky, Tolstoy, Proust. The three friends gathered on the island of Corsica that spring; the plan was to hike for ten days, explore the wild island in the Ligurian Sea south of France, then go on to Sardinia.

The three young Americans selected Corsica for its peaks, high enough to produce snow; for its ancient isolation and rugged splendor; its hiking trails, beaches and mild Mediterranean climate. Its Napoleonic connection might have tempted them as well, the little French emperor having been born in the town of Ajaccio a century and a half earlier.

They were young men on the cusp. Weighted by expectations from without and within, they were beginning to settle into paths, both professional and personal, expected of the gifted and privileged, a description that fit all three. Jeffries Wyman and John Edsall—both from old Boston families and exceedingly bright—had become close friends at Harvard and would remain so all of their lives. Initially, Wyman had read philosophy while Edsall studied chemistry; by their postgraduate year, both had declared for science. Wyman took advanced courses in mathematics, thermodynamics and organic chemistry while Edsall was a first-year medical student. During their last year at Harvard, they had become friends with an undergraduate named Robert Oppenheimer. Edsall found the younger man to be "a phenomenal person, with immense intellectual power and intense interest in literature, philosophy and other subjects that went far beyond science." Wyman found Robert to be "a little precious and perhaps a little arrogant but very interesting, full of ideas."[43]

The young men were of that subset of students who find romance in science, wonder in ideas gleaned from books, delight in study. Consequently—this was true especially of Oppenheimer, easily accepted as the most intelligent of the three—they had a certain ineptness in matters social and emotional.

Almost two years earlier, in the summer of 1924, Wyman and Edsall had made their way to England together on a slow steamer also carrying 700 cattle—a crossing they would not forget. A year later, Oppenheimer arrived at the Cavendish Laboratory at Cambridge, to work in the new field of quantum physics. The three found each other, as well as another Harvard friend, Francis Fergusson, who was studying at Oxford and had known Robert since the Ethical Culture School and their boyhood summers in New Mexico.

Not long after his arrival in England, Robert found himself navigating a series of terrifying shoals between late adolescence and manhood. For the first time, his great advantage—his intellectual superiority—was no longer enough. At Cavendish, the emphasis was on experimental physics; he needed to be able to manipulate complicated laboratory equipment. But he was not good at it. Neither were his social skills up to British standards. It didn't help that Francis Fergusson talked about invitations to the salon of Lady Ottoline Morrell, whom Robert described in a letter to a mutual friend as "the high priestess of civilized society and the patrons of Eliot and Berty." (T. S. Eliot and Bertrand Russell, as well as members of the Bloomsbury Group, Virginia Woolf and John Maynard Keynes.)[44] Robert was intensely jealous of his old friend's social status, and his old friend seems not to have made any attempt to alleviate Robert's envy, or for that matter to include him. Increasingly miserable in life as well as in his science, Robert for the first time felt his future to be in jeopardy. Reason enough for his emotions to become unstable, his behavior bizarre, and for his parents to come steaming across the Atlantic to the rescue. To complicate matters, Robert had left what has ever after been referred to as "a poison apple" on his tutor's desk. Exactly what that was has never been fully explained. [45]

Robert's breakdown coincided with the rise of psychoanalysis; it was the age of Freud and Jung. Although he was to read widely in the field of psychology, which would become one of the enduring passions of his life, at this time Robert was not convinced of the value of analysis. His mental condition continued to deteriorate: one psychiatrist delivered a diagnosis of dementia praecox (schizophrenia). For the holidays, Robert's parents whisked their troubled son away to Brittany, a landscape they must have felt would calm him. It did not; his mood darkened and he contemplated suicide.[46]

Fergusson joined the family in Paris, where Robert became increasingly troubled, and especially when Fergusson announced he was contemplating marriage. Fergusson described how Robert attempted to strangle him one afternoon without warning.[47] After the initial surprise, Fergusson easily held Robert off, then comforted him when he broke down in tears. Another day Robert locked his mother in her hotel room, which was enough reason to be sent to yet another analyst in France. (The move was not original. On an earlier Oppenheimer family holiday in Paris, Frank had locked Robert in their shared bathroom, then blithely told their parents that his brother had decided not to join them for that day's outing.) This time, according to Fergusson, the French psychiatrist attributed Robert's troubles to a *"crise morale"* and recommended aphrodisiacs and *"une femme."* Robert attempted to act on the advice, with humiliating consequences. Many years later—long after Robert's status had eclipsed his friend's—Fergusson would say that Robert "went to bed with several whores, but without being able to raise the slightest enthusiasm."[48]

After returning to Cambridge, Robert wrote a conciliatory note to Fergusson, promising to make it up to him someday (which he did). Then he saw his third psychoanalyst in four months. This seems, according to some versions, to have been a requirement for being allowed to stay on at Cambridge. In the midst of his turmoil, Robert had still been able to apply himself. Edsall noted that he was joining the right science clubs and was beginning to understand the kind of physics he wanted to pursue. He was, in fact, beginning to position himself to be in the right place at the right time, and to play a central role in one of the most exciting scientific upheavals in history.

BY SPRING, WHEN ROBERT JOINED Wyman and Edsall on a ten-day walking vacation in Corsica, he was already getting a grasp on his science and his life. Edsall had earlier noticed in Robert a "tremendous inner turmoil, in spite of which he kept on doing a tremendous amount of work; thinking, reading, discussing things, but obviously with a great sense of inner anxiety and alarm."[49] It was Wyman—a veteran hiker—who thought a walking vacation on Corsica and Sardinia would do all three of them good.

The young men shouldered their packs and began their walk around the narrow, rock-strewn pathways of the island, stopping now and again to study the beauty of the ancient landscape. They endured drenching rainstorms and flea-infested inns with the tolerance of the young and hardy. Sometimes they slept in the open, under a cork oak tree or alongside one of the tafoni rock formations that mark the island landscape.

Robert's anguish did not stop them from enjoying the good wines of the region, the food, the fresh air and their debates over the relative merits of poets and novelists. Dostoyevsky is superior to Tolstoy, Robert insisted: "He gets to the soul and torment of man."[50] At night, by flashlight, he tore through Marcel Proust's *A La Recherché du Temps Perdu* (*In Search of Lost Time*). The words spilled off the page, in long and lingering sentences that seemed to speak to him.

At a time when Oppenheimer's friends began to vanish into marriage, he read in Proust about a kind of love that "possesses one's soul before love has yet entered into one's life, then it must drift, awaiting love's coming, vague and free, without precise attachment, at the disposal of one sentiment to-day, of another to-morrow, of filial piety or affection for a friend."[51]

Long years later, Robert Oppenheimer would be able to recite from memory another passage—in which a lesbian laments the cruel words said to her father: "Perhaps she would not have considered evil to be so rare, so extraordinary, so estranging a state, to which it was so restful to emigrate, had she been able to discern in herself, as in everyone, that indifference to the sufferings one causes, an indifference which, whatever other names one may give it, is the terrible and permanent form of cruelty."[52] For the rest of his life, he would consider evil to be an unavoidable part of the human experience.

Robert had immersed himself in the contemporary works of Freud and Jung. In Corsica he would combine those two disciplines with Proust; the three would provide him with a new vision of his universe. Robert's contemporary, the critic Edmund Wilson, would say that *In Search of Lost Time* was the literary equivalent of Einstein's theory, insisting: "Proust has re-created the novel from the point of view of relativity; he has supplied for the first time in literature an equivalent on the full scale for the new theory of physics."[53] Proust's relentless probing of personality, his fascination with detail, his close analysis of the human condition had, in some profound way, provided answers the young Robert was seeking, and lifted his spirits above the pall of his depression.

As their Corsican holiday was drawing to a close, the group was having dinner at an inn when the waiter approached to tell Robert when the next boat for France was departing. Surprised, the others asked him why he was leaving early. His answer was that he had done "a terrible thing." He told them that he had left a poison apple on the desk of his tutor, Patrick Blackett, and said he was going back to Cambridge to face his fate.[54]

This could not have been the same "poison apple" he had mentioned some months earlier, when his emotional torments had threatened his Cambridge career. Edsall and Wyman decided the apple must be a metaphor, a hallucination.[55] Neither thought to ask. It was one of Robert's obfuscations, a shimmer of a mystery, but with Blackett at the heart of it.

Nonetheless, the gray fog that had descended on Robert's mind and heart indeed seemed to have dissipated. After Corsica, he felt lighter, more content, "much kinder and more tolerant," as he would say. He was ready to face his future. Back in Cambridge later that same spring, Robert would write to Frank, his fourteen-year-old brother, at home in New York, "Some day you must come with me to Corsica. It's a great place, with every virtue from wine to glaciers, and from langouste to brigantines."[56]

As the years passed and Robert's fame grew, the story of an epiphany on Corsica would be added to the literature of his legend, with variations on the theme of a woman and a life-changing love affair. When an early biographer asked Robert to explain what had happened to him in Corsica in that spring of 1926, he reportedly said: "It was a great thing in my life, a great and lasting part of it." And then: "What you need to know is that it was not a mere love affair, not a love affair at all, but love."[57]

5

RUTH WEIGHS HER FUTURE AND ENCOUNTERS THE OPPENHEIMER BROTHERS, AND BOTH KITTY AND JEAN GO TO EUROPE FOR THE SUMMER

By April 1930, Ruth and Richard Tolman had been married for more than five years. She would be thirty-seven in October. She knew Richard must be disappointed, the women in his family having produced so many children. "Oh Darling, I want to be able to give you babies. I am so sorry that I am no good," she had written when he was on one of his frequent trips. Each new month held the promise of pregnancy; each month, tears came easily. She called Richard her "darling lamb."[58] Yet she had not been brought up to be a lady of leisure. If children weren't to be part of their lives, she had no time to lose in considering her future. What she needed was meaningful work.

Ruth's husband made a good living, and there were plenty of volunteer jobs she could take. She chose instead a half-time job, paying $900 a year—a substantial salary for the time—as an assistant in the clinic at Los Angeles' Juvenile Hall.[59] Her main responsibility was to give psychological tests to the young wards of the court—delinquents—and to report the test conclusions to the court referee. Day after day she found herself facing angry, tough, disturbed young people, almost all from poor families in areas of Los Angeles that she had never encountered. But as a minister's daughter, she had seen her share of families in crisis and she did not shrink from the harsh realities of life.

Two years later she moved to another half-time position—for $1,200 a year— at the University of California, Los Angeles. Her experience at Juvenile Hall qualified her to do research and counsel students. Her title, associate in psychology, allowed her to audit courses. Though not for credit, the courses would help her decide if she wanted to pursue a graduate degree, which in turn would qualify her for more responsible positions. Ruth eventually enrolled at Occidental College, some 10 miles from the Tolman home, to begin work on a master's degree. A young friend, Natalie Raymond, was around when Ruth was writing her master's thesis and helped with the details: "Nat and I have been working like horses . . ."[60] But even with Nat's company and her own career in the making, Ruth missed Richard intensely when he traveled. She would write in more than one letter, "Darling, the house is empty and seems all wrong with you away, and I so lonely for you."[61]

While Ruth developed her own future, she applied her considerable charm to Richard's university obligations, including the recruitment of bright young physicists to the select faculty at the California Institute of Technology. Robert Oppenheimer, who had completed his Ph.D. at Göttingen, was high on the list. His reputation preceded him: intellectually brilliant but tightly wound. Tense. He excelled in what could be learned. He fancied himself a connoisseur of food and wine. His manners were immaculate. Most of all, he was one of that small band of bright young men newly returned from the continent, ready to spread the gospel of nuclear physics to America.

Every major college in the country wanted him. Robert was known to love the Southwest, particularly New Mexico, which gave Caltech a geographic advantage; more important, the school had the only strong theoretical-physics department on the West Coast, thanks in large part to Richard. Four hundred miles to the north, at Berkeley, the University of California had Ernest Lawrence doing groundbreaking work in experimental physics, but the school had no theoretical-physics department. Helping to coax Robert to Caltech was an unwritten part of Ruth's job description.

ROBERT AND HIS SIXTEEN-YEAR-OLD brother Frank had breezed into Pasadena that August of 1928, driving an eight-cylinder Chrysler roadster, new but battered, its cloth top in shreds. Robert, twenty-four, sported a broken arm, which he carried rather tenderly in a bright red sling, a color chosen, he said, to cheer up his brother. Frank was wearing a suit that threatened to come apart at the seams—it had been sprayed with battery acid when the two had flipped the roadster on a high mountain pass between Colorado and California. The roads indicated on the map were, they had discovered, mostly wishful thinking, and the roadster and its occupants were dusty but somehow elegant after the brave but futile effort.

Robert's manners were strangely old-fashioned. Frank was perfectly natural and easy, as if to balance his brother. Despite the difference in their ages, it was clear that the two were friends as well as brothers, each deferring to the other. It was Frank who told the story of the road trip west. Ruth would have listened carefully to the story he told. [62]

They had joined their parents at the Broadmoor Hotel in Colorado Springs to spend a few days together before Robert was to return to Caltech to pack up his belongings. At that point, their father decided it would be a grand idea for Brother—meaning Robert—to have a new roadster for his tour of the West Coast. And then it occurred to the ebullient father that Frank should ride along. He would, after all, be off to college soon, and it would be good to have a look at the West Coast universities.

Never mind that neither brother knew how to drive; in Colorado, the father signed them up for a few lessons and waved them off. The logical route would have been to drive south to Route 66, a new interstate that twisted through Gallup, New Mexico; Flagstaff, Arizona; and on to Winona, Kingman, Barstow, San Bernardino and then to Pasadena. Easy enough, especially at a cruising speed of eighty miles per hour.

"Easy enough" was never Robert's style; he thought it would be interesting to experience the splendor of this unknown country, so he spread out the maps, noticed roads marked with a dotted line throughout the high mountain wilderness, and plotted a different course, one that would cut across Utah and northern Arizona, on through Cortez, Moab and Lees Ferry—through some of the wildest mountains in the American West, the kind of country where outlaws could vanish when necessary.

The "roads" indicated on the maps turned out to be no more than two ruts in a dirt path. At each fork, the brothers learned to take the least traveled road, because the other would inevitably end at the entrance to a ranch. They decided to take turns driving as they passed through Pueblo, then climbed up and into the Sangre de Cristo Mountains, over icy La Veta Pass, which even late in the season had remnants of snowpack at its 9,413-foot crest. Onward then to the next pass, called Wolf Creek, elevation 10,863, teetering on the Continental Divide. At that elevation, it was cold and the air was thin. Frank commented, "Although it was my brother's turn, he broke out into such rivers of sweat that he could hardly see and asked me to drive."

They carried on, passing through Durango and Cortez. Not long after Cortez, the Chrysler made it up one steep incline and sailed down again, gathering speed. Frank tried to negotiate a close turn, but the car skidded in loose gravel and went flying, landing upside down in a ditch alongside the road.

"You okay?" each asked the other when the car came to a rest.

Frank thought he felt warm blood spreading over him, but realized it was battery acid. They managed to crawl out. As Frank explained, "The only damage to

the car was that the cloth top was completely ruined and the windshield was broken. As was my brother's arm." In fact, Robert's arm was fractured and two bones
in his wrist were broken. Eventually a local came along, pulled the roadster upright and towed it back to Cortez. Robert had his arm set and chose the red sling.

The next day they tried again, this time with Frank at the wheel for the duration. By dark they were almost at Moab. Almost. The car got hung up on a high
rocky rut in the road, unable to go either forward or back. Robert spent the night
on the ground, hungry and cold and in pain from his arm. He lay sipping from a
bottle of spirits of ammonia and sucking on some lemons while Frank, "bit by bit,
jacked up the front wheels of the car and built a rock runway so that by morning
we could back off the rock."

Finally mobile again, they gave up the quest, and headed south to pick up
Route 66 at Gallup. The trip, as plotted by Robert, had been foolhardy. Still, it
should have been a fine tale to tell, the kind that gets better with embellishment.
Frank was having none of it; he would insist that it had not been an adventure; that
they were never in any real danger. What was good, Frank insisted, was that they
had come through it together. And there would be other, more difficult challenges
ahead for the brothers.

Ruth would have been attuned enough to the vagaries of human behavior
to wonder about those "rivers of sweat" that poured over Robert's face at a chilly
10,000 feet and kept him from being able to drive. Was it fear? And there were
other questions to ponder: Did this episode expose something about how Robert,
this genius everyone was talking about, looked at the world and railed at its limits?

In the end, Robert divided his time between Berkeley and Caltech, spending
most of each year in Northern California. Berkeley's academic year ended early in
the spring, allowing him to move to Caltech. In a letter to Frank, he explained that
he wanted to keep the connection so he could be checked by the Caltech theoreti-
cians "if I got too far off base." He also had an open invitation to stay in the Tolman
guest cottage, and wanted to see more of Richard Tolman's "extremely intelligent
and quite lovely" wife,[63] and to hear her stories about her work with psychologi-
cally troubled youth.

&

ABOARD SS *MINNEKAHDA*, ATLANTIC TRANSPORT LINE, 1928

"O snab of all snabbists," Jean Tatlock would write on the first day of the
crossing to England, "I would stand 4 years of seasickness if this boat were going the other way."[64] The fourteen-year-old lost no time in finding a quiet corner

in one of the ship's public lounges to write the first of many impassioned letters to her friends at home. The "snab of all snabs" was her close friend May Sarton. With Letty Field, Jean and May had formed their own exclusive little triumvirate at Cambridge High and Latin School in Cambridge, Massachusetts. Jean's father, and May's as well, were professors at Harvard; Letty's father was Herbert Haviland Field, a humanist and Quaker pacifist, who had died of a heart attack when Letty was eight.[65] She was fifteen now; May, at sixteen, was the eldest of the three. Two others, the Clark sisters, Margot and Jean, were on the edge of the group. All the girls were vibrant, passionate, precocious and often charming, as well as sure of their own intellects.

Snab, the name they adopted for themselves, was probably meant as a play on *snob,* which they agreed was a label that applied to them, not out of any sort of social conceit but on the basis of their obviously superior literary skills. The girls read incessantly and wrote poetry and plays. They adored Ibsen's *Hedda Gabbler,* shared bits of gossip about Edna St. Vincent Millay, critiqued her new poems while immersing themselves in Galsworthy, Khalil Gibran and Amy Lowell. Their bodies were beginning to bloom, feelings they didn't understand to stir, and the three shared it all—pouring out their unformed desires, often in bursts of poetry.

In Cambridge, the trio rode their bicycles around the neighborhood, bought chocolate ice-cream sodas at Gomaos', had dinner or stayed the night in one another's homes, smoked Pell Mells, called each other "darlingest," and swore that all boys were fools. (Though occasionally either Letty or Jean would timidly admit to running into a boy who wasn't totally awful.) They went to the theater as often as they were allowed and became infatuated with their favorite actresses, Jean with Katherine Warren and May with Le Gallienne, at twenty-nine a doyenne of the American stage.

The girls haunted stage doors, begged for photos and autographs, wrote the actresses fawning notes, invited them to tea with their mothers, and swooned when they responded. The actresses clearly enjoyed these educated and, for the most part, charming young fans, and offered them advice. Eva Le Gallienne was certain that a college education was totally unnecessary, even an impediment, for an actress.

May had declared her intention of forgoing college to become an actress. Jean followed suit, announcing in one of her letters, "May, I *have decided not to go to college!* Oh boy. Everybody I know says that when you have a specialty, college is death to it. No actresses ever go. I have terrible faith in my powers of acting. I'm perfectly sure I can do it. I don't always feel this way, but I will henceforward. I know, I know."[66] Jean wrote her way across the Atlantic in long letters, filled with longing to get back to Cambridge, and to Boston and New York and the theater.

May—petite and self-confident—was clearly the ringleader of the Snabs. She had one more year at Cambridge High and Latin, and Le Gallienne had offered her a place in her student repertory company in Gloucester for the summer. And now that Jean had declared her intention to become an actress, May would speak with Eva about making a place for her Snab friend in the company.

⤿

THAT FALL OF 1928, ROBERT returned to Europe for his last postdoctoral studies. He started at the University of Leiden in the Netherlands. In his first six weeks he managed to learn enough Dutch to deliver a lecture in the language, which earned him the nickname *Opje*. When he returned to California, it would become "Oppie," which would stay with him for life. From Leiden, he went on to Zurich to study under Wolfgang Pauli.

⤿

THE TATLOCK CHILDREN GREW UP reading aloud in the evenings, memorizing Shakespeare, becoming familiar with the cadences of Old English. In the summers they went to outdoor performances and to the theater in Boston. Marjorie understood that she had contributed to her darling daughter's decision to become an actress. And there were other reasons to worry about Jean, now clearly in the full throes of adolescence. Marjorie would have noted her daughter's mood swings, though it was difficult to say how much of Jean's emotional distress could be attributed to adolescent angst, and how much might have signaled problems to come.

Before they embarked from New York, Marjorie had convinced her husband to leave Harvard and return to Berkeley. Professor Tatlock did not want to go; he had been at Harvard only four years, and, as the head of the English Department, was at the apex of his career. He was happy with his position at Harvard. Of course, the English department at Berkeley was delighted to add such a distinguished scholar to its roster. He made his discontent clear; it was Marjorie who insisted they return to the coast, but her motives were confusing. She was making a sacrifice by putting a continent between herself and her son, Hugh, at Phillips Academy in Andover, Massachusetts. And between herself and her dearest friend. But Marjorie was adamant. She was intensely interested in psychology, and from her time at Stanford was aware of the pioneering work in psychotherapy being done in the Bay Area.[67] Possibly she had also seen something in Jean that alarmed her, warned her of storms to come, and felt she would be better able to face them in this far west conclave of psychotherapy.

While the professor prepared for the move to Berkeley, Marjorie sailed off to Europe with Hugh and Jean. Marjorie's plan was to get Jean settled, then return to the States to make arrangements for the move to the West Coast. She set about convincing Jean to stay on in France for a month or more; it was a marvelous opportunity, she said, a chance to become adept at French and to practice being on her own. Marjorie's hope was to find an "angelic" family for Jean to stay with, and a tutor or a school where she could take classes. If all went according to plan, the family would collect Jean in France and sail from Cherbourg to New York in time to celebrate Christmas with John's sister in New York, then on to California for the New Year.

Aboard the *Minnekahda*, Jean continued to write longingly about returning to Cambridge High and Latin. Jean pleaded with May to convince her parents to allow her to stay with them for her junior year. When May's mother came through with the invitation, Jean burbled, "I can't get over your mother's wonderfulosity … Tell her again that I will be an angel."[68] Marjorie did not want her daughter to stay behind, but Jean was unrelenting. And Mabel Sarton, May's mother, was both liked and admired among the faculty wives.

At the moment, steaming toward England, Marjorie looked forward to joining Winifred and Priscilla at Stratford on Avon; she was counting on her best friend's counsel. At Vassar, Winnie had accumulated years of experience in guiding bright, starstruck young girls through their tempestuous adolescences. In London, they stayed at a boardinghouse near the British Museum, where Jean found the original scripts of English poems, including the sonnet of Rupert Brooke that begins, "If I should die, think only this of me …" She decided, "I didn't used to like it, but now I adore it."[69]

In their meanderings between museums, Jean occasionally noticed a different London: "The first two or three days I had the most uneasy feeling that I was living in the nineteenth century. Everything was so old and pleasant and cruel. The poor were so terribly poor and haggard and hopeless. The rich were so inconsistent and tasteless. The city was so silent and yet busy in a make-believe way."[70]

Marjorie, Jean, Winifred and her niece Priscilla went off to Stratford on Avon. Priscilla was eighteen now. She and Jean had corresponded over the years since their trip to Colorado, sharing their feelings. In England, they took off as they had before, this time swimming and rowing on the Avon. Jean didn't mention to May that she and Pris were meeting friends and going to the theater and having adventures. She wrote to explain that Priscilla was a junior at Vassar, adding rather formally, "You see her aunt, Winifred, teaches drama there, and is mother's best friend."[71]

MAY'S OWN LETTERS WERE LONG and splashed with poetry and gossip about the theater; she copied letters written to her by the actress Katherine Warren, sending Jean into paroxysms of envy. May's mad crushes were almost always attached to older women, often her teachers. She had not experienced that "sort of mechanical instinct" that made Jean, for the first time, aware of the physical effects men can have on women.

In August, the Tatlocks made their way across the Channel to France. Jean found a quiet place on the ship to write to May: "So very much has happened since I've seen you." Jean was still hoping for a reprieve that would send her back to Cambridge, where she could stay with the Sartons for a year, before she returned to California and the new family home.

⤳

"INTELLECTUALLY SUPERIOR" IS HOW ONE of Kitty Puening's high-school boyfriends would remember the petite brunette who graduated from Aspinwall High School in Pennsylvania in June of 1928. For four years, the Puening's capacious home on woodsy Delafield Road had been headquarters for the circle that revolved around Kitty. Small and pretty, lively and ambitious, she was popular and certainly a flirt. Her parents regularly took Kitty to Europe to visit relatives. Kitty hinted that her parents were titled, that there was a family castle; she would obliquely mention Belgium's royal family. She was bright, outspoken, daring.[72] Her high-school boyfriend would remember that she had moved decidedly to the political left in her senior year. While her father most likely tolerated her political interests, he would have been less pleased by the cadre of young men who seemed to circle around Kitty—or by the fact that Kitty didn't discourage the attention.

The girlfriends Kitty admired and courted were those who dreamed of personal success and accomplishment. One boyfriend would remember how determined Kitty was to succeed academically. In chemistry class, possibly after someone repeated the popular canard about women enrolling in college to get an M.R.S. degree, she stamped her feet and insisted, "I'm going to be a Ph.D."[73] No one seemed to doubt that Kitty Puening was serious, even if at the time not many high-school girls with ambitions of their own were in the habit of broadcasting them. Having ambition almost always meant these women were willing to forgo marriage and children for a career. The majority of bright young women chose to marry a man of consequence and become a silent partner, living in his reflected light. A doctor, perhaps. Or a lawyer. Or an academic. Only a few women declared that they were determined to achieve a level of success on their own.

After Kitty graduated from high school in June of 1928, she enrolled for the fall semester at the University of Pittsburgh as Katherine Vissering Puening. She and her mother then boarded a steamer bound for Europe, arriving in Bremen, Germany, at about the same time the SS *Minnekahda,* with the Tatlocks aboard, put in at Plymouth, England.

6

JEAN WISHES THAT "SOMEBODY WOULD
PAINT CHRIST AS A LIVE, INTENSELY STRONG,
DREAM FIGURE." SHE IS SICK OF CRUCIFIXION,
OF BLOOD AND OF WEEPING

Hugh Tatlock had two weeks before the start of his senior year at Phillips Academy, so for the last weeks of summer, he and his mother and sister crossed the Channel to St. Jacut, an ancient fishing village in Brittany, on the rugged northwest coast of France. Named for an Irish saint from the Dark Ages, the area held the remains of an abbey and the impressive ruins of the medieval Chateau du Guldo. Fishing boats lay stranded at low tide on the long empty beaches. In the village, the old houses huddled together against the winds. "St. Jacut is rather sweet," Jean wrote to May, "the type of French village made up of stone walls, cats, dogs, chickens and utter filth."[74]

The young visitors roamed the beaches and climbed the rocks, joined by fifteen-year-old George, the son of the friend who had invited the Tatlocks to St. Jacut. George presented a problem for Jean, who was content with writing about her strange new attraction to men, but not ready to confront it in real life. "He is sensible in that he isn't silly about girls and can talk decently when he wants to," she wrote, "but otherwise I hate him." What she would call "a sort of feud" erupted between them. Young George could not understand Jean's moods, or she his clumsy reactions. "Every night," Jean tried to explain, "he would get horrid and make the most sarcastic inane remarks about me and to me. He only began it three nights before they left, so I think he was mad at me for some unknown reason. He said things that made me want to slap him, but, like a Spartan, I kept silent until he made more remarks about my never speaking. It was unbearable with everyone listening attentively . . . Boys are perfect fools, I am convinced."[75]

AT SUMMER'S END, HUGH SAILED for home and Jean wrote May that she "almost died" when his ship pulled away, wanting so much to return to Massachusetts with him. But she dutifully agreed that staying was "probably doing me more good than being in America and Boston ever could."[76] Jean was beginning to trust her mother's judgment; to accept that she was indeed thinking of her future, and of what was best for her. Even if it meant leaving her on her own for a month in Paris.

With all the fresh air and swimming and rock climbing, all the snacks of Petit Buerres and chocolate amid the ruins of the ancient chateau, Jean juggled an adolescent's adoration of favorite actresses with a growing critical thinking inspired by the books she was devouring. (Galsworthy's *Saint's Progress* was "perfectly horrible in every way. Badly written, sentimental, untrue and Victorian-tinged, it made my blood boil.") She managed also to copy reams of poems, some her own and others from contemporary poets published in books or magazines. Her life that summer flowed out in her small, unfaltering hand onto the fronts and backs of letter paper, addressed to May and Letty and the Clark sisters. And always, somewhere in all those solid pages of handwriting, she would manage to squeeze in, "Cambridge again in three months . . ."[77]

Cabarets, Gertrude Stein, Shakespeare & Company, sidewalk cafés, waiters in black with long white aprons. For Jean, Paris was at once the most beautiful city she had ever seen, and something more: "The sort of grand effect of space and un-hurried sure loveliness of the whatchucallit square, the Champs Elysees and L'Arc de Triomphe. The vistas and fountains and the art oh . . . Jeanne d'Arc too. I'm glad there is so much of her in Paris. I don't know what but Shaw's play and everything about her have taken a tremendous hold on me. . . . After I finished it I thought I'd burn up or drown and I tried like a fool, to do parts of it. It'll be a long time before I try again, methinks."[78]

She haunted the art museums, lingered in front of the *Mona Lisa* and Da Vinci's *Madonna,* found it all unbelievably beautiful. She wished, she said, that "somebody would paint Christ as a live, intensely strong, dream figure. I'm sick of crucifixions. After all, his life and words and revealing actions were the main thing. Not his blood and people weeping. Anybody can weep and shed blood."[79]

The images that bombarded Jean's mind, of blood and intense dream figures, would presage the struggles to come, of color and movement and a racing mind, everything suffused with velocity and energy until she plunged into depression and despair. All now suffused with the religious images that filled the vast, soaring spaces of Saint-Sulpice on a Sunday afternoon. Jean would write: "I've never been through such a variety of moods as I did in that hour. I gazed most of the time at God in a white beard sitting on a velvet cushion in the clouds. It made me quite ill to think that humanity thought that way, and I almost cried about it but then I decided it wasn't any more worth crying about than dreams or stories." The theatrical pulpit atop dual staircases, with its gold-encrusted canopy, made her want to "ask how many hairs there were in God's beard." She thought that a shocking thing to say—she knew most people believed you shouldn't make fun of other people's ideals and dreams—but she was adamant. The sooner people "crawl out of the shells of other centuries the sooner we'll progress," she wrote. "At any rate, we can't stand still."[80]

She didn't intend to stand still, and a letter from May's mother arrived, formally inviting her to stay with the Sarton family for the spring semester. Jean wrote May to say she hadn't words to express how much the letter had meant and promised that "I shall be like the shepherdess, unlike Mary Jane, Tartuffe, Edward Jones, The Vicar of Wakefield, Uriah Heap . . . In short, I shall be a model to you. Please tell your mother, do. I really want to compliment you on the bravery of asking me; I had no idea you were so lion-hearted. But I will be good."[81]

Before her mother left in September, Jean moved into a pension near the American school to live with a French family named Boué. She reported to May: "Mme. Boué is most respectable with dyed red hair and an irritating manner of calling me 'ma pauvre petite.' She is the kind (not necessarily French) that strokes your hand on the slightest provocation and tries to get under your skin by breathing in your face . . . The only nice thing about her is that she calls her dwarfed parent 'petite Maman' . . . I've been in bed with a cold since I got here. I always did have a grudge against people who mess around you when you're sick. It's my ungrateful nature. I like to be left alone in emotional and physical crisises."[82]

Then, like the fourteen-year-old she was, Jean changed the subject: "I did meet Monsieur Sympole, a young gentleman boarder here, just as I entered the door. He looked nice, but was terribly scared of me. Which is rather exciting for a change. I wish I would fall in love with him or somebody different. (I don't really; I detest men.) This point of view was given me by Isadora Duncan. She must have been a perfect bug-bear; I can't imagine anything more wonderful than being able to fall in love any moment, and to have it realized. She was a bit too sensual. I don't think she was exactly wrong morally though . . . Of course, personally it disgusts me that she should let herself go so easily; just like a gluttonous person eating. After all, she was primarily an artist; not a writer or a saint. (This whole paragraph is slightly unbalanced. Don't take it to heart.)"[83]

IN OCTOBER, JEAN CONFIDED TO May in one of her long, discursive letters: "I'm in an awful mess of mind . . . I go through more stages and nightmares in one day than I would have thought possible in a year. I think 'Oh, what's the use' and then get sudden glimpses. I get into a streetcar and am astounded at the apparent happiness of everyone; this is during black moods. Then I see lights into the past and the future, and smile sardonically, very forced, very self-conscious . . . I can't understand myself . . . Of course, I know that this is all pure and simple adolescence which everyone goes through, but that makes it all the worse." In the next breath she added, "Another thing that makes me perfectly ill is that though I detest men wholly, I am beginning to take small notice of them. Before I never even looked at them; now something utterly outside of myself, something without the slightest feeling, some sort of mechanical instinct makes me aware of them as men." Another gasp and her mind leapt: "Today . . . I got a sudden wild desire to be naked in the night. It is an impulse I get very often; to be alone among trees and wet grass with room for movement and sound; I don't know why I tell you this; it means nothing."[84]

With no close friend to talk all this over with, and in the absence of any experience, the teenager's typical sensations and confusion about sex, about love, life, art and morality spilled out into letters to the Snabs. What was remarkable was that Jean had the intelligence to recognize that her line of thought was, in fact, "slightly unbalanced."

Her failure to make friends could have been caused by a developing intellectualism; at fourteen, Jean had some definite and, for the time, even radical, opinions as well as the vocabulary to express them vividly: "You agree that there are too many people in the world, don't you?" she would demand in a letter. "I mean poor people having five or six children because of ignorance and religion. And other people because of ignorance and laws. It seems to me the most human and inconsistent thing that America should have two such broad and contradictory laws as Prohibition and lack of Birth Control. In one it wants to control a strong instinct; in the other, it doesn't want to control a stronger. In this, a so-called age of science, it will not accept what it puts forth and what must eventually become one of the main stays of humanity. (Birth-Control, not Prohibition.)"[85]

All through October, more or less on her own, she rambled about Paris and wrote poetry. ("With me, poems are the inevitable outcome of good and conflict; any kind of expression has two forces behind it to make it be.") She searched out the Rodin sculptures and Napoleon's tomb and went running home to write it all down in a letter to Letty or to May, how it had a "sort of powerful, mystic quality which terrifies me. Those still, solemn figures around it, the sudden aching color . . . the unflinching serenity and sternness of it all."[86]

Early in November, John and Marjorie returned to Paris and in December the three Tatlocks sailed from Cherbourg in time to arrive in New York just before Christmas. John's sister Jessie was there to meet them. For the past two years, Jessie had been teaching history at Mount Holyoke College in Massachusetts, and she was happy to spend the holidays with her brother's family before they left for the West.

Jessie Tatlock adored her niece. One summer years before, when they had all been together at the shore, Jessie had taught Hugh how to swim. Jean had been only four at the time, but so determined to learn that she would walk out into the water until only the top of her head remained in sight and Jessie would have to rescue her.[87]

For Christmas, Jessie had made plans to take Jean to the theater to see Le Gallienne in Chekhov's *The Cherry Orchard* and also had booked them a room at the Women's University Club on East 52nd Street. All across the Atlantic Jean dreamt about this night and about her plan to see the actress. Finally in the theater and seated, she sat through the first act so excited she was "shivering, but I was very sure of myself the way one is before acting. Not that I was going to act."[88] At the first intermission, she gave the usher a note to take to Le Gallienne. At the second intermission, the usher returned to say that the actress would meet her after the last act.

At the end of the play, the usher led the girl to a bench outside of Dressing Room No. 1, and motioned for her to sit. Jean felt she "would throb to death." She sat patiently, drawing her feet close under her to let people pass. She didn't move for five minutes, feeling "that everything was inevitable and wonderfully tragic, that everything was sure." Then a woman in "a mottled leopard skin coat with a loose face" walked into the dressing room. Jean heard kissing, talking, and laughing that went on for a time. Then Le Gallienne came out, "her hair wild and her face splotched," and told the slender, polite girl waiting on the bench that she had picked a bad night to come. Gallienne asked, "Was it anything special you wanted to speak to me about? Can you come some other night?"[89]

Jean managed to make her way through the stage door and move into a dark space to be alone, to regain her composure. Then she returned to her waiting aunt, who took her arm and "talked unbearably all the way home about how it didn't really matter."[90]

Jean cried herself to sleep, and wrote to May the next morning, describing the whole humiliating experience. She was not giving up, she said. She might have left Le Gallienne kissing "vile ladies," but she was not giving up her dreams of the theater.

7

JEAN AND MAY INDULGE IN THEATER AND
PLAN FOR A NIGHT IN NEW YORK CITY, AND
THE OPPENHEIMER BROTHERS DISCOVER A
LOST MINE IN THE SANGRE DE CRISTOS
AND STAKE A CLAIM

The Tatlock family took the train west and celebrated the first day of 1929
in California. Soon after Jean crossed the country again, through the snow-clad
Sierra Nevada, rolling on through the plains and into Chicago, where she changed
to a Boston-bound train. Her final destination was the Sarton house in Cambridge.
Marjorie and John had agreed to let Jean finish her junior year at Cambridge High
and Latin; at last the Snabs were together again.

For May, an only child whose parents had always treated her with a kind of
benevolent neglect, who had been lonely through much of her childhood, life with
Jean in the household was simply "scrumptious." Jean behaved as well as she had
promised to, and was as delighted with Mabel and George Sarton as they were
with this cerebral, tender, wistfully beautiful girl.

The Clark sisters, Margot and Jean, previously always on the fringes, now became
more a part of this intellectual "in group." All the girls immersed themselves in writing poetry, imagining emotions they had not yet experienced, then running to each
other's homes to compare their efforts.[91] They talked at length about love and life and
their futures. The group was a force of its own, and May remained its magnetic center.

Several of the girls' mothers had gone to college before World War I, when
"smashing"—conducting romantic friendships that mimicked crushes on

boys—was considered innocent. (Marjorie Tatlock and Winifred Smith came from this period.) "Smashing" became a rite of passage—a practice run before marriage. But early in the new century, thanks in part to Freud and the rise of psychoanalysis, it began to be seen as abnormal and deviant.[92] The result, for girls who came of age in the 1920s, was a confused and relentless preoccupation with the nexus between emotional and physical love.

FOR JEAN AND THE SNABS, always a step or two ahead of their classmates, "smashing" began while they were still in high school. They loved and trusted and held onto one another. Precocious enough to know about adultery and homosexuality, they would read *The Well of Loneliness,* the novel about lesbianism banned in England the previous year as obscene.[93] Yet custom still permitted girls to walk the halls of Cambridge High and Latin holding hands, to sleep over at each other's houses, to curl up together and share a bed, to kiss and hug and pledge their enduring love. This friendship among Jean and May and Letty was, perhaps, more intense, more intellectual, more introspective about sexuality than others, but the girls were alike in the feelings that arise in the tumultuous teenage years: loneliness, uselessness, often out-of-control emotions. They squabbled with one another, pouted, cried, made up and fretted over the inevitably of leaving the safety of childhood. They felt as if they were about to fling themselves off a cliff and into adult life, and they both thrilled at and feared this development. May, for one, couldn't wait.

As spring moved toward summer and the end of the 1929 school year, Jean went to nearby Andover to join her parents for Hugh's graduation from Phillips Academy, then returned for May's ceremony a week later. Before an audience of 1,500, May read the class poem. Immediately she wrote her mother, "Graduation is over … You can't imagine how happy I am!" As an afterthought, she added, "Jean left yesterday. It's awful without her—except that I'm so busy."[94]

In fact, May would only see Jean one last time that year. May planned to go to New York for a day before making her way to the Gloucester Little Theatre. Jean would meet her on June 16; a hotel room would give them the luxury of absolute privacy for their last night together before May left to begin her theatrical career, and Jean would begin the long continental crossing to face her own last, lonely year of high school in Berkeley.

The girls walked Manhattan and talked, about the theater and all that May was doing, about the people she was working with and the excitement of it all, about how wonderful it would be when Jean could join her and begin her own career. May had enough confidence for both of them; she had already spoken to Eva Le Gallienne about Jean.

Jean rose early the next morning, left the hotel room and caught a bus to New Hampshire, where she joined Priscilla, who was going west as well, and at eighteen was old enough to be Jean's companion. It was not until they boarded the Union Pacific's Gold Coast Limited that Jean found a private place in the observation car to write to May. "I want to know," she asked. "I have been puzzled ever since then, did something really happen the last night or did I dream it all? The next morning after everything you are always untouched and oblivious."[95]

If May had given her no hint of how she felt, Jean at least wanted her to know that she had "felt a passion that night that was pure beauty and full and fulfilling. I have never been so deeply happy in my life. I love you . . . I didn't know so much before, I am horribly thankful that I do now. Isn't it wonderful that it should have happened the last night so now nothing can break it? Even if you should say in your next letter that you hate me, it would be just as perfect."[96]

It is easy to imagine Jean, sitting alone in the observation car, crossing through Iowa or Illinois, lighting one of her Pell Mells and writing with all the honesty she could muster: "I suddenly thought once that it might have been lesbian love, but it wasn't, and if it was I don't care." After a few drags on a cigarette, blowing smoke into the air and picturing it drifting off to May, she changed the subject: "I am dying for my mother; aren't mothers nice sometimes? I think mine is almost saintly. I think it is peculiar and a crime that she should have such a daughter as I."[97]

May did not hate Jean, but she did know that whatever had happened between them that last night was not lesbian love. Jean had been "too shy," May decided. They were not, after all, alike. For May, erotic love with a woman would happen, but it would not be with Jean.

⌒

In 1928, on one of the visits to New Mexico, the Oppenheimer brothers and Katherine Page set out on horseback to explore Grass Mountain, only a mile or so from her dude ranch at Los Pinos, and came upon a plot of land with a primitive cabin for lease. "Hot dog!" one of the Oppenheimers said. Katherine—now called Katy—repeated in Spanish: *"perro caliente!"*[98]

The cabin had no running water, no indoor plumbing—no amenities at all. The brothers wanted it, and their father quickly signed an agreement to lease the cabin and surrounding acres. They named it Perro Caliente; that summer was the first spent on Grass Mountain, with any of Frank's friends and Robert's colleagues who were willing to rough it. They slept on cots on the porch, warmed by piles of Indian blankets, and ate food out of cans. Katy Page supplied them with horses, and when she wasn't tending guests at Los Pinos, she would join the gang. Katy had placed the adolescent Robert in her regal inner circle; now she was invited into his. The Tolmans visited, and Ruth and Katy became friends, part of the widening gyre of the Pasadena-Berkeley circle.

"Sometimes we took along camping gear and stayed in the mountains," Frank would remember. More often, he went on, they would ride all day, then drop into the desert to stay at one ranch or another where people always seemed willing to put them and their horses up for the night. One day he and Robert planned to go to Truchas, a town at 8,000 feet on a high plateau, surrounded by 13,000-foot Truchas peaks, and looking across at the Jemez Mountains and down at the Rio Grande Valley. There they knew the man who ran the general store and the post office. Their usual route to the south was about 30 miles; this time they were planning to go the long way around to the north, in a remote swath of mountains they had never covered, figuring it would be about 50 miles. They left early and stopped at Los Pinos; Katy waved them off, jokingly instructing them to keep their eyes open for the legendary Lost Mine.

What the brothers thought would be 50 miles turned to 60, much of it through unmarked wilderness with no signs of humans, not even a lonely sheepherder's initials carved into trees. The brothers navigated over and around and sometimes through gravel slicks and rock slides that covered the trails. When they stopped to rest, Frank wrote, Robert "looked up and saw a cluster of columbine growing out of the dirt covered roof of a small log cabin." They probed as far as they dared and discovered first a horizontal shaft, then a vertical one filled with water. They had found the Lost Mine. Robert collected a small crucible from the forge, which became his ashtray, a totem that he'd keep for years.

The last part of the ride was as formidable as the first; another long drop was covered with masses of fallen timber. Their horses could jump some of the logs, but the brothers had to remove the horses' saddles to scramble under others. Finally they had to chop their way through; it was midnight before they reached Truchas. Not long after the excursion, the two made their way to the county seat and filed their claim. Later that summer they rode back to survey the mine. The Oppenheimer boys were living the legends of the Old West.

Soon enough, they would return to another plateau in these mountains, where another legend would be created.

8

JEAN GOES WEST TO A NEW LIFE IN BERKELEY, WHILE ROBERT MEETS LINUS AND AVA HELEN PAULING AT CALTECH

Her junior year behind her, Jean left Cambridge in 1929 and returned to Berkeley and her family. She wrote to May, "Our house is marvelous and big with weeping willows and rocks and eucalyptus and bushes. The tennis court is perfect. But I haven't found any people yet."[99] Marjorie had discovered the house on San Antonio Avenue, high in the Berkeley Hills, a scant two miles from the university. It had a wide entry hall that looked through to a library, an elegant staircase that wound to the second floor and seven bedrooms scattered throughout. There was room for every family member, including Jean's grandmother, with several rooms to spare. A basement had servants' quarters and a music room with remarkable acoustics; a second staircase connected all the levels. Every west-facing room had large windows that looked out onto San Francisco Bay and the Golden Gate; in four years, the family would use binoculars to follow the building of the great bridge that would span this gateway to the Pacific.

Jean thought the summer-brown hills that rose, soft and round, to the east looked like sleeping elephants. Walking trails meandered through woods heavy with the scent of eucalyptus, and opened up to views where Jean could watch the sun throw great swaths of pink and orange skyward before being swallowed by the Pacific. There was a small flat roof on the house, next to a deck, and Jean found a way to climb onto it. [100] She spent clear nights there watching the moon float above her and dreaming of joining Eva Le Gallienne's theater group. Art was beauty and she lived for beauty, she continually reminded herself and May in the letters that flew between them. Jean also wondered whether high school would ever end, and life would ever begin.

With the months of July and August looming, long and empty, Jean's letters began to pose questions, concerns that she was not progressing as she had hoped. The changes she had expected in herself were not happening. She had wanted to be rid of the anxieties of adolescence, to grow up and emerge into a calmer, clearer time. She wrote that perhaps she was expecting too much. In letters, she told May of the added distress that the poems she wanted to write were not coming—and she needed them because she had so much to say.

Her languor was aggravated by a fight she'd had with Priscilla on the journey west. It should have been a small thing. Pris asked to read Jean's poems. Jean had, very politely, she thought, explained that she would rather not show them to her. Pris had pushed, and tried to wrest the book from her. Jean had panicked, she was shaking, her adrenaline pumping. At last Pris had backed off, but not without pouting and telling Jean that she acted as though she were a mother protecting her child.[101] More likely, Jean was a child protecting her mother—from the love poems she had written to May. If Pris read them, Jean suspected she would tell her aunt, and Winifred would tell her best friend, Jean's mother. She couldn't let that happen. Jean vowed never to forgive Pris after their incident on the train.

THE TATLOCKS' FRIENDS ELIZABETH AND James Whitney were medical doctors who had gone to Zurich in 1926 to be analyzed by Carl Jung, and had returned to San Francisco to practice psychoanalysis. The Whitneys became part of the psychoanalysts and psychologists who were drawn to the Bay Area. Berkeley turned out some of the earliest psychologists. Edward Tolman and Jean Macfarlane (the first female Ph.D. in psychology from the university) and her husband, Donald, were also part of an early group, along with other followers of Freud and Jung. Jean often joined Marjorie and Elizabeth Whitney on their hikes.[102] The women took long walks in the hills together, Jean sometimes tagging along, tuning in and out of their conversations but dismissing most of them as boring—"they talk about rats," she wrote a friend. In fact, much of the groundbreaking research that psychologists were doing on human behavior was being done by Edward Tolman—Macfarlane's mentor, Jean's future teacher—at Berkeley's psychology program, and rats were at the center of many of his laboratory experiments.

MARJORIE, INCREASINGLY AWARE OF JEAN'S moods, and wanting to find a way to ease them, found a theater group that happened to be putting on *Saint Joan*, a play that fascinated Jean: the Maid of Orleans had visions when she was thirteen, led the army that vanquished the British at eighteen, and was martyred in 1431 when she was nineteen. Jean got a walk-on part. Her role in *Saint Joan* helped earn Jean the lead part in three more plays that summer—and revealed an obstacle to her dream of an acting career. She confessed to May that she was "stricken with unbelievable stage-fright so that I didn't see how I could utter a word or move. I was mortally afraid that I would forget my lines and was so self-conscious that I shook. Unless I can do something about it I certainly will never be able to act." She added: "I can tell you I died more than once, this summer."[103]

She was determined to learn to settle her nerves. Marjorie thought that per- haps going to camp would help. It would get Jean out in nature, to sing songs around a campfire, to have a new experience. Jean agreed only because, as she wrote May, "one night I just about went insane with despair and would have done anything under the earth."[104]

Enormous coastal redwood trees—great giants that reached to the skies as if planted just to make humans feel insignificant—surrounded many Northern Cal- ifornia campgrounds. Around the campfire one night, as a talented young camper played the violin, Jean was transported, as if "some curtain seemed to be lifted from me and I was laid bare to a sort of blind and all-powerful pain and beauty. I became nothing, and everything became nothing; it was unbearable and yet it was the greatest thing that can happen to a human, as far as I know. All the trees and the blackness and the whole world was one and 'immensity was made manifold.'" She wrote, "I ran away from everyone and looked at the violinist, till I became her soul and she became mine, and everything together was Beauty choking us and yet deadly clear."[105]

The quote "immensity was made manifold," is from the Edna St. Vincent Mil- lay poem "Renascence."* The poet was a favorite of the Snabs; any of them could recite the verses, written when Millay was just nineteen. The poem describes with compelling accuracy the progression of the kind of psychotic interlude that thera- pists would come to label manic-depressive.

Jean's experience that night—girls gathered around a campfire, sparks ris- ing in the night air, the sound of a single violin piercing the darkness—sent her from ecstatic revelations to a painfully beautiful awareness. And it was not the only time: in November she would write that, "The other night when the moon

---

*Edna St. Vincent Millay was a friend and classmate of Winifred Smith at Vassar. She would write "Renascence"—a favorite poem with adolescent girls for almost a century—the year before she entered Vassar. She would receive a Pulitzer Prize for Poetry and would suffer from recurring bouts of depression later in life.

was up . . . I had a religious ecstasy."[106] She understood that something alarming and important had happened, so suffocating that to regain her breath she needed to share the intensity of it with her closest friends. She wrote to May, Letty, and Jean Clark. Alarmed, all three girls responded. Jean's visions were intensifying and she was desperate to understand them.

⤚

Two tall, good-looking young Americans, Robert Oppenheimer and Linus Pauling, were on similar levels intellectually and professionally; Pauling, though, had already made a professional mark in chemistry. A few years older than Robert, Pauling had the same sort of questioning, profound mind as Robert—the kind of mind that seemed to operate at higher RPMs than those of most people. Each man was at the beginning of a career that gave every sign of being spectacular; each had been courted by the same top universities. It was not surprising that they should become instant friends at Caltech.

But in fact, the two men were different in more ways than they were alike. Born and reared in Oregon, Pauling had a decidedly western outlook. He had grown up poor and his widowed mother saw no need for college, no matter how precocious he was. He went anyway, working his way through Oregon Agricultural College by mopping floors and chopping wood, and very quickly was drafted to teach basic chemistry in freshman home economics. It was not Harvard; his social skills were not up to "Old School" measure. Older faculty at Caltech, including Richard Tolman, found him a trifle too brash, perhaps a little too ambitious. When Harvard made him a handsome offer, Pauling used it to leverage a better deal with Caltech, one very much like Oppenheimer's, whereby he could work at other universities for part of each year.

But the major impediment, in terms of the Oppenheimer-Pauling friendship, was Pauling's wife, Ava Helen. The same age as Robert, she was high-spirited and flirtatious, "smarter than any girl I'd ever met," Pauling said.[107] And she had definite ideas of her own about how the world should work. The tenth of twelve children, Ava Helen had grown up on an Oregon farm with a schoolteacher father who was a socialist and expected his clan to be aware of what was happening in international politics.

The Paulings found the Caltech senior faculty stuffy and boring, and avoided them socially. But Robert was their own age, and the couple was intrigued by the hints of scandal (the poison-apple affair) and gossip (was he a homosexual?) that swirled around him. Before long, Robert asked Pauling for help with his lecture techniques, and Pauling asked Robert to work with him on the mathematics of carbon's tetrahedral bonds. Socially, they formed a threesome. Robert's old habit of gift-giving resurfaced—he could not resist. Armloads of flowers, always for her; and no less than his entire, extensive, and very expensive mineral collection for him. He also gave Pauling a collection of his poems, some with sexual references, which Pauling found "obscure and troubling."[108]

Ava Helen grew up expecting to participate in conversation, to introduce ideas and have opinions. And she couldn't resist flirting. She didn't seem to realize that her actions might be misinterpreted. Wasn't Robert a man of the world? A rich New Yorker, sophisticated world traveler, experienced with women?

In fact, at this juncture in his life, Robert Oppenheimer was almost as inexperienced in the rituals of love and sex as was Jean Tatlock, a teenager, reading a novel about lesbians and wondering whether she might be one, then deciding that she was not because she didn't look masculine. Robert's confusion on matters sexual was about to take a fateful turn. On one of those nice pastel days in Pasadena, after Pauling had left for his chemistry laboratory, Robert appeared at the Pauling house. Ava Helen answered the door, happy to see him but puzzled by a sudden awkwardness and confusion in one of the most articulate people she had ever known. Suddenly he blurted out something about going to Mexico. The two of them. Together. Ava Helen, the disingenuous coquette, could be forgiven if she was thoroughly confused, before she realized that Robert must have completely misunderstood her. She said the only thing she could say: No, of course not. She took her marriage seriously, and she had no intention of going off with him to Mexico.[109]

She had the rest of the day to consider her part in the debacle, to decide how to present it to her husband. When Pauling came home, she very calmly told him what had happened. She was not angry; she may have even smiled. Her husband was not amused. He was furious. At the man he thought was his friend, yes. But at Ava Helen too, for what he perceived to be her too-calm reaction. As if she took pleasure in being propositioned, like she were some femme fatale.

Pauling would never again be anything but cool to Robert, and eventually "the Oppenheimer affair" would become part of Pauling family legend. Many years later, Ava Helen would say to her husband, "I don't think Oppenheimer was in love with me. I think he was in love with you." Pauling, with the passage of time, and with reflection, decided that was probably true.[110]

Either way, Robert's bumbling proposition to Ava Helen at the end of those flirtatious years illustrated a serious flaw in Robert's persona. He had figured out how to present himself as charming and self-assured to the point where women found him attractive. But when it came to reading sexual innuendo, he was still in poison apple country.

IN THE FALL OF 1929, Jean started her senior year in Berkeley at a private, progressive school originally named the Institute of Creative Development, and now called simply the Williams School, founded by the innovative educator Cora Williams. With its focus on poetry, music, language and literature, the school seemed right for Jean. It also offered interpretive-dance instruction in the style of one of Jean's idols, Isadora Duncan. Performances were held in the nearby Temple of Wings, where Duncan herself had danced. The Tatlocks' new home was no more than a three-minute walk up the road from the expansive school property. Once on the grounds, Jean passed by fountains and a reflecting pool on her way to the grand Spring Mansion, a two-story Beaux Arts building modeled after the Empress Elisabeth of Austria's Achillion Palace in Corfu, and now the school's main building.

Friends and adults used the word *brilliant* to describe Jean. Effusive in her Snab letters, she was in fact a quiet girl, intellectual and with definite opinions, but not yet a rebel. Having been transplanted from one coast to the other, she knew she should make new friends, but resisted, perhaps feeling it would be disloyal to replace the Snabs so easily. She settled in to read poetry and books, and to write long, aching, lonely letters. In her concise hand, with excellent grammar and punctuation and spelling, Jean again poured all her yearnings and love and terror onto multiple pages and mailed them off to May and Letty, and the Clark sisters. Once, Jean wrote to May: "I am in deep despair about boys. Haven't you had any experiences yet? You are so old. Letty seems to be growing up rapidly."[111]

And she fretted about her relationship with May. "I ache and ache for your presence," she said in one letter, the longing almost palpable. Then she added: "But I am not a lesbian. Are you?" Soon after, she wrote about a boy she had run into in Carmel, a favorite vacation town on the coast. Jean reported that he "fell in love with me. It was silent, as things are apt to be with me . . . The feelings he inspired in me were humorous. First excitement, then distain, then terror."[112] He walked up and down a few times, glanced at her without speaking. He left. The terror prevailed.

Fog shrouds summer mornings in Berkeley. At about eleven, the fog lifts and the sun comes out. It graces the sky until close to four in the afternoon, when the fog rolls back in through the Golden Gate and floats up and over the hills, wafting like a sea of chiffon. It isn't until September, when school starts, that true summer weather arrives, with bright-blue skies and temperatures that move toward 80 degrees.

Hugh and Professor Tatlock spent their days that September on the university campus. Hugh made new friends, but stayed in touch with those from Phillips Academy who had gone to Harvard. Even with the natural beauty, the dramatic geography of the Bay area, he preferred the East. Jean couldn't shake off her longing for Cambridge. Of the four Tatlocks, only Marjorie seemed to want to be in Berkeley.

III

FOREBODINGS

9

Jean worries that high school will never end, Robert's parents come to Pasadena for a visit and Ruth finds herself with parallel versions of the same man

The golden decade was over, the optimism of the '20s shattered by the stock-market crash of 1929. Banks failed, steel mills went dark, topsoil blew away in clouds of dust, farm boys' dreams of college and career evaporated as they helped pile family possessions on trucks to join the procession west. The madness crossed the Atlantic and wreaked havoc there as well. The world moved inexorably into chaos, both economic and political.

The Oppenheimers, Tolmans, Tatlocks and Puenings remained above the economic maelstrom but could not escape the social upheaval. They managed to afford private schools, comfortable homes, trips to Europe and elaborate presents (for Easter, Robert's mother gave the Tolmans "a beautiful crock of stuffed figs ... It must have cost a million dollars"[113])—but they could not deny the misery that was all around them.

In the 1930s, the movements of Robert, Ruth, Jean and Kitty had one or the other skimming up and down the West Coast, covering the 350 miles between Pasadena and Berkeley and back again. They looped out and over the mountains and plains of the country's vast interior on steam trains with names like *Gold Coast Ltd.* and *Zephyr;* then moved routinely up the East Coast, from Pittsburgh to New York City, to Vassar in Poughkeepsie and on to Harvard and Cambridge; and they sailed over the Atlantic on the great steamships—the SS *Europa,* SS *Kaiser Wilhelm*—to land at Southampton, Cherbourg or Bremen.

Robert spent the decade moving with the academic calendar between Pasadena and Berkeley, with a wide, high summer swing over to Perro Caliente (the wilderness cabin that he and Frank had discovered and the family had subsequently purchased) in the mountains of New Mexico. The Tolmans had been among the first to stay at the cabin on Grass Mountain (Frank would remember their visit as a "lovely, lovely" memory).[114] Ruth continued to make summer trips to New Mexico with her friends Ruth Valentine and Natalie Raymond,* as well as frequent forays north to Berkeley to see her family and friends. Jean divided her time between the West and East Coasts and Europe until midway through the decade. Both Jean and Kitty—four years apart in age—were moving urgently, if for different reasons, to commit themselves to a cause, and to respond to the turmoil that arose from competing ideologies: the Fascism that spawned Hitler in Germany, Mussolini in Italy, and Franco in Spain and the Communism that shaped the USSR.

Jean's greatest fear in 1930 was that high school would never end, that her future would never arrive. Ruth was facing her own personal disappointment and the need to rethink her future. Kitty was in college, frantic for life to begin. As for Robert, who was twenty-six that year—he was so intensely excited by all the discoveries in the esoteric world of physics, the sweetness (his word) and thrill of it, that he could scarcely break away long enough to notice life beyond the classroom and the lab. His students, caught up in the same great excitement, often followed him from Berkeley to Caltech and back again, sensing that they were part of an exciting new age, and that the work they were doing would change the world.

Even Robert, who had never had to consider money, who had little interest in politics or economics, became aware that times were hard, that most of his students were struggling, that family members in Germany were being persecuted because they were Jews. It was an adventurous, formative, intense decade for Ruth, Jean and Kitty, and for the man whose love each would claim.

∽

THE SENIOR OPPENHEIMERS ARRIVED IN Pasadena during their elder son's spring semester. They rented a Packard with a chauffeur, so they could come and

---

*Natalie Raymond was born in Pasadena, daughter of a well-to-do lawyer. She spent a lifetime weaving in and out of the lives of Robert, Frank, Ruth Benedict, Ruth Valentine and Ruth Tolman, among others. She at one time talked of becoming a psychologist or an anthropologist or a medical doctor. She was a talented writer and freelanced for various magazines, including *The New Yorker.*

go as they pleased. The Chrysler Roadster his father had bought Robert in Denver two years before had suffered several accidents and was now unreliable. When setting out with Robert, you never quite knew if you would get to your destination. Ella knew her son's reckless side only too well, and she knew how fast he drove.

The Tolmans invited Robert's parents to tea on several occasions. Julius was particularly taken with Richard. Ella noticed that her husband seemed somewhat less charmed by Ruth, perhaps because he was not used to a woman who took such an active part in conversation. Invariably, Julius liked to lead a lively exchange. Sometimes too lively, according to Robert, who in the past had been embarrassed by his overly ebullient father. But Ella found both Tolmans charming. Ruth kept a beautiful house and dressed with style, on the conservative side. She not only appreciated music but was a fine pianist herself. She took them to a Tchaikovsky concert in Los Angeles.[115] It probably occurred to the woman who had spent so many years fearful for her son's well-being that Ruth Tolman was the kind of wife she would wish for Robert.

That spring Robert did not stay in the Tolmans' guesthouse, but in a one-room "efficiency" apartment. Ella approved, but she worried about Robert's cough that wasn't going away, and there was the memory of that awful winter in Brittany and Paris, when he had been so distraught that he had locked her in her room. Now, with Robert in such good spirits, she hoped he had found his place in the world. And she thought it quite a fine world. People were drawn to Robert; his students were clearly devoted. He and Richard were engrossed in something called "cosmic ray theory." And, of course, Julius was beside himself with pleasure that his Roberty had succeeded magnificently. Only twenty-six, and already an important Herr Professor. America had worked magically for the immigrant Julius Oppenheimer, who had sold his share of the family business shortly before the previous year's stock-market crash, so the Oppenheimer fortune was secure.

Near the end of their Pasadena visit Julius bought his son an early birthday gift—a new Chrysler. After insisting that he could manage with the two-year-old roadster, Robert graciously accepted the new car and named it *Gamaliel*, Hebrew for "reward of God." A proper thank-you to his father and, in a way, an acknowledgment of his Jewish heritage.

⸺

JEAN SPENT HER DAYS AT the Williams Institute quietly avoiding new friendships, and tucked into her room with a view of the Golden Gate. Throughout the rainy winter months, her door closed, she read the letters from Cambridge. Then, pen firmly in hand, she emptied her thoughts onto page after page. At times it was difficult to know which Jean was appearing on the page: sometimes her words mimicked the novels and poems of the books she and her friends were all reading and recommending to each other, or she would lapse into the rhythms of Edna St. Vincent Millay—*my candle burns at both ends; it will not last the night*—or echo May's theatrical prose. But the question that began to plague Jean no longer troubled May, who now understood that she preferred women. For her, their last night in New York had been a disappointment, while for Jean it remained an exciting yet disturbing enigma.

Jean did not know how she could love May, could hunger so much to be with her, yet not be certain that this love was sexual. She told May: "Last year there was a period when I thought I was a homo-sexual. I am still in a way, forced to believe it, but really, logically, I am sure that I can't be because of my un-masculinity. Do you ever think of it?" Then she lapsed into a kind of poetic concatenation of a "curious torturing feeling . . . of the pain and passion and desolation . . . the dying joy and utter weakness" that flashed through her, and she wanted an explanation. "Wasn't that night a leavening, an equaling, a molding, a dissolving?"[116]

Finally, tired of the subject, she wrote, "Beloved, life is so short; reality and beauty, just be true; it isn't unbalanced. I don't love you that way. Only I have to give in to this beauty, any beauty." Plaintively she added: "You are my friend this year, as I have said, lots, I am friendless. I suppose I am a sly self-conscious and repulsive creature. . . . Adolescence is harder even than I had thought."[117]

ON THE LAST DAY OF January 1930, spring blew in soft and warm and the Williams Institute student body emptied out to watch a tennis match. Jean sat on a stone bench, going through what she described as "tortures of self-consciousness," which made her feel like crying because she was turning out so differently from the person she had "vaguely supposed and desired" she would become. Gusts of the warm spring weather propelled her up the hill to home, where she took her violin and spent the rest of the afternoon practicing, feeling some kind of fresh new hope rising. Finally she put down the bow and began to commit her spring-fed feelings to paper: "I want to pull myself straight and clean—I am now really going to try to get into Vassar." In the next paragraph she backed off, saying she didn't really mean it, that she still planned to be an actress. Adding there was little hope that she'd get in to Vassar—because she was failing chemistry.[118] Yet she interjected a note of hesitation, a hint that she might go to college after all, and made it real by mailing the letter off to May.

‿〜

VIENNA'S ALFRED ADLER WAS THE first of the European psychoanalysts to arrive in the San Francisco Bay Area in the late 1920s. He gave a lecture on "Understanding Human Nature" at Berkeley's Wheeler Auditorium. The following week, he spoke about the "Inferiority Complex" at Mills College. He was pleased enough with his reception, and the San Francisco area, to let Cora Williams talk him into teaching a summer course at Williams Institute.

Almost certainly, Marjorie Tatlock went to one or more of these early Adler lectures, along with her friends Elizabeth and James Whitney. The psychology group included Jean and Donald Macfarlane and opened its doors to academics in other fields, as long as they had a grasp of the discipline—primarily the teachings of Freud and Jung—and a desire to explore the field of psychotherapy.[119] Robert Oppenheimer became part of the group.

During his fall semester at Berkeley, Robert lived in an elegant if spartan guest room at the University Faculty Club, tucked into a grove of live oaks on campus. During these early years at Berkeley, Oppenheimer met John Tatlock. The two men had a great deal in common: a Harvard education and a sense of loyalty to that university, ambition and a love of medieval literature.

In June, Hugh Tatlock finished his freshman year at Berkeley with both an award for academic excellence and a determination not to return. Marjorie was aware that neither of her children was happy. Hugh was fair and slender—the brother and sister resembled each other more than they did their parents. Although he had been a bit shy as a boy, he had fit in easily at Andover. Called "Tats" or "Hugo" (his father called him "Hughby"), he swam and played tennis for his school, but baseball was his love, the Boston Red Sox his team. All San Francisco had to offer was the minor-league Seals.

Hugh had been accepted at Harvard, but he decided he did not want to go back to school at all. He wanted to go to sea. Professor Tatlock must have felt a certain exasperation with a son who would rather go to sea than to Harvard and a daughter who wanted to become an actress. The observant Marjorie waited, wrote her own long letters to her friends and tried to be as patient as a saint—an effort that her daughter, in her better moments, acknowledged. Marjorie watched her daughter challenge and charm a dinner table of distinguished scholars, listened as she filled the house with soaring music, and the next day appeared so full of woe that she locked herself away in her room. This was a girl who wandered about at midnight or in the early hours of morning, climbed on the roof of the house and swam alone in the pool, who wrote a friend: "I am despairing. I am a different species from you and from the rest of the world . . . I don't know what to do."[120]

On his next trip to New York, Jean's father—following in the footsteps of his erstwhile Harvard colleague George Sarton—appeared at the office of Miss Eva Le Gallienne. She seemed vague about Jean; she hadn't remembered promising her a place in the student company. Soon Jean received a letter written by a secretary at the theater, saying that she would have to apply and go through the usual routine. Jean's feelings were bruised, but she did not intend to give up. She *would* audition, and she *would* do well. She knew that Vassar was still an option. The first choice of her parents, certainly. But she had to give her father credit for going to see Le Gallienne, though how earnestly he pled his daughter's case could only be guessed.

⤳

THE TOLMAN HOUSE AT THE edge of the Caltech campus was well positioned to become an unofficial headquarters for the friends Richard and Ruth had brought together. Some were Richard's colleagues, though not all were physicists and not all senior faculty. Charlie Lauritsen had received his doctorate the year before; he was on the physics faculty, working on the use of X-ray tubes for radiation therapy on cancer patients, a new field altogether. His wife, Sigrid, was in medical school at the University of Southern California, also intending to work in radiation therapy. Lauritsen was a dozen years older than Robert, who slipped easily into this group. Ruth provided friends as well, most with links to Berkeley and to psychology.

As a discipline, psychology was considered a soft science by most of the physicists, not something to pursue when the hard sciences presented such tantalizing questions. But, like Robert, Richard found psychology intriguing. He was twenty-three years older than Oppenheimer, but the two were fairly well matched in their abilities—with quick and inclusive minds drawn to the unknown, and interests ranging from music and literature to ethics and the new study of human behavior. Both had younger brothers with whom they were close. Richard's younger brother Edward was leading the field of behavioral psychology at Berkeley, while Robert's brother Frank was at Johns Hopkins, getting his undergraduate degree, and then would be heading for Caltech.

Richard introduced Robert to astrophysics, and on his monthly visits, Robert would stay in the guesthouse and the two would spend hours in the study that Ruth dubbed "Richard's Folly," involved in lively arguments. With Richard, and a covey of remarkable graduate students, Robert would accomplish some of his most original work in physics at Caltech, including studies of compressed stars known as "white dwarfs."[121]

Ruth was halfway, in years, between what seemed like parallel versions of the same man—one a New England patrician, and the other a first-generation German Jew. At the beginning of the 1930s, both Richard and Robert encouraged

Ruth to find her own place in the world. She would complete her master's in psychology at nearby Occidental College. Ruth, though, was acutely aware that as she approached thirty-eight, the prospects of having a child had diminished.

RUTH WAS A POPULAR NAME for girls at the turn of the twentieth century. Ruth Sherman would likely have met Ruth Valentine*—always called Val—at Berkeley, where she was getting a doctorate in psychology. Val was also working with Lillie Margaret at the YWCA, as a secretary and managing the Y's Golden Lantern Lunchroom. Ruth and Val were the same age; Val had graduated from Vassar in 1915, and stayed there long enough to get a master's degree before returning to her wealthy—and troubled—family in Oakland. Val had a somewhat bawdy sense of humor and a direct manner combined with a sensitivity that made her appealing to both men and women. When she finished her doctorate under Edward Tolman, she went to work in the Los Angeles school system as a psychologist. It would not have been an accident that she bought a house in Pasadena with a back garden that adjoined the Tolmans'. Val became Ruth's closest friend,[122] and a regular member of the homegrown, informal *stammtisch*—a relaxed gathering of Tolman friends and colleagues. A gate was built to connect their gardens.

The Tolman/Oppenheimer/Valentine vortex drew in other friends: the psychologists Donald and Jean Macfarlane—Marjorie Tatlock's close friends—traveled between Berkeley and Caltech and some of them to Perro Caliente. Natalie Raymond, the renegade daughter of a prominent Pasadena family, added excitement. Nat was a year younger than Robert and game for any exploit that promised relief from boredom and restlessness, which seemed to be her main afflictions. Ruth and Val treated Nat like an errant but lovable little sister who had a habit of putting herself in untenable situations. Nat was attractive, bright and unconventional in her search for herself. For the group, there was something oddly compelling about Nat's misadventures. A friend described her as a "dare-devil, an adventurer, as was Robert to some extent."[123] Her reckless approach to life almost ensured that she and Robert would become friends.

NAT WAS WITH ROBERT IN the roadster one day when a train came rumbling down the tracks that paralleled the coastal highway. Robert couldn't resist racing it. ("I have driven him 95 without opening the throttle wide.") He lost control, the

---

*Val's father had been president of the Wells Fargo Company but had died when Val was eight years old. Her mother was a socialite who had Val's brother Philip declared incompetent because she felt he was squandering his inheritance. A year later another court his inheritance. In 1934, he was arrested for highjacking a taxi in Oakland. *Oakland Tribune,* November 15, 1921:21; Ibid. April 21, 1934:1. Val had been caught in the middle of family wars almost all her life.

car careened, and when it came to rest, Nat lay motionless. Robert, unscathed, was certain she was dead. She was unconscious, but after a time came around, miraculously intact. A close brush, another improbable story to attach to Robert and Nat's respective growing repertoires. Julius Oppenheimer considered it yet another disaster narrowly averted. For having the good grace not to perish because of his son's irresponsibility, Julius gave the young lady two works of art from his collection: a Cézanne drawing and a small Vlaminck painting.[124]

Nat moved in concentric circles made up of friends, acquaintances and lovers, both male and female, whose lines sometimes crossed. Robert fondly described Nat's "jams" as "her always new & always moving miseries."[125] Like Jean Tatlock's friend May Sarton, Nat was drawn to older women. She turned to Val and Ruth for advice, then to Dr. Ruth Benedict, already an important name in the field of anthropology, who was seventeen years older.

Like Val—who gave Nat a bed when she needed one and a place to hide out when things went wrong—Benedict was captivated by Nat. In June of 1931, Benedict was in Santa Fe doing field studies on the Apache Indians. "Nat came, and as a bed in my room was vacant [and] she very much at loose ends, she is staying on til she is put out, she says," Benedict wrote to her former student and lover Margaret Mead. Benedict tried to describe Nat: "She is used to amusing herself—boring herself would be more descriptive—and I go on working with the Apaches. In the evening she joins in the poker games, and daytimes she walks in the pouring rain or drives one of the boys miles back country to find an Indian.... She's not in love with me, but she's used to holding everybody at arm's length and she is at ease with me." Then she asked the question both Ruth and Val, and all the others who marveled at Nat, were pondering: "What will become of her?"[126]

Later, Benedict wrote Mead, who was on her way to New Guinea for fieldwork. "Natalie's jam seemed worse to me the more I knew about it," she confided. "Her plan is to take the Medical School course at the University of California, and that's even second rate as a medical school. She is way above the level of anything they're used to, and gets cum laudes with everything."[127] Benedict told Mead that there were other issues that would make medical school a problem for Natalie: she could not stand to look at a corpse, and blood unhinged her completely.

"She might be able to come to New York. I'd be glad if she could." Benedict went on, perhaps to convince Mead, or possibly herself: "She's a desperate, unhappy child and that doesn't seem such a strange state of affairs to me as it does in her home city, so she feels more at home with me. I wish I could talk to you about it. I know well enough that I could hurt Nat irreparably—as human 'irreparable' go—but I think it would be all right even if she came to New York. I care about her a lot, and it would be a no more insulting offer of benevolence. On the other hand, there's all the difference of age and the rest, and her complete unplacedness, that make me to her a symbol of security and peace rather than any end-all and be-all."[128]

That August, Robert wrote to his brother Frank, who was in England, "I have seen Val and the Tolmans and Nat . . . Nat has gone east, having worn out the Pacific coast. She will be in New York, probably at the Cornell Medical School or the Rockefeller."[129]

Nat and Benedict moved into an apartment on West 72nd Street and lived together for most of the decade, with Nat taking classes, being distracted, starting one thing and moving on to something else, with time out every summer for regular excursions west, keeping her place in the Tolmans' circle. Sometimes she turned up at Perro Caliente, and occasionally she met Robert when he happened to be in New York City. She continued to move through life delighting and exasperating her circles of friends with her small insurgencies and "always moving miseries."

Jean is overwhelmed, Ruth and Robert grieve, and Kitty falls in love

The spring of 1930, as graduation approached, Jean's handwriting changed from the precise, bold, upright script to a rather chaotic, right-slanting scrawl. "*I would anything were real, even my body*," she wrote to May. She then leapt into fantasy: "*Had I a man, I should give myself to whatever that is. I can easily imagine becoming drunk over his body and more over his delight in mine. He could have all that and whatever of the rest of me he could find. I imagine, were he a fine man he could make something out of me.*" Then she added, with a certain poignancy, "*I'm in terribly deep, Snab.*"[130]

Jean graduated from high school early in June, predictably contemptuous of the ceremony: "It is the most awful graduation I can conceive of. So hypocritical." She went through the motions because she couldn't bear to hurt her mother, who she felt was saintly for tolerating what Jean called her "overwhelmings."[131]

Just when she finally decided to apply to college, Jean received an invitation to audition with Eva Le Gallienne and worried that she might faint—her doctor had said her blood pressure was much too high for her age. "In the last year my body has gotten more and more out of hand. I can't be sure of anything, and these silly overwhelmings are omnipotent," she wrote May.[132] The word became a code for those times when Jean felt unable to move, to think, to act. All she could do was shrink into herself, close down, try to control her breathing. Her parents hoped this was all part of adolescence. Her father wanted her to grow up, to get on with it. Her mother wasn't sure. She did not share her husband's attitude that Jean was going through an annoying but passing phase, to be ignored as much as possible.

IN LETTERS TO LETTY, THE Clark sisters and May, Jean complained that her parents wanted her to be more active, to take summer classes at the university so that she would be able to get into Vassar. She revolted and decided she must go to Europe before she could do anything else. When her mother suggested they were "too poor," Jean shook it off as an excuse to deny her the trip.

Jean's dear friend Letty had been having troubles of her own, but hers were physical. Jean owed her a letter—a point Letty chided her about in typical Snab melodramatic style: "Unless you write to me immediately I shall pray God to condemn you to live forever upon this painless earth." Doctors were having difficulty diagnosing Letty's problem. Jean wrote May to ask whether Letty was in pain, adding, "Last year I used to feel sometimes in great surges that she was greater than any of us and anyone else."[133]

On June 9, a week before she was to graduate from Cambridge Latin and High, Letty Field underwent surgery. The fifteen-year-old died that same day of peritonitis. A shock washed over her friends in Boston and New York, Berkeley and Switzerland. The news all but buried an already tenuous Jean Tatlock. May and Margot and Jean Clark were stunned, but Jean could not shake loose the dread. Death became a recurrent theme in her letters.

"Dears," she wrote, "I am so tired and small and young, the only thing Letty's death has done to me is to make death seem too sweet." She echoed Joan of Arc: "Sometimes a fear grips me. I don't know what it is. It's supernatural. I see in little things, that God has been preparing me for this all year, all my life. A miserable creature, he." Her impulse was to run, as far and as fast as she could. To Cambridge first, to be with Mrs. Field and live in Letty's room if possible (it was not), then on to Europe—to Geneva, where Letty had lived when her father was alive. Or to France or Italy or anywhere; she felt she could not stay in America. Jean announced that she was going to "ditch my heart-felt plan of going to Eva's . . . But I am in such a state . . . that I don't think I could give much to it. I am quite empty and all tied up inside . . . This is the time in my life when I must find salvation or go without forever."[134] Shaken by their daughter's tortured reaction to Letty's death, and perhaps relieved that she would not be going to the theater school, the Tatlocks decided that a year in Europe might give Jean time to gain equanimity. They hoped the year would also help her decide in favor of Vassar, where Winifred could watch over her. The Clark and Tatlock families conferred and decided that Margot Clark would go with Jean to Geneva.

The girls sailed from New York on the SS *Pennland* early in October. That fall, Hugh Tatlock put off Harvard for a year, and signed on as a cadet on the merchant marine vessel SS *Golden Coast,* and later as an ordinary seaman on the SS *Golden Star,* sailing between San Francisco and Hong Kong. John and Marjorie Tatlock, left in their big house overlooking San Francisco Bay, had to wonder why their two privileged children so readily turned down the opportunities offered them. John sought solace in *The Canterbury Tales*. Trying to understand, Marjorie asked help from the people who were probing human behavior—just as Ella Oppenheimer had done in Cambridge and Paris and Brittany, just four years earlier, when Robert was in such despair that he'd had thoughts of suicide.

FRIENDS WERE BECOMING WARY OF Jean's obsessive need to talk about Letty, even May. Lashing back, Jean wrote: "I think you idealize silence in me. There is no need to. Silence for its own sake can be unbearably, disgustingly sentimental . . . I am sorry, but I must say this: think of Letty and her silences which were always natural, elemental, terrifyingly strong. Yet she was not a silent person, nor was she ever sweet, only terribly terribly to take to one's heart."[135]

A family friend of the Fields, a German tutor named Leni Cahn, was there to watch after the girls. Jean would write to May that she loved Leni "in a constructive satisfying way," but that she was "not eaten by passion so disgustingly (I detest and abhor passion) as I was for K and for you too some of last year in California." Jean also wrote to May to say, in rather blunt terms, that she now found homosexuality abhorrent and "unnatural."[136]

For the Christmas holidays, Jean went to a ski resort in the Alps with her mother's friend Elizabeth Whitney and her husband, James. Both had close ties to Carl Jung, who had analyzed them three years earlier. Elizabeth was aware of Jean's "overwhelmings," and her struggle to come to terms with Letty's death. James Whitney was "a very heavenly person," Jean reported. She skied with him and they had long talks; she came away claiming to trust him more than any other man she had ever met. About her time with Elizabeth, she was more guarded, saying only, "She is all but a practicing psycho-analyst, and understands very well things ignorable by others."[137]

As winter wore on, a new equilibrium emerged. Jean wrote to May, "I feel very strongly that I have done exactly right for this year." Jean began to consider Vassar seriously enough to take the college boards at the beginning of summer. May had plans to be in Paris, and Jean looked forward to seeing her, even if she expected a tirade about college being a waste of time. To give May fair warning, she wrote, "I am not sure about acting. I feel at times there is something indisputable and absolutely surely set for me to do later, only I have not seen it yet. I now almost want to go to Vassar for a year or so."[138] She need not have worried; May had become embroiled in her first real love affair, with a woman who lived in a boardinghouse on McDougal Street. She had moved on.

◡

IN THE FALL OF 1928, Kitty went to the University of Pittsburgh and continued to live at home. Kitty's father worked at the Koppers chemical company and was successful in developing patents for blast furnaces and coking coal.[139] There was enough money to send Kitty and her mother to Germany for summer visits with Vissering and Puening relatives.

Kitty's academic interest was botany; her love of plants would prove enduring. She would create gardens wherever she lived, and was proud of what she called her "gardener's" thumb. Her freshman classes included biology, mathematics and chemistry. Determined since high school to get an advanced degree, she managed to complete her first full year at Pitt, during which she learned that even an undergraduate degree required a certain amount of time and patience. She ran out of both by the end of the term, and did not return to school until the spring semester. She managed to stay through summer school and the next fall semester.[140] Then she left again.

Kitty convinced her parents that it would be a fine idea for her to travel around Europe. She could study modern languages, maybe take classes at the University of Munich, or at the Sorbonne, even the University of Grenoble. She could go skiing in the Alps with aunts or cousins. She sailed from New York in March 1930 with a ticket to return in May, in time for the summer session at Pitt.

If she registered at the Sorbonne, she didn't bother to go to classes. Much later, vivacious, fun-loving Kitty would admit that in those months most of her friends were musicians and that "I spent little time on school work."[141] One of those musicians was a handsome young Harvard graduate named Frank Ramseyer, who was studying in Paris that year with Nadia Boulanger, the composer and conductor who taught a generation of famous musicians on both sides of the Atlantic, including the American Aaron Copland.[142]

Frank, who was five years older than Kitty, had a job as a teaching assistant in Harvard's Music Department, and planned on pursuing his master's degree at the university. He had an easy sense of humor, he made delightful music, and he could be spontaneous. American jazz had just arrived in France, and Frank would sit down at a piano and accompany a singer in an impromptu session. For Kitty, it was a storybook romance, clinging to the arm of a good-looking young American who loved Paris— walking along the Seine in the lavender light of a Paris evening, spending days at the picture galleries, exploring the Tuileries and the Jardin de Luxembourg.

She was scheduled to sail from Bremen on May 19. She and Frank said their goodbyes, and pledged to meet again. Pittsburgh wasn't all that far from Boston. Kitty left; Frank returned to America soon after. He returned to his position at Harvard and to his family home on Adelaide Street in the historic district of Jamaica Plain. It had taken Frank's father twenty years to become a cotton broker and to buy the house the family had rented since 1910.[143]

⟞⟝

IN THE MIDDLE OF JUNE 1931, Ruth's father, the Reverend Warren Sherman, died in Berkeley; at almost the same time Robert's mother was diagnosed with leukemia. In October, he was with her when she died. When a family friend offered his condolences and said, "You know, Robert, your mother loved you very much," the son muttered: "Maybe she loved me too much."[144]

After Ella's death, Robert gathered his father into his life; Julius visited both California campuses and stayed for weeks at a time. In Pasadena, Ruth took the father under her wing just as she had the sons. She included Julius in her group of friends, taking him to the symphony and to musical evenings.

In the early years of his rotation between Berkeley and Pasadena, Robert's social life centered almost entirely on his students and colleagues. He took the students to dinner in San Francisco and always picked up the tab, knowing how pinched they were for funds. The wives of his colleagues invited him to dinner and then fluttered over the flowers he inevitably had delivered. He was having a good time: creating a new field in theoretical physics at Berkeley was a romance of its own. He was becoming known as an eligible bachelor, and while he had dalliances here and there, so far there were no serious contenders for his attentions.

During the last month of summer, Robert would return to New Mexico. Katherine Page—now Katy—who had seen promise in Robert when he was still a boy, remained an important part of life at the camp. The main attraction at Perro Caliente was the horseback rides into the high mountain country. Some of Robert's guests were excellent riders; others had never been on a horse. It didn't matter. They rode with graham crackers and whiskey in their saddlebags, in the rain or by the light of the moon, over trails and through trees and brush.[145] Perro Caliente tested everyone's mettle, and it allowed Robert to appear the mountain man.

⟞⟝

CHANGE CAN BE MEASURED IN the smallest things: an escaped sigh, the shadow of moving leaves, an errant thought. The moments gather, deepen over the course of a day, a week, a month. A year had passed since Letty's death; Jean took the college boards. Then she and Margot went to Paris, and were waiting when May arrived. May found Jean "wonderful and strange . . . so wise, *anciently* wise in some ways, and then suddenly childish." Margot agreed; Jean thought deeply about so many things, worried them in the far recesses of her mind. And all the while on the surface, she was this tall, eloquent girl with dark eyelashes so thick, they clustered when wet.[146]

According to May, the reunited Snabs spent two "glorious weeks" swimming naked in "fiery blue seas." May was too besotted with her new love to keep it secret, but the news didn't seem to unsettle Jean. "Love" meant different things to the two of them. For May, Jean would always be too "modest" to experience physical love. Jean's ideal involved the perfect merger of emotional love and physical love. One without the other would never work for her. And—aside from that one night with May in New York, about which she remained uncertain—she had had no experience with either at this point in her passionate young life.

Still, Jean spoke with precision when she thought her friend was acting the fool. May's talent as a writer was beginning to earn her some money, and she was considering a year in Russia to research a book. Jean told her that the idea was "certainly excessively exciting," but wondered how much May could possibly expect to "get of the heights and depths" of present-day Russia, to be able to write a proper book about it, when she couldn't even speak the language. Jean was clear: "It seems to me impossible . . . I think you cannot help either idealizing it entirely, or being broken by it."[147] The Russian Revolution had taken place scarcely fourteen years before; the Communist Party was gaining in popularity as the Depression closed in on America and Europe.

Jean's thoughts that summer in Paris were not on the shifting politics of the world, but on how a just life should be lived. "The farther I went from Letty's death the more I felt the strongest need in the world was for compassion and kindliness," she wrote, "something to combat the cowardly puritanism and sickly stoicism which the stupid western world has somehow gleaned from Christianity."[148] Jean was growing up; personal tragedy had stirred her deepest convictions.

After France, Jean traveled to Florence, where she found herself in what she called "an agony" of homesickness. She was ready to go home. Her mother was waiting for her at the dock in New York. She would be going to Vassar in the fall.

〜

KITTY RETURNED FROM PARIS IN time for summer school at Pitt. Caught up in the incandescence of romance, she did not want to be locked into summer classes—she wanted to be in Boston with Frank Ramseyer. She told her parents he was a wonderfully talented musician, a pianist who could work on complicated scores. He was quiet, well-read, loved art and design and good books. She was certain her parents would approve. And his family? The name was German; his *grosspapa* had come to America from Switzerland. Kitty's mother's family had roots in Switzerland as well. The Visserings were related to the de Blonay family; the family seat was a castle, built in the eleventh century, high above Lake Geneva. Her great-grandfather, Bodewin Vissering, who had married Johanna de Blonay, owned an estate in Hannover, and was a member of the German parliament. The Visserings and de Blonays were much more prestigious, in the European scheme of things, than the American Ramseyers. Frank's grandfather had been a clock-maker; Kitty's a professor in Munster.

It took all the patience Kitty could muster to get through summer school at Pitt, completing her junior year. But the rest of the degree would have to wait. She had to be with Frank.

On the day after Christmas 1932, Kitty and Frank were married before a Justice of the Peace in Pittsburgh. Then, with pieces of her family silver which were engraved with the Vissering initials as part of her trousseau, the couple moved into an apartment near Harvard.[149] He had hoped to begin work on a master's degree, but with a wife to support, that would have to be delayed.

Confusingly, Kitty seems to have enrolled at Pitt for the semester beginning in January of 1933, almost immediately after her marriage, and to have returned to her parents' house in Aspinwall. She also sailed for Europe, returning in June 1933 to New York; on the passenger list she was Katherine Ramseyer and her address was the one she shared with Frank in Cambridge, but Frank was not on the ship with her. That summer he was in residence at Harvard. Soon after, Kitty registered at the University of Wisconsin, but never turned up for classes.[150]

On December 20, 1933, Kitty claimed to have been granted an annulment of her marriage from the Superior Court of Wisconsin. The testimony, she would later tell a friend, was ruled by the court to be so obscene it did not become part of the public record. That December, ten days before the annulment, Frank was in Cambridge, playing Handel and Beethoven sonatas with a string trio at Lowell House.[151]

Kitty's version, told much later when she was speaking more freely, was that several months into the marriage, she had found a diary of Frank's, and discovered pages of "mirror writing." Kitty got a mirror. What she read, she said, shocked and disgusted her, and caused her to conclude that her new husband was a homosexual and a drug addict.[152] Some time during that same year, Kitty became pregnant.

Who arranged for the abortion, how and where it was done, who paid for it, and who if anyone was with her at the time—none of this information appears in any records. It couldn't: abortion was a criminal offense in 1933. It was also a common practice during the Depression, when many women simply could not feed the children they already had. That was not Kitty's reason. She wanted the marriage and the pregnancy to be erased. It seems likely that Frank was with her during the abortion because he would later tell his second wife that the fetus had been a boy.[153]

By Christmas, Kitty was back in Aspinwall with her parents and Frank was in Cambridge, playing in a Christmas recital. He had been expunged from Kitty's past, along with his unborn son.

Ruth makes a decision; Jean goes to Vassar; Kitty falls in love again and Robert has a perfect summer at Perro Caliente

Ruth was forty and childless; she had skipped all of those years when academic wives were having babies and worrying about their husband's tenure. Physicists' wives joked that they would always be second to physics in their husbands' affections; as with most such jokes, there was a kernel of truth to this. Ruth knew what Richard's family thought, even said to each other: that the terriers they owned were their children, that Ruth "didn't really want children." In fact, Richard tolerated the dogs; away on one of his frequent trips, Ruth wrote him, "I let Nitz sleep in the room with me last night, but I certainly will not do it again, as he barked much of the night and in general behaved very restlessly and badly. I told Nat that for once all the unpleasant and unflattering things you say about him are, or were, pretty close to true."[154] But to Ruth, the dogs were so responsive to her moods, such good companions, that they filled a need. The little terriers would follow her around, crawl into her lap whenever they could.

Fulfilling the social obligations of the dean's wife, running his house, playing the piano like the talented amateur she was, were not enough. Had there been a child, Ruth would have established a certain kind of work schedule—it was always a given that Ruth was going to work. Now, she needed to be part of a larger and more demanding world. At her part-time job administering psychological tests to delinquents at Los Angeles Juvenile Hall,[155] the young people she worked with were angry, sullen, in despair; their families had fallen apart, their lives were stunted. For Ruth, these young people became an antidote to the ivory tower, and the work gave her an idea of the practical applications of psychology.

When Ruth went to UCLA—with the title Associate in Psychology—counseling students and doing research, she was able to audit psychology courses. She stayed in this holding pattern for two years, keeping up with the field. In 1929, she enrolled at nearby Occidental College, which had ties to Caltech. In little over a year, she completed her master's degree and started a new job—half-time again—lecturing, counseling, and giving aptitude tests to freshmen at Occidental. After that she began working, again part-time, at Scripps, one of the prestigious Claremont colleges, where she was paid smartly—$250 a month,[156] a big leap from the $75 she had earned at Juvenile Hall. Still, the real-world troubles of the young people must have challenged this preacher's daughter, for teaching was to prove only a way station.

In the fall of 1934, after a semester at Scripps, she signed on with the Federal Emergency Relief Administration in downtown Los Angeles as a consulting psychologist. Ruth became witness to the devastations of the Depression, to the most afflicted populations in a country struggling to regain its balance. At the agency she had access to a world most Californians never enter, one that offered rich material for a dissertation. She became engrossed in the field of criminal behavior; she wanted to understand the prisoners themselves.

Ruth brought some of the reality of life in downtown Los Angeles up the hill to Pasadena. Val had seen her share of troubled children in the public schools, and both understood better than Richard or Robert the toll poverty was taking. Robert was far from any contact with the barrios or with those who lived in "the Nickel," Los Angeles's Skid Row (named the Nickel because it was on Fifth Street) or, for that matter, the growing urban poor regions of the city—the places that served as breeding grounds for criminals.

After a year, Ruth decided—obviously counseled by her brother-in-law Edward—she could combine her consulting work at the Relief Administration with study for a Ph.D. at Berkeley. Richard was pleased that his wife had taken on a challenge equal to her energies and needs. For her studies, Ruth had to appear regularly at Berkeley, which meant she was able to spend time with the two Lillies—her mother and her sister—in the house on Ashby Avenue, and with her cousin Alma, who had married into the socially prominent Chickering family in nearby Piedmont.

EACH SPRING THROUGHOUT THE 1930S, Robert appeared as usual in Pasadena, trailed by his own small troupe of admiring grad students who would rent cheap rooms, take classes and stay close to their leader. "He was like a comet coming with his stream of students," one admiring Caltech colleague said. "There was an electricity in the air."[157] One year the group arrived in time for a birthday celebration for Robert at the Tolmans', where Ruth served a first course of avocados brimming with caviar and, for dessert, apple pie decorated with candles.

Robert's graduate students adopted his mannerisms, even his walk. It seemed as if everyone always had a cigarette balanced between nicotine-stained fingers. (During one of the department's Monday night Journal Club meetings at Berkeley, where reports were given on recently published articles, an acrid smell filled the room. It took several minutes to discover that Oppenheimer's cigarette, held too close to his head, had set fire to his bushy black hair.)[158]

THE SUMMER BEFORE RUTH STARTED at the Federal Emergency Relief Administration, she drove to Perro Caliente with Val. Nat was already there; she had stopped in New Mexico on her way home from New York to help open camp.

~

JEAN WAS JUST SEVENTEEN IN 1931, when she started at Vassar. The prescribed courses in nineteenth-century Italian literature, zoology and medieval history didn't thrill her. The second year, she granted, sounded better: economics, political science, music theory and singing, and German. The year in Europe had steadied Jean, produced in her a new grace, an ease of movement. Her classmates at Vassar didn't seem to know what to make of this tall, elegant young woman who spoke French fluently, who recited John Donne and critiqued Galsworthy. She did not flaunt her achievements, but had a depth of knowledge most of them did not. Not surprisingly, Jean made many of them uncomfortable. Priscilla, who had graduated but stayed close to Jean and to Vassar, explained that from the first Jean "seemed set apart from the other girls." Some were scared of her, Priscilla surmised, and it took the brighter girls time to figure out that there was nothing superficial about Jean, that she did not posture. Eventually, she found a niche, writing for the *Vassar Miscellany News* and the *Literary Review*.[159]

Jean Tatlock finally began to make new friends, among them Eleanor Clark and the poet Elizabeth Bishop. Jean continued to correspond with May, though sporadically. As if to apologize for going to college, she wrote, "I know that this college business is irrelevant and therefore fearfully mask-like and artificial as anything—being a beauty specialist for instance. My best friend there at Vassar, Eleanor Clark,* feels it so strong, she's probably going away to England, maybe

---

*Eleanor Clark attended Vassar and contributed, along with poet Elizabeth Bishop and Mary McCarthy, to the college magazine, *Con Spirito*. Elizabeth Bishop would, among other honors, win a Pulitzer Prize for Poetry in 1956 and was Poet Laureate for the United States in 1949–1950. Eleanor Clark would win a National Book Award in Arts and Letters in 1965, and marry the two-time Pulitzer Prize winning Robert Penn Warren. Mary McCarthy would write the bestselling novel *The Group*, about eight Vassar graduates.

to Oxford." Still, she closed the letter with, "Honestly, I love you wildly now, and surely all the time."[160] But her letters were now absent the emotional abandon of her younger years.

The atmosphere at Vassar was accepting of loving and intense relationships between women, sexual or not. The college had a reputation for being discreet about lesbianism. By the time Jean arrived, she seemed to have navigated the worst storms of adolescence and was able to write, "My darling, I'm glad we couldn't lay hands on one another. With me at least, it would have been a giving in, not a consummation. . . . I hope to God we may one day simply love one another."[161]

Within a few years the exuberant, talented May would abandon the theater for a successful writing career and a succession of lovers who served as muses. Jean had longed to understand the completeness of emotional and physical love; now she was intent on finding something to believe in that was larger than herself: a crusade, a quest worthy of a Joan of Arc.[162]

Even at this oasis of privilege, the Depression made its mark. More than a hundred women of Vassar's class of 1934 would withdraw before graduation, many for financial reasons. Capitalism and democracy were increasingly called into question as solutions to the country's ills, and Americans, especially in college settings, began to see an answer in socialism. Aunt Winifred—Vassar's Dr. Smith—would be remembered by some as one of the college's "greatest rebels," while others lambasted her as an "indefatigable Socialist Agitator." In the 1930s, she would travel to Russia to see how the new form of government was working. Jean took up the cause so vehemently that one of her professors gave her Max Eastman's "Artists in Uniform," hoping that the book, written by one of the country's most avid radicals with solid socialist credentials who had turned skeptic, might temper her passion.[163] It did not.

After her freshman year at Vassar, Jean took a summer course in psychology at Berkeley, perhaps to learn more about her own emotional turmoil. She began to think seriously about medical school and a career in psychotherapy. Jean returned for a second year at Vassar and, like many other college students, became increasingly involved in protesting the inequities of capitalism. She elected to do her third year at Berkeley, living at home. It would turn out to be a momentous, troubling and inspiring school year.

In May of 1934, just as Jean was finishing her Berkeley year, the ports of San Francisco and Oakland exploded with the General Strike; some 65,000 dock workers were demanding the right to unionize and the ship owners resisted. The struggle continued for weeks. Strikebreakers were called in and July 5th became known as "Bloody Thursday," with police and tear gas, shots fired into crowds, bricks and stones thrown, trucks overturned and men killed.

One afternoon during the strike, Jean went with some members of the League Against War and Fascism to the Oakland Police Department to ask about the jailing of strike sympathizers. The group got little sympathy from the police inspector, who instead lectured them on the Constitution. When one of their group asked to speak to the prisoners, he was "bellied out the door by a big policeman, and told not to show his face around there again."[164]

Jean returned to Vassar with a story for the October issue of the *Vassar Miscellany*. An editor's note explained it was "The fourth in a series of articles by students whose summer experiences showed them some particular aspect of Americans' social and economic life." The headline read: "Account of the General Strike in San Francisco as Told by an Eye Witness/Jean Tatlock Describes Campaign to Break the Strike With the Red Scare." Jean recounted how she had heard about the strike from two members of the International Longshoremen's Association (ILA) who spoke at the University. Neither of the two was a Communist, she quickly pointed out. They were striking for the right of collective bargaining, and asked for an increase in wages, from 85 cents an hour to $1, and $1.50 for overtime.[165]

Jean had seen and heard enough that spring and summer, when tear gas drifted over the Oakland and San Francisco waterfronts, when bricks crashed into police cars and billy clubs smashed skulls, when finally the National Guard was called in and bayonets fixed, to know that her sympathies were altogether with the workers. By the end of the year, every port on the West Coast was unionized; the longshoremen's strike had worked, and Jean understood that radical action could be effective.

⌒

THE SUMMER OF 1934 AT Perro Caliente was close to perfect. The alpine weather was cool and clear, a wood fire sent up a warm, smoky scent that permeated the cabin in its grassy clearing—it was rough-hewn, primitive, cheerfully spartan. Pipes that lay above ground carried water down from a spring, but there was still no real plumbing. No electricity, no heat for the chilly nights, except for the stacks of Indian rugs for warmth.

Frank's college friend Roger Lewis from Johns Hopkins came early that summer and helped Nat Raymond set up camp. Ruth and Val came next. Then Robert arrived, gunning his big Chrysler *Garuda* up the mountain, and bringing with him physicist George Uhlenbeck and his wife Else, a young couple from the Netherlands who would become great friends of Robert and his father. Else's forté was Indonesian food, spicy enough to thrill Robert; the couple would stay all summer and Else would do much of the cooking.

"Camp works like a charm," Robert would report to Frank, who was in England. "The chief innovations are kerosene lamps and stove, and two army cots, both to meet the fluctuating and exorbitant demands of the summer's hospitality." Those who knew Robert only in his university habitat were astonished: no coat, no tie, jeans and old boots. And Robert was an absolutely fearless, fine horseman.[166]

Robert continued, "This summer more than ever we have been grateful for Vixen and Dink, who are fast, completely competent, full of spirit and even of a good deal of sense." The same could not always be said of the campers; on one trek that summer, Robert, Roger and the Uhlenbecks camped high in the Sangre de Cristos. The men were suddenly seized with altitude sickness; they all shivered through an especially cold night, and when the sun came up, two of the horses were missing. The men revived enough to set out to climb Truchas anyway. A thunderstorm caught them at the peak, and they arrived back in at their campsite wet and cold and miserable. A stop at Katy Page's for a shot of whiskey seemed to set them right. The two delinquent horses appeared early the next morning, and Robert ran out in his pink pajamas to hustle them into the corral. Else would remember the trip as one of the best parts of that summer.[167]

The scientists tried not to talk physics at Perro Caliente. They talked mountains, and trails, and Else's recipe for *nasi goreng*. Before bed they played a wickedly complicated version (devised by Oppenheimer) of the simple child's game Tiddlywinks in front of the fire. Katy, Ruth and Val collected "Robert" stories. Val had a favorite, probably apocryphal: "Imagine this," she would begin, "you're riding on a mountain ridge at midnight in the middle of a thunderstorm, lightning hitting all around you; you come to a fork in the road, in the trail, and Robert says, 'this way it's only seven miles home, this way it's a little longer but it's much more beautiful.'"[168]

Those few who had sailed with him on the east coast knew something of this Robert. A different picture of Oppenheimer was emerging. Summer ended with Else and George piling into *Garuda* with Robert at the wheel, driving north to Berkeley for the fall semester. He was the most fun, the most completely spontaneous person to be around, Else would tell anyone who wanted to know.

NINE MONTHS EARLIER, THE UHLENBECKS, Robert and Nat had started the year together in New York City. The holidays had been a gay and hectic time, with all of them crowded into Julius' new, smaller apartment on Park Avenue. The 21st Amendment to the Constitution had been passed only weeks before, repealing Prohibition, and by New Year's Eve spirits were flowing. Robert wrote to his brother, "An even greater change: Nat has learned to dress. She wears long graceful things in gold and blue and black, and delicate long earrings, and likes orchids, and even has a hat." He added, intimating that he knew that Nat was living with Ruth Benedict, "To the vicissitudes and anguishes of fortune which have brought this change to her I need say nothing."[169]

Robert described the party itself as "wild, confused, very amusing." The problem, this time, wasn't about Nat's tendency towards chaos but with one of the *"jeunes filles"* brought along by Frank's friend Roger Lewis. According to Robert, Roger had terrible taste in women. They were, he wrote, with an adolescent streak of viciousness, "indescribably and mournfully dreadful little bitches."[170]

∽

THAT SAME NEW YEAR'S EVE, Kitty celebrated her successful escape from both marriage and motherhood by going to a party in Pittsburgh. Her good friend Zelma Baker, home for the holidays from graduate school at the University of Pennsylvania, thought it was just what Kitty needed: have some fun, meet some new and exciting people. Zelma, who was finishing her Ph.D. in biochemistry, promised to bring along a "real Communist," a novelty from a different world.[171] Her guest turned out to be more real than a novelty.

Joe Dallet was big with dark eyes and a thick thatch of unruly hair, the result of an amateur haircut. One friend described him as a "handsome sonofabitch. Just a gorgeous guy." He spoke in a kind of longshoreman's patois, yet he was perfectly at ease in this crowd of young university people. The men found him hard to fathom. According to one comrade, "He astonished them when he quoted Eliot and Yeats and Rilke at them out of the corner of his mouth."[172] He fairly breathed Marxist theory, and delivered the kind of impassioned rhetoric that married idealism with action. At twenty-seven, Dallet was already at the front of the Communist Party's struggle in the U.S.; he proved his devotion to the cause on March 6, 1930, when he showed up in Chicago with 600 other activists to mark "International Unemployment Day." Dallet was one of the fourteen leaders rounded up by the city's brutal "Red Squad," while planning the march, for a select beating with blackjacks. The battering didn't keep Dallet from turning up two weeks later to march with the 75,000 who were rallying for the establishment of unemployment insurance for the workers.[173] Dallet was on the dangerous front lines, and Kitty was in awe. He seemed invincible, his life filled with fervor and direction. Instantly, she turned on whatever it is that makes some women irresistible to men.

In the course of the night, the two finally found themselves alone. He was working in Ohio, in Youngstown, organizing for labor unions in the steel mills. It was in the center of the most important steel-making region in America, about a two-hour drive from Pittsburgh, which meant he was challenging some of the same people who employed Kitty's father. But Kitty wasn't thinking about her father or her mother, she was thinking about Joe, and the exciting life he was living.

Joe was not quite what he seemed to be. While he believed that class war was inevitable, that the proletariat—the workers of the world—would triumph, his own background embarrassed him. His family was affluent; his childhood had been spent with art and music, with piano lessons and travels to Europe. He had spent more than two years at Dartmouth College and, restless, left to work in the insurance industry in which he made more money than he felt he needed. The execution of Sacco and Vanzetti, anarchists accused of murder, when he was twenty, was critical for Dallet (as it was for many of his generation). To make the conversion to the working class, he went to Illinois to work in the coal mines, then east to do a stint on the docks.

Had Kitty's mother had any idea what was happening that New Year's Eve, especially after seeing their daughter through the previous disastrous year, she would have been furious. Yet all Kitty would ever say was: "I fell in love with him at this party, and I never stopped loving him."[174]

12

JEAN WRITES FOR THE *WESTERN WORKER* IN SAN FRANCISCO, KITTY SELLS THE *DAILY WORKER* ON THE STREETS OF YOUNGSTOWN AND ROBERT BECOMES A PART OF HIS LIFE AND TIMES

Everyone was in motion.

Robert was pushing Garuda flat-out up and down Highway 101, top down in the sunshine, barreling to and from Pasadena, often a couple of graduate students in the backseat.

Jean had written the year after Letty's death: "I feel at times there is something indisputable and absolutely surely set for me to do later, only I have not seen it yet."[175] She would see it by the time she graduated from Vassar in 1935 and returned to the West. That left only Kitty in the East, poised to begin another life, one promising the fulfillment she longed for.

Ruth made frequent trips to Berkeley working on her doctorate. She and Robert sometimes met there, building their friendship. Frank returned from England and came west to Caltech to do his doctorate in physics. He arrived with his flute and proved so talented that, with Ruth at the piano, they began playing Friday night concerts at Val's, across the garden.

At Berkeley, Robert was attracting some of the best young minds in theoretical physics. In 1934, Robert Serber heard him speak at a summer seminar in Wisconsin and changed his plans completely, deciding to go to Berkeley to work with Robert. Serber was small and brilliant and spoke with a lisp; with his smart and funny wife, Charlotte, they slipped easily into the Caltech-Berkeley–Perro Caliente coterie. Serber became Robert's lieutenant—his alter ego some would say—content to stand slightly to his side and behind.

⤫

WHEN SHE MARRIED RICHARD, RUTH'S family in Berkeley grew to include not only Richard's brother Edward, but his wife Kathleen and their three young children, who were especially fond of their "Uncle Dickie." The children didn't quite know what to think of Ruth, perhaps because their mother didn't seem to know what to make of her either. Ruth was elegant and competent, yet she didn't have any children, which seemed to make Kathleen Tolman uncomfortable. The Tolman children would remember how the men would drift into one conversation, the women into another. But Aunt Ruth seemed always to be included in the men's group;[176] there was no comfortable in-between for professional women, which would be one reason they sought each other out for important friendships.

⤫

ROBERT'S SOCIAL LIFE IN BERKELEY included his grad students and sometimes their wives or girlfriends. They went to Mexican restaurants for dinner, or into the city to Jack's Restaurant. He dated a succession of women, mostly pretty and young. Eventually Robert found an apartment near Edward Tolman's home and within walking distance of campus. On the lower level of a house that perched above a canyon filled with manzanita and bay trees, the apartment had three fireplaces and a deck. Even on cold nights, he'd often sleep on the deck—it reminded him of Perro Caliente. Robert often entertained, even making his own version of Else Uhlenbeck's spicy *nasi goring.*

The house belonged to the Washburns, who lived on the upper level. John Washburn was a public accountant and politically conservative; his wife, Mary Ellen, was younger and more left-leaning. The FBI had her listed as a Communist, even though she and her husband had registered Republican in 1926. Since 1932, Mary Ellen had registered to vote as a Socialist.[177] She was tall and brashly elegant, with an eclectic array of friends. As "a modern woman," she was tolerant of deviations from the social norms. (Indeed, there were murmurs about her own sexual preferences.) Mary Ellen's home became a center for the intellectuals of Berkeley, including many Communists. Robert liked the house, the apartment and his new landlady. He was ready to emerge from his singular love affair with physics to become, as he put it, "a part of [his] life and times."

⌒

KITTY'S PARENTS HAD MOVED TO London, where her father represented a Chicago company in England. Even though they were a continent away, Kitty still had to be careful. She knew her mother, especially, would find it repugnant if her daughter took up with a Communist, a Jew at that, and even worse an agitator in the very industry that employed her father. Kitty could not afford to break with her parents until she had another source of income. Joe was agitating for her to join him in Youngstown; he was sure she would be a great addition to the Party; he had a place for her right by his side.

Dallet believed in Communism with an intensity that could be exasperating to his family. When his sister confided that she wanted to become a social worker, he wrote that he felt social workers, "No matter how good their intentions, are objectively harming the workers (the 'poor'). They try to make them 'better adjusted' to the world about them, to 'help the misfits fit' etc. In other words, they try to make it easier for them to exist under capitalism . . . The only solution is to have the workers own, control and operate the means of production, in other words—Socialism, which the workers and peasants in Soviet Russia are building today."[178]

Joe Dallet was going to change the world, and he wanted Kitty to change it with him. She agreed; first, she said, she needed to meet her mother in Germany. Using her Katherine Ramseyer passport, she visited relatives including her Aunt Hilde, the unmarried one, who would later work for an infamous Nazi filmmaker. Kitty's German family would not have approved of Dallet and he would have been even more repulsed by this part of Kitty's family. Kitty left Bremen on the SS *Europa*, arriving in New York on August 3, 1934, less than a month before the Nazi Party rally in Nuremberg where *Triumph of the Will* was filmed.

Dallet was waiting for her in Ohio; he took her to the rooming house to meet some of her new comrades. She became known to them as Kitty Dallet, though the FBI would label her a "common law" wife, which probably means they could find no record of a marriage. In writing to his mother in the summer of 1934, presumably after he and Kitty had married, Joe told her a bit about Kitty: "You asked for information about K. . . . Born in Germany about 24 years ago . . . Studied at Pittsburgh U., Wisconsin, and also abroad for a year or so. Used to play the piano quite well. Family had some money until the depression. Father an engineer. Parents living in Germany the last few years." He went on to describe her: "Pretty good head. Plays good bridge. Rather slight of build, tho well-proportioned. Weight about 112." He told Hilda that Kitty was in charge of selling worker's literature and working hard to set up a worker's bookshop.[179] And, yes, she had become a member of the Communist Party USA.

Dallet might have been a gorgeous guy, musically talented and brave; he was also doctrinaire. He eschewed personal wealth for the greater good, and felt that the state, corrupt capitalist entity though it might be, had a responsibility to care for its workers. He had no compunction about writing home to tell his family his shoes were worn out and asking them to pay for a new pair, nor did he hesitate to live on the government dole ($25.00 a month) while he agitated against the system. He showed his devotion to the working classes by living in a boardinghouse with other comrades. As Kitty described it, in the shared kitchen, "the stove leaked and it was impossible to cook. Our food consisted of two meals a day, which we got at a grimy restaurant."[180] An ideologue, Joe expected Kitty to be one too. She wrapped herself in his arms, and said of course she would.

"I AM DEVOTING MY TIME, precious to me only," Jean wrote to Priscilla, "to reporting and writing for the *Western Worker*, Pacific Coast organ of the Communist Party. This means attending a couple of weekly meetings . . . Then there are sudden excitements such as . . . the trial of 25 workers for participating in a riot which never took place, in a faraway lumbering town called Eureka, to which I will get a ride in a couple of days." Jean went on: "I find I am a complete red when anything at all." But then, "I find it impossible to be an ardent Communist—which means breathing, talking and acting it—all day and all night." [181]

Jean was back on San Antonio Avenue in the Berkeley hills after graduating from Vassar in 1935, at age twenty-one. She was dividing her time between political activities and attending Berkeley to complete the prerequisites necessary for medical school. When her political spirit was exhausted, she wrote Pris, she visited a "heavenly" family who was "completely oblivious of the dialectic as of the conflict under their noses—so with them I enter a Never Never Land." She felt no moral compunction, she wrote on, "As perhaps good comrades would," because, "I still have a feeling for the sanctity and sense of the individual soul."[182]

The people she could not avoid quarreling with were those whose interest in psychoanalysis prevented them from believing in any other form of social action. She was especially aggravated by those who treated psychological theory as a hobby, who didn't realize it, "like surgery, is a therapeutic method for specific disorders."[183] Jean spelled out for Pris one of the major conflicts of her life. She wanted to make a difference as an individual by going to medical school, but at the same time she felt a need to be part of the larger struggle that Communism represented.[184]

~

KITTY DALLET, AS SHE WAS known, sold the *Daily Worker* on the streets of Youngstown, and when she handed out Communist Party leaflets at factory gates she wore tennis shoes, she said, "so that I could get a fast running start when the police arrived." She taught a class in English to workers who didn't speak English well, ran errands, was given the title "literary agent" which meant prodding Party members to read Marxists tracts.[185] She stood at Joe's elbow when he ran a quixotic race for mayor of Youngstown, and listened to speeches, which could seem endless.

The summer of 1934 was the hottest on record in Ohio: long days of temperatures climbing above 100 degrees, stifling nights with people sleeping on porches, or on lawns, to escape their suffocating houses. Drought parched the Great Plains, followed by dust storms so thick it was impossible to breathe; hurricanes ravaged the Florida Keys. The summer floods and tornadoes were followed in winter by great drifts of snow which buried the north of the country.

Kitty persevered in Youngstown for almost two years, trying to be Comrade Kitty Dallett. The trouble with Kitty, Joe told one of his friends, was that "she was a middle-class intellectual who couldn't quite see the working class attitude." She needed a time-out, and he had no patience for people who needed time-outs. He did not tolerate weakness or wavering. They quarreled. The poverty and the heat and the unrelenting dialectic of the Communist Party wore her down. "Finally in June, 1936, I told Joe that I could no longer live under such conditions and that I was separating from him."[186]

She ordered a new passport, using the name of Katherine Puening (which would seem to confirm that she and Joe had never married), and had it mailed to Zelma Baker in Philadelphia. With her passport in hand, Kitty sailed off to England. Her parents were waiting for her, probably with more than a little trepidation.

~

JEAN MIGHT HAVE WALKED FROM her Berkeley home to the Washburn's more modern house on Shasta Road, something over a mile away, in the spring of 1936. The walk would have given her time to consider some of the dilemmas confronting her. Psychiatry was anathema to Communism, which she wanted to believe was the best hope for a world in despair. But she also wanted to become a psychiatrist.[187] Once she had finished all the prerequisites, which were keeping her busy enough now, medical school would be far more demanding and time-consuming. She needed to make some choices—could she maintain her level of commitment to Communism? Did she want to?

Mary Ellen was one of the few good friends Jean had made in Berkeley. The older woman (she was thirty-two, born the same year as Robert) was well known for her parties, where she regularly gathered an esoteric mix of left-leaning Berkeley professors and dock workers, some of them Communists. Others in the room would come to be called "fellow travelers." Talk merged and rose like the smoke from guests' cigarettes, Camels and Lucky Strikes from the cluster of workers, Pell Mells and a pungent whiff of Gauloise from the academics.

At twenty-two, Jean might have been the youngest person there, yet nothing in her manner would have suggested timidity. Tall and slim, her tousled hair cut casually short, she had ample breasts, a small waist, and boyishly narrow hips— a beautiful body, but it was her face that fascinated. A slight droop in one of her eyes was her only discernible flaw; it should have detracted but in fact it added an oddly melancholic cast to her face, so that even when she smiled, as she often did, it seemed tenuous, as if part of her were held in reserve.

Jean was a serious woman with a serious mission. As the Depression continued to rage, the West Coast was shattered by labor unrest and besieged by refugees fleeing the poverty and dust of the country's interior. The major European powers had just signed a non-intervention pact in what those in the Washburn living room believed was a doomed attempt to ward off a civil war in Spain, the first open battle between communists and fascists. The British and the French for the most part held to the agreement not to interfere; the Soviet Union actively supported the democratically elected Spanish Republican government, with fascist Germany and Italy lined up behind General Franco and his Nationalists.

Jean had no patience for those who chose to ignore the threat of fascism, especially members of her own privileged class. She was determined to live the resolute life, yet at this critical point in her life the battle within had become more acute than the battle without. In a month, Jean would be accepted at Stanford Medical School in San Francisco. Becoming a medical doctor and a psychiatrist was going to be her way to give, to help others, and, she hoped, to help herself as well.

Mary Ellen would have welcomed Jean into her living room party with the smile another friend described as being so warm that "in her presence one felt like a small state suddenly granted diplomatic recognition by a major power."[188] Mary Ellen often wore bohemian costumes, perhaps that night a full-length dress in a batik print, her pale face framed in a tangle of curly black hair. She would have introduced Jean to her new tenant, the young man with a stand of wiry black hair that made him seem even taller than he was.

Jean would be in no hurry to meet yet another academic. Perhaps Mary Ellen insisted, and ushered her toward the tweeds and ties. The man holding forth would have been characteristically waving his cigarette in the air as he spoke, keeping the attention of the circle around him. He was some kind of star in the physics department. Smart, but a political naïf. He was thirty-two and rich. His gray suit was well tailored, the blue shirt and tie gave him a professorial air.

Jean Tatlock. Robert Oppenheimer.

Robert knew Jean's father and she would discover soon enough that he also knew a great deal about her father's passion, medieval literature; in fact he knew a great deal about a lot of things. As he did when he talked with anyone who interested him, he gave her his undivided attention, concentrating his shockingly blue eyes on her in the way that unnerved others, keeping up a small undercurrent of murmurs—"yes . . . yes"—to show how intently he was listening. Jean had grown up surrounded by academicians she sensed to be, under all the facile charm and quick wit, oblivious to the desperate realities of the world, and very often incapable of action. Mary Ellen's new tenant certainly spoke eloquently; Jean wasn't sure whether or not that was all he could do. Her life was full, and complicated. She really didn't have time for a man. Yet she responded to Robert Oppenheimer.

Robert left for Southern California and Caltech shortly after the Washburn party, then headed east to Perro Caliente. It was not until the fall when he returned to Berkeley that he called Jean. She said yes, she would like to see him. Robert discovered Jean to be "a lyrical, uplifting, sensitive, yearning creature." For the first time in his life, he found himself pleasantly out of control, strangely euphoric, having somehow experienced whatever biological or chemical reactions could have made him suddenly vulnerable to falling in love.

⟿

KITTY DIDN'T FALL OUT OF love with Joe; she simply could not take being on the front lines of the labor wars in America. She had said she was ill, surely he could see that. Certainly she didn't want to have to go back to her parents in England, but there was no place else she could go. And she couldn't stay.

Her parents now lived in a house called, in classic British understatement, "The Cottage," in the village of Claygate in Surrey, some twenty miles from London—a short train ride. Soon Kitty found village life stifling. She wrote to Joe, but got no answer. She waited, went to Germany to visit relatives, went skiing. She found Germany changed, less friendly, strained. Living with a Jew was something she knew not to mention, not even within the family. On her return to England, she became increasingly restless; she had nothing important to do, no work other than a few English-German translations. Then she discovered that Joe had been writing to her after all, and her mother had been intercepting his letters.

Kitty was furious. She wrote Joe to say she wanted to come back to him; he answered that he was on his way to France, he would be on the *Queen Mary*. They could spend a few days together in Paris before he made his way over the border and into Spain, where he would be fighting with the International Brigade. Kitty was waiting at the dock in Cherbourg when he arrived.

IV

LOVE AND WAR

13

TWO MARRIAGES AND TWO FUNERALS

For the first year of medical school, Jean was required to spend time on the Stanford campus an hour south of San Francisco. Robert and Jean would see each other on weekends and when he drove to Stanford for one of the frequent seminars he had organized with physicists there. Or the couple would meet in San Francisco; the San Francisco-Oakland Bay Bridge had opened that November, replacing the ferry service.

When Jean came home, Robert would pick her up at the Tatlock house on San Antonio Avenue. He would have paused to visit with Jean's parents. Then Robert and Jean would have been off together, going to lectures on campus or to political meetings in Oakland. Jean's friendship with Mary Ellen deepened; with Robert living in the Washburn house, she spent even more time there.

When Robert first presented one of his exotic corsages to Jean, she rejected it politely but firmly; there was no time for flowers when people were standing in breadlines only a few miles away. (When he forgot and did it again, she threw them on the ground and refused to go out with him.)[189] But she admired his ability to grasp a difficult concept and explain it with exquisite clarity and she spoke up when she thought his rhetoric was obscuring his reason. He, in turn, was amazed and delighted with this young woman who did not see him as a brilliant aberration. (She would defend him to a friend who found him pretentious, "Remember that he never had a childhood so he is different from the rest of us.")[190] Jean became his guide through the turbulent political state of the world.

In the Pacific, Japan moved ever more aggressively into China, and in Europe, the civil war that so many dreaded had started in Spain in the summer of 1936. The world waited to see if the Fascists would prevail. If that happened, it seemed obvious to those who met at the Washburns that the conflagration could spread throughout Europe. It could mean another World War, not twenty years after the first one. Robert became increasingly troubled as well by the problems his graduate students faced. He could pay for their dinners in San Francisco but he could not find jobs for them. Even more immediate, he was alarmed by the treatment of Jews in Europe, and began making arrangements for relatives in Germany to come to America.

Robert, along with Haakon Chevalier, a strikingly handsome professor of French literature at the university, became involved in the teachers' union and the movement to help migrant workers. Like many of their friends, both Robert and Jean became caught up in the effort to support the Spanish Republicans. And both began to meet the refugee psychoanalysts—students of Jung and Freud—who had fled Europe for San Francisco.

Robert didn't share Jean with his students as he had the other women he had dated; the intensity of the relationship set it apart. Their friends tended to be people with shared political views. When Pris wrote a chatty letter about people they knew, and where they were, Jean answered, "most of my friends and I have the habit of not noticing events like commencements and departures—so I thought I didn't care, but letters like yours with mystical combination of casual friendliness and apropos-ness are strangely pleasant to get, I find."[191] Even so, it is likely that Robert and Jean avoided socializing with the physics senior faculty, especially Ernest Lawrence, who disapproved of any of his colleagues dabbling in politics. The Tolmans were different; Jean had studied under Edward at Berkeley and Robert would have wanted her to know his great friends Richard and Ruth.

Much about Jean would have pleased Robert: Her Vassar/Harvard connections and New England pedigree; that she was fluent in French and a quick and critical thinker; that she was comfortable in academia and yet not in awe of it. She had a brother who was soon graduating from medical school at Harvard. Her formidable and kind mother balanced the too-distant father. Jean also moved easily in the wider world outside academia, the world Robert was just beginning to explore. She loved poetry, and was fascinated with the promise of psychotherapy. Looking forward, Jean was young enough to get her medical degree before they need think about a family; he was of an age to think of a family of his own. That year, though, their future was obscured by the gathering war clouds.

Robert was convinced that Frank had not thought about consequences when he had announced, in 1936, that he planned to marry Jacquenette Quann, a Berkeley student who was working as a waitress. Seven years older than Frank, Robert had relished his role as something between a father and an older brother. Now he objected strenuously to Frank's choice, told his brother he was being "infantile," pointed out that he was already twenty-five and hadn't yet finished his doctorate.

But it was Jackie—he called her "that waitress"—to whom he objected. It wasn't so much her waitressing he disliked as it was her seeing it as a badge of honor, and for dismissing him and most academics as "highbrows."[192] Frank married her anyway, and Robert had to make a choice. He loved his brother too much to give him up, so he accepted Jackie with all her rough edges. Robert's rejection understandably offended her, but she loved her husband enough to join the brothers at Perro Caliente for a few weeks that summer. Jean may have had something to do with the détente; she was friends with both Jackie and Frank, all but Robert were members of the Communist Party USA. Yet none could have had any idea of the enormous repercussions their act of joining the Party was to have on the Oppenheimer brothers.

As 1936 wound to an end, Marjorie Tatlock knew that she was seriously ill. This was probably why her husband accepted a teaching position at Columbia, in New York City, for a single term beginning in January. Marjorie could be seen at New York Cancer Hospital for treatment for lymphoma. John Tatlock wasn't going to give her up without a fight. Hugh was in Boston and had another reason for wanting his mother to come East. He had proposed to Anne Fisher, and he wanted his mother to get to know her and to be at their wedding.

Marjorie must have worried about leaving Jean just as she was beginning medical school, as well as a serious romance. What if her daughter was waylaid by one of the depressions that overwhelmed her? Jean, as it happens, had found someone who could understand her depression even better than her mother. Robert knew what it was like to balance on the thin edge of sanity; his fascination with psychiatry was rooted in his own terrifying experiences in Cambridge. He had helped himself, he believed he could help her find a way to overcome them, as he had.

Before Jean entered Vassar, she had written May Sarton to admit she was glad they had never "laid hands on each other" in Paris, and asked, "Doesn't it seem to you a sad and futile thing to let beauty pain and weaken you instead of absorbing and growing with it into impersonality and vitality. The former is what I do. I observe it and compare it with the commonplace, and am hurt by the immensity and transiency and unattainability. Why is this? Paradoxes come over me as answers. Sometimes I think it is because I know too much of the mechanical working of myself, sometimes too little. Everything seems conscious and exposed to me, yet not taut enough to make these mean anything."[193] What Jean sought was consummation both emotional and physical. One without the other would not be enough. And, possibly, that need intensified her depressions.

She loved Robert Oppenheimer at the same time that she hurt at "the immensity and transiency and unattainability" of the beauty she longed for which, for lack of another name, was love. Robert loved her enough, he felt confident, to vanquish her hurt, and he began his campaign to convince her. But there was an issue other than depression that may have troubled Jean; even though as a teenager she had decided she was not a lesbian, she was still uncertain about her sexuality. That too Robert could understand.

෴

THE SPANISH CIVIL WAR WAS on everyone's mind. In Pasadena, Ruth and Frank—she at the piano and he on the flute—rented a hall and gave a benefit concert in support of the Spanish Republicans. In Berkeley, John Tatlock, Robert Oppenheimer, Haakon Chevalier and a few others donated $1,500 to buy an ambulance for Spanish refugees. At Stanford, Jean introduced Robert to Dr. Thomas Addis, a professor of medicine who became both her mentor and friend. A cultivated Scotsman, Addis was both an acclaimed scientist—a pioneer in the treatment of kidney disease—and a renowned humanitarian. He was also sympathetic to the Communist Party and chairman of the United American Spanish Aid Committee, and recruited Jean and Robert to the cause. Robert gave generously, and together he and Jean sponsored benefits to raise money. Initially Robert took the attitude that while he supported the "underdog," he would have to settle for remaining on the periphery of political struggles. Jean responded: "Oh, for God's sake, don't *settle* for anything."[194] After that, he didn't.

෴

WHEN JOE ARRIVED ON THE *Queen Mary,* he and Kitty embraced, happy to be together after a full year apart, and excited to be a part of a movement of such magnitude. Traveling with Joe was his good friend Steve Nelson, an organizer for the American Communist Party. The three boarded a train for Paris. Most of their conversation centered on how Kitty could join them in Spain, Joe railing against a Party rule that allowed neither wives nor girlfriends. Kitty said she wanted desperately to go, and Joe vowed to find a way.

She found a small hotel for them and, as she reported in a letter to Joe's mother, Hilda: "Joe and I had a lovely five days in Paris. We didn't do much, danced one night, went to a meeting another, but mostly just walked, sat, and talked; ate quantities of oysters and snails, drank Vermouth and enjoyed each other. And Joe bought me a Camellia and some Violets. In return, more prosaic, I made sure he had warm socks, gloves, shirts, and shoes."[195]

When Steve rounded up the group of some twenty-five volunteers waiting in

Paris, Joe rejoined him and the group headed south, all "conspicuously trying to be inconspicuous," where a French fishing boat was to be waiting to smuggle them into Spain. The boat, however, was late; it didn't appear until the first light of dawn. Just when the coast of Spain was in sight, a fast-moving French police boat approached, and the officers arrested everyone.[196] Although the French often turned a blind eye to volunteers going to Spain, this time they decided to uphold the nonintervention agreement.

Even before she returned to Surrey, Kitty began a correspondence with Hilda that was a marvel of equivocation: "I know there is no use in my saying anything to you about what Joe is doing," she wrote. "It was as great a shock to me as it will be to you, when Joe told me where he is going. I can offer you no help, nor you me, except perhaps that we know there are two of us who feel more or less the same way about it. It's a superbly great, and preposterous, thing—to think that each one who goes there feels that he is making the world the place it should be. In that respect what you and I feel doesn't matter." Then she added, "When Joe gets back we are going to take a holiday someplace, perhaps in England or on the Continent, or in the Soviet Union. Then we shall both come home and settle down, and I shall try to persuade Joe to try to live in New York. I am sure he will come back, Hilda, I don't know why, but I'm convinced of it."[197] She added that her address was on the back of the envelope, in case Hilda wanted to write.

A few days later, Kitty wrote Hilda again to report she had heard from Joe, that he was in jail in the town of Perpignon in the south of France, not far from the Spanish border. "He says there is nothing to worry about, which is quite true (at least they can't get shot while they're in jail)."[198]

⤴

IN LOS ANGELES, RUTH SPENT a good part of 1937 working on her dissertation, using her connection as a psychologist to arrange interviews with the young men in the Adult Division of the County Probation Department. She wanted to determine if it was possible to predict which men would become recidivists, and perhaps offer some new insights into criminal behavior itself. Her approach was not going to depend on what she described as the "highly technical methods of psychoanalysis," nor was it limited to the broader sociological view that connected poor work habits and damaged family relationships with criminal behavior.[199] Ruth had enough experience with prisoners to believe it reasonable to listen to what the inmate had to say about the forces that affect his life.

All that year she sat across from a succession of sometimes-angry white men, asking them extremely personal questions. What kind of relationship did they have with their mothers and with their fathers? How were they punished? How about nagging, spoiling, affection, their own fears? Most of the men were down on their luck and suspicious; they had seldom confided in anyone, much less an attractive, self-assured woman in a position of authority. Yet she gave them time, gained their confidence. And slowly they told her of problems with their marriages and their children, their grievances.

Nat, being back in California for the summer and, as usual at loose ends, was staying with Ruth while Richard was away. She sat at the dining room table in Pasadena typing Ruth's report from her interviews. The work would serve as a basis for Ruth's doctoral thesis. She received the degree of Doctor of Philosophy from Berkeley in 1937. The following year the Genetic Psychology Monograph series published a full report on Ruth's doctoral study; the year after, so did *The Journal of Criminal Law and Criminology* at Northwestern University.

IN THE MIDDLE OF APRIL 1937, while visiting Winifred at Vassar, Marjorie became so ill that she had to be admitted to Memorial Hospital in Poughkeepsie. Winifred saw her every day. Marjorie wrote to Priscilla from the hospital in a faltering hand, "I have this one piece of paper and a tiny bit of energy," and she wrote the important news: "We shall be staying around here longer than we had expected to help Hugh get married the 18th of June. He has picked out a fine person," she went on, adding that Anne was twenty, lovely to look at, an artist as well and that she was especially fond of painting horses as her models. Marjorie reported what she wanted Pris to know, that Jean was prospering at Stanford. She did not mention Robert, or even hint at the seriousness of her own illness, but said only that Jean was coming East to be a bridesmaid at the wedding, and added. "She will hate it, but she'll do it!"[200]

The wedding took place not on the 18th as planned, but almost two weeks earlier, on the 5th of June, probably because Marjorie was failing. It was a small, family affair in a chapel at the Cathedral of St. John the Divine in New York City, some eighty miles from Poughkeepsie.[201] Jean was there, and becoming increasingly upset with what she saw as unreasonable demands being made on her mother, especially by her father. Marjorie clearly was not well enough to go home to Berkeley, so they returned to Winifred's house in Poughkeepsie. Jean was with her mother when she died on June 20.

FROM HIS LETTERS, IT SEEMED that Joe was having a fine time in Perpignon prison. The arrest of the twenty-five Americans was front-page news in France. "We saw beautiful snow capped mountains and lovely flowering fruit trees in the alleys below during our tour of Southern France," Joe wrote to Kitty, "Some day you and I must travel this land together and hire us a small sailing boat and sail along the coast." His next letter described going to a hearing at the court, finding a piano in a room, and sitting down to play Chopin to a group of gendarmes, lawyers and prosecutors. "Kitty darling, there's lots of personal things I'd like to say, but the censorship, the lack of privacy . . . forbid. Besides, you know everything."[202]

Their trial was held on April 16, with Joe translating for the Americans. The group was sentenced to twenty days, most of which they had already served, and suddenly they were free, sitting in cafes and being feted by the Young Communist Leaguers. They couldn't walk the streets without a crowd gathering, according to Joe. Kitty had been sending him snapshots, which he had been proudly showing off to his French comrades who "fell in love with your pictures and insisted that when all is over you must come here with me for a real visit. They add that we won't have to sleep in straw but in the best feather bed in town."[203]

He told her there was some talk about him remaining in France to do some work for the Party. "That'd be a heluva place to be at a time like this. The one redeeming feature would be that we could be together. But as much as that would mean to me, I'm obviously against it."[204] Joe loved Kitty, but nothing was going to keep him away from the fight. Steve Nelson had been the first to leave for Spain; now a guide had appeared to lead seven others over the Pyrenees.

⟳

BY JULY 11, JEAN HAD returned to the house in Berkeley, and was writing courtesy notes to those who had sent letters of sympathy, in which she said such things as: "It is pretty bad that such a person as my mother should be no more on earth—so very much of life she was. There are things she said in the last months and even things that happened that make it not exactly a bitter thing."[205] Jean would have confided to Robert, the man she had come to love and trust, what her mother had said.

Robert understood the grief Jean felt. But the recent years with his widowed father had been a salve for that ache. He had made Julius part of his life and the affection between them had grown. Jean was not inclined to embrace her father; she was angry with him for what she felt was his stubborn and selfish refusal to accept the inevitability of her mother's death, and for not allowing her a peaceful last few months. The one "unmitigated blessing," as she wrote Priscilla, was that her mother had died in Winifred's house.[206]

But the summer's sorrow was not done; in September Julius died of a heart attack, just two days before his sister Hedwig and her family arrived from Germany.

14

JOE GOES TO WAR, JEAN MEETS SIEGFRIED BERNFELD, ROBERT RESCUES GERMAN JEWS AND IS WARNED THAT HE IS "TOO GOOD A PHYS-ICIST TO GET MIXED UP IN POLITICS OR CAUSES"

From Spain Joe wrote to Kitty that the guides took them up and down narrow goat paths and dry creeks. "The Pyrenees," he wrote, "are magnificent, and cruel. . . . Some have crossed in such darkness you had to hold the coat of the man ahead." Joe had to help carry one of the men the last part of the way. Still, he had time to notice the stars, how the moon glistened on the snowcapped peaks and the lovely pattern the lights of the French villages made far below. When finally they were in Republican territory, he shouted for joy and said if she had been there he would have crushed the breath out of her.[207]

At the camp outside of Albacete, Joe wrote again: "Today was a rich day. I got three letters from you. I was overjoyed by your desire to come here and work, but I am compelled to say no for the present at least. We have made a decision that no wives are to be allowed to come here unless an emergency arises." But he added, "Personally, I think you'd make a first rate tank-driver." In fact, Joe did agitate to make an exception for Kitty, and a month later he thought she might be able to come: "All the dirty work you did for years, cranking leaflets, passing them out in snow and sun, visiting contacts, etc. was not in vain. Everything we worked for years is coming true in steel."[208]

Kitty wrote to Hilda, "Joe is, I gather, although he does not say so, as usual well beloved by his fellows and their leader in thought and action." His fellows did not agree. Joe Dallet was a cultivated man trying to be part of the proletariat, complete with tough-guy accent, expletives and fractured grammar. More than that, his reading of the Communist Manifesto required him to refrain from fraternizing with the men and to ignore their suggestions and complaints if he decided they were not valid. He followed the rules as he understood them, and brooked no exceptions; as a result, many of his men disliked him. Even his good friend Steve Nelson—who was popular with the men—would later admit, "He was trying to do the right thing, but the right thing was wrong. Discipline has to come from political conviction, not from military books."[209]

‿

IN 1937, THE WRITING WAS literally on the walls in Germany: *Jude Raus* (Jew Out). "I had had a continuing, smoldering fury about the treatment of Jews in Germany," Robert would explain.[210] After his father's death, he helped his Aunt Hedwig Stern, her pediatrician son Alfred, and his wife Lotte settle in Berkeley; his father had left Robert with another part of the family to embrace, and he had also left a substantial inheritance. Robert did not hesitate to use it to help others escape the Nazi threat.

Soon after Hitler took power in 1933, the Nuremberg Laws were passed, prohibiting employment of all Jews in the civil service. The faculties of the state-run universities in Germany included some of the country's most celebrated scientists, many of them Jews. Some found a way to England, others came to the U.S.; most were in their thirties and forties, at the apex of their powers, a concentrated treasure of scientific knowledge. These included Alfred Einstein, John von Neumann, Stanislaw Ulam, Edward Teller and Leo Szilard. Immediately after receiving his 1938 Nobel Prize, physicist Enrico Fermi and his Jewish wife Laura fled Italy. Oppenheimer regularly donated to a fund established to help his Jewish colleagues—a number of them were men he had befriended in his days as a student in England and Germany.

‿

WITH THE DEATH OF HER mother that summer of 1937, Jean was stunned by sorrow. Robert too was feeling the strain. He would write a friend, "By the summer I was fairly worn out with a long & in some ways a hard year & thought some weeks in the mountains were more than ordinarily a good idea."[211]

The very perversity of the times provided Jean with some extraordinary new friends. She was at Stanford Medical School just when some of the most inspiring refugees would arrive in the San Francisco area. One of these was a medical doctor named Hannah Peters, a young German woman working at Stanford on a research project with Thomas Addis. Jean admired Hannah: She was brave, had strong political principles, and was a compassionate doctor. She had fled Europe with Bernard Pietrkoiwski; when the two arrived in the United States, he changed his Polish name to Peters, and they married. He had been an engineering student in Munich but because of his left-wing politics, the Nazis had forced him into the concentration camp at Dachau. He escaped and then wrote a moving account of the horrors he had witnessed. When they came to the Bay Area, Peters found work as a longshoreman.

Jean and Hannah became close friends and she introduced Robert to the couple. When he found that Bernard Peters was interested in physics, Robert managed to get him admitted to Berkeley's graduate program as his student. Peters' obvious intelligence, intensity and gravitas impressed everyone. Along with the research at Stanford, Hannah had a medical practice in a poor, racially mixed section of Oakland and became Robert's physician.

In 1937, Siegfeld Bernfeld arrived in San Francisco, and Jean's life took another turn. Bernfeld had a doctorate in philosophy from the University of Vienna; he had studied with Freud (who called him his most gifted student), became a psychoanalyst, and went on to explore, with equal fascination, education and biology. A gifted teacher, Bernfeld embraced both Zionism and Marxism. When he was twenty-seven, in Berlin, Bernfeld had founded a school for some 300 Jewish refugee children from Poland. He came to believe psychoanalysis should be treated as a natural science, based in biology—that there was a genetic connection for mental disorders.[212] Jean became his student, and as part of her training in the 1940s, would be psychoanalyzed by Bernfeld. His approach seemed tailored for Jean. His search for scientific answers to psychological problems echoed Jean's search for therapy as "a surgical tool"—a way to find a cure for herself, to be free of the burden brought about by her "overwhelmings."

⌒

ALL THAT LONG HOT SUMMER, letters passed back and forth: Joe to Kitty, Kitty to Joe's mother Hilda in New Jersey, Hilda to Kitty, and both to Joe. Kitty hadn't met the Dallets, but now she inserted herself into the family. In June, she wrote a burbling dispatch to Hilda from England: "We've had two weeks here of the most glorious sunshine—something I had begun to believe never happened in England. At the same time the temperature went up to 78° and once to 83° and as a result the papers are full of headlines about the 'Heat Wave.' . . . I've spent my afternoon lying as naked as my conscience permits—mine only, since there's no one who could possibly see me, and we lock the gate—and whenever I'm nicely warm take a dip in our pool. As a result I'm quite nicely brown already. However I think it's too bad that civilization should have brought anyone to the point where he cannot comfortably lie quite naked when in absolute privacy."[213]

On July 11, Kitty wrote to Hilda that she kept asking Joe to get her to Spain, but the answer was always "no." That said, she went on to explain that she needed an operation to remove her appendix, but her father's two sisters were coming from Germany for a three-week visit and she would need to help her mother. And after that her very good friend Zelma Baker would be coming to stay for the month of August. So the surgery would have to wait "until all our guests have come and gone.... So i suppose it will be the end of september or more until I can go traipsing off to spain [sic]."[214]

Joe seemed unaware of her August plans. In a letter dated July 19, he declared: "Wonderful news. You can come. Get in touch with Jack in Paris, for whom I enclose a note. He will put you through. I love you."[215]

⤺

IN AMERICA, THE INTENSITY OF the Spanish Civil War had become the rallying cry for the Communists, the progressives and left-wing liberal intellectuals. Ernest Lawrence at Berkeley, who was fond of Frank and Robert, told them it wasn't proper for scientists to get mixed up in politics. The brothers didn't listen. Robert was beginning to enjoy being part of a wider community, Jean sometimes by his side. He joined the East Bay Teachers' Union, the Consumer's Union, organized for FAECT,[216] and signed on to the American Civil Liberties Union. He lent his name to any number of organizations that one day would be labeled "Communist fronts" by the FBI. Robert saw himself as a loyal American, eager to do his part.

⤺

JOE WAS EXASPERATED WITH THE war, with the wait, with Kitty's appendix. "Why in God's name does it have to pop now?" he wrote, after telling her how worried he was about her, "Please have it fixed up immediately so you can start your trip here."[217]

At the beginning of August, Joe was sure his unit would be sent to the front imminently. He waited now for the letters from Kitty, and fussed when she skipped a week or two. But that month, Kitty and Zelma went to Paris to the 1937 World's Fair—officially the *Exposition Internationale des Arts et Techniques dans la Vie*

Moderne. There the massive German Pavilion designed by the young architect Albert Speer stood across from the equally gigantic Soviet Pavilion, a giant eagle and swastika on a stone colossus faced the hammer and sickle. Nearby in the Spanish Pavilion, the central feature was a mural that was to become an enduring and powerful anti-war statement: Pablo Picasso's *Guernica,* depicting the German bombing of that small Basque town.

Joe had no real experience in the front lines, so he wrote what others who had been there told him: that some of "best" people crack up here, some of the worst are heroic. He had heard that up front the changes came so fast he wouldn't see them. It was "a bloody interesting war and the most bloody interesting job of all the bloody interesting jobs I've ever had," he wrote to Kitty, was "to give the fascists a real bloody licking."[218] And he continued to beckon her to come to Spain.

But Kitty was enjoying herself in Paris and chattered on in one of her letters to Hilda, describing the Paris office, which acted as a clearinghouse for the international volunteers: "There is an amazing number of fine young fellows there from America and England—university students, young scientists, all kinds. We went out with them several times and enjoyed ourselves tremendously."[219]

On August 26 in Germany, the doctors operated and discovered that Kitty didn't have appendicitis after all. She gave the details to Joe's mother: "They burned out about 15 or 20 tiny ovarian cysts and sewed the uterus into place; it was almost upside down." Which meant she was being forced to spend another three weeks doing nothing, to give her uterus time to become firmly anchored. She was, she said, dreadfully disappointed. The doctor had told her that she should have a baby within the next two or three years, "so I'll have to see what I can do about it!" Released from the hospital, Kitty and her mother traveled to a spa in Wildbad in the Black Forest. Kitty supposed she might as well take advantage of being there. She wrote to ask Hilda, "I wonder if you've heard anything from Joe lately. Naturally, being here I haven't."[220]

On September 15, Joe wrote to Kitty to say that he'd received several letters and cards from Paris, and "I'll be glad when I get a letter which assures me that you are well and getting ready for the trip." He was writing in an olive grove by candlelight with artillery and avion bombing in the distance. He ended with: "It is all quite picturesque. Much love, Joe."[221] But he was having problems that he would not likely divulge to Kitty or his mother. The men of the battalion—antagonized by Joe's unwillingness to divert from a strict Communist line—were on the verge of rebellion. Commissar Dallet had finally gone too far when he'd accused one of his men of malingering, and threatened reprisals. The men's anger resulted in a meeting that lasted into the night. For eight hours Dallet was battered with complaints; at last, a good Comrade, he experienced a "personal transformation" and apologized, then offered to resign as commissar.[222] It was too late. They were called to the front. For redemption, he needed to prove himself in battle.

In the offensive against the town of Fuentes de Ebro, Joe would lead First Company over the parapet. At 1:40 P.M. on October 13, 1937, he was first out of the trenches, directly into returning fire. Within yards he was hit by machine gun rounds; he began to crawl back to the trenches, waving off the first-aid men. The battalion's machine gun commander watched helpless as Joe struggled in terrible pain, until a second burst of enemy machine-gun fire silenced him.

15

KITTY DECIDES WHAT TO DO, ROBERT TALKS

OF MARRIAGE, AND JEAN SINGS, "SHE NEVER

TOLD HER LOVE, BUT LET CONCEALMENT, LIKE

A WORM IN THE BUD, FEED ON HER DAMASK

CHEEK"

On October 18, 1937, Kitty was back in England, unaware that Joe had been killed five days earlier. She wrote a breathless three-page typewritten letter to Hilda, not taking the time to capitalize words: "i hadn't heard from you for a long time and was beginning to worry lest something had happened to you. and now I haven't written to you for ages either and feel quite bad about it, but I've been rather depressed since I got out of hospital and didn't feel like writing to anyone at all." It had been rainy and cold at the spa at Wildbad and at the end of two weeks, she could no longer stand Germany "with its dreadful feeling of tension. . . . no one dares to talk to a stranger, in fact no one dares speak at all except of the most trivial matters. and its heil hitler all over the place. . . . everyone seems to believe that everyone else except his most intimate friends is a spy. i shall certainly never go back as long as the nazis are in power." [223]

Kitty was now ready to go to Spain, she wrote Joe's mother, but when she went to the office in Paris for Spanish War volunteers to make arrangements she was told she couldn't go immediately. She had waited in Paris for a week, and "would very much liked to have stayed in Paris" had there not been "complications." Kitty explained, "two of the chaps there had fallen for me which made it rather embarrassing and tended to spoil the good time i could otherwise have had with them." [224]

Not knowing her words were pointless and painful for Hilda to read, Kitty rattled on: "i'm back in claygate, still waiting. heaven knows now when i can start, or if i will ever be allowed to go." She confided that her family had felt she would be foolish to go, but then "joe is waiting for me and will be worse than disappointed if I don't come. besides which i can't believe that he would allow me to come if he thought i wouldn't be all right." She added petulantly, "also i hear seldom from joe because he is expecting me all the time and no doubt thinks it useless to write."[225]

On October 25, she learned that Joe had been killed.

She fired a cable to the Dallet family in New York: NEWS TODAY JOE KILLED / DON'T KNOW WHEN /STOP/ COMING BACK IN FEW MONTHS IF I CAN THINK OF SOMETHING TO DO/ ALL LOVE KITTY.[226]

The Dallets had been the first to hear of their son's death. It was two weeks before Hilda responded to Kitty, who wrote back: "evidently you knew about it before i did. that was because nobody here had the courage to tell me about it, since they all knew me personally, and they put if off as long as they could."[227] More likely, his parents were listed as next of kin.

When Kitty learned that Steve Nelson was passing through Paris, she arranged to meet him. Nelson would later remember that "She literally collapsed and hung on to me. I became a substitute for Joe, in a sense. She hugged me and cried." When Kitty pleaded with him to tell her what she should do, he impulsively suggested she return to the States and move in with him and his wife Margaret—Maggie—in Brooklyn, for a time.[228] Kitty considered her options. She despised wet and dreary England, where her father was contracted to stay for at least another year, and she had no place else to go—nor anything to occupy her—elsewhere in Europe. Worse yet, her father seemed to be putting some financial constraints on her. She wrote to Hilda: "i am returning to the u.s. next week. for one thing the only possible way I could please joe is by staying as a good communist and anti-fascist ... as it is possible for me to be. for another, my home is in america and not in this god-forsaken country." She wrote that before Joe, she had planned to be a chemist. Now she was returning to get a Ph.D. from the University of Chicago, but "the only trouble is managing the money end. ... i remembered the other day that joe said he still had some money with you, and that if anything happened to him i was to have it." She said it was painful for her to ask, "but i'm going to be in a position soon where i <u>have</u> to earn my own living and any little bit that will help me on the way is necessary to me. so i hope we can fix it up when i get to new york, although i know in advance that i shall be terribly embarrassed."[229]

The Dallets kept an apartment in New York, as well as a home on Long Island. It seems doubtful that she was ever given the chance to be "terribly embarrassed" when asking for the money. Hilda must not have responded because Kitty moved into Steve and Margaret Nelson's cramped Brooklyn apartment and stayed for two months.

She would turn twenty-eight that August and was still financially dependent on her father. Joe became a celebrity in certain circles: a committed Communist Ivy Leaguer who had become a hero in Spain. Kitty offered his letters for publication, and the Party had them printed with the title *"Letters from Spain by Joe Dallet American Volunteer, TO HIS WIFE."*

As Kitty had told Joe's mother in her telegram, she now had to think of something to do.

⟿

ONE SUMMER DAY IN 1939, Jean put the top down on her roadster, picked up two friends and headed north toward Mendocino, a small fishing and lumbering village perched above the sea. One of the friends, Edith Arnstein, was a year younger than Jean. The two had earned their radical credentials at the same time and their mothers moved in the same circles.

Edith would write that they sang their way up Highway 1, tracing the coastline, hair flying in the ocean breeze. Edith taught them Orlando Gibbon's famous madrigal, "The Silver Swan."

> *"The silver Swan, who, living, had no Note,*
> *when Death approached, unlocked her silent throat.*
> *Leaning her breast upon the reedy shore,*
> *thus sang her first and last, and sang no more:*
> *Farewell, all joys! O Death, come close mine eyes!*
> *More Geese than Swans now live, more Fools than Wise."*

In turn, in her strong contralto, Jean sang a few lines from *Twelfth Night:* "She never told her love, but let concealment, like a worm in the bud, feed on her damask cheek."[230]

JEAN AND EDITH HAD DISCOVERED the metaphysical poets at about the same time, but for Edith, all the music and poetry ceased when she became totally immersed in the Communist movement. She explained, "I am not sure Jean was ever so doctrinaire, though we shared the same political beliefs." There was much that Jean did not share, Edith admitted: "Jean was private about her despair. She had always been close about her life and her decisions, so that although I was surprised when she told me as a fait accompli that she was registered in medical school, I felt the decision came from some place in her that I never had presumed I knew. When I saw her after her first year, she had already decided to become a psychiatrist."[231]

If Jean was private about her deep depressions, she was just as private about her relationship with Robert. "All of us were a bit envious," Edith wrote, "I for one had admired him from a distance. His precocity and brilliance already legend, he walked his jerky walk . . . with his blue eyes and wild Einstein hair."[232] Edith was also a friend of Mary Ellen Washburn, and between Jean and Mary Ellen— and the increasingly frequent gatherings at the Washburn house about the war in Spain—Edith came to know Robert well enough to call him "Oppie."

Poetry had always been a way for Jean to express her most profound yearn-ings. At Berkeley, Robert was learning to read the 700 verses of the Hindu holy book, the *Bhagavad Gita,* in the original Sanskrit. As a girl, Jean had copied long stanzas from her favorite works. Now, the two read together. Jean confided in him, and he in her. They discussed her depressions, and he struggled to help her under-stand them. He knew how demons filled the mind with dread and fear and worse, hopelessness. He did not discount the pain he knew she was enduring, a form of torture that distorted and twisted all of life until all that mattered was a way to escape. He had, that time in Brittany, thought about suicide. But his terror had dis-sipated; he had come through intact. He could not believe that someone as loving and yearning and good as Jean could not be rescued.

Robert was a fine man, she knew. As she had written several years prior: "Had I a man, I should give myself to whatever that is. I can easily imagine becoming drunk over his body and more over his delight in mine. He could have all that and whatever of the rest of me he could find. I imagine, were he a fine man he could make something out of me."[233]

They talked of marriage, but she hesitated.[234]

He asked again, and she refused.

Jean had watched her mother bend her life to accommodate her father. Even at the end, John had held on to Marjorie, made demands, had not allowed her to go easily to her death. Her father clearly needed a woman to anchor his life. (He would, in fact, marry their old friend Elizabeth Whitney at the end of September. Jean would have had to wonder how this late marriage would work out; she ad-mired Elizabeth as a Jungian psychiatrist and must have assumed she knew what she was doing. Certainly it would relieve the pressure on Jean to offer emotional support to her father.)

Would it be any different with Robert, who was already a star in the academic firmament and thinking about marriage and family? Twice they had come close to declaring themselves engaged. But how was it possible to think of fulfilling his needs, of becoming a mother and caring for children?

Sometime that year she told him she could not marry him. Not now. There was no sharp break, no dramatic end. They remained close—to each other and to many of the same people—Bernfeld, the Peters, Mary Ellen, and Thomas Addis. They cared too much for each other to stay far apart. Most of their circle still considered Jean his "sweetheart," not knowing exactly where the relationship stood, and Robert and Jean were silent. When he started to see other women, it seemed obvious that it was with Jean's understanding.

∽

NEW YORK HADN'T TURNED UP anything to occupy Kitty, and she couldn't stay at the Nelsons much longer, so she made her way to Philadelphia to see Zelma— also known as "Bake." It is likely that Zelma urged Kitty to finish her bachelor's degree, as Kitty enrolled at the University of Pennsylvania for the spring semester. She would graduate in June, and go straight into graduate school—if she could find a way to support herself. She complained that her parents had said it was difficult to send money out of England.

Bake was on the staff of the Cancer Research Laboratories at Penn's Graduate School of Medicine. She had introduced Kitty and Joe, and it was likely she also introduced Kitty to a colleague visiting from California[235] named Stewart Harrison. A medical doctor also in cancer research, he happened to be a good-looking British bachelor as well.

Harrison's degrees, both undergraduate and medical, were from Oxford. He wasn't a Communist. He wasn't homosexual or a drug addict. Harrison wasn't Joe, she would tell her friends; she would never stop loving Joe. She was, however, twenty-eight, and alone.

Harrison quickly proposed. Kitty accepted but with a proviso: she would need to stay at Penn long enough to finish her bachelor's degree, which meant that Harrison would have to be in California without her for the first six months of their marriage. And when she joined him, she intended to begin graduate work in botany at the University of California at Los Angeles. Harrison agreed to it all.

In November of 1938, one year and one month after Joe's death, Kitty married Richard Stewart Harrison in Philadelphia. Soon after, he made the train journey across the country alone to California and his research at the California Institute of Technology.

∽

RUTH'S AND VAL'S LIVES MOVED along apace, back and forth through the garden gate that connected their homes. Both had demanding jobs; when at home Val tended her roses and Ruth entertained; they visited their families and friends in Berkeley. Ruth had worked at the Federal Relief Administration from 1934 to 1936, attempting to apply new principles of behavioral psychology. By 1937, she had completed her dissertation, and chose to continue working, part-time, for Los Angeles County as a senior psychological examiner for the County Probation Department. Even part-time, the work was challenging.

꿍

KITTY ARRIVED IN CALIFORNIA FROM Philadelphia. She and Harrison had been married ten months and separated for six of them. It had taken her nine years to get her bachelor's degree, but at last she was enrolled at UCLA's graduate school—on her way, she said, to a Ph.D. Her life seemed like a series of interruptions and the party they were going to the night of her arrival in California might have seemed like just one more. Harrison was popular, and his Caltech friends wanted to meet the woman who was lucky enough to catch him. Tall and handsome in his summer whites, his dark hair carefully trimmed, Harrison was eager to introduce his bride.

The party was in the Lauritsen garden. For the past three years, Harrison had worked with Charles Lauritsen in Caltech's high voltage X-ray lab which, when it wasn't being used in physics research, was available for the experimental treatment of cancer. Charlie or his wife Sigrid welcomed Kitty and Harrison, made sure they had drinks, and began the introductions. Kitty was twenty-nine years old that August, small and vivid, not beautiful in any usual way, but engaging and confident. Her eyes were dark and expressive and she laughed easily—there was nothing coy or timid about her. She was the kind of woman whose appeal could never be explained by a photograph. Men were drawn to her; if some of their wives were hesitant, it was because they couldn't quite tell who Kitty was, where she fit.

"Meet the new Mrs. Harrison," someone would have said, then the conversation would have turned back to Europe and war. Talk would have been tinged with a sense of dread. Most of the academics at the party had studied in Europe, many of them in Germany. A few, like Robert Oppenheimer, were Jews and were anxious about their relatives.

It was late in the summer of 1939. On August 23, the Soviets signed a non-aggression pact with the Nazis, removing for Hitler the threat of a Russian attack on his Eastern Front. On September 1, Hitler would invade Poland and three days later, Britain and France would declare war on Germany. The Republicans in Spain were finished; Franco—with the backing of Hitler and Mussolini—would emerge the victor and the Fascists would be in command.

The Tolmans were at the party. Ruth would have engaged Harrison's young bride with her usual warmth. Others would have sought out Richard, as a veteran of the First World War, to hear his thoughts. The guests were scientists, influenced by facts more than hopes, and the facts coming out of Germany told them the atmosphere there was poisoned.

Kitty could describe Germany. How she found "Heil Hitler this, and Heil Hitler that," and the dirty looks she got when she refused to respond. She could explain that she had been visiting family in Germany all of her life, and how now everyone suspects everyone else. (She would not have revealed that she had family connections to Hitler's top generals.)

Harrison would have been the one who pointed Robert out to Kitty, whispered that he was already something of a legend in the field of physics. Kitty, moth to flame, could see for herself: Robert holding a cigarette and waving it ever so slightly as he spoke. His soft speech, the effect he had on the others. How he was "interested in almost anything you could think of. His mere physical appearance, his voice, and his manners made people fall in love with him—male, female, almost everybody ... He was terrifically attractive."[236]

By the time she left the party that summer evening, Kitty Harrison wanted Robert Oppenheimer.

ECHOES OF WAR RUMBLE OVER BOTH COASTS,

RUTH MAKES A DECISION, JEAN FINDS HER

VOCATION, AND KITTY CHALLENGES THE

SANGRE DE CRISTOS

The year 1939 marked the end of one grim decade and 1940, the beginning of an even more tortuous one. Roosevelt had begun to prepare the United States for war. For those whose lives intersected most intimately with Robert Oppenheimer's, some changes were abrupt, others came so quietly they were noticed only in retrospect.

Robert continued to make the monthly drive between Pasadena and Berkeley, and in the summer to New Mexico and Perro Caliente, where he exchanged the car for a horse named Crisis. The mainstays gathered there as well: Frank and Jackie, and Bob and Charlotte, who made the long drive out from Illinois in both 1939 and 1940. An assortment of other friends also came for shorter periods.

Jean, who loved riding and mountains and mystery, seems never to have been part of the gathering because of the demands of medical school. Jean's father's marriage to family friend Elizabeth Whitney did not last long. In a letter to Hugh, who was concerned about his father's health, Whitney attempted to explain that she felt his father's symptoms—exhaustion and the feeling that he could not work productively—stemmed from his need to find lost elements in himself through a woman—friend, sister, daughter, wife. "He cannot <u>bear</u> to <u>live alone</u>," she wrote. He had refused to go into deep therapy to find a fresh source of energy within himself, which she had urged.[237] And though she didn't spell it out, it was clear that she didn't choose to become an acquiescent wife. Her erstwhile stepdaughter, who had neither the time nor the inclination to tend to her father, would have seen this failed marriage between her father and her mother's good friend as a cautionary tale.

IN 1940 RICHARD TOLMAN RETURNED to government service. Soon he was traveling across the country to Washington, D.C., meeting with James Conant, president of Harvard and chairman of the National Defense Research Committee, and Vannevar Bush, a former MIT professor and current president of the Carnegie Institution. Ruth would sometimes see Richard off on the *Super Chief* out of Los Angeles on the four-day trip to Washington, D.C. If he was needed urgently, Richard would fly American Airlines and be there within sixteen hours. Ruth carried on at home with her terrier named Tim (Nitz's successor), her work and her friends. She wrote Richard loving letters, told him she was always lonely without him. Both knew that their comfortable world of garden parties, pure research and *stammtisches* was coming to an end.

⤳

KITTY AND STEWART HARRISON'S APARTMENT at 553½ South Coronado Street was not far from downtown Los Angeles, and almost equidistant from the new University of California, Los Angeles campus to the west, and Caltech to the north. Kitty enrolled at UCLA as Katherine Stewart Harrison, and she said she was exempt from paying the registration fee because her father could not send her money from England. Kitty intended for UCLA to be her path to the doctorate that would make her one of the exceptional women, like her friend Bake and like Ruth. It would also put her on par with Robert Oppenheimer's "sweetheart" in San Francisco, a medical doctor on her way to becoming a psychiatrist.

⤳

LATE IN 1939, RUTH BENEDICT and Nat Raymond's relationship was sputtering. Nat had spent much of the 1930s living with Benedict in New York, and now left the country, exuberant with a new idea to become a travel guidebook writer. Benedict traveled west to stay with her mother in Pasadena while waiting to see if her brother and his wife had managed to get on a freighter out of Europe. With the war declared, Americans were scrambling to return on any ship that would take them.

Later that month, Benedict visited old friends in Berkeley and spent some time at the university. She wrote to Margaret Mead that she had met Nat's good friend Ruth Valentine, that they had much in common—they had both gone to Vassar—and that they had driven back south "along the magnificent coast drive that is new since I lived out here—down through the Robinson Jeffers country—and that was something I'd always wanted to do. It was magnificent."[238]

The next month, Benedict would write to Mead that she was staying at Val's, and was part of a new group, one that included Ruth Tolman: "It's been a great pleasure. . . . Wednesday nights some eight or ten highly selected men and their wives have dinner together that they call the Stamtisch; they're liberal and are most of them Cal Tech faculty but there is a psychoanalyst, etc. I've met some people there I enjoy." Benedict wrote on, "I'm very happy living with Val . . . She's spent her life picking up the pieces of a disappointed and violent family; she's been tied to it, and she's never taken life into her own hands and planned for herself. Now the last one of the family is dead—three have died in the last two years—and it's meant everything to her that I've been here."[239]

She would stay for four months, not leaving Val's home until April 1940.

⌐⌐

THERE IS NO RECORD OF who made the first move, of when Kitty and Robert first saw each other after they'd met in the Lauritsens' garden. The fall semester in Berkeley started in mid-August, taking Robert north until he returned to attend the requisite monthly meeting at Caltech.

With the wives of his friends and colleagues, Robert had earned a reputation. Ten years earlier, he had taken Ava Helen Pauling's flirtation as an invitation to a tryst, and acted without regard for her husband. The year before, in 1928, also in Pasadena, Robert had attempted to romance Helen Campbell, who at the time was engaged to marry Sam Allison, a colleague of Robert's at Berkeley. Helen admitted that before her engagement, she had found herself attracted to Robert, but decided that he had an eye for women, even married ones, "and that his attentions to her should not be taken too seriously." She added that she thought he was drawn to "slightly discontented women and seemed specially sensitive to lesbianism."[240] Since Jean, he had been dating a number of women in San Francisco, none of them seriously. And there was no reason to believe he was serious about Kitty Harrison either.

Kitty had no doubts about her sexuality, and shared Robert's lack of compunction about allowing marriage or friendship to interfere with what she wanted. (Especially if what she wanted was more permanent than what he had in mind—she told a friend that she had "set her hat for him. . . . and did it the old fashioned way, got pregnant. And Robert was just innocent enough to fall for it.")She was soon seen happily enthroned on the passenger seat of Robert's big car. They had only to be seen together more than once for the gossip to begin in academic circles. Robert would remember that time as a "highly charged passionate falling in love"—something never easy to hide.[241]

For most of that year, Kitty remained at UCLA and continued to live with Harrison. Later, she would tell one of the Tolmans' inner circle that her marriage was all wrong from the outset, that she continued to live with him only because he was concerned that a divorce would affect his reputation as a young doctor. She also stayed because she had no other place to go, and no income of her own. As the fall progressed into winter, Kitty and Robert saw each other on his monthly trips to Pasadena, and somehow, when the Christmas holidays rolled around, Kitty managed to make her way north to Berkeley—without her husband.

The first time Robert's friend Haakon Chevalier met Kitty, "was a not altogether happy occasion," Chevalier would write. Estelle Caen* had been the last in a "string of 3, 4, 5 mostly very attractive youngish girls" Robert had dated in the last year or so, according to Chevalier, who considered his good friend "Opje" to be a paragon of fine manners. "[Estelle] with whom he had broken a short time before, was giving a holiday dinner party in her house in San Francisco for a dozen or more close friends . . . Being a good sport, she had also invited Opje. To everyone's consternation he appeared, very late, bringing with him, uninvited and unannounced, his new fiancée, wearing a big spread of orchids."[242] Kitty was hardly Robert's "fiancée" at the time, since she was married to, and living with, Stewart Harrison.

If Jean was both beautiful and deeply intellectual, she could also be unsettling, removed and complicated. Kitty, in contrast, was bright and laughing and fun; she didn't think before acting, didn't anguish over "social conscience demands." Kitty elaborated on her background, hinted at her aristocratic connections. And she surprised Robert with her history in the Communist Party; she had actually been a Party member, had lived the life, had been on her way to the war in Spain when her first husband was killed in action. But it would have been her exuberance, her blatant disregard of boundaries, that especially appealed to him. He described her as "golden."[243]

As his brother Frank pointed out: "In fact one of the most important characteristics of my brother . . . involves the way in which he made people into heroes. He could like all manner of people but in liking them they became special and

---

*Estelle Caen, born in Sacramento, studied at the San Francisco Conservatory of Music and the Juilliard School in New York. She was an accomplished pianist and strong supporter of left-wing causes all her life. Her brother was Herb Caen, well-known *San Francisco Chronicle* columnist.

exceptional."[244] Kitty had found the man she believed would meet all her needs: he was charming, powerful in a world she relished, clearly admired by his peers and adored by their wives. His Harvard was not Frank Ramseyer's scholarship Harvard; he did not count poverty a virtue, as Joe had; he lived a larger life than she sensed Harrison desired. And she had managed to get his attention. Now she had to find a way to keep it. Her chance would come in the summer of 1940.

〜

RUTH WAS FEELING OUT OF sorts at the start of the new decade. Richard remained in the nation's capital living in a hotel room when he wasn't flying to secret destinations. Her neighbor and confidante Val was preoccupied with Ruth Benedict, her new love. While Ruth was pleased to see Val happy again —after the last two miserable years, which had included the death of her brother—she would have missed the closeness with her friend of twenty years.

Though Ruth and Richard were open-minded and accepted Val's and Nat's various relationships with women, they frowned on Robert and Kitty's *coup de foudre*. They liked Stewart Harrison and were dismayed to see hurt and humiliation inflicted on a friend. The Proust quote Robert liked to recite was about an indifference to suffering as the "most terrible and lasting form of cruelty." Robert's friends did not want to believe he was capable of cruelty. Robert Serber said, "He was . . . so sensitive to other people and their feelings; there was just an aura around him." But not all the time.

〜

JULY BECAME A MONTH FOR decisions: Benedict's sabbatical ended and it was time to return to her life in New York City and she wanted Val to go with her. Val had not been sure—leaving her house, her friends. But she screwed up her courage and decided to join her new love in the East. As for her friend Ruth Tolman, she knew that with England and France now at war and America on the fence, Richard could be in Washington for a long time. Going East herself would mean giving up her work and her home and probably even her dog. Ultimately, though, she wanted to be with Richard and to be part of what was happening in the country. In mid-July 1940, she and Val closed their homes, piled their things into Val's car, and drove across the country in the heat of summer. They paused in Detroit long enough for Ruth to buy a new car for Richard; she drove it into Washington on a sweltering August day.

In a letter to Benedict, Nat wrote that Ruth "sounds doleful; and why not? I think she's been virtue personified to come at all, and I don't begrudge her a load of neuroses, indecisions and complaints. . . . I do hope she finds something to do that will take time and energy. I can't quite picture her in a hotel, caring for Richard who just isn't around most of the time, and without her house to play with, her job to run, and the innumerable chores that result from having lived in one community for some 15 years." [245]

⌒

BEFORE HEADING TO PERRO CALIENTE in the summer of 1940, Robert returned to Berkeley. Frank was now at Stanford. The other regular summer visitors to the cabin, Bob and Charlotte Serber, had arrived from Illinois, ready to move on to New Mexico. Robert had a plan and turned to the ever-accommodating Serber, explaining that he had invited Stewart and Kitty Harrison to Perro Caliente in the spring, but that Harrison had told him he was caught up in research and could not make it. (To justify herself, Kitty would say that Stewart had other reasons for wanting her to go without him.) Kitty might come alone—if she could find a way to get there. Robert then suggested: "You could bring her with you. I'll leave it up to you. But if you do, it might have serious consequences."[246] Serber was adept at translating Robert. As a good friend, of course he and Charlotte would detour to Pasadena. Robert, Frank and Jackie were waiting at the cabin in New Mexico when the Serbers drove up the rough road with Kitty in the backseat.

The Oppenheimers had become excellent horsemen. Jackie learned to ride as she did most things, by grit and hard work. Charlotte had a few lessons, but Serber had never been on a horse in his life. The diminutive Serbers seemed unlikely candidates for the rugged life in a high mountain wilderness. Their first summer at Perro Caliente, Robert had chosen a horse named Blue for Charlotte, and one called Cumbres for her tremulous husband, then promptly sent them out by themselves on an overnight trail ride. Six years later, by the summer of 1940, the Serbers were veterans. Horseback riding and camping out were what Serber would come to call "the business" of a summer at Perro Caliente. He explained, "We rode in the wilderness area, in the pine and birch forest, the high grassy and flowered meadows, and along the ridges of the Sangre de Cristo Mountains." [247] The quest was to camp out with a minimum of food or equipment, to live a lean and active life far from academia. Riding was required, so a visitor's first confrontation with a horse became a defining moment.

The group watched expectantly as Kitty Harrison approached the young mare that Robert had selected for her, "lifted easily into the saddle . . . touched her heels to its flanks and took the east fence at a leap." Robert looked on with "undisguised affection." They watched as she rode as fast and fearlessly as Robert did on his horse, Crisis. Like most girls of the middle and upper classes in America at the time, Kitty had learned to ride early. Aspinwall had its own riding trails and was close to the Mellon Hunt. Even Jackie, as proud of her working class credentials as she was repulsed by what she saw as aristocratic pretensions, had to admit that Kitty knew how to handle a horse.

By firelight that first night, the group played the ritual, complicated version of tiddlywinks that Robert had concocted, then bunked in as usual on cots on the porch. A day later, Robert announced he was riding to Los Pinos with Kitty to introduce her to Katy Page and would stay over. Robert and Kitty returned the next day. Soon after, Katy appeared on her big bay horse, looking as imperious as ever. The reason for her trip, she announced, was to return Kitty's nightgown, found under Robert's pillow, which she held out like a flag.[248]

Charlotte and Jackie quickly saddled their horses and took off, Jackie in the lead. When they came back, Jackie's neck ached from turning around to talk to Charlotte. Suspicions were confirmed. The "serious consequences" had begun.

⤳

"I FIND IT QUITE UNCOMFORTABLE being so out of touch with you," Jean wrote to Winifred Smith. "But this shall be remedied this summer when I come to New York to work in the psychiatric clinic of an institution called The Children's Village." Jean explained that it was for "what they call unadjusted or antisocial boys and girls." Founded in 1851 in New York City as an asylum for homeless immigrant children, the Children's Village moved in the 1920s to a farm in Dobbs Ferry, barely an hour and half from Vassar. It was the first residential treatment center in the country to establish a psychiatric clinic on the campus. Jean was expected to interview the children and study the behavior and progress of the boys. "As you know," she wrote, "I am interested in the psychology of it and also very much in the environmental—that is social—background of such conditions."[249] Jean had one more year of medical school to complete before she moved into her specialty. This summer would give her an idea of the challenges, of how psychology as a science might address some of the problems these most vulnerable children faced.

Jean added, "I sometimes wonder if I have become a different person from Vassar days," then paused to add, "And then I fear—not enough. But I do know that whatever has happened to me has been in line with experiences of that adolescent period—the deepening though not the solution of the conflicts that came to light in that period. I can hardly tell you how horribly I miss some of you older enlightened ones—and my friends none of whom I ever see and who are irreplaceable."[250] Jean continued to search for solutions to the conflicts that had bedeviled her adolescence and to which Winifred had been both witness and protector (as she had been in the two years since Marjorie's death). Jean may have been referring to a lingering confusion about her sexual orientation, but it is more likely she meant the debilitating depressions that continued to plague her. She was now twenty-five, and neither conflict was resolved.

From Dobbs Ferry, she took time to go north to Massachusetts to see Winifred, and to pay a visit to May Sarton and her parents. May reported that Jean brushed past her to embrace her parents, who opened their arms to the girl who had lived with them a decade earlier. (They found her "tall, slim and stunning . . . very left fringe.") May had admitted to herself, if not her parents, that she was a lesbian. Rumors had sifted back to the Sartons that Jean had a lover at Berkeley, a professor.[251] Jean didn't mention Robert, or that the relationship had floundered.

In May 1940, the Nazi Wehrmacht had invaded Belgium, the Sartons' homeland. In the next month, France surrendered and England stood alone, desperate for America to enter the war. The summer of 1930, after Letty's death—when May and Jean swam naked in the seas off the coast of France—seemed a lifetime away.

⁓

TWO RIDERS ON HORSEBACK COULD find whole forests full of secluded places in the high mountain wilderness, and Kitty and Robert discovered their own. Kitty had no reservations about how she felt for Robert. By the time they were ready to leave in August, when Robert had to be back in Berkeley for the fall semester, Kitty was pregnant but barely. She would not know for sure until late September. What Kitty did know for sure was that something had to be done about her current husband.

When he returned to California, Robert called Harrison to say he wanted to marry Kitty, that she was going to have his child, and that he hoped Harrison would agree to a speedy divorce. Harrison would later claim that the three remained "on good terms" and that they "had modern views concerning sex."[252]

Kitty appeared in Berkeley a week or so later. She was with Robert when he was the featured speaker at yet another Berkeley fundraiser for Spanish Civil War refugees. Robert talked of the fascist victory in Spain as being the precursor to the war now raging in Europe; brave men had fought a delaying action, men like Steve Nelson, sitting with him on the platform that early autumn evening. Newly arrived to take over as organizer for the Alameda County branch of the Communist Party USA, Nelson had never heard of Robert Oppenheimer before that evening. After the speech, Robert approached Steve with a smile and said, "I'm going to marry a friend of yours ... I'm going to marry Kitty."[253] Nelson looked perplexed. Kitty Dallet? He had not heard from Kitty since she'd left his apartment in New York. Kitty was sitting in the back of the hall, and Robert waved her up. Steve opened his arms and hugged his comrade.

THAT SEPTEMBER OF 1940, KITTY was no longer interested in the Communist Party; she had other things to do. The first was to establish a six-week residency in dusty, sinful Reno—the Nevada gambling town at the foot of the Eastern Sierra, filled with shabby boardinghouses ready to welcome people who needed a quick divorce. In October, as Kitty sat waiting in Reno, her parents returned to the United States via Lisbon. Kitty had some news for them. Robert called the Serbers, to say he had some news for them. Except Serber wasn't sure if he heard "Kitty" or "Jean." Even those closest to Robert seemed surprised—either that he would choose to marry Kitty, or that he would give up Jean. What none of them knew was that Robert was wild about Kitty, and that there was a reason for rushing into marriage.

ON NOVEMBER 1, 1940, KITTY'S divorce was granted, and that same day she and Robert were married in the county courthouse in Virginia City, Nevada— once the richest boomtown in America. A court janitor and a local clerk served as witnesses, and signed their names to Kitty's most recent marriage license.

When the Oppenheimers returned to Berkeley, one of their first dinner invitations was from Molly and Ernest Lawrence. Molly was taken aback to notice the new bride obviously pregnant. Other department wives were furious with Kitty; they believed that she had somehow stolen Robert from his "sweetheart." It created quite a stir, Serber said: "Robert was the most eligible bachelor around in the academic world there, and the wives of all his friends were also his friends but they were very possessive about him." He added, "Kitty really was in a difficult position. She had to prove herself and defend herself at all times. It was pretty rough for her for a year or two."[254]

The leftist community—except for those who were close to Jean—was considerably warmer to Robert's new wife. Haakon Chevalier, a regular at Mary Ellen's soirees and someone who had known Jean and Robert as a couple, was among the first to welcome Kitty. The same Chevalier who would one day begin a book about Robert with the explanation: "Our friendship was to be, in a negative sense at least, epoch-making; and in a positive sense—for myself certainly and for Oppenheimer also, perhaps—one of those rare, selfless, profound attachments that leave an indelible mark upon a life."[255]

V

LOS ALAMOS AND WASHINGTON, D.C.

17

Kitty gets a baby boy, a Cadillac, and a house on a hill while Jean earns her M.D. and moves away

As 1940 closed, the familiar old routes were replaced with nothing in the least routine. Lawrence and Oppenheimer and a select group of physicists in universities around the nation began making quick, hushed trips to Boston, Chicago and Washington, D.C. to talk about "the uranium problem." Others quietly appeared at MIT for a secret research project on a system of radio waves called radar. It was only a matter of time before the United States would enter the conflict. America stood by as London was bombed, and hesitated as Churchill begged the U.S. to come to the rescue. Behind the scenes in Washington, the government prepared for what they called the "Emergency."

In the fall, psychologists and anthropologists at the National Research Council formed the Emergency Committee in Psychology to coordinate the personnel they anticipated would be needed. Fairly early in the effort, female psychologists protested that they were not being adequately included in the planning. A special "Subcommittee on the Services of Women Psychologists in the Emergency" was established with Ruth as the chair.[256] She was also working as a Department of Agriculture "social science analyst," planning public opinion surveys. In FDR's Washington, an alphabet-soup of acronyms gave shorthand to agencies that were being set up. In her four years in Washington, Ruth would serve at four of them.

By 1941, a feeling of nervous excitement infused the nation's capital. The devastation in England and Europe and the rising threat of Japan triggered a new patriotism. People flocked to the capital; hotels and boardinghouses were packed;

women clerical workers were living five to a room. Roosevelt's government and particularly the President's wife, Eleanor, recognized that the social sciences could analyze civilian and military morale. Margaret Mead declared that Hitler's manipulation of his people's minds called for all-out psychological warfare. Who better to wage that war than the people who study human behavior? Mead would spend weekdays in the capital, sharing a house with Ruth Benedict and Val. Even Nat turned up, eager to get in on the action.

Somehow, Ruth and Richard found a spacious colonial house in a leafy neighborhood on the northwest edge of the District. On the main floor were two formal parlors, a full dining room and a large kitchen. A back porch looked onto woods. The bedrooms were upstairs and on the ground level, a separate guest apartment that seemed always to be occupied by friends, relatives and occasionally a foreign scientist traveling incognito.

EARLY IN 1941, KITTY WAS rapturous. After six solitary weeks and one glorious day in Nevada, she had returned to her new home in Berkeley with the husband she "simply adored"—a phrase she would repeat in French and German. Robert was the center of her universe.

Kitty swept into this new life vivacious and captivating. Her slim figure bulged in what could have been an embarrassing admission, had she not acknowledged the pregnancy with one of her impish smiles and no trace of regret. She was Mrs. Robert Oppenheimer now. In the spacious home that Robert sublet, the new couple quickly put the kitchen to use. They began to cook together and entertain; Robert was a connoisseur of good food and wine; their dinner parties always started with one of his perfect and powerful martinis. One of Kitty's first invitations was to the Nelsons; they had been kind to her after Joe's death and were, really, the only people she knew in the area. The Nelsons were also committed Communists and the FBI—already watching the radicals in Berkeley—had taken note.

ALTHOUGH THE FERVOR OF KITTY'S early Communist Party days had died with Joe Dallet, she went with Robert to many left-wing fundraising events and meetings. Robert had not, he would insist, joined the Party,[257] but he had given generously to any number of causes it championed, sometimes funneling the money through friends such as Thomas Addis. Robert also bought Kitty a new Cadillac convertible that they named, prophetically, "Bombsight." As winter moved into spring and they prepared to leave for Caltech, Kitty busied herself with family matters. And she began to explore the graduate program in mycology at Berkeley for the time when they would be settled long enough for her to resume her work on a Ph.D. But not everyone took Kitty's academic aspirations seriously. Jackie Oppenheimer, never one to mince words, called her a "schemer." "I remember one time when she got it into her head to do a Ph.D. And the way she cozied up to this poor little dean of the biological sciences was shameful. She never did the Ph.D. It was just another of her whims. She was a phony. All her political convictions were phony, all her ideas were borrowed." [258]

AT BERKELEY, ROBERT DROVE DAILY down tree-lined Arlington Avenue with its large homes, onto the campus and to Le Conte Hall. Inside those walls, he was quickly lost in the "sweetness" of physics, with its "rigor and austerity and depth" that he felt no other science could match. Physics, though, was in creative turmoil. When fission was discovered in 1938–1939, physicists knew a stupendous weapon was theoretically possible. The most respected leaders, including Einstein, were facing the daunting task of convincing the top echelon of the government that a bomb might well be developed. Those who knew Werner Heisenberg—one of the top theoretical physicists in the world—were sure he would lead a formidable German team. The British and Americans thought it possible that Heisenberg already had a secret laboratory up and running. The agonizing question then became: What if Hitler got the bomb first?

ONE BY ONE, ROBERT'S COLLEAGUES began to receive appointments. Ernest Lawrence wanted—and needed—Robert to be in on the planning stages but there was a problem. Robert would need a security clearance to work on such a top-secret project. It was clear to Lawrence, and it aggravated him to no end, that Robert had been foolish enough to involve himself in left-wing politics. That Kitty's mother's cousin was a member of Hitler's inner circle didn't seem to alarm Army security or the FBI nearly as much as her Communist connections. It didn't help that Robert was surrounded by friends of all shades of red, and had three Communists in his own family.

⤳

TOO OFTEN HISTORY ERASES THE trenchant moment; no one knows what Robert said the first time he saw Jean either before or after Reno, if he told her he was to be married, if he confessed that he was about to become a father, if he tried to explain anything. His relationship with Jean always had been private and remained so. (Serber, who was close to Robert, had never seen them together except for once at a distance, walking along an avenue near Robert and Kitty's home.) Some of the conversation between Robert and Jean can be inferred by what was not said. He did not say, "I cannot see you again." He did not say that his marriage would exclude her from his life. He did not say that he no longer loved her.

And much later, when asked if, after he met Kitty, his relationship with Jean had become "fairly casual," he answered no, it would be wrong to say his feelings for her were casual; there was always deep feeling when they saw each other. And they did continue to see each other. Sometimes he would drive to the hospital to see her, or to her home in the city. They had been together at New Year's in 1941. Once they had met at the elegant bar in the Mark Hopkins hotel, the "Top of the Mark," at the very peak of Nob Hill, one of the highest points in the city. It was a poignantly romantic place, often fog-shrouded. During the war, the Top of the Mark would become legendary as a place where young men in uniform took their girlfriends or wives to say goodbye.

IN THE SPRING OF 1941, Kitty and Robert drove the Cadillac south to Pasadena, where they rented a house with a garden and a guest cottage. The Tolmans and Val were in Washington, and with Kitty in her last month of pregnancy and Robert down with a case of mononucleosis, their social life was drastically curtailed. On May 21, their eight-pound son was born—"premature," Kitty would offer with a grin. They named him Peter. Two weeks later, Robert and Kitty invited the Chevaliers to visit and stay in their guest cottage. They came at once; sometime that week the Oppenheimers hosted a party for about twenty-five physicists.

On Sunday, June 22, the Germans invaded the Soviet Union. The Oppenheimers and Chevaliers sat up until early in the morning listening to the radio newscasts, to Churchill's speech excoriating Hitler and offering the Soviet Union British aid. Chevalier remembered that Robert said the invasion was a major blunder on Hitler's part, and would probably cost him the war. "The communist and democratic forces were now allies committed to fighting their common fascist enemy," Chevalier wrote.[259] He did not guess that the security apparatus of the U.S. government was not so sanguine about America's new ally.

Both couples returned to Berkeley later that July. Robert did a quick walk-through of a house for sale only a few blocks away from their sublet, at the top of a knoll at One Eagle Hill. The Spanish style house had a baronial living room with high ceilings, a massive fireplace and windows that offered wide views of San Francisco and the Bay. A tiled dining room opened onto a terrace; there was a modern kitchen and laundry, a servant's room, and gardens dripping with wisteria. Perfect for entertaining, for raising a family and for hanging some of the paintings Robert had inherited (then in storage at a San Francisco museum). He made an instant decision on the house, paid the full asking price ($22,500 plus $3,500 for the adjoining lots). Robert and Kitty said they would move in a month later. They wanted to spend the rest of the summer at Perro Caliente. The only problem was six-week-old Peter.

"Opje and Kitty came to us with a proposal that deeply flattered us," Chevalier would write. "Opje felt that Kitty badly needed a thorough rest. They would like to go and spend several quiet weeks on Opje's ranch in New Mexico. But the ranch was too remote and conditions there too primitive for them to think of taking the baby with them. Besides, Kitty needed to be relieved for a while of the responsibility of taking care of the baby."[260] Opje proposed that they leave Peter with the Chevaliers, along with their newly-hired German nurse. Peter and the nurse were deposited with the Chevaliers, and Kitty and Robert turned Bombsight south towards Perro Caliente.

SINCE THE PREVIOUS SUMMER WHEN Kitty had appeared so dramatically, the social situation had shifted. Kitty now saw herself as part of the academic elite, or at least assumed that she would be when she got her doctorate. The Serbers did not turn up until mid-July that summer and when they did, they found Jackie, who took pride in her working class origins, and Kitty locked in conflicting roles.[261] It was a situation that was to tear at the brothers.

That summer Kitty pitched in to help shingle the roof of the cabin, and entertained the others by standing on her horse while circling one of the meadows. But Serber complained that it was "a bad luck summer." In the corral, Charlotte's horse had kicked Robert on the knee, leaving him with a painful bruise. A few days later Kitty was driving the Cadillac into Santa Fe when she slammed into a car in front of her, hurt her leg and had to go to the hospital. With Kitty and Robert unable to ride, the ranch didn't offer enough excitement. They were suddenly eager to get back to their new house, so they left New Mexico at the beginning of August—not a moment too soon for Jackie. She, Frank, Charlotte and Bob immediately saddled up and headed into the wilderness for a six-day pack trip before closing the cabin for the season.

The Serbers had a month before classes started in Illinois, so they drove back north to help with the move into One Eagle Hill. Kitty and Robert were to leave Peter and his Germany nanny at the Chevaliers for another month. Looking back on this period, Robert would wonder if, so soon after the intensity of their courtship, Kitty had been ready for motherhood. Certainly she did not see herself as the kind of wife and mother who would make family her life's work. What she had at the moment was a baby and no doctorate. It was Robert who showed Peter off when friends came; Kitty spent time hiring household help and continuing her studies.

With her botany classes starting later in August, she had little time to spend cooing over a newborn.

⌐

ONE MONTH AFTER PETER OPPENHEIMER's birth, Jean graduated from Stanford. During the winter of 1940–41, not long after Robert married Kitty, Jean had applied for an internship at St. Elizabeth's Hospital in Washington, D.C. She may have wanted to get away from the Bay Area. For someone who wanted to become a psychiatrist, with a focus on children, St. Elizabeth's was a good choice. It was the nation's oldest public facility for treating the mentally ill.

By June of 1941, the imposing redbrick Gothic Revival structure had more than 1,000 psychiatric patients. By the time Jean arrived, the director Winfred Overholser had begun to introduce innovative treatments—therapy, art, psychodrama, electro-shock therapy and tranquilizing drugs. As an intern, Jean would have started her intensive training working with mentally ill children, many of them poor and black. Six months after she arrived, St. Elizabeth's opened a new Theater for Psychodrama. Dr. Jacob Levi Moreno, who rejected reliance on Freudian methods, began to develop alternate treatments that stressed interpersonal relationships, including group therapy and psychodrama. Jean, with her love of acting and the theater, would have been fascinated with the therapy Moreno described as "'Shakespearean' psychiatry as we are all improvisational actors on the stage of life."[262]

On December 7, 1941, Ruth and Jean were living on opposite sides of the District of Columbia when they heard the Japanese had made a sunrise attack on Hawaii, decimating the American fleet in Pearl Harbor. Across the continent in Berkeley, Kitty and Robert heard the news as they were finishing breakfast that Sunday morning. The night before, they had attended a Spanish Relief party. Robert suddenly decided he'd had enough of the Spanish cause, and turned his attention to the coming crises. On December 8, the United States declared war on Japan, and three days later, on Germany and Italy.

18

Work begins on the bombs,
Richard Tolman vouches for Robert,
and Ruth thinks, "though the woods are
full of wonderful people, maybe there
ought never to have been any
psychologists in D.C."

With America suddenly in the war that Sunday in December, the government began to take the building of an atomic bomb more seriously. In the spring, Britain's uranium research group, the MAUD Committee,[263] reported that the bomb was not only feasible, but would take only a year or two to develop. (Patrick Blackett, Robert's one-time tutor at Oxford, and the recipient of "the poison apple," was a MAUD committee member.) The British, preoccupied by the Germans in North Africa, and without the considerable resources such a project required, turned to the Americans.

Robert suddenly found himself with the odd title of "Coordinator of Rapid Rupture"; his job was to gather a group of the country's top theoretical physicists to confirm that the British were right about the bomb, and if they were, to come up with a design. Robert brought in, among others, Hans Bethe and Edward Teller—Jews who had fled the Nazis. Richard Tolman was there in a dual role, as vice chairman of the National Defense Research Committee and as a physicist. He took part in the discussions about not just how to make an atomic bomb, but how to make one small enough to be dropped from an airplane. The theorists agreed almost immediately: the bomb was possible, and they drafted a potential design.

The Secretary of War Henry Stimson, and Army Chief of Staff General George Marshall approved the project, code named Manhattan Engineering District, usually called the Manhattan Project. What had been the physicists' deepest dream—to unlock the secrets of nature—shifted to making an astounding new weapon that would almost certainly win the war. In September 1942, Army General Leslie Groves became Military Director of the project. Groves knew how to get things done—he had supervised the building of the Pentagon—but he knew little, if anything, about nuclear physics. Richard became Groves' personal scientific advisor and helped him select a director to coordinate the building of the bomb.[264] Robert's name was on a short list of the men deemed capable, but the War Department made it clear that he would not be given security clearance. Too many close Communist connections, and there were rumors that he had even joined the Party himself, though he consistently denied it.

Groves was an arrogant, self-assured West Pointer, brusque of manner, with solidly embedded conservative opinions, and was often dismissive of academics. Robert was his polar opposite. Richard, who commanded respect in both military and academic worlds, assured Groves that Robert had "integrity, discretion, and loyalty to the United States."[265] The General had no patience for those who dabbled in what he considered political nonsense, and he was not impressed with Robert's breadth of esoteric knowledge. But he sensed something in Robert—and to everybody's surprise, Groves named him director of a secret laboratory that did not yet exist. Suddenly, all the university cocktail-party chatter fueled by physicists about weapons of almost unimaginable destructive power ceased. Official secrecy wrapped around the project, until all talk of atomic bombs was stifled.

During the Christmas holidays that year, Oppenheimer took the first of what would become a series of recruiting trips. Serber signed on as Robert's assistant. When Charlotte and Bob arrived in Berkeley some months later, they were amazed by the changes war had brought. The Richmond shipyards were up and running, workers had flocked in, and vacant housing was all but nonexistent. The couple moved into the room over the garage at One Eagle Hill. Blackouts were enforced at night; cars had headlights painted black, with only a slit to let out light. The only problem, Serber pointed out, was that from Eagle Hill, the night sky was lit up by what would be a major target: the Richmond shipyard, which was turning out warships at a record pace.[266]

Robert took a leave of absence; Kitty gave up her graduate classes to sign on for 50 cents an hour at one of the labs at the university, working with the Department of Agriculture. She was also presiding over dinners for the many physicists who kept turning up in Berkeley and a household staff that included a maid and the German nurse for young Peter. Robert and Kitty now had less time together; during the week they would drive to campus, park the Cadillac, give each other a goodbye kiss and go to their separate buildings.[267]

⤳

JEAN HAD RETURNED TO SAN FRANCISCO from the East Coast, to a residency program at Mt. Zion Hospital, where she worked alongside some of the Stanford psychologists that Robert admired. Their circles remained intertwined. He continued to attend the psychoanalytic study group started by Siegfried Bernfeld, along with Edward Tolman, Erik Erikson, Jean Macfarlane and a host of other Bay area luminaries in the field of psychotherapy. Bernfeld remained Jean's mentor at Mt. Zion, and would also become her psychoanalyst.

Kitty could tell herself that she understood how Robert might feel about a former lover. She had loved Joe, would always love Joe. Still, it must have rankled that Jean was well-connected and warmly accepted by academics as well as the left-wing political movement. Even if Jean, like Joe, dismissed the idea of social class and professed herself a Communist, Kitty would have recognized that Jean was part of the American elite. Kitty herself had spent a short stint as a Harvard man's wife; she knew the terrain.

⤳

WHILE WORKING IN THE CHILDREN'S wards at St. Elizabeth's, Jean had become painfully aware of the many ways a child's mind can be ravaged. She wanted to believe that Bernfeld was right when he said there was a correlation between psychoanalysis and scientific principles, but the field of child psychology was still in its infancy, and could not yet offer effective treatments. The same was true of her own malady; there was no course of action that could ease the despair she felt when in the throes of one of her deep depressions. They could start with a period of elation, of excessive energy and racing thoughts, followed by feelings of utter desolation. Yet even as she struggled with depression, she was to present herself as the intelligent and engagingly competent young doctor she was.[268] Most of her colleagues were not aware of her affliction.

In the months after Jean's return from Washington, she would have guessed that Robert's frequent trips out of town had to do with his new role in the war effort. Jean was not the kind of woman who left things unsaid. They had been lovers and confidants. They knew each other too well not to explore what might be, and that would include how much they wanted or needed to be in each other's lives.

That he made the effort to see her, not often but consistently, indicated he was conflicted. For Jean, the questions became: How strongly did she feel about him? And did it matter that he had a wife and child?

About the imminent future, Robert would have given Jean some oblique hints. He had taken a leave of absence from the university and would be leaving Berkeley, but he couldn't say where he was going, or how long he would be gone. It was the same story thousands of young men were telling the people they loved as the country girded for war.

Jean asked to see him before he left, and he said yes, he would see her to say goodbye.

❧

KITTY BEGAN TO MAKE REGULAR trips to the San Francisco airport to drop off or pick up Robert. He was using all of his charm and powers of persuasion to put together a team that would be "willing to disappear into the New Mexico desert for an indeterminate period."[269] One by one they signed on; many were still graduate students, their doctorates would have to wait until after the war. Robert could not tell his new recruits exactly where they would be going, only that it would be for the duration. They could bring their families, but once they were on site they were not to leave, and those who left families behind could not divulge their location. The scientists were not to speak of their work to anyone, not even to the wives who might come with them to the secret mountain.[270]

❧

RUTH TOLMAN'S U.S. GOVERNMENT PERSONNEL file noted that the color of her eyes was brown; her hair, gray; her complexion "dark." She was 5 foot 5 inches tall and weighed 125 pounds. She had a slim, youthful figure, even if her hair was beginning to turn gray. According to one of Edward Tolman's graduate students, one of Ruth's many young admirers, "She's 50 years old but she is as charming as a woman of 30."[271]

In 1942 Ruth was transferred out of Agriculture, where she had been following trends in public opinion and attitudes, to the domestic branch of the Office of War Information, where she became a "Public Opinion Analyst," responsible for studying popular attitudes on war-related subjects. Ruth Benedict also came to the Office of War Information and analyzed overseas cultures, particularly the Japanese. (The Japanese studies were the basis for her book, *The Chrysanthemum and the Sword,* which would become a bestseller.) She and Val stayed in the house that

Margaret Mead had rented, but the two spent many weekends at the Tolmans', especially when Richard was away.[272]

Nat Raymond found what seemed, for her, an improbable niche. As she wrote to Ruth Benedict: "I simply must tell you about induction into the Quartermaster Corps . . . I survived the four-page forms, to be filled out in duplicate; and the residence form for the FBI, and the application form for the Army; and the form saying that I could get to Jersey City without either gas or tires; and the form asking for fingerprints (and getting them); and the form asking for identification disk (and getting it). I survived sitting and waiting, and two colonels, and the accounting department, and a physical examination with emphasis on flat feet. But when it came to going down last night to the Barge Office, and getting a Coast Guard identification card I gave up. When the yeoman asked, in line of duty, 'What do you want this for?' I said, 'I don't want it.' But they gave it to me anyhow, after another five forms, and another set of fingerprints for the FBI. And now I am on the government payroll for three weeks."[273]

WHEN A COLLEAGUE IN THE Psychology Department at UCLA wrote to Ruth with questions, she answered: "I don't wonder that you feel mystified by the problem of 'what Washington wants' and confused as to what happens to all the psychologists swallowed up here. To give you a little notion . . . the Bureau of Intelligence, in which Jack Hilgard, Ruth Tolman, Dan Katz and others [labored], has been liquidated . . . This is the second time in four months that some of us have been in one of these collapses." She added, "It's kinda frustrating—maybe there ought never to have been any psychologists in D.C."[274]

Ruth ended the letter on a strangely pensive note: "It is actually a curious life. The woods are full of wonderful people, and everyone is so driven that we never get a chance to see them . . . It is as if you are running in a dream and your legs won't move . . . With the physicists now things are better. They went through a hellish hard time at the start, trying to convince the army and the navy that the scientific developments they knew should be done were any good. Now they've won their game and are going full tilt." Richard was now at General Groves's side, solidly placed among the politicians, the military and the scientists, interpreting and advising, with a heavy load resting on his aging shoulders.

⸻

GENERAL GROVES WAS EVERYWHERE AT once, barking out orders, brooking no dissent, tightening his grip on the Manhattan Project. He had *carte blanche* to give the scientists everything they needed to complete the mission; Los Alamos alone was to cost more than 74 million in 1940 dollars.[275] (The entire project, including new facilities at Hanford in Washington State, Oak Ridge in Tennessee, and Argonne in Illinois, was to cost about two billion 1944 dollars). It was Robert who had mentioned to Groves that New Mexico had enough empty space to build and test a bomb, and Robert who knew about the Los Alamos Ranch School on a mesa at 7,500 feet, a boarding school established in 1917 to give boys "a life of rigorous outdoor living and classical education." It was only a few miles from where Robert himself had been introduced to his life of rigorous outdoor living. The mesa was undisturbed except for a row of houses built of logs and stone for the faculty, a larger structure for classes and dining, a dormitory with outdoor porches where the boys slept year round, and a barn with a supply of riding horses.

Groves took one look and requisitioned it. The boys were sent home, and a parade of bulldozers and a thundering herd of heavy Army trucks crawled up the narrow winding dirt road with its hairpin curves, steep cutbacks and sheer drop-offs. They churned up the pristine mesa, slashing the woodland wilderness into a mud-covered warren of brown wood apartments, barracks, Quonset huts and laboratories. All of it was then surrounded by a high fence topped with barbed wire and sealed with gates manned by sentries. Anything Groves needed, he got.

The top-secret city would be peopled by a collection of the most brilliant physicists in the United States, Canada and Great Britain, and the cream of the graduate student crop. Those who did not know this part of America were astonished by the beauty of the high desert mountains, the utter wildness of the place where they were to spend the war years. The average age of the scientists was twenty-five. Oppenheimer himself had not yet reached his thirty-ninth birthday when he drove the Cadillac up what came to be called "The Hill."

In Berkeley, Robert said his goodbyes. Oddly, he made a point to call Steve Nelson, Kitty's friend and a Communist Party organizer, to meet him for lunch. "We met at a restaurant on the main strip in Berkeley," Nelson would remember, "and he appeared excited to the point of nervousness. He wouldn't discuss where he was going, but would only say that it had to do with the war effort. We chatted, mostly about Spain and the war, and exchanged good-byes."[276] Neither was being watched by the FBI or Military Intelligence at the time, but this would soon change.

In the winter of 1942–1943, the Chevaliers came to dinner at Eagle Hill. Robert went to the kitchen to make his famous martinis, and Chevalier followed. In the course of the conversation, Chevalier said that he had been approached by a chemist at Shell Oil whom they both knew. This man said he had contacts at the Soviet Consulate who wanted to know if Robert would be willing to share the research he was doing. Chevalier said his answer had been a quick and emphatic "no," but he had felt that Robert should be informed of the inquiry. Chevalier did not remember exactly what else was said during the conversation but he did remember that Robert was "visibly disturbed." Chevalier, for his part, said he dismissed the incident from his mind. They rejoined their wives and had another pleasant evening. Robert remembered that when Chevalier told him that the contact had a way to transmit information to Soviet scientists, "I thought I said 'But that is treason,' but I am not sure. I said anyway something." Kitty was to claim that she was the one who'd said, "But that would be treason."[277]

In March, the Oppenheimers turned Bombsight toward New Mexico and Los Alamos. Despite his promise, Robert left without seeing Jean.

Kitty and Robert go to Los Alamos and
Robert says goodbye to Jean

In the spring of 1943, General Groves decided that the only way to protect secrecy was to keep each group of scientists working separately on their individual projects, with no exchange of information, no talk about work at all. It fell to Richard to convince the General that scientists could not work that way, there would be no bomb without collaboration. Richard was also the liaison between the U.S. and British governments. Some of the top British physicists came to Los Alamos. Sir James Chadwick came. So did Italy's Enrico Fermi; both were Nobel Laureates. One physicist, the most revered of all, was still at risk. The British were standing by, ready to spirit Niels Bohr to England as soon as he would agree to leave Denmark. Richard Tolman would then arrange Bohr's passage to America.

When Richard and Ruth managed to find a few days together, they would head for Massachusetts. An inveterate sailor, Richard felt at home on Cape Cod and especially in the village of Woods Hole. In the fall of 1943, he took Major Robert Furman out on a little skiff into Buzzard's Bay. Furman was the head of intelligence for the Manhattan Project. He was planning a foray into Italy and Germany, named the Alsos Mission. In the middle of the bay, Richard drilled Furman on fissionable material and bomb assembly, prepped him on the questions he would need to ask for the American scientists to discern how close the Germans were to developing their own atomic bomb.

THE OWI, WHERE RUTH WORKED, was to keep the home front informed about the progress of the war and more important, to bolster morale, considered crucial to the war effort. It was also to convince women to enter the workforce.

OWI published stacks of posters with slogans like, "We're All in This Together," or, "Are You a Girl with a Star-Spangled Heart? Join the WACs Now." That spring, Ruth was one of eighteen women chosen to be part of a country-wide effort to select female officers for the Women's Army Corps. Ruth was in the Third Corps Area; out west in the Ninth Corps her old friend Jean Macfarlane, now Professor of Clinical Psychology at Berkeley and one of the tightly entwined psychology clan, was also interviewing candidates.[278]

⤳

THE OPPENHEIMERS WERE AMONG THE first to wind their way over the old road that rumbled through the Indian pueblo of San Ildefonso, across the Rio Grande, then up through a series of dizzily treacherous switchbacks before emerging at the top. There they were rewarded with glorious views of the mountains Robert loved, a gift that would sustain that wartime generation through the hard months ahead.

Robert and Kitty had first pick of the single row of substantial houses inherited from the Ranch School. Made of rock and logs, the house had a high vaulted ceiling with exposed beams, and a large window that provided northern light for the expansive living room. It would serve well for the entertaining Kitty was expected to do, except Kitty did not see herself as the social arbiter of an Army outpost. Martha Parsons, the wife of the ranking Navy captain in charge of ordnance, stepped up and filled that role. Kitty did throw the first big party on the Mesa on May 22, to celebrate Robert's thirty-ninth birthday. For the fete, Robert had his thatch of black hair cropped close to his head, which emphasized his handsome face and penetrating eyes. The cut also gave him the aesthetic appearance of a monk; he looked older and wiser.

The Corps of Engineers stretched a fence around the whole mesa top, with gates that required official passes and implacable Army MPs who insisted on compliance. Another, even more sequestered enclosure, was built inside the fence, accessible only to the theoretical and experimental physicists, chemists, metallurgists, ordnance experts and engineers—those whose job it was to create the bomb. Called the Technical Area, it was the secret heart of Los Alamos, a secret within a secret. It housed the laboratories where scientists would spend their days and many of their nights, working on what was no longer to be referred to as a "bomb"—someone might slip and mention the word where enemy ears could hear—but instead "the Gadget." Nothing said inside the Tech Area was to be repeated outside. The obsession with secrecy was to settle over the camp, spreading even to those young wives who knew nothing at all.

Kitty and Charlotte understood the magnitude of Los Alamos: Charlotte be-cause Robert had appointed her as librarian, with access to The Tech and all of its top-secret files; Kitty because she did not intend to be shut out of any aspect of her husband's life. In fact, quite a few of the husbands confided in their wives. "Los Alamos was not a casteless society," one of the scientists' wives explained, "Lines were drawn principally not on wealth, family, or even age, but on the position one's husband held in the laboratory."[279] This made Kitty first among the wives. And while she liked the idea, her reality was less glamorous. All the wives were ex-pected to stay within the compound except for a monthly trip to Santa Fe, where they were not to talk to anyone who wasn't from the mesa. Kitty was virtually trapped. Unlike most of the others, Kitty did not thrive in the company of women, and she was only minimally interested in the basic organization required of the wives and mothers to create a sense of community. For Kitty, Los Alamos was not so different from Youngstown in her Communist days. Except that at Los Alamos, she was responsible for a rambunctious two-year-old, and the men still did all the important work.

Indian women from nearby pueblos were allowed to work in the scientists' homes, freeing some of the wives to take jobs. Kitty worked for a while in Dr. Hempelmann's laboratory doing blood tests as part of a study of the dangers of radiation. (The doctor judged her competent but "bossy.") She also found time to plant a flower garden, and to make regular forays down the hill to pick up fresh vegetables and chickens from a local farm, to be distributed to other families. Kit-ty began to entertain a parade of important men who turned up regularly, often from Washington, D.C. Richard came, along with General Groves. The General was abrupt and demanding and dismissive, not a favorite of those who came into con-tact with him. But Groves was important to her husband, so Kitty gave him her full attention, and the General seemed to respond.

TO THE AMAZEMENT OF MANY who knew him well, Robert was able to trans-form himself into an excellent manager, both inside the Tech Area and out in the community. On any given day, he would appear in the Tech Area where he made a point of understanding what each scientist was working on, or he might be han-dling the complaints of the women who railed against the monster stoves that dominated their kitchens—the "Black Beauties" that consumed coal and wood. Robert became the thread that kept them all connected.

"The Tech Area was a great pit which swallowed our scientist husbands and kept them out of sight, almost out of our lives," one of the wives wrote. "They worked as they had never worked before. They worked at night and often came home at three or four in the morning. Sometimes, they set up army cots in the laboratories and did not come home at all. Other times, they did not sleep at all. Few women understood what the men were seeking here or comprehended the magnitude of the search. The loneliness and heartache of some scientists' wives during the years before the atomic bomb was born were very real."[280]

Lonely for some. But for others, Los Alamos offered excitement and adventure. The young group on the mesa worked hard all week, but with their director's encouragement, they managed to play hard on the weekends. They drank too much, danced until dawn, went to each other's homes and shared whatever food they mustered from the Army PX. Horseback riding was a favorite way to explore the mountains; Kitty set the pace in an active riding group. As spring moved into summer, groups began to ask permission to go on hiking expeditions and explore some of the ancient Indian ruins in the region. Robert coaxed the security detail into allowing the outings. The General was determined to "satisfy these temperamental people" so they could keep their minds on the work at hand.

To keep track of anyone who breached security, a covey of undercover Army counterintelligence agents was in place at Los Alamos. Offices were wired; individuals checked in and out through gates. Army security officers regularly questioned Robert about possible security lapses by different scientists, until he wondered if counterintelligence was trying to get rid of them all. Head of security was Captain Peer de Silva, a singularly humorless man, who seemed determined to expel not only Director Oppenheimer but anyone with any connection to Communism—including both Serbers. The enemy, it often seemed, was neither Japan nor Germany, but the USSR. For a time, MPs were stationed around the Oppenheimer house and even Kitty had to show her pass before she could enter. It was only when she started using the sentries as babysitters for Peter that they were withdrawn. Outgoing mail was routinely censored. At one point an envelope from her parents was sealed clumsily, with bits of wool caught in the glue, and Kitty complained loud and long. She believed it had been opened. Los Alamos security could not give her an answer, so they sent an agent to the Puening home in Pennsylvania, and discovered that Kitty's father had sat on the envelope—wearing his wool pants—to make certain it sealed properly.

Kitty could be forgiven for overreacting; the Oppenheimers had been plagued by intense security for months, and it was wearing on them. Kitty endured several long interviews with Lt. Col. John Lansdale, the lawyer who served as General Groves' head of security for the Manhattan Project. She impressed him with "how hard she was trying. Intensely, emotionally, with everything she had." She had been frank and open about her membership in the Communist Party, about Joe, about her later disillusionment with Communism. Although Lansdale had earlier described Kitty as "a curious personality, at once frail and very strong," he would report that: "Mrs. Oppenheimer impressed me as a strong woman with strong convictions . . . She didn't care how much I knew of what she'd done before she met Oppenheimer or how it looked to me. Gradually I began to see that nothing in her past and nothing in her other husband meant anything to her compared with him. I became convinced that in him she had an attachment stronger than communism, that his future meant more to her than communism. She was trying to sell me on the idea he was her life, and she did sell me." He told General Groves that Kitty's "strength of will was a powerful influence in keeping Dr. Oppenheimer away from what we would regard as dangerous associations." Kitty as well as Robert regarded the project as "his outstanding career opportunity."[281]

The FBI and Military Intelligence had tracked the Oppenheimers in Berkeley, had tapped their home phone, read their mail. Robert complained so bitterly that some of his friends thought he was becoming paranoid. He felt he could scarcely speak to his own brother without being questioned. Once at Los Alamos, the Army Intelligence called off the FBI, saying they had taken over full-time physical and technical surveillance of Oppenheimer. J. Edgar Hoover was not so easily dismissed; he directed his agents in San Francisco to keep watch on any of Robert's Communist friends.

Jean Tatlock was on the list.

⌒

BY JUNE, PRESSURE WAS BUILDING on Robert. His main responsibility, enormous in itself, was to follow the work of all of the scientists in order to grasp the whole. It was a performance that required an extraordinary mind and memory, combined with the temperament that he had developed; the scientists gave him full credit for acting as a translator for the body of work. When the community came together and made this raw young society work, Robert was given full credit for that, too.

During the first summer at Los Alamos, Robert finally admitted his exhaustion to Bob Bacher, a physicist from Cornell who headed the experimental physics division at Los Alamos, and someone whom Robert admired and trusted. He told Bacher he felt inadequate to the task; said he was on the verge of giving up. Bacher listened and then pointed out that quitting wasn't an option because there was no one else who could do what was, at best, an impossible task.[282] Bacher was sincere; like the other scientists, he was amazed at Robert's capacity for grasping the Gadget, and each man's role in building it. Robert was key to the project's ultimate success.

⤻

June 14, 1943

At the beginning of the summer of 1943, Robert had to be in Berkeley to confer with Ernest Lawrence at the Berkeley Radiation Laboratory. It was Robert's first trip back and he had unfinished business. He had not seen Jean before he left, and she had sent messages saying she needed to see him. No matter how many Army intelligence agents were tracking Robert, how miserable they would make his life, he was going to keep his promise this time.

The light was fading by the time he finally left Le Conte Hall. He walked across campus at his usual fast clip, heading for the streetcar that would take him into San Francisco. He would have allowed his mind to skim over the consequences. It would be more of an exercise to keep his mind occupied, to block the uncertainty of how he would find her. Jean present or Jean absent. Radiant or remorseful. Perfect, or flawed.

The simple act of seeing her meant there would be hell to pay, he knew. Seldom without a cigarette, Robert would have stopped to light one, maybe taking the opportunity to take a quick look around for the security agent he knew would be there. His signature porkpie hat made an easy target to tail. From the moment he met her, the security agents would inform Lt. Colonel Boris Pash, chief of Counter-Intelligence for the 9th Army Corps headquartered in San Francisco, and Pash would be delighted to inform General Groves and the General would be livid.

The idea would have been so disturbing that Robert would have shoved it into a compartment in his mind and slammed it shut. Neither would he have allowed himself to consider Kitty and Peter, left in Los Alamos. She did not like it when he left; she could not know, or control, whom he would see in Berkeley, what he would do there.

He took a last deep drag of the cigarette, flicked it away, then swung onto the Key System train that carried him over the Oakland Bay Bridge and into the city. He had celebrated his thirty-ninth birthday only a month before. Jean was twenty-nine; they had known each other, loved each other, for seven years now. Even when she wouldn't—couldn't—marry him, he continued to love her.

Perhaps he had not seen her before he left for Los Alamos because he wasn't allowed to tell her why he was leaving or where he was going, or especially what he was doing. Jean, who believed above all else in the sanctity of life.

It was dark by the time the train rattled over the lower level of the Bay Bridge. The FBI would have a file on Jean, on their relationship. What could they possibly know about that relationship, what could anyone know?

On that June evening in 1943, he knew that an agent would be lurking somewhere near her at the terminal in San Francisco where she would be waiting for him.

OPPENHEIMER, ARRIVING AT 9:45 PM, the FBI report reads, *rushed to meet a young lady whom he kissed, and they walked away arm in arm.... They entered a 1935 green Plymouth coupe ... and the young lady drove.* [283]

SHE WAS SMILING, NOT HURTING—Robert could see that—but glowing, happy. The Jean that kept him coming back. He smiled as she fit into his arms and kissed him. He would have studied her with that intensity that so unsettled others, the blue eyes riveted, as if he could study the very synapses of her brain. She slipped her arm into his and led him to the roadster.

She drove east along the Embarcadero—scene of much of the labor unrest she had reported with such righteous indignation in the *Western Worker*—then turned north and west on Broadway. She had decided where they would eat; not one of the posh restaurants he would have chosen, but a shabby place not far from her apartment on Telegraph Hill, good for the hot spicy food he favored and some proletarian privacy.

AN AGENT WAITED OUTSIDE, WHERE he could watch the door. He would report: *Drove to Xochiniloc Cafe, 787 Broadway at 10 pm. Cheap type bar, cafe, and dance hall operated by Mexicans. Had few drinks, something to eat.* [284]

Robert would later say that they did not talk about Communism. It was always an on-again, off-again thing with her, he would explain. Nor did they talk about where he was and what he was doing. "Military secret," he might have intimated. By now, though, Jean would have known something about his war work—they had several good mutual friends who had some knowledge: Bernard and Hannah Peters, whom Robert had tried to recruit for Los Alamos; or even Mary Ellen Washburn, who was close to the Serbers and knew how to contact them. He might have mentioned Peter, but probably not Kitty.

Perhaps Jean told him that her brother was an Army doctor at Fort Bragg, North Carolina, studying infectious diseases. Or they talked about Churchill, who was in Washington at the moment with Roosevelt. The newspapers were full of the war. Maybe they spoke of the Europe both remembered from what now seemed long ago. The Allies were making progress in Tunisia, the tide seemed to be turning. Yet there was no doubt that this war was a fight for survival.

What Jean wanted—needed—to tell him was that she loved him. He needed to know that it didn't matter if he had married, had started his family, had moved ever more deeply into the world of science that was his one pure love. What mattered to her was that he knew she had never stopped loving him.

Perhaps she told him at the Xochinoloc Café. Or maybe it was later, when they went to her apartment on Telegraph Hill, where a car with two agents sat watching. The report reads that the couple went to 1405 Montgomery, where Jean lived on the top floor: *At 11:30 pm the lights in the above mentioned apartment were extinguished. . . . The relationship of Oppenheimer and Jean Tatlock appeared to be very affectionate and intimate.*[285]

PERHAPS SHE WAITED TO TELL him when finally they turned out the lights. They may have made love or simply held each other for the night. They had to have known it might be their last time together for a long while. The next morning they left in her roadster; she kissed him goodbye at the East Bay Terminal and he caught a streetcar back to the Berkeley campus and his meetings. They made plans to meet later that day at the airline office in downtown San Francisco, and she drove on to the hospital.

That afternoon, the FBI picked up the surveillance: *Tatlock arrived on foot and Oppenheimer rushed to meet her. They appeared very affectionate and walked to her car nearby . . . they then went to Kit Carson's Grill.* After dinner, she drove him down the Peninsula to the San Francisco Airport.[286] Perhaps he kissed her goodbye before they left the car, mindful that he was meeting a colleague. She watched him walk onto the tarmac and board the plane, first to Los Angeles, then on to Los Alamos and his other life.

WITHIN TWO WEEKS, LT. COLONEL Boris Pash would send a memo to the Pentagon recommending that Dr. Oppenheimer be denied a security clearance and be fired as Scientific Director of the Los Alamos Laboratory, citing among other things his overnight tryst with Jean Tatlock, identified as his mistress and a known Communist. The General was livid, but he did not fire Robert. By now, Groves felt that the success of his mission depended on this man. But there was a limit to his patience, and to how long he could hold off the hounds of the Counter-Intelligence Corps. Military Intelligence immediately requested that the FBI conduct an investigation of Jean and recommended *installation of a technical surveillance on the residence of Jean Tatlock for the purpose of determining the identities of espionage agents within the Comintern Apparatus for the* *further purpose of protecting secret information regarding this nation's war effort.* Her phone was tapped, "informers" questioned.[287]

When Robert returned to Berkeley the following month, he did not see her.

Ella Friedman Oppenheimer with Robert, who was born in 1904.

Robert in an ID photo taken on February 13, 1942, at the beginning of the atomic age.

Kitty Puening's 1936 passport photo; she was 26.

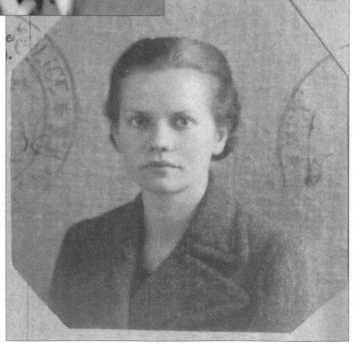

Teenager Jean Tatlock in Cambridge, Massachusetts.

Ruth Sherman Tolman, Berkeley, c. 1931.

*Kaethe Puening
with baby Kitty,
born in Germany
in August 1910.*

*Kitty in a German
garden with Kaethe
before the family
emigrated to
America in 1913.*

*Robert with doting
father Julius.*

*Jean spent her first ten years in
California, where her father was a
professor at Stanford.*

In time Jean would dispense with the long curls,
but the direct gaze would remain.

Jean, 10, with brother Hugh, 12, about the time the family moved east to Cambridge, where their father would teach at Harvard for four years.

Robert at home in New York City; already interested in everything.

After World War I, Kitty and her mother resumed frequent visits to Germany; here with her grandparents.

Kitty's relationship with her mother became strained; her father, like most men, was charmed by his daughter.

Germany, 1927. The seventeen-year-old Kitty (standing) and her mother, on right, with members of the Vissering family. Family visits were interrupted by two world wars.

Kitty met Harvard-educated classical musician Frank Ramseyer in Paris in the summer of 1932, when she was 22. They married the following Christmas; within a year Kitty had the marriage annulled.

Joe Dallet in Spain; Kitty referred to him as her first husband. A doctrinaire Communist, he would die fighting in the Spanish Civil War.

*Kitty
was an
accomplished
equestrian.*

Jean, during the stormy adolescent period when she was writing May Sarton, her best friend in high school.

Jean and Hugh were close in childhood, but saw little of each other after college. Both became medical doctors.

Richard Tolman was twelve years Ruth's senior.

The Tolmans' Spanish-style home in Pasadena, next to the Caltech campus, was a lively center for their eclectic circle of friends.

*Jean while in
medical school in
San Francisco . . .*

... *when she was*
active in the
Communist Party
and was seeing
Robert Oppenheimer.

Haakon Chevalier, professor of French Literature at U.C. Berkeley, a Communist, and Robert's close friend until the 1950s. Chevalier played a key role in the Hearing that caused Robert to be expelled from service to his government.

Professor John S. P. Tatlock, eminent medievalist at Stanford, Harvard and Berkeley, and Jean's father.

John and Marjorie Tatlock with daughter Jean at her Vassar graduation.

Robert rubbing liniment into the leg of his horse, named Crisis.

The newly married Tolmans in a Caltech classroom where Richard taught physics.

The Tolmans at home in Pasadena, adjacent to the Caltech campus.

Richard Tolman, like Robert, was a polymath, and one of the most respected physicists in the country, serving as a top science advisor in both world wars. Friends found the Tolmans to be perfectly suited to each other.

Ruth Sherman, at 29 and listed as a "secretary," was the witness on this passport issued in 1922 to Eliza Ruth Valentine – her best friend, Val.

Fatherhood as practiced by Robert with baby Peter.

Friends said Robert took delight in his new role.

Kitty's third husband, Stewart Harrison, on left in white suit, at Caltech's high volts lab where he did medical research.

Robert kept this photo of Kitty and Peter on his dresser.

Jean in her 20s, when she and Robert were together.

A "master's cottage" when Los Alamos was a boy's school, this house was occupied by the Oppenheimers during the war years.

The living room, with windows that offered fine northern light.

The same room, its stone walls white-washed, ready for wartime parties.

At Berkeley, Kitty worked in the
university's mycology lab;
at Los Alamos, for a time she
would work in a doctor's office.

Robert at one of
the many parties
held in their
Los Alamos home.

Kitty tucked into a chair in their
home on "Bathtub Row."

Jean, in her medical
whites, as she appeared
when Robert last saw her.

Kitty (above) on one of many nights spent with shades drawn, in dressing gown, with cigarettes, a drink and two books close by. Robert (below) is happily surrounded by a group of scientists including his one-time friend Linus Pauling, all of them enjoying the thrill of science.

After the war, the British honored Richard Tolman with the Order of the British Empire; he died two years later, at 67.

Ruth in her later years; she would die in 1957 at 64.

Kitty's parents on a rare visit to Olden Manor; Kitty and her mother would become completely estranged.

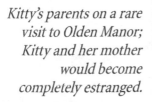

Invited to Japan in 1960, Robert was received with excessive civility. The Oppenheimers with Kiyokata Kusaka and his wife.

With the excesses of the McCarthy era over and John Kennedy in the White House, an effort was made to bring Robert back into service to the government; here with Pearl Buck at a dinner for Nobel Laureates.

The Oppenheimer family at the White House where, on December 2, 1963, only ten days after President Kennedy's assassination, President Johnson presented Robert with the Fermi Award.

St. John in the Virgin Islands would become the Oppenheimer family's sanctuary, where they would spend Christmas and part of each summer in their beach house.

Toni Oppenheimer took refuge on St. John after the death of her mother.

Kitty Oppenheimer found freedom and joy in sailing.

RUTH LEARNS HOW ONE OLD SHOVEL CAN HELP
MAKE FOUR HAND GRENADES, RICHARD IS SENT
ON A SECRET MISSION TO ENGLAND, JEAN SENDS
"ALL LOVE AND COURAGE" AND ROBERT TAKES A
LONELY WALK IN THE WINTER WOOD AND MEETS
THE PALE ANGEL OF MISERY

———————

On the Home Front, rationing tightened supplies of almost everything: gas, tires, sugar, meat, nylons—the list was long and affected everyone. The War Production Board's mission was to speed up manufacturing, as well as to set priorities and designate allotments of materials. The Board was expected to rally civilians. One statement exhorted: "We are faced with a serious shortage of metal scrap, rubber and other vital materials." The search was on for "the ordinary junk that today is lying around in barn yards and in the gullies of farms, in the basements, attics and garages in homes and stores throughout the country." Children helped by saving tin cans and newspapers, and taking them to a pickup point at their schools. The message was that everyone needed to help: "Even one old shovel will help make four hand grenades."[288]

After two years of pitching in, civilians began to grow weary and even protest about shortages, putting morale at risk, so the War Production Board set up a Civilian Surveys Division to look into shortages. George Gallup was brought in, as were four psychologists, one of them Dr. Ruth Tolman. At the WPB, Ruth met Jerome Bruner, a recent Harvard Ph.D. in psychology. After being assigned to the Psychological Warfare Division of Supreme Headquarters in London, Bruner came to know Richard well, and was one of their friends who had a key to their Washington house, where he stayed when he was in town. Another frequent guest in the war years, according to Bruner, was Robert Oppenheimer—"brilliant, discursive, lavishly intolerant, ready to pursue any topic anywhere, extraordinarily lovable. I had no idea what he was doing, only that it was war work and in the Southwest. We talked about most anything, but psychology and the philosophy of physics were irresistible."[289]

⤳

AT LOS ALAMOS, AN ARMY base replete with military supplies, the scientists' wives weren't affected by rationing as much as the rest of the country was. But that didn't keep them from complaining about a lack of fresh fruits and vegetables. Luckily, while there were no shops on the Hill, there was also little need for formal dress. Jeans and slacks were standard apparel; Kitty favored blue jeans and a Brooks Brothers shirt, or sometimes a short, pleated skirt and sweater, with bobby sox and saddle oxfords. In the winter, ski pants and parkas became everyday wear. Men switched from the coats and ties that had been their university uniforms to jeans or khakis and flannel shirts. For many of the young couples, the years at Los Alamos were one of life's grand adventures.

KITTY'S DISCONTENT, HOWEVER, WAS GROWING, fueled by her loneliness and the demands made on her. Like most of the scientists, Robert vanished into the Tech Area where she was not allowed to follow. Other people at Los Alamos had more access to her husband than she did, and he seemed always to make time for them. When he traveled to Berkeley or Washington, she stayed behind. Once again, Kitty found herself in a place where living conditions were rough, where she felt she was expected to do menial work, living with a man who was the center of her universe, only to find that she was not the center of his. She became jealous of any woman she imagined had designs on her husband. Robert's first secretary, Priscilla Duffield—who had felt Kitty's sting—described her boss's wife: "She was a very intense, very intelligent, very vital kind of person, and no question at all that she was difficult to handle. She didn't get along very well with women." Duffield added, "I'm sure she had romantic ideas about herself that she didn't carry through and I think this went on for years and her frustration got worse and worse."[290] At Los Alamos, working on a doctorate in botany was impossible. Even the flower garden she had coaxed out of the high desert soil had to be sacrificed when there was a shortage of water.

Kitty had a small coterie of women who rode the trails with her, and some-times drank with her, but she had no close friends.[291] She was becoming increas-ingly isolated, both emotionally and physically. The government-issue fence that wrapped around the community began to wear on Kitty; and so, it seems, did the little boy who needed her attention.

⌖

ALL THROUGH THE SUMMER AND fall of 1943, Richard was in and out of Los Alamos, bringing Ruth news of the Oppenheimers. He often returned to Washing-ton with gifts of silver and turquoise jewelry for her—purchased from Indians on the plaza at Santa Fe. In the first week of November 1943, Richard left for London. His mission, top secret, was to bring back Niels Bohr, the Dane who was at the very heart of the nuclear revolution.

Germany had occupied Denmark since April of 1940, but it wasn't until October 1, 1943 that Hitler ordered Denmark's Jews be deported to concentra-tion camps. The Gestapo had specifically ordered the arrest of the great champion of quantum theory. At last, Bohr was convinced to leave; that night the Danish Underground smuggled him and his wife across the choppy seas of the Oresund Strait to Sweden. Their sons were among the 8,000 Jews that made the crossing into Sweden in the next few days.

The British sent a modified Mosquito bomber to Sweden, its bomb bay fitted for one passenger. Bohr climbed into an insulated flying suit with a helmet but he didn't listen to the instructions on how to operate his oxygen mask. When the plane reached 20,000 feet and Bohr did not respond, the pilot dove to a danger-ously low elevation, figuring his passenger had passed out. Once on the ground in England, Bohr roused, telling his welcoming party that he'd had a nice nap.[292]

Bohr and his physicist son Aage sailed on the SS *Acquitania* across the Atlantic to New York. General Groves sent one of his aides to met Bohr, with instructions to handle the situation "with extremely soft kid gloves." Richard had called him "an extremely superior person."[293] Two days later, Bohr was on a train to Washington.

ONE WINTER THURSDAY IN 1944, psychologist Jerome Bruner arrived at the Tolmans as usual, and noticed two cars parked outside the house—both of them occupied by quiet, stoic men. "I thought it rather odd," he noted. He let himself in, and found himself "face to face with a kindly and rumpled man who introduced himself as Mr. Baker. Ruth and Richard, he told me, had gone to a

Ration Board Appeals sitting." Mr. Baker had been told to expect Bruner, and the two settled down for a drink. They were happily discussing "the complementarity of the human mind" when Ruth and Richard appeared. As soon as he could, Bruner took Richard aside and, considering the Army security parked outside, queried if, perhaps, the Mr. Baker he was chatting with was actually Mr. Bohr. Richard conceded. [294]

Niels Bohr had a habit of thinking out loud, murmuring in long run-on sentences, talking through any problem. In Denmark, he had been convinced that building an atomic weapon was impossible. Now, hearing what the British and Americans had already done, he saw that the bomb was feasible. His thoughts quickly turned to what he now saw as the overwhelming problem: What could be done to control such an apocalyptic weapon? The problem, he repeated, was "what is going to happen *afterwards.*"[295]

In Washington, Bohr bustled about seeing influential people, explaining that he felt the only way to avoid a postwar arms race was to share the information with the Russians from the start. General Groves was apoplectic, and became even more intent on getting this "extremely superior person" safely behind the fences at Los Alamos, and keeping him there as long as possible.

‿

IN OCTOBER, THE ASPENS IN the Jemez Range flamed yellow; by November a chill was in the mountain air and for that first Christmas on the mesa, snow fell softly, camouflaging the rough gashes inflicted by the Army Corps. By mid December, a steady stream of British scientists, two and three at a time—some twenty in all—began arriving on the mesa. Sir James Chadwick arrived with a few of his countrymen and an assemblage of German, Austrian, Swiss and Polish scientists.

The snow brought with it some holiday spirit and everyone rallied; soldiers were ordered to cut Christmas trees of all sizes, including a huge blue spruce for the great room of Fuller Lodge. Decorations were scrounged or made from what could be found; dinners in formal dress were planned; hunters were sent out to bag wild turkeys; parties were scheduled for every weekend. It was a curious mix of European formality and American openness in the wide-open Old West. Kitty managed to procure a goose for Christmas dinner. A chorus of carolers rode around town on the back of a truck, breathing in the cold mountain air, gaping at the splash of stars in the clear, dark night sky—an inadvertent gift from General Groves, who refused to allow street lights for fear of giving away the location of his secret city.

〜

THE BRITISH CONTINGENT WAS FASCINATED by this desert mountaintop and by the Sangre de Cristo Mountains at sunset, blushing the cold pink of alpenglow, and bewildered by the quiet after the steady pounding of the London Blitz. While the Americans fussed over a lack of fresh vegetables, the British and those who had escaped from Europe luxuriated in the fresh eggs and what must have seemed like abundant food.

The European refugees gave the people of the mesa pause; when the Americans asked about the damage inflicted by the German bombardment of England, a young British mathematician named Bill Penny gave a straightforward report that left the listeners stunned. "His presentation was in the scientific matter-of-fact style, with his usual brightly smiling face," recalled physicist Rudolph Peierls. "Many of the Americans had not been exposed to such a detailed and realistic discussion of casualties." It would be some time before they learned that Penny's wife had in fact been killed in one of the bombing raids on London. Peierls and his Russian wife Eugenia had fled Austria for England; the blitz had so traumatized them that they had sent their two young children, four and six, to Canada.[296] After four years, they would be reunited in Los Alamos. Others had families, wives and parents on the Continent, and wouldn't know their fate until after the war. As 1943 came to an end, the one thing they had in common was concern about how close the Germans might be to developing an atomic bomb; some of them knew Werner Heisenberg and did not doubt his abilities.

IN THE LAST FEW DAYS of that first year at Los Alamos, Richard Tolman and General Groves were once again on the *Super Chief* train heading west, this time escorting the irrepressible Dane to Los Alamos. They agreed to take turns sitting with Bohr in his compartment so he didn't wander around, as he tended to do. Richard took the first watch; after an hour he came out, exhausted by listening to the continual murmurings from Bohr's fulsome mind. "General," Richard said to Groves, "I can't stand it any more. I am reneging. You are in the Army, you have to do it."[297]

The Bohrs—now known as Nicholas Baker and his son, James—were greeted warmly at Lamy railroad station in what seemed like the middle of nowhere. The scientists were eager to meet the man who was at the very center of their world and who possessed the kind of moral authority that gave their work an imprimatur, quieting the restless questions that were in the backs of many of their minds. Robert would recall that Bohr was marvelous and that, although he took a lively technical interest, "His real function, I think, for almost all of us, was not a technical one. He made the whole enterprise seem hopeful, when many were not free of misgiving."[298] That night, a reception was held in the great room at Fuller Lodge. The first question Bohr put to Oppenheimer was: "Is it big enough?" Would the power of the bomb be destructive enough to put an end to all war?

General Groves left the following day, the last one of the year. Richard stayed on to celebrate the New Year with old friends at a party at Fuller Lodge, while most of the younger group celebrated with the usual high spirits. Given the altitude, it was easy to get drunk and more than a few residents of the Hill stumbled home in the early hours of the first day of 1944.

In England, General Eisenhower began to prepare for the long-awaited invasion of France and the Red Army was only 200 miles from Poland. In Italy, there would be 55,000 Allied casualties at the bloody battle of Monte Casino. The U.S. Marines began to push the Japanese out of the Marshall Islands, often in vicious hand-to-hand fighting. And the American press reported that Hitler claimed he had a secret weapon that would end the war. It was a year in the balance, and death was the fulcrum.

⤳

SAN FRANCISCO, JANUARY 1944:

The coroner's report read: *Body is that of a well developed, well nourished 29-year-old female. Rigor mortis pronounced. Height: 5 foot 6 inches. Weight: 117. Eyes: Hazel. Hair: brown. Heart: 240 grams and measures 13x7x6 centimeters. There is female external genitalia, the ovaries and fallopian tubes are normal. Uterus normal. Death had occurred 12 hours earlier.*

Stomach contained considerable recently ingested, semi-solid food. Toxicological: 4 barbituric acid derivatives, derivative of saliacylic acid, faint trace of chloral hydrate (uncorroborated). Conclusion: Cause of death: Acute edema of the lungs with pulmonary congestion.[299] Death by drowning.

Death was pronounced at 5:30 P.M. January 4, a Tuesday. On Wednesday, January 5, about 1:00 P.M., body found by father, Professor John S. P. Tatlock, of the University of California, Berkeley. Identification confirmed by Dr. Siegfried Bernfeld, her colleague at Mt. Zion Hospital and her therapist. The distinguished scholar of medieval literature and the esteemed psychotherapist, favorite student of Freud, stood together in the San Francisco Coroner's Office that rain-drenched Wednesday night, identifying the dead, still beautiful body of Jean Tatlock.

A front-page headline of the *San Francisco Examiner* called out the news: "Dr. Jean Tatlock is found dead; note hints suicide."[300] The story explained that the body was discovered resting on a pile of pillows next to a bathtub, head and shoulders underwater. A scrawled yet unsigned note seemed to try to explain: "To those who loved me and helped me, all love and courage. I think I would have been a liability all my life. I wanted to live and to give and I got paralyzed somehow. I tried like hell to understand and couldn't. . . . At least I could take away the burden of a paralyzed soul from a fighting world . . ." The words had trailed off the page.

BEFORE SHE KNEW ROBERT, BEFORE her soul became paralyzed and when poetry was the only language in which Jean could reveal herself, she had written:

> *This kneeling to you*
> *In the dark dawn*
> *With their bareness*
> *And their grayness*
> *Dissolved to melting silver*
> *And your love,*
> *Is even this*
> *Not enough to appease your awful pain*
> *You gaunt terrible bleeding Jesus*
> *Fils de Dieu?* [301]

BY THURSDAY, THE SHOCK OF Jean's death rattled over the telephone lines. To Mary Ellen Washburn in Berkeley, to Jean's brother Hugh, and Winifred Smith and Elizabeth Whitney, the Tolmans—Edward in Berkeley and Richard and Ruth in Washington—to the Sartons and May, to Steve Nelson and Haakon Chevalier and Hannah Peters and Edith Jenkins. The news reached those Jean Tatlock called her "heavenly friends," and others whom she did not.

As happens after a young and vibrant woman takes her own life, friends and relatives—even those who had rarely seen her in the past decade—felt compelled to look for signs, for signals missed, for any possible reason that could explain and ameliorate their sense of loss. Hugh was told that psychoanalysis had been hard on Jean, that records showed she had called her analyst fifteen times in November. Letty Field's mother surmised that Jean had been obsessed with death ever since Letty died. May, who had scarcely seen Jean after high school and knew only that she was rumored to be having an affair with a college professor, decided that Jean "drugged and drowned" herself because of lesbian tendencies. A Tatlock family friend who had met Jean only once, on holiday with Jean's sister-in-law Anne, and Aunt Jessie, remembered that she was "quite withdrawn—purposely withdrawn and quiet." [302] Only a few knew that Jean's battle was within; that she had looked to science for a cure, and that it had escaped her.

J. Edgar Hoover was informed of Jean's death by teletype from the local FBI field officer: "Informant" it began, had indicated she was a Communist party member, and added that "she was very loose morally." Then he suggested that direct action might create some bad publicity, but "Direct inquiries will be made discreetly."[303]

One day Robert would defend her, declaring, "She was a person of deep religious feeling. . . . She loved this country, its people and its life."[304]

Her physician brother would question the coroner's report. Chloral hydrate? *Uncorroborated.* Death by drowning? It made no sense to him. Not Jean. Never Jean. His sister, the one person in the room, he would say, that you would always remember. Always.

On a remote plateau deep in the Jemez Mountains of New Mexico, Robert would receive the message that first week of the New Year in his office, delivered by the Los Alamos head of security. He sat at his desk, silent, and wept. Then he walked out into the winter woods, head bent. His guards hung back, offering him as much privacy as they dared.

Ten long years later, he would be forced to explain to people who had not known her: "I met her at a time when I had suddenly become vulnerable to falling in love. She was a lyrical, uplifting, sensitive, yearning creature."[305]

They had, in those first lyrical months, read poetry together, and almost certainly the sonnet by John Donne that begins, "Batter my heart, three-person'd God."

And before even he knew her, Robert wrote a poem that would seem prophetic:

> But for us, who are not angels, for us
> You, whom the angels inhabit, are so precious
> That we learn to cherish equally
> The red angel of joy, and the pale angel of misery.[306]

VI

THE ATOMIC BOMB

21

PROFESSOR TATLOCK STRUGGLES WITH THE "HIDEOUS GASH" IN HIS LANDSCAPE, RUTH BECOMES INVOLVED IN THE NEW WORLD OF SPYCRAFT, AND KITTY IS PREGNANT AGAIN

It had rained in San Francisco those first few days of January 1944.
Heavy showers and gusty winds assailed the northern coast of California. The temperature dipped into the chilly 40s, as it does during the rainy season when the winds blow south out of Alaska. In Jean's top floor apartment on Telegraph Hill, the rain splashed silver against the windowpane, obliterating a view of the docks below and erasing the East Bay hills in the distance.

At Mt. Zion, all psychiatric residents spent six months in child psychiatry; the hospital was the center for analytic practice in California. Jean's hours had been long; holidays were a difficult time for her patients, and for Jean as well. The only family she had on the West Coast was her father. They had never been close, she did not confide in him, in fact she resented him. He maintained a proper distance, having convinced himself that he should not encroach on her private life. John Tatlock was stoic; he believed that humans could endure profound troubles, if they set their minds to it. "Nothing," he had written, "marks a well-educated man . . . more than clear thinking, discrimination."[307] But as Elizabeth Whitney had discovered, this particular well-educated man could not be without a woman— "friend, daughter, wife"—and the only woman in his life at the moment was Jean.

New Year's Day was a Saturday. It was Monday before Jean drove over the Bay Bridge to visit her father. She might have stopped to see Mary Ellen. There had been rumors about Jean and Mary Ellen, that they were lovers.[308] There were always rumors about women like Jean who didn't marry.

Her father had no idea how disgusted she was with herself for being neurotic, for having to work so hard to stay emotionally intact, for feeling like a burden in a time when their whole world was in a death struggle. That Monday he could see that she was in one of her despondent moods. When she left, he was worried enough to ask her to call him the next day. She said she would. Tuesday passed with no call. Instead, Jean telephoned Mary Ellen to ask if she would drive over to be with her. Mary Ellen declined.[309] It was raining and blustery and dark, difficult to drive at night in the blackouts, with all the talk about Japanese subs along the coast. Jean understood it was too much to ask. She had dinner alone.

Sometime during the tortured hours of that long night she filled the bathtub and piled pillows on the floor next to it. She emptied some powder from an envelope into a glass of water, drank it and waited for the relief. As she felt the numbing begin, she fumbled for a scrap of pencil to scrawl a message on the back of an envelope: "To those who loved me and helped me, all love and courage . . ."

The next morning, a Tuesday, John dialed his daughter's number—Sutter 0169—and when she did not answer, he phoned the hospital to see if she was at work. The dread began. At about noon he pulled on his raincoat and drove across the bridge, made his way through the downtown financial district on Montgomery Street and drove to the north end, just below Coit Tower. He parked and walked to number 1409. It was not yet one o'clock when he rang the doorbell. No answer. Alarmed now, he pushed through the wet foliage, climbed a back stairwell, and lifted a window to crawl into the silent apartment.

He found his daughter in the bathroom, kneeling on the pillows, her head and shoulders submerged in the cold water.

His heart would have pounded, his eyes and mind unable to grasp the reality of what Jean had done. He waited, weak. Somehow, the sixty-seven-year-old managed to lift her and then lower her carefully on the sofa in her living room, her dark hair and sweater wet. He began to search her apartment, grief swelling, tinged with anger. He found a cache of letters and photographs and went through them methodically, the same way he researched the details of other lives, from other centuries. And all the while Jean there beside him, on the couch, beyond reproach.

He sorted out some of the letters and photographs and put them in the fireplace. What did he not want other eyes to see? Possibly Jean had kept the letters that May Sarton had written when they were young and struggling with sexual identity. Or there may have been letters from Robert that should not be exposed. Tatlock was sympathetic to his daughter's political views. (He and Robert and Haakon Chevalier had purchased an ambulance to send to Spain during the Civil

War.) But he was also aware of how, in the current political atmosphere, his daughter's Communist ties might cause damage to others. Other letters might have revealed a continuing sexual ambiguity. He attempted to protect her memory, which was all that was left.

In his pain was a protective flare of anger: How could she have done this? Didn't she think about the pain she would cause him? And after that: I am not to blame for this. Why wouldn't she grow up?

WHOM SHOULD HE CALL? NOT the hospital, she was dead. Finally he found the phone book, and dialed the Halsted Funeral Home. (The FBI tap on Jean's telephone recorded the call, which prompted the teletype to J. Edgar Hoover.) After listening to the grieving father's confused explanation, someone at the funeral home phoned the police. Then he set fire to the letters and photos in the fireplace, watched as the fire caught, flamed, and burned bright. When the police and a deputy coroner arrived at 5:30, the winter light gone, the fire was still smoldering. By then, Tatlock had been alone with his dead daughter for more than four hours.

He watched as the attendants wrapped her body and carried her away to the city morgue. He was told to follow, to make an official identification, and that he needed another person as well. He called Siegfried Bernfeld. Among the things Tatlock had found in Jean's papers was a bill for $760 from Bernfeld. It was the amount she owed for the psychotherapy she was undergoing as part of her training. The newspapers would report the item, inferring that she had sought psychiatric help.

Hugh wanted to come home, but his father said no, he did not want him to, much to his son's regret.[310] The coroner's report raised questions that, as a medical doctor, Hugh could not accept. It made no sense to him. He wrote to request notes from Bernfeld, who replied that he couldn't find them. Hugh would try later to explain: "We never found enough details to satisfy either of us or know what happened. I lost her as a sister. We went to different places. I never really knew her after college age . . . we were good friends but it was pure chance that we were separated." He had been at Harvard, she at Stanford. He didn't want to believe that she was a Communist.[311] But he loved her, she was his astonishing, remarkable sister and he could not believe she would kill herself. He felt there had to be more than the depressions. Her death shocked the people she worked with, who were with her every day. Hugh knew his father was being protective; he refused to talk about Jean.

Hugh did not know about Boris Pash, or that Jean's phone had been tapped, or that J. Edgar's agents had been tracking his sister.

∽

WHAT DID KITTY FEEL WHEN she learned about Jean's death? Probably that it was such a waste, all that fine education, Vassar and Stanford, a medical degree and a residency in psychiatry, and only 29. (Kitty had once blithely dismissed the popular Dorothy McKibbin for having done nothing with her fine Smith College diploma, even though Dorothy had all but singlehandedly run the Los Alamos office in Santa Fe, a prodigious feat.) But in the case of Jean, what Kitty would have felt most acutely was that she was no longer a threat. Kitty had her Joe, now Robert had his Jean.

The winter wore on, the longest and coldest in living memory on the Pajarito Plateau, temperatures plunging below zero. On the weekend, the boys' school ski run was rigged up, the ice on the pond scraped for skating, and if the weather calmed and the skies were bright blue, the families went hiking and exploring. In the evenings, they partied and danced and drank too much. Sometimes Robert and Kitty joined them, Robert dancing in an old-fashioned style he probably learned at dancing school.

When Kitty had had too much to drink, she would divulge extremely personal details about her sex life to the woman she happened to be befriending at the time. She confessed that Robert did not bother with foreplay, had no sense of fun, no playfulness at all. She had to teach him, she said. Because, she continued, she believed sex should be fun,[312] not necessarily a religious experience. If Jean had been looking for ecstasy, Kitty wanted playfulness and pleasure. At Los Alamos she wasn't getting much of either. It might have been because her husband was working all day and many nights, the pressure so intense he was losing weight (his six-foot frame would go down to 104 pounds) and the belt with the big silver buckle had been drawn in several notches. Exhaustion might have explained his lack of energy for sex; so might a wife who was often drunk. Or it may have been Jean's death that made him less than responsive to the wife who thought sex should not be taken so seriously.

That Kitty was a very sexy dame, as one of the women at Los Alamos called her, was a given. Men responded to her, she was adept at flirting, a tease when she needed to be. Sex was how she had assured her marriage to Robert.

There was enough sex on the Hill to provide what would become a bumper crop of babies. RFD, they called it: Rural Free Delivery, just like the mail. Since the Army was paying the bills, and the young couples were stuck on this mountaintop, many of them figured they might as well take advantage of the time and the price, and produce their families. General Groves didn't like it, but there wasn't much he could do about it, since his director's wife would be adding to the RFDs before the year was out.

〜

By the end of January 1944, the 872-day siege of Leningrad was over. The brutal cost was the deaths of a million people. In the spring when the snow finally melted, corpses were exposed in the streets. The Allies made their first daylight raid on Berlin and two months later they entered Rome. On June 6, the long-awaited Allied invasion of Normandy began. In the Pacific, the U.S. Marines had landed on Guam, and the painful task of extricating the Japanese from island strongholds across the Pacific was underway. For years to come, the names of the islands would echo in the collective American memory: Saipan, Iwo Jima, Guadalcanal. In the high desert mountains of New Mexico, far from the battlefields, the scientists followed the news and intensified their already-long hours. Work on the atomic bomb was now at fever pitch; time for making a difference was running out.

〜

Almost from the beginning in Washington, Ruth moved quickly from planning studies on public opinions and attitudes, to conducting interviews and interpreting psychological experiments, then designing research methods that would validate or disprove data. By mid-1944, her reputation for excellent judgment brought her to the attention of the Office of Strategic Services—OSS—the national agency responsible for intelligence gathering, espionage, subversion and psychological warfare, and the forerunner of the CIA.

Hastily organized in June of 1942, the OSS was headed by William J. Donovan—known for good reason as "Wild Bill"—who convinced his close friend President Roosevelt that the country needed an intelligence service based on the British system. Sent into the field to work as spies, clandestine radio operators and saboteurs, a significant number of OSS agents broke under the stress, often at the cost of their lives. The British and Germans used psychologists to assess the emotional strength of their spies. Donovan decided the Americans should do the same.

In July of 1944, the OSS requested Dr. Ruth Tolman "on loan" from her current assignment at the War Production Board. She would interview potential candidates to assess who would be most likely to perform well under stress. Ruth worked in OSS Station W, located in a townhouse in the District. Her brother-in-law, Edward, was working with OSS at its secret "S" station in nearby Fairfax, Virginia. Officially, Ruth was to instruct the staff of what was euphemistically called the "Evaluation School for Overseas Personnel." Three "assessment centers" had been established to administer the tests and questionnaires that Ruth had helped develop. The aspiring spies would move on to trials that would determine their tolerance for frustration, verbal resourcefulness and emotional stability. After that, the number of agents who experienced "neuropsychiatric breakdowns" decreased dramatically from that reported before the training.[313] The job gave Ruth a preview of what to expect when the war was over and many young combatants came home suffering from psychological traumas.

Both Tolmans were caught up in webs of secrecy. Ruth, though, was secure in Washington while Richard was flying across the Atlantic in drafty Army planes, or rattling across country on trains packed with soldiers.

POSSIBLY IT WAS RICHARD WHO told Ruth about Jean's death or, more likely, Lillie Margaret or Edward's wife Kathleen. Or Robert. Possibly someone sent the newspaper clipping from the *San Francisco Chronicle*. The Bay Area psychology group was intertwined; the Tolmans and the Tatlocks knew each other, professionally and socially, even politically. Jean Macfarlane had been a good friend to Marjorie Tatlock. All of them had known Robert's "sweetheart."

Long before he knew Jean, Ruth had been Robert's good and close friend. She had been a witness to his courtship of Jean, to his attempts to help her. It would be Ruth who would understand the nature of his time with Jean, Ruth who was to become his touchstone to a life and a love that was now lost to him.

22 JULY 1944

"My dear Winifred," John Tatlock wrote to his wife's best friend, "The hideous gash in my landscape stands out the same as ever; I wonder if it will ever fill with vines and shrubs. I wonder too if such a tragedy is not worse for a man than for a woman, because more serenity and usual activity is expected of a man—which of course in the long run is best for him. Most people, though not quite all, have been perceptive and have helped me to carry on.

"I know full well your loyal love for darling Jean (as well as for Marjorie). One of the hardest things has been her exclusion of me from her thoughts and intimacy, as she tragically excluded everyone. I could never show her that she had no idea what pain a human being can go through, and pass on beyond, even; for my policy was always to try to make her feel that I was always there, serene and with what solidity the Lord had given me, these to back her up; but never to encroach. I overdid this last. Yet in the worst moments my judgment tells me that I have not been blameworthy. So the inevitable self-vivisection of the last months does not prevent me from carrying on. At bottom the cause of the tragedy was a pitiful resistance to growing up.

Yours most sincerely,

J.S.P. Tatlock."[314]

THE SUMMER WORE ON IN Los Alamos, with August temperatures in the 80s. Kitty was bored and tired and five months pregnant. The unseen weight on Robert's shoulders was pressing him into a stoop. There was nothing Kitty could do about it; she scarcely saw him.

As librarian, Charlotte Serber had her own little duchy, and it became an insider's center for social gatherings. Kitty was left outside, with all the young twenty-something mothers whose hands were full managing babies and the difficulties of keeping house on the Hill. She might have found friends in what Oppenheimer's secretary called "the Frau Doctor sorts of people," but most were European Jews who may have been uncomfortable with Kitty's background. Even if they did not know her Nazi connections, they would have resented her sense of superiority; in short, she made people nervous. Kitty was just thirty-six, but she could not work up enthusiasm for the women's clubs and teas or community-building efforts. She had her house, the American Indian woman who worked more hours for her than for any of the others, and her own horses. And some of the Army wives joined her afternoon cocktail group.

Emily Morrison, wife of one of Robert's protégés, explained, "Kitty was a very strange woman. She would pick a pet, one of the wives, and be extraordinarily friendly with her, and then drop her for no reason. She had temporary favorites. That's the way she was. She did it to one person after another . . . She could be a very bewitching person but she was someone to be wary of."[315]

One of the women Kitty turned her attention to for a time was Shirley Barnett, the young wife of the project's pediatrician. Kitty would ask Shirley to lunch and shopping trips to Santa Fe, or even Albuquerque. "Kitty always had a bottle of something with her when she was driving," Shirley remembered, "and you could always tell when she was getting drunk because she would talk more freely . . . She was fascinating but not very nice. She was not very happy and you got the sense that she never really had been."[316]

ONE YEAR INTO THE ASSIGNMENT, Los Alamos was beginning to wear on its residents. Louis Hempelmann didn't mind saying what others were thinking: At first it was lots of fun, but "after a while everybody got tired and tense and irritable." On December 7, exactly three years after the Japanese bombed Pearl Harbor, Kitty gave birth to a daughter at the Los Alamos hospital. Named Katherine for her mother, her first nickname was "Tyke," but her lasting pet name became "Toni."

It was cold that January and Kitty spent her days with drapes drawn, stretched out on the sofa, smoking cigarettes and probably drinking as the afternoon wore on. The pediatrician's wife came to visit and was alarmed by Kitty's languor. The house seemed morose. Then Kitty declared she had to get away, to go home to Pennsylvania. She would agree to take Peter—her mother could deal with a three-year-old, but not with a four-month-old baby. Kitty had trouble dealing with either of them.

No doubt General Groves wished that the families had never been allowed to come to Los Alamos, but he knew that if he were to succeed with this $2 billion project that would define his career, he was going to have to keep the "crackpots" as he referred to the scientists, focused.[317] He decided it was time to loosen security and allow the civilians a few days off, even a week. He made an exception for Kitty and granted her request to go home to Pittsburgh for an indefinite period, even if her mother was the cousin of one of Hitler's top generals.

Henry Barnett, the pediatrician, crafted a plan to help Kitty get away. Pat Sherr, the wife of one of the young Princeton physicists, had a four-year-old daughter and was expecting again. But she was also in mourning for her son Michael, who had died that winter. Barnett asked Pat if she would consider taking care of a baby—the director's baby—for a short time. Kitty, he explained, was feeling depressed and needed to go home to her parents. Pat didn't know either of the Oppenheimers, she was just twenty-four, her husband, Rubby, twenty-seven. And she didn't understand the request. Barnett tried to explain: he thought it would help her come to terms with Michael's death. And it would be doing a tremendous favor to the Oppenheimers, to know that someone so responsible would be taking care of their baby.

After Peter's birth, the Chevaliers had cared for Peter for two months so Kitty could get away. Now Pat Sherr was taking on a four-month-old whose parents were all but strangers. Kitty would be gone for three-and-a-half months; Robert would stop by the Sherr's house twice a week, as if fulfilling a responsibility. At first he would sit and visit with Pat, and not ask to see his daughter. When Pat brought Toni to him, he held her awkwardly. "He held your attention by speaking in the lowest of low voices so that you had to sit at the edge of you chair to catch all of those gorgeous words," Pat recalled. And yet one afternoon, after several months of these duty visits, Robert—usually so verbally adept—mumbled out a few words about how much Pat seemed to love the baby. He then asked Pat if she "would like to adopt her?" Pat was dumbstruck. Her answer was unequivocal: "Of course not ... She has two perfectly good parents." Why, she wanted to know, would he even think of such a thing?

Robert's reply was heartbreakingly simple: "I can't love her."[318]

At that moment his wracked body was eroding under the pressure of the battalions of people that needed his time and attention. The science was only part of it; the demands of family only part; since his arrival at Los Alamos, and especially after what was to be his last time with Jean, the intelligence officers had pushed at him, questioned him, challenged him. They read his mail, tapped his phone, followed him, prodded him for something—anything—that might turn up an enemy spy ring or a lingering Communist connection.

Kitty, sensing it was the right maneuver, and ambitious for Robert, now vehemently denounced Communism and her past. Robert had alarmed the security officers in August 1943 (not quite two months after his last visit with Jean) when he told them that the Shell Oil chemist who had spoken with Chevalier "might bear watching." All the alarms had gone off. Lt. Colonel Pash immediately questioned Robert, who gave him the later-to-be-famous cock-and-bull story of two, maybe three, persons being involved. Chevalier had been the messenger, but Robert refused to bring his friend's name into it. For a time he gave Pash and Military Intelligence obscure answers instead of a name; he embroidered the story, a strategy that was to backfire. Finally, after holding off for many long months, when ordered by General Groves, he named Haakon Chevalier.

The security detail at Los Alamos spent their days checking passes, reading mail, keeping a watchful eye over everyone in their search for spies, and hounding Robert Oppenheimer. As it would turn out, they were looking in all the wrong places. The elaborate security apparatus in place at Los Alamos failed to find the several real traitors in their midst who did pass information to the Soviets: the most important of these was Klaus Fuchs, a physicist with the British contingent.[319]

FRANK JOINS ROBERT FOR THE COUNTDOWN
TO TRINITY, AND KITTY WAITS TO HEAR IF SHE
SHOULD CHANGE THE SHEETS

Early in the spring of 1945, Kitty and Peter boarded the eastward-bound Acheson, Topeka and the Santa Fe at Lamy station and headed for Riegelsville, Pennsylvania. The journey would take them almost 2,000 miles to the Puenings' comfortable home near the city of Bethlehem. Keeping a lively four-year-old occupied on the crowded trains, with soldiers standing or sitting in the aisles, was demanding. But somehow they made their connections and arrived at Kitty's parents' home. Most likely, an agent tracked Kitty and Peter all the while, and probably kept watch on her parents as well.

Kaethe and Franz had experienced enough of their daughter's unexpected homecomings to wonder what she was running away from this time. She had all but disappeared from sight for two years, and if her letters offered any hint of where she might have been, it was redacted with heavy black pen. Her parents had no idea of what their son-in-law's mysterious role was, except that it seemed important.

IN AMERICA'S REVOLUTIONARY WAR, GENERAL George Washington had crossed the Delaware at Riegelsville to attack the British. George Washington didn't seem particularly historic to Kaethe Puening, who liked to repeat the family lore that one of her noble ancestors had fought in the Crusades in 1150.

Kitty's parents were living in England when the war broke out. In 1940 they had made their way back to America via the "spy route" to Lisbon, where they departed on the SS *Exochorda,* a luxury steamer that picked up stranded Americans and deposited them in New York City. By 1944, Allied forces were demolishing the German war machine. It was cause for celebration in most American homes, but though the Puenings wanted the Allies to win and the war to be over, the vanquished enemy included their families and the victory over them would involve destruction of places they knew and loved.

All across America, families listened to bulletins from the front on CBS's *World News.* Americans scoured newspapers, followed the battles on maps. The Puenings listened for mention of Münster, where Franz's sisters lived and which, as a headquarters for Panzer and Luftwaffe divisions, had endured heavy Allied bombing. On October 5, 1944, as the Allies advanced across France and entered Germany, the *New York Times* wrote "1,100 Flying Fortresses and Liberators, escorted by 750 Thunderbolt and Mustang fighter planes had 'delivered a series of smashing blows' on Münster."[320]

On April 3, about the time Kitty and Peter arrived in Riegelsville, the *New York Times* headlines reported fighting on the streets in Münster, and that the German commandant was refusing to surrender. The following day, a front page story reported that the tanks of the British Second Army and doughboys of the U.S. Seventeenth Airborne had found the city in flames. Some 90 percent of the old city was destroyed.[321] The story that gave heart to Americans longing for an end to the war would have distressed the Puenings, worried about the fate of their brothers and sisters, aunts and uncles, and their nephews who were still fighting for Germany.

Kaethe, sixty-three that spring, was the eldest of six in the Vissering clan. Two of her sisters had sons fighting in the war, and her brother's son was a Panzer commander. Another sister, Hildegard, was an assistant film director, most notoriously on the film *J'Accuse,* a Goebbels sponsored film supporting the Nazi euthanasia program in 1941.[322*] Kaethe had other cousins who were officers in the Wehrmacht. Field Marshall Wilhelm Keitel was now the head of the Oberkommando der Wehrmacht (Supreme Command of the Armed Forces); his brother Bodewin Keitel was a Lieutenant General and First General Staff Officer. On July 20, 1944, Kaethe and Franz would have heard radio reports of the failed assassination attempt on Hitler; from the front page headline of the *New York Times* the next day, they learned that Wilhelm Keitel, far from supporting the assassination attempt, "issued all the necessary instructions to all the fighting services and . . . military commanders" that Hitler was alive and in

---

*Kitty's aunt Hilde had worked with Wolfgang Liebeneiner, director of *J'Accuse,* a film supporting the euthanasia of a woman with multiple sclerosis, in collaboration with Josef Geobbel's Nazi Propoganda Ministry. He also directed, in 1956, the film *The Trapp Family,* which became the hit musical and film, *The Sound of Music.*

command, and that the suspects were to be arrested.[323]

Kaethe no longer mentioned that she had once been engaged to Keitel.

On May 8, 1945, after Hitler had committed suicide, Field Marshal Keitel was left to sign the official surrender to the Russians in Berlin.[324] That day was declared VE Day: Victory in Europe.

In the U.S., all radio programs were interrupted, a short burst of static and then the voice of President Harry Truman proclaimed, "This is a solemn but glorious hour ... The flags of freedom fly all over Europe." In Washington, spontaneous celebrations broke out. In England, Prime Minister Winston Churchill intoned, "We may allow ourselves a brief period of rejoicing; but let us not forget for a moment the toil and efforts that lie ahead."[325]

GENERAL GROVES, WITH RICHARD TOLMAN'S assistance, had ordered the top-secret Alsos Mission to determine Germany's progress on an atomic bomb. In command of Alsos was Colonel Boris Pash, a passionate anti-Communist (the same Boris Pash who had attempted to have Robert removed as director of Los Alamos after he spent the night with Jean, and who had Jean's phone tapped). Alsos headquarters in London was under the command of Major Robert Furman, the intelligence officer Tolman had briefed in the middle of Buzzard's Bay. Once again, Richard became the liaison between the Americans and the British.

The mission began in 1943 in Italy, its agents following immediately behind the Allied army as it battled across Europe. Finally, when the armies made their way into Strasbourg near the end of 1944, the Alsos team found what they had been looking for—the documents revealing that the Nazis did not have an atomic weapon. There had never been a race.[326]

Alsos' goal shifted quickly to keeping the German scientists and their laboratories out of Soviet hands. Between mid-April and VE Day, Pash and his men rounded up leading German physicists, including Heisenberg; they were then spirited them off to a country house in England.

VE DAY AT LOS ALAMOS was a mass of colliding emotions. Joy from the many who did not know the secrets of the Tech Area, and who assumed that with the Nazis defeated, and the Allies moving toward victory in the Pacific, they would all be going home soon. Some who did know the truth were disappointed that they hadn't produced an atomic bomb in time to shorten the war in Europe. Many felt a sense of relief that the Germans didn't have the weapon after all. Still others, including some scientists, wondered why work on the Gadget should continue now. Some admitted, in the exhausting buildup to complete this doomsday weapon, to having qualms. Yet no one actually stopped working; they were close now. And the government was footing the bill for the whole Manhattan Project, including other centers in Hanford, Washington and Oak Ridge, Tennessee, and the Met Lab in Chicago. With such an enormous investment, results were expected. The race to develop the bomb shifted its focus to ending the war against Japan and the postwar struggle with the USSR.

Prime Minister Churchill was for staying the course: "Japan with all her treachery and greed, remains unsubdued."

JUST OUTSIDE OF GENERAL GROVES' office in Washington sat Anne Wilson, a pretty and spirited twenty-year-old who, when Groves offered her a job as his secretary in 1943, probably wrinkled her nose and told him, "you're too ornery." Groves and Wilson had played tennis at the Army-Navy Club—her father was an admiral. Anne did take the job despite Groves' temperament, and found herself privy to the secrets of the Manhattan Project. She was often asked to listen to Groves-Oppenheimer conversations so she could take notes. When Robert came to Washington, he would stop by Anne's desk to chat. "I was just practically dumbstruck," Anne recalled, "because here was this legendary character and part of his legend was that all women fell on their faces in front of him."[327] Anne did not fall on her face; Robert was twice her age, after all.

When Robert needed a new secretary in Los Alamos, he seemed in no hurry to find a replacement and turned down several possibilities. Finally Groves, exasperated, asked if he had anybody in mind. Robert rather coolly answered, "I think I'd like to have Miss Wilson." Groves called Miss Wilson. Knowing something about the exciting project in New Mexico, she said yes, she would like to go. (But when Lansdale, head of security for the Manhattan Project, offered to pay her to send monthly "reports" on Robert, she retorted that he should forget he ever said such a thing.)[328]

Then a curious thing happened. Anne had scarcely settled in at Los Alamos when, every three days, a florist from Santa Fe delivered a single rose. Pretty young woman that she was, Anne wondered out loud if she had a "secret lover." No one knew anything, but finally one person floated the notion that it was just the kind of thing Robert would do. Anne didn't know the identity of her secret admirer, but the whispers moved like the wind: the Boss was having an affair.

The whispers somehow reached Kitty. She went straight to Anne and, dispensing with the pleasantries, asked if she was seducing her husband. Anne must have stared at her as if she had lost her mind. Robert was ... old. How could Kitty think she would be in the least interested in her husband? Kitty could not have misread the look on Anne's face. Anne and Kitty began a friendship that would survive for many years.

Anne never found out who had sent the roses.

⤳

RICHARD WAS AT LOS ALAMOS in May, and could not have escaped the growing tension and exhaustion among the scientists. General Groves pressed for a test of the Gadget before Truman's scheduled meeting with Stalin in mid-July; Robert hesitated, still wanting to make adjustments in the bomb design. Three months earlier, one of Air Force General Curtis Le May's B29 bombing raids on Tokyo had sent a storm of flames and gases that killed some 100,000 Japanese civilians. On Okinawa that spring there were just short of 50,000 American military casualties; kamikaze attacks alone killed more than 4,900 Americans. Japanese military and civilian casualties were reported to have been near 200,000. These obscene numbers splattered across the headlines of newspapers and on news programs nationwide. Americans were sick of war, sick of death, sick of the Japanese culture that seemed to prefer death over surrender. Robert finally agreed: they would test "the device" on July 17 in a desolate New Mexico desert site 239 miles south, in a valley called the *Jornada del Muerto*—Journey of the Dead. Robert named the test "Trinity." He would later say that he wasn't certain why he had chosen the name, recalling that it came from a Donne poem, *"Batter my heart, three person'd God"*—one he and Jean were likely to have shared. Could Robert remember her voice? Did he remember that she would have wanted nothing to do with what was about to happen?

KITTY RETURNED FROM HER PARENTS' home only weeks before the Trinity test. She collected seven-month-old Toni, healthy with big, sparkling baby smiles. Pat, seven months pregnant, was proud of the little girl, and yet relieved to turn her over to her mother. Kitty was obviously grateful, but managed to offend Pat by showering her with gifts, as if to pay for her help, until Pat had to ask her to stop.

ROBERT HAD ASKED FOR HIS brother to be with him for the first test, and General Groves obliged, bringing Frank out in May 1945 from the Oak Ridge, Tennessee facility where he had been working on extracting pure U235 (the uranium isotope that could sustain the fission chain reaction necessary for a bomb). Jackie and the children had not moved to Oak Ridge; Jackie could not stomach the people and politics of the South, especially segregation. As much as she wanted to be with her husband, she had stayed in Berkeley. In the summer of 1945, she and their two children came to Los Alamos for a visit. She was there when Kitty returned from her parents and resumed late afternoon cocktails. She included Jackie in the gathering upon her return. "It was known that we didn't get on too well," Jackie remembered, "and she seemed determined that we should be seen together ... When I arrived, there was Kitty and just four or five other women—drinking companions—and we just sat there with little conversation, drinking. It was awful and I never went again."[329] Jackie felt about Kitty much as she felt about the South, she simply couldn't take her.

AN ELECTRIC SUSPENSE HOVERED OVER Los Alamos that summer, an increasing feeling of anticipation. Most of the 5,000 residents did not know what was about to happen 239 miles to the south. The wives who did know weren't sure to whom they could talk freely; sometimes they seemed to be taking a breath between every syllable.

⤙

ON JULY 15, 1945, THE tension at the Trinity site was palpable. Most of the scientists had arrived; generals and VIPs began to fly into the Army Airfield nearby. In Santa Fe, Dorothy McKibbin got a phone call from a friend on the Hill, asking if she would like to join a small group that was planning an overnight camping trip to the Sandia Mountains, near Albuquerque. She understood immediately; the Sandias would offer the best view of Alamogordo and Trinity. She packed her gear.

Robert had made a pact with Kitty: if it worked, he would send her the prosaic message: "You can change the sheets." She gave him a four-leafed clover for luck.[330]

Scorpions and rattlesnakes, field mice and frogs populated the scrubby desert. A tall tower was ready, the Gadget in place for the 4:00 A.M. test. As darkness fell, the winds rose, then great flashes of lightning slashed the night sky and thunder echoed off the surrounding hills. The air seemed filled with portent. Frank would remember the frogs, how they seemed to migrate to a pond, and then filled the night with the sounds of wild copulating. He would remember, "The only living things around there [were] coming together."[331] He joined his brother, lying outside the control bunker; they would see the thing through.

At Los Alamos in the first dark hours of that day, Jane Wilson, whose husband, Bob, was one of the first of the physicists to question the morality of the project, would remember, "the air seemed empty and bitter cold, although it was July." Those wives who knew kept vigil. Some watched from their porches.

A small group of wives gathered on Sawyer's Hill near the ski run, where the view to the south was wide. The pine trees stood black against a starless sky. Four o'clock came and went. They waited, scanning the sky, silent and afraid for their husbands at the test site. Jane would write: "Four thirty. The gray dawn rising in the east, and still no sign that the labor and the struggle of the past three years meant anything at all." They continued to wait.

At 5:30, Jane saw a "Blinding light like no other light one had ever seen. The trees, illuminated, leaping out at one. The mountains flashing into life." And then the slow, monstrous rumble that announced the birth of the atomic age. [332]

⤳

THE BROTHERS LAY FACE DOWN, 6.2 miles from ground zero, side by side, their eyes closed and arms covering heads. "But the light of the first flash penetrated and came up from the ground through one's lids," Frank said. Then there was the fireball, and very quickly "this unearthly hovering cloud. It was very bright, and very purple and very awesome . . . And all the time . . . the thunder of the blast was bouncing back and forth on the cliffs and hills."[333] The brothers looked at each other and said simply, "It worked."[334] This band of unlikely warriors in their jeans and porkpie hats, the men General Groves had called "the longhairs," had figured out how to unleash the fury of the universe. Bohr's question had an answer: It was big enough.

One of the generals rushed over to Groves and all but shouted, "The war is over." General Groves, solemn, answered: "Yes, after we drop two bombs on Japan."[335]

23

NAT DISCOVERS THAT RUTH "SAW THE END
WRITTEN LONG BEFORE MOST OF US KNEW EVEN
THAT THE BEGINNING OF THE END HAD BEEN
STARTED," ROBERT WANTS TO GO BACK TO
CALIFORNIA FOR THE REST OF HIS DAYS, AND
KITTY GLIMPSES THE HALLS OF POWER

On July 16, a few short hours after Richard Tolman witnessed the birth of the atomic age in the skies over New Mexico, Ruth arrived at her desk at the OSS for the last time. She had spent four years, one month, and twelve days in service to her country. That same afternoon Richard boarded an Army plane at Alamogordo Air Field bound for the nation's capital. With him was General Groves, his executive officer, Tom Farrell; James Conant, Vannevar Bush and Ernest Lawrence. The scientists, Conant wrote, were "still upset by what they had seen and could talk of little else, to the annoyance of Groves, whose thoughts were already grappling with the details of the 'upcoming climax' in Japan."[336]

When Richard arrived home, he was weary but excited, overwhelmed by what he had witnessed and eager to talk to his wife. Ruth understood the magnitude of the event described by their close friend Conant: "A cosmic phenomenon like an eclipse. The whole sky suddenly full of white light like the end of the world." Or Tom Farrell in his religious incantation of the detonation wave that had followed the flash as a "strong, sustained roar which warned of doomsday and made us feel that we puny things were blasphemous to dare tamper with the forces heretofore reserved to the Almighty."[337]

None of this could be revealed to the Tolmans' ubiquitous houseguests, who at that moment included Nat, just returned from three months in Germany with the Quartermaster's Corps, with a trove of new stories. Again at loose ends, she decided to set off, that first week of August, for California in a car in such poor repair that getting across the country was itself an adventure. Ruth reminded Nat to take notes about good places to spend the night; she was imagining her own imminent journey home.

Nat had chosen a fateful week in which to cross America.

On August 6, the question first asked in Berkeley in the summer of 1942—could an atomic bomb be delivered by an airplane?—was answered. The airplane was a Boeing B-29 Superfortress bomber named *Enola Gay* and its target was Hiroshima.

THE NEWS CAME OVER THE airwaves: The largest bomb ever used in the history of warfare had been dropped on a Japanese city. President Truman explained, "It is a harnessing of the basic power of the universe. The force from which the sun draws it power has been loosed against those who brought war to the Far East."[338] Three days later, on August 9, another atomic bomb dropped from the bay of another Superfortress, obliterating Nagasaki.

ON SUNDAY, AUGUST 12, 1945, Nat wrote from Palos Verdes, California:

Ruth darling:

I was in the middle of Tennessee when I heard the exciting and awe-full news of the atomic bomb. It didn't take very great deduction to realize that Dicky's long absence must have been at the bomb testing site, especially when such familiar names as Conant, Oppenheimer, Bohr began to tumble from the newsprint. And I wondered whether the important occasion last week, when he dressed in his blue suit, had been to talk over our surrender ultimatum with the Sec. of War."[339]

Nat continued: "What an exciting life Dicky must have been living these past years!" She wanted details, especially whether, during the New Mexico test he had been his usual intent scientist self, or if "for one minute he relaxed and grinned and said, 'I hope the darned thing goes off.'"

Nat was close; most of the scientists at Trinity, including Robert and his brother, had said something like "it worked," followed soon after by a ground-swell of doubt (Wilson would talk of the "terrible thing we made"). Now the job was done, and they were going to have to face the consequences of their success. Niels Bohr had warned them; it was the future use of the bomb that would trouble many of the men who had created it.

Nat had no qualms. She wrote: "Few people can have such a feeling of immediate contribution to the war's end. But it must be an anticlimax to you and to all those who have been engaged in this work and who saw the end written long before most of us knew even that the beginning of the end had been started."

Her letter burbled on, offering a glimpse of America in the last week of the war:

"And now surely you can come home. Even by the time you come, things will be so different. Gas will no longer be rationed, more traffic will be on the road, food will be easier, everything will have changed. I took careful notes as I went along, for your benefit—of food, gas, roads, mileage—but it is out of date already. But this will not be out of date—beware the housing problem. I was all right through Arkansas but didn't find a place to sleep west of that state. Every town seemed to be near an Army base or a large war construction of some kind, so the thousands of tourist cabins were filled long before I would be interested in stopping . . .

"I haven't driven these roads for ten years and therefore don't know how much of this change has resulted just from the war. All the tourist cabins, all the neon lights, all the beer joints, all the polluted and crowded West amazed and bewildered me. I came through to San Diego and the traffic in California was almost the most amazing part of the whole trip: the thousands of cars traveling fiercely over the highways at a minimum speed of 65. They seemed never to have heard of gas rationing, of tire shortage, of car shortage. I saw more fine cars, and saw more go whizzing past me, than in a year's driving in the East. California looked just like a fair ground filled with blue-uniformed sailors."

Nat ended the letter by sending her congratulations "On what you have done, both of you, in these years of crisis."

THREE DAYS LATER, JAPAN'S EMPEROR Hirohito broadcast an announcement to his "Good and Loyal Subjects" that he had ordered his Imperial Forces to surrender. General Groves' mission had been accomplished.

〜

PHYSICISTS PHIL MORRISON AND BOB Serber had gone to Tinian Island in the Pacific to help prepare the bombs destined for Hiroshima and Nagasaki.

In the aftermath, they were sent into the ravaged cities. The two returned to Los Alamos, stunned: the horror had begun to sink in. Of Hiroshima, Morrison said, "One bomber and one bomb had, in the time it takes a rifle bullet to cross the city, turned a city of three hundred thousand into a burning pyre." Jean Bacher, after listening to Morrison, said she finally understood it all—and wrote that she "shook all night—it never leaves you."[340]

As for Robert, though he would consistently defend the use of the bombs against Japan, he now seemed to express himself in terms of sorrow and terror. He would recall that after Trinity, a few people laughed, a few cried, most were silent, and that he had remembered the line from the Bhagavad Gita: "I am become Death, the destroyer of worlds." After Hiroshima and Nagasaki, he would speak of scientists having blood on their hands, of knowing sin, of being guilty of a complicated hubris in their creation of a new world. The gods were battering his heart. When Robert seemed dangerously close to a breaking point, physicists Bob Bacher and I. I. Rabi calmed him.

Kitty and Robert took off for Perro Caliente for a week, his first break in almost three years. Fall was approaching and the ranch offered the illusion of being removed from the madness. The two took long rides through the woods and into meadows scattered lavishly with penstemon and blue gilla and yarrow, through all the places that had given him pleasure and peace before the war. And for much of the time he sat on the porch and answered some of the letters that had poured in from old friends and from universities offering him faculty positions.

On August 7, Haakon Chevalier wrote from the San Francisco area, "Dear Opje, You are probably the most famous man in the world today ... we are very proud of you." He continued in a more solemn tone: "There is a weight in such a venture which few men in history have had to bear. I know that with your love of men, it is no light thing to have had a part, and a great part, in a diabolical contrivance for destroying them. But in the possibilities of death are also the possibilities of life, and these I know have been uppermost in your mind ... You have made history. We are happy for you."[341] Robert answered obliquely, making excuses for not writing, speaking of the strain and fatigue of the last years, avoiding mention of the bomb, or of the fact that he had spoken Chevalier's name to military security.

Robert wrote letters to those institutions that approached him, sending his regrets to some because, as he would explain to Conant at Harvard, "I know now ... that I would like to go back to California for the rest of my days; that I have a sense of belonging there."[342] In a long letter responding to Charlie Lauritsen at Caltech, he wrote at length about his own requirements, then reminded him that he had twice proposed getting Rabi to Caltech. Robert pushed: "Has this fallen through? If so, is it lack of money, is it reluctance to add another Jew to the faculty?" Caltech's president had his doubts about Robert as well, reminding Richard Tolman that he could get two younger men for the price of one Oppenheimer, and that Caltech already had enough Jews on the faculty.[343] (The war, the Holocaust, the number of Jewish physicists working on the atom bomb, had not changed attitudes about quotas for Jews in American universities.)

Robert's first choice was Berkeley, the place he felt most at home. But he knew that some there had reservations about him, and held his political views against him. Still, Ernest Lawrence wanted Robert. In the end, both Berkeley and Caltech offered Robert everything he asked; he would return to Caltech and requested an extended leave of absence from Berkeley.

When Robert and Kitty returned to Los Alamos from Perro Caliente, Kitty told Jean Bacher that Robert was in such a state that she didn't know how she could stand it.[344] Robert left almost immediately for Washington for a two-week trip; there he would talk to Ruth and Richard about the struggle for control of nuclear arms that—as Neils Bohr had predicted—had already begun. Some Los Alamos scientists wanted to outlaw atomic weapons; another group, led by Edward Teller, was pushing to create thermonuclear "super" bombs, massively more destructive than those dropped on Japan. The majority of the Manhattan Project scientists believed the answer was in international controls and in an open exchange of information with all countries, including the Soviet Union—in effect, giving up any advantage the U.S. monopoly might offer in exchange for a chance to prevent an arms race. Other countries would, the scientists knew, build their own atom bombs. It was only a matter of time.

SUDDENLY ROBERT WAS CATAPULTED INTO a new and very public role. The American press presented him as a hero, the "Father of the Atomic Bomb," even as Robert told the American Philosophical Society that, "We have made a thing, a most terrible weapon that has altered abruptly and profoundly the nature of the world . . . an evil thing."[345]

What Robert didn't yet know was that FBI director J. Edgar Hoover had decided he still warranted being watched. Hoover alerted his agents that Robert obviously would be valuable to the Soviets.

⌒

THE TOLMANS RETURNED TO PASADENA, Frank and Jackie to Berkeley with the Serbers, Val and Ruth Benedict to the apartment on Central Park West in New York City, with trips to Val's house in Pasadena. Most of the senior scientists—

after three remarkable years in the mountains together—went back to their old schools. Robert, Kitty and the children headed first for Pasadena, then north to Berkeley. Rabi ended up at Columbia, not Caltech. Anne Wilson went home to Washington, D.C.

In November of 1945, Robert and Kitty and the children settled back into One Eagle Hill, above the bay in Berkeley. Robert had agreed to return to Caltech to teach one course a term, which meant he again would be staying at the Tolmans' guesthouse once a month. Although he was living in Berkeley, he continued to put off a decision about teaching there. During the war he had come to know and admire such scientist-statesmen as Conant and Bush. Now, in his frequent trips to Washington as a scientific advisor, he was discovering the exhilaration of shaping government policy. Robert had begun to believe that his only chance for absolution from what he would describe as "the scientists' sin of pride" came with the power to influence.[346] Kitty was more than ready to become his executive officer.

In New York, the newly formed United Nations had created an International Atomic Energy Commission. President Truman appointed Dean Acheson to chair a committee that would recommend U.S. nuclear policy. Robert and David Lilienthal, who had administered the Tennessee Valley Authority before the war, were to provide technical advice. Robert called up his dazzling powers of persuasion, and convinced Lilienthal, Acheson, and Acheson's aide Herb Marks that the U.S. should give up its monopoly on atomic weapons immediately. Robert became the primary author of the thirty-four-page Lilienthal-Acheson Report, which offered some radical ideas on the control of atomic weaponry and supported the idea of international control of nuclear information, which he thought essential for world peace.

Acheson passed the report on to Secretary of State James Byrnes, who said publicly that he found it impressive and sent it on to Truman. The conservative Democrat Bernard Baruch (Byrnes' business partner) was selected as U.S. Representative to the UN Commission,[347] which would prove to be the death knell for the Lilienthal-Acheson report. Baruch, unduly protective of American atomic interests, added provisions of his own that were unacceptable to the Soviets.

Acheson was discouraged; Lilienthal felt Baruch had sabotaged their report and felt "quite sick." Oppenheimer said, "We have failed."[348]

⌐⌐

THE OPPENHEIMERS HAD ACQUIRED A retired Army dog named Buddy, who became Peter's shadow. (If Peter slipped out of Buddy's sight, the dog was known to barge into neighbors' homes, and would not leave until he had searched every room.) Kitty was again driving to and from the train station or the airport. She hosted dinners, arranged Robert's schedules, accepted or declined their many invitations. For the first time, she was part of the substance of Robert's working life, even when he was away.

Compared with academia and the life of a faculty wife, the struggle building in Washington seemed infinitely more interesting, and more important. Kitty was thirty-five that year; with no Ph.D., two young children, and a husband she adored (as she often said, sometimes in public when she'd had one too many drinks), she was enjoying Robert's access to the power brokers in Washington. Kitty knew by then that the FBI was taping their conversations. She would have been pleased when they copied Robert telling someone he couldn't give them an answer until he communicated "with my boss."[349] That Boss being Kitty.

THERE WAS NO REASON FOR Kitty to go with Robert to Pasadena; the train trip was long and boring, he used the time to read and work. At the Tolmans' he could talk with Richard, who was also making regular trips to Washington. Kitty and Ruth had spent little time together; Kitty must have felt that at fifty-two, Ruth was not a threat. She didn't realize that neither Ruth's energy nor her ambition had ebbed. Or that Ruth had good friends—men and women alike—who had been with Kitty at Los Alamos and had tales to tell about her erratic behavior. So although Ruth was scrupulous about inviting Kitty to join Robert at their house, she was mostly relieved when Kitty remained in Berkeley.

AT THE WAR'S END, RICHARD looked decidedly older than his sixty-four years. He had spent the months immediately before Hiroshima helping to prepare the important—and controversial—Smyth Report, which recommended what nuclear information could be disclosed to the public, a subject that was to divide scientists and the American political establishment in the years to come. Robert was still rail thin, but was regaining his strength. Ruth, once again, found herself the confidante of two of the most revered scientists on the planet, both struggling to find a way for the world to live in peace with the nuclear threat they had helped to create.

⌐

RUTH KNEW, FROM RICHARD AND Robert, the anguish that was corroding the consciences of many of the scientists from Los Alamos. Nat's letter wasn't the only one Ruth received the week after news of the atomic bomb broke, when it became obvious that Richard was intimately involved in the biggest story of the war.

On August 7, after Hiroshima, an old friend and admirer of Ruth's—a photographer she had corresponded with during World War I—sent her a letter that she tucked away to keep. The friend wrote that from the radio and newspaper accounts of Hiroshima, he had learned of Richard's involvement, and that he "can no longer lay the flattering unction to his soul that he never did any harm." He went on to say that if the world "can't adapt this discovery, conceived in a destructive spirit, to constructive uses even in the low spirit of realization that all hostile groups are mutually check-mated, they deserve to be destroyed utterly. I congratulate the doctor on attaining the eminence of avenging angel. 'Vengeance is mine—I will repay, saith the lord,' through Richard Tolman and his scientific colleagues."

Having said what was on his mind, which must have jolted the preacher's daughter, he shifted to a tough but affectionate tone that seemed to define their former relationship: "You are a lousy correspondent in this war and you were a wonderful one in the last war. Your letters were the most interesting and stimulating of any I ever received. How about composing one to me and let me see if you are as good as you used to be. . . . When you come to New York, remember that I still have a passion for you and would love to see you." Then he added a postscript. "I regretted the death of your relative, Bill Chickering, whom I met in Honolulu. He was a charming fellow and was getting to be a good writer."[350]

Bill Chickering was cousin Alma's son, the little boy that Ruth and Lillie Margaret had adored as a baby. They had watched him grow into a tall and handsome man. He was beginning a career as a writer when the attack on Pearl Harbor interfered. Time Incorporated took him on as their first war correspondent in the Pacific, reporting for both *Time* and *Life* magazines. The cousins kept close touch during the war. Alma sent copies of some of the letters Bill wrote home. In January of 1945, he was standing on the bridge of the battleship New Mexico, along with its captain and two Royal Navy men, waiting to cover the landing on Luzon. A Kamakazi appeared, then plunged his Zero into the bridge, killing all of them in the explosion. Bill Chickering was the only *Time* correspondent lost in the Pacific war. Ruth did not escape the kind of devastating news that was being delivered to families in cities and towns throughout the country as the war wore on. For the families of men already on the high seas, in troop ships ready to take part in the invasion of Japan—code named "Operation Downfall"—the atomic bomb seemed a miracle. They were thinking of the American lives saved if Japan surrendered rather than the 200,000 Japanese dead in Hiroshima and Nagasaki.

For Ruth, as for most of the scientists who were instrumental in building the first atomic bomb, the lives saved—some casualty estimates escalated to as high as a million—helped to justify the use of this almost unimaginably destructive new weapon on a civilian population. Ruth, close as she was to Richard and Robert, could not have questioned the decision. But echoes from her early years in her father's church, cadences from the King James Bible, the "thou shalts" and "thou shalt nots," and her own moral code would have compelled her to confront the ethical questions raised by this new threat to civilization. That was yet to come; first she had to face an aftermath of the war, the battered returning army.

～

WAVES OF GIs WITH DEBILITATING emotional and neurological injuries were coming home with symptoms that ranged from a pounding heart and racing pulse to prolific sweats and terrifying flashbacks. In World War I it was called "shell shock," in World War II, "combat fatigue." In all, some 44,000 veterans returned from the war with some degree of emotional trauma. The Veterans Administration, established in 1930, was responsible for these traumatized soldiers, a difficult task given the serious shortage of psychiatrists in the country.

At the time, psychiatrists were supposed to treat patients, and psychologists to devise studies to assess them; but now the psychologists were needed to treat patients as well.[351] This meant they needed to be trained. Ruth, who had been assessing and training OSS candidates during the war, was in the right place at the right time to help educate psychologists to see patients.

Ed Boring, director of the Psychological Laboratory at Harvard,[352] had been at OSS with Ruth, and they became friends. When, as part of several studies that he and Alice Bryant did on women psychologists, Boring asked Ruth to explain her success in a predominately male profession, she answered that it was hard "to abstract 'being a woman' from being a particular woman and [that she tended] to hold responsible my particular idiosyncrasies rather than my sex for the arrangements of my life."[353] Ruth was one of the few women at the top of her profession, and she was treated as an equal by men who were acknowledged to be leaders in their field. Realist that Ruth was, she acknowledged that this was the result of her skills but also of her relationship to her brother-in-law, Edward. Although younger women seem to have found her somewhat threatening, with the men and professional women with whom she worked, she was regarded as an excellent colleague; she was a serious researcher and teacher, made no overt demands, and asked for few if any exceptions. And she had powerful connections in the field of psychology and in the government.

In 1946, the Division of Clinical Psychology in the Neuropsychiatric Service at the Veterans Administration created five types of facilities where veterans could be treated. The largest number would go to what were called Mental Hygiene Clinics, for outpatient care which would allow the veteran to stay in his community. Group therapy was one of the innovations introduced in these clinics. Although

Ruth had taught part-time at various colleges before the war, she spent most of her postwar years doing research and developing training programs for clinical psychology, one of the few fields in which women outnumbered men.[354] In 1946 she was assigned to the clinic in downtown Los Angeles, the largest in the West.

She would write to David Shakow, a colleague and friend, that the VA program offered rich research possibilities that should be integrated throughout the system. To help solve her quandary of what, exactly, was effective therapy, Ruth argued that the first step would be to define and measure what "efficacy" means.[355] Throughout her career Ruth would place great importance on defining terms, to make psychology as precise a science as possible, something she undoubtedly learned from the physicists in her life.

IN PASADENA, THE PRE-WAR camaraderie revived; Robert confided in Ruth his growing doubts about teaching. Before the war it had been his life, he would say, but now the thrill was gone, and all the calls from Washington were distracting. Having Robert to herself for a few hours each month gave the two, after the rigors of the past four years, time to grow closer. He had always, in some ways, been a younger, more intense version of Richard.

It wasn't long before rumors of an affair between Ruth and Robert began to circulate. A young acquaintance recalled stopping by the Tolman house one morning to find Ruth and Robert alone and in their dressing gowns.[356] It was enough to start talk. Those close to Ruth didn't believe it, but the Oppenheimer marriage had become such a topic of gossip in academic communities that the hint of an affair between Robert and not just any older woman, but the wife of his good friend Richard Tolman, created a frisson of speculation.

⌣

VII
REPERCUSSIONS

24

J. Edgar Hoover monitors life at Eagle Hill, Robert finds that teaching seems irrelevant and Kitty has a premonition

Immediately after the war, Robert at forty-two was a celebrity. Richard just wanted to go home to Pasadena.

Robert was meeting important people in Washington, including Secretary of State General George Marshall and President Truman. But he was beginning to find the practice of democracy an aggravating, often disappointing business. Not nearly as clean and orderly as physics. Many of the political leaders he worked with were thoughtful men, others he dismissed as either too simple to grasp a concept, or fools. But he could not dismiss Edward Teller and others who refused to understand that taking the atomic bomb to another "super" level could be catastrophic.[357]

On Eagle Hill, Kitty entertained a steady stream of guests, juggled Robert's schedule, and continued to drink. At one in the morning one night in 1946 Kitty fell in her driveway. FBI wiretap reported that she fractured her wrist in seven places, and spent the early morning hours in Alta Bates hospital. It was just another in a series of bone breaks and bruises collected in car crashes or on horseback, some fueled by recklessness, others by alcohol.

The FBI recordings of the Oppenheimers' phone conversations produced a tapestry of daily events: Peter had traumatic nightmares, Toni would soon be out of diapers. Kitty called a domestic help agency to explain that while they felt it was wrong to have servants, they needed a second maid. They were happy with their current help, she said, because she "went around with a completely detached attitude; she did not bother them at all and Robert liked that."

In May of 1946, Kitty's mother came to visit. Robert was in the East at the time, and arranged to see Kitty's father in Pittsburgh and meet his boss, the head of research at Bethlehem Steel. Kitty suggested, "If you can say the right things, it won't do [father] any harm. So be nice to him."[358] She also said she wanted Robert to come home before her mother left.

ON THIS TRIP, ROBERT DELIVERED the fifth in a series of lectures at Cornell University. He unabashedly described the event to Kitty as "wonderful." She was desperate to be part of the excitement so he appeased her by saying how much "everybody misses you, many people wished you had come." Then he ended the conversation quickly by saying he would call again on Sunday "for Pete's sake too." But if it turned out he was too busy, he said, he would call as soon as he could. When Robert finally did call, it was to tell Kitty he would be delayed.[359] He finally flew home on May 25, missing Kitty's mother by one day.

Kitty distracted herself with an interest in the flourishing romance between Anne Wilson and the married Herbert Marks. Kitty invited Anne to come west to stay for a time. One day on the phone Herb asked Anne, now at Eagle Hill, what kind of spirits Oppie was in when he left for New York. She answered, "not good." Anne had delivered to Robert some news that had depressed him terribly, and she felt like a "skunk ... Kitty almost slit my throat, for which I do not blame her." Anne described Kitty as a tigress, determined to protect her mate. Herb, who knew what news she had delivered, reassured her, "No, I think it was best that you did what you did ... he needs to know things as they are, for his own sake."[360] One of the things Robert "needed to know" was that Bernard Baruch's speech before the United Nations Atomic Energy Commission had included provisions that the Soviets would not and did not approve. Lilienthal noted in his journals that "O. was deeply troubled."

Lilienthal also wrote that Robert had told him, "I am ready to go anywhere and do anything, but I am bankrupt of further ideas. And I find that physics and the teaching of physics, which is my life, now seems irrelevant." When Lilienthal was appointed chairman of the new U.S. Atomic Energy Commission the following year, he would write: "God grant in the coming year that I may by a bit lessen the cloud of dread and fear that hangs over the world since Hiroshima."[361]

In Washington, Oppenheimer increasingly relied on Marks, now the Atomic Energy Committee counsel. Marks was at Robert's side as he worked to operate effectively in government. Anne and Herb, struggling to make a life together, were becoming mainstays in the Oppenheimers' lives. If Kitty were running true to form she was growing confessional as she drank, and Anne was learning more than she probably cared to know.

THE FBI RECORDINGS REVEAL KITTY'S continuing hopes of being a more integral part of Robert's public life. When he was invited to dinner with "a flock of brass coming through" Berkeley, Kitty asked if she could go—"I would like to meet General Farrell, I am so fond of him"—but she was rebuffed. Wives were not included, which frustrated Kitty, who felt she was so much more than a "faculty wife." One day Robert called from Washington and reported to Kitty that he was with Richard, that soon Ruth was joining them, and they were going to Martha's Vineyard. Kitty—who had pleaded to join him—now pleaded that he wouldn't go. In another conversation, Kitty offered a problem of her own: her mother had written to say she was lonesome for reasons she was not yet willing to disclose.[362] The FBI tapes make it clear: although he called Kitty frequently, Robert was not interested in the family problems he had heard time and again. No matter how much she wanted to deny it, Kitty was the wife left at home with two small children.

JACK TENNEY WAS A CALIFORNIA state senator and chair of the state's new Committee on Un-American Activities who liked to say, "You can no more coexist with communism than you can coexist with a nest of rattlesnakes."[363] By the late 1940s, with fears of Communist espionage escalating, the Tenney Committee began to issue subpoenas. Frank was on the list. Robert, calling from Washington, said (with a nod to the FBI on the line) that he "wondered what it was all about," then told Kitty he had spoken to Frank and he seemed "not worried." As the Hearings began in California, Robert was on a train from New York to New Jersey, where he was to meet Lewis Strauss at the Institute for Advanced Study in Princeton.

⌐⌐

ROBERT WAS CERTAIN IT WAS a chimera to think the U.S. could contain atomic energy. He had confidence in his formidable powers of persuasion, but was finding people he could not persuade. His conversion to realpolitik was inevitable. If he wanted to continue to have influence in government he must, as Herb Marks had put it, "know things as they are, for his own sake." He, unlike many of the scientists still at Los Alamos, would have to settle for what was possible.

Kitty, whose own reactions were consistently visceral, would have been in complete agreement. She was smart, but without Robert's ethical compunctions; she did not question the morality of building an atomic bomb. She made decisions on what was best for them, and had no problem cutting off a friend who might detract from Robert's success. In fact, in the early Los Alamos years, when it was clear that Army security considered Communism a threat, she was quick to renounce all her past involvement.[364] When Kitty's old friend Steve Nelson, still an entrenched member of the Party, tried to contact them after the war, Kitty slammed the door shut. Nelson never saw them again. Frank, as Robert's much loved brother, was inviolable. Jackie and Frank had left the Party, but not their left-wing views, and they would not betray their friends. Like many of the young activist scientists, Frank had been disappointed in what seemed like Robert's willingness to work with those in government and the military who were "pro-bomb." Still, he would say of his older brother, "he'd been in the Washington scene, he saw that everything was moving—he felt he had to change things from within."[365]

⮑

THE INSTITUTE FOR ADVANCED STUDY was founded in 1930. The intent was to create a world center for intellectual inquiry to "pursue advanced learning in fields of pure science and high scholarship." Built on one square mile of beautifully wooded land just next to the Princeton University campus, the two were separate, but shared close ties. The Institute offered no classes, no exams, no degrees; most of those invited already had advanced degrees from some of the world's most formidable universities. Both setting and idea were idyllic: those invited would be free to think about whatever they wished and, in the community of thinkers, perhaps arrive at altogether new knowledge. (After a visit to the Institute twelve years before, Robert had written to Frank that it was "a madhouse, its solipsistic luminaries shining in separate and helpless desolation."[366]) The place could accommodate 150 visiting members, along with a small number of permanent faculty. Albert Einstein was the most celebrated; he spent the war years there, and would stay for the rest of his life.

In 1946, as Robert continued to put off final decisions about teaching, the Institute's Board of Trustees asked him to be their new director. Robert was known for the wide range of his intellectual pursuits, not only history and literature, but also some of the new social sciences (which many of the mathematicians did not consider to be science at all).

The trustee chosen to ask Robert was Lewis Strauss, who was on the Atomic Energy Commission. A self-made man, Strauss had not gone to college, but had worked his way to Wall Street, where he made millions. Jewish, and from the South—where his name was pronounced "Straws"—he would maintain his Southern drawl. As a protégé of Herbert Hoover, he had managed to get an appointment in the Office of the Navy during the war, and emerged an honorary Rear Admiral. Strauss, who liked to be addressed as "Admiral," understood how bureaucracy could be manipulated. Though Robert didn't realize it, the Admiral was a man to be reckoned with. Like Robert he could be critical and arrogant; but unlike Robert he was also petty and vindictive.

In December, Strauss had flown to Berkeley on business for the Commission; Ernest Lawrence and Robert met his plane. Strauss drew Robert aside and right on the tarmac offered him the directorship of the Institute. Robert played for time. Berkeley felt like home. Still, he was determined to keep trying to influence the nation's atomic energy policies, and that could only be done in Washington. The Princeton position would give him better proximity, and time. He knew now that he was talented as an administrator, and the Institute needed strong management. Finally, Robert decided that if he planned to continue taking part in the fate of the atom, the Institute would be an ideal home base from which to make an even greater impact in his field.

To tempt Kitty, he told her that Strauss had said the gardens were elaborate. Before long, she couldn't wait to get to New Jersey. This time she was sure her life would be different.

Not realizing that Strauss would be insulted by his wavering, Robert continued to delay. At the same time, he was undergoing another full security check for the top secret "Q" clearance required for his appointment as chairman of the General Advisory Committee (GAC) on scientific matters for the Atomic Energy Commission (AEC).

As part of this clearance investigation, FBI agents questioned Robert's colleagues. The chairman of the Berkeley physics department said that Robert was "about as radical as Franklin Delano Roosevelt." Ernest Lawrence, Robert's old pal, said he regarded Dr. Oppenheimer as "a grand person in every way." At Caltech, Linus Pauling told the FBI Robert was "unpredictable because he was volatile, complex and brilliant." For good measure he added that while Oppenheimer "might be an extreme radical," he now seems to "hold the views of the more conservative scientists such as those associated with the Army and Navy." Either Pauling was having fun with the FBI, or he was being sarcastic. Only Richard kept it to the point and curtly reminded the FBI agent that Oppenheimer had been in charge of the Los Alamos Scientific Laboratory.

One of those permitted to read the FBI reports was Lewis Strauss, the most conservative member of the Commission. He was shaken by the extent of Robert's liberal, pre-war politics. But in the end, he came to believe the new investigation had turned up nothing that should prevent Robert from becoming the GAC chairman or the director of the Institute of Advanced Study. The rest of the commissioners agreed. The government granted Robert's "Q" clearance.

On April 5, 1947, an FBI teletype was sent from San Francisco to J. Edgar Hoover, advising that J. Robert Oppenheimer had accepted an important position at Princeton. The agent noted that Robert had returned to Berkeley, and that it was his opinion that "physical surveillance in this area has indicated no association with known communists, and is being discontinued today."[367]

J. Edgar Hoover did not agree.

Richard is an "appreciator of the odd forms the human spirit takes," Robert rediscovers the "sweetness" of physics, and what Kitty does well

"My heart is very full of many many things I want to say," Ruth wrote to Robert on August 24, 1947. "Like you," she went on, "I am grateful to be writing. Like you, I cannot yet quite accept the fact that the monthly visits will not be resumed." The Oppenheimers were spending the end of summer at Perro Caliente before leaving for Princeton and their new life. Ruth was writing in answer to what she called a "weary little letter" from Robert. The correspondence had troubled her, she told him, because of what, at first, she thought was his "sense of panic" about the future. She corrected herself and said, "It was not really panic.'Appalled' was the word you used." Earlier in the summer she had written Robert, saying, "I think of you often there in that marvelous spot, riding the horses, enjoying the country ... Here we miss you badly ... thinking wistfully of your monthly calls."[368]

Robert had found himself in the West. He had built the most important theoretical physics program in the country at Berkeley, had become excited about teaching, had made close friends. He and his brother had challenged the mountains together and gathered their friends at Perro Caliente. It was in the West that he had found Jean, and had lost her. In the West he had been swept away in a tempestuous romance with Kitty, and had married her. It was where his children were born.

In the two years after the war, Robert's connection with Ruth had become more profound. Her love and respect for Richard was not diminished (a close friend would judge Ruth and Richard to be "totally suited for one another"[369]), but a growing intimacy with Robert seemed inevitable, stemming from the remarkable events they had witnessed together and from their mutual interests in each other's fields. Ruth radiated warmth; she would tilt her head when speaking to someone, inclining slightly toward them as if to indicate: tell me more. She had a curious mind; she made few demands; she listened and, at the right moment, offered thoughtful advice or asked the right question.

Robert and Ruth would speak often on the telephone—but rarely from his home or office lines, monitored by the FBI. They consistently worked to find little islands of time together. At the end of August in 1947, Ruth ended a chatty letter, "I am going East ... but only to Detroit. If you should be there (I confess I can't quite imagine why) I am going to APA meetings. My address will be Hotel Statler. Come to us when you can, Robert. The guest house is always and completely yours."[370] Her affection floated between the lines.

Even so, neither Ruth nor Robert had any intention of damaging their marriages. Richard had known Robert for almost twenty years (and was "close and dear to him," as Robert would say many years later) and he knew Ruth's capacity for affection. Richard was, as Jerry Bruner of Harvard (one of those who had a key to the Tolman house in Washington) noted, "A man of wry humor and enormous generosity, an appreciator of the odd forms the human spirit takes."[371] He seemed to understand the nature of his wife's relationship to his younger friend. Kitty, congenitally jealous, could not.

In one letter to Robert, Ruth wrote that she and Richard had just returned from Northern California. With Lillie Margaret, they drove to the Chickering family summer home in the Sierras. "It was interesting after ten years," Ruth wrote, "seeing the huge family of children and grandchildren—such a great clan now, with a most heartening stability and closeness. This way of life which is theirs provides a wonderful cushioning against neurosis and anxiety, in large part, I suppose, by its promise of security against loneliness."[372] Ruth's perception of her cousin Alma's "great clan" as an antidote to loneliness would explain her need to hold close her small family and her circle of friends, especially after the upheaval of war.

⌒

ROBERT AND KITTY CLOSED, BUT didn't sell, the Eagle Hill house. They intended to spend part of their summers in the Bay Area. They went to a series of going away parties, and then arrived in Princeton in the middle of a very hot July.

In 1947, Princeton's population was 25,000. The Institute was situated on 600 acres of rolling meadows and woodlands. Olden Manor, the three-story colonial house set aside for the director, was right in the middle. Kitty and Robert, with six-year-old Peter and three-year-old Toni, had landed in a historic Early American countryside—George Washington had fought the Battle of Princeton there in 1777. The original Olden farmhouse had been built in 1696, a wing added in 1720. Generations of Oldens had added parlors, a music room, a library, a capacious country kitchen and ten bedrooms—eighteen rooms in all. The house was not grand, but pleasant and commodious enough for entertaining. It also came with a full-time live-in cook and groundskeeper. Robert and Kitty were expected to host cocktail parties and frequent dinners for visiting luminaries.

But all too soon, Kitty must have felt she had been banished to the countryside. The town had only one stoplight; Manhattan was about an hour train ride to the north and Washington, a three-and-a-half-hour ride south. Good for Robert, not so for Kitty. The people Robert was seeing to the north and south were the ones she wanted to know. Princeton, it has been said, was a community with character but no soul. Kitty had no interest in becoming part of the social life of this small and stuffy university town.

The Oppenheimers preferred an austere setting. Almost every room had been lined with bookshelves, and Robert had most of them torn out, leaving only one wall in the library. The "pictures" as he tended to call the art he had inherited from his father, were brought out of storage and Van Gogh's *Enclosed Field with Rising Sun* (Saint-Rémy, 1889) took the place of honor over the formal fireplace in the living room. For the dining room he chose a Derain, and a Vuillard for the music room.

Kitty put on her jeans and shirt and started on a large flower garden, enclosed by the crumbling stone remnants of an old barn. There was a paddock for their horses as well, and Topper and Step-up joined Peter's dog Buddy. To the outsiders, a perfect young family had moved in (even if the horses occasionally got loose and trampled the neighbor's garden[373]).

Robert understood Kitty well enough to play to her strengths; his gift-giving was legend and for her birthday not long after their arrival he had a large greenhouse built and attached to the back of the house. It was Robert's statement: she was a botanist. At least one guest was impressed by how seriously she took this work; others dismissed her passion for plants as pretentious. Kitty's particular interest was orchids; for birthdays or holidays Robert had exotic varieties shipped to her from the Big Island of Hawaii.

FOR ROBERT, THE INSTITUTE FOR Advanced Study was the base from which he launched the rest of his life, and where he would pick up where he had left off in

Berkeley. The Institute became one of the centers where new boundaries of theoretical physics would be set. Robert's plan was to integrate other disciplines—literature, history, psychology—with the sciences. For Kitty, the Institute was simply a stage from which to begin yet again, a new and dynamic life.

Robert's office in Fuld Hall, the Institute's main building, was an easy quarter of a mile from the house. Across a grassy field, Kitty had a clear view of the hall. On any given day she might see Albert Einstein walking to or from his corner office, or Robert heading for his, which looked out on woods and meadows.

But it was not all bucolic. Stationed just outside of Robert's office was a stolid, no-nonsense safe filled with classified documents, with it a military guard. Like an elephant in the room, the safe was a constant reminder that Robert was chairman of the General Advisory Committee of the Atomic Energy Commission—the group that advised the commission and the government on scientific and technical matters. The trustees encouraged Robert's participation in government work, but before many months had passed, Rear Admiral Strauss would be having serious doubts about his director.

⁓

BACK IN PASADENA, THE TOLMANS continued to gather with friends including Stewart Harrison, who had remarried and, as a physician, treated various Caltech faculty members including Linus Pauling, the Tolmans, and friend Ruth Valentine. Nat came and went; Ruth Benedict and Val too. The war had worn them all. Bob Bacher had, with Robert's strong recommendation, taken his position at Caltech, and he and his wife Jean quickly became part of the Tolman circle.

"For a decade after the war," wrote close friend Jerry Bruner, now at Harvard, "Ruth Tolman played an incomparable role in holding together her friends—psychologists, psychoanalysts and physicists from all over the world. She did so whether at her home in Pasadena, or whether visiting in Berkeley, in Cambridge, in Princeton at the Oppenheimers', wherever." She was, he wrote, "the perfect confidante, a wise woman. It is difficult for me to separate what is personal from what is 'profession' or intellectual about Ruth. And that, of course, was part of her genius."[374] Robert may have been Ruth's favorite correspondent, but he was far from her only one.

RICHARD NOW MOVED LIKE AN old man, his once handsome face weighted with accumulated weariness. Still there were moments of surprise and delight. On July 23, 1948, Ruth and Richard boarded the 12,000-ton British cruiser HMS *Sheffield,* docked at the U.S. Naval Base on Terminal Island in Long Beach. In a ceremony marked by the pomp at which the British excel, Vice Admiral Sir William Tennant presented Richard with the Order of the British Empire from a grateful King of England. The whimsical Richard, who always referred to himself as "of the yeomanry not the gentry,"[375] accepted the King's honor with his usual grace. Though his part in making the infernal bomb had sometimes troubled his Quaker ethos.

⤴

WITHOUT INFLUENCE FROM ROBERT, THE University of Minnesota offered Frank a position on the faculty of the physics department at the University of Minnesota in 1947. He would be researching the high-altitude cosmic rays that continually bombard the earth. The Minnesota group, including a friend from Los Alamos and Berkeley days, Ed Lofgren (one of "Lawrence's boys"), began building cloud chambers, detectors encased in spheres and packed with sensors to load on huge helium balloons that could reach high into the atmosphere. Ernest Lawrence had clapped Frank on the back and told him he could always come back to Berkeley.

Frank was making discoveries and his group was having an exhilarating time, according to Lofgren[376], on U.S. Navy ships, releasing the balloons in different parts of the world and then racing to retrieve them. Sometimes this involved slashing their way through jungle terrain, Indiana-Jones style. (And losing them, which was always "heartbreaking.") Frank was teaching, which made him happy. Then, in July of 1947, the *Washington Times-Herald* ran a front page headline trumpeting: "U.S. Atom Scientist's Brother Exposed as Communist." Frank was accused of being a card-carrying Party member. The dean at Minnesota told Frank he would have to deny the charges. He did. Emphatically. With the Minnesota administration tugging at him, he had a lawyer draw up a statement with what was becoming standard phrasing: "I am not now nor have I ever been a member of the Communist party."[377] It was only a matter of time before Frank would be called before a committee that would require him to swear to tell the whole truth, and he would admit he had lied.

Two years later, trouble was also on Robert's horizon. His chairmanship of the General Advisory Committee (the GAC) was about to become more complicated, thanks in part to Lawrence and Teller's insistence that the U.S. government should focus on the "Super." Lawrence sought lucrative government contracts for ever-bigger laboratories. Soon Lawrence and Teller were on their way to Washington to promote a new generation of nuclear weapons. To a man, the scientific advisors on the GAC believed this to be a formula for genocide. As long as the U.S. had a monopoly on atomic weaponry, they agreed that there was no reason to plunge ahead with expensive bigger bombs.[378]

When Kitty arrived at Princeton the summer of 1947, she knew one person: Pat Sherr, who at Los Alamos had cared for Toni for the months when Kitty had escaped to her parents' home. After the war, Pat's husband had rejoined the Princeton physics faculty. Kitty had asked Pat to recommend a school for Peter, and soon after their arrival that hot summer, she invited the Sherrs to Olden Manor for a picnic. It had been two years since Los Alamos, and Pat was eager to see Toni. After a time a maid came out, carrying a sleepy little girl, who crawled into her father's lap and rested her face against his chest. Pat gave herself credit for having nurtured this pretty little girl; even so, she had a lingering feeling that she had been badly used.[379]

For the next five years, though, Pat and Kitty maintained a peculiar friendship, and like others before her, Pat found herself in the uncomfortable position of bearing witness to the intricacies of the Oppenheimer marriage. According to Pat, Kitty repeated the patterns she had established at Los Alamos, where she would "latch on to someone, bare her soul and I mean bear her soul, tell you absolutely everything . . . about herself, about her sex life with him, about anything." Kitty would, Pat recounted, later disparage whatever friend she had divulged too much to, publicly attempting to discredit her. In an effort to be somewhat even-handed about the director's wife, Pat said, of Kitty's social abilities: "She was outwardly gay and exuded some warmth . . . I think the general appearance was one of ease with people and warmth."[380]

Kitty's parenting skills are less well documented. In 1947, *Life* magazine ran a cover story on Robert and included photographs of him reading a bedtime story to the children. The dog is curled at his feet, Kitty watches on lovingly. A happy family. And a few standard stories are repeated in most of the articles and books about Robert: how Kitty and the children liked to search the lawn for four-leaf clovers for good luck, how Toni carried tea in a delicate French china cup to the horses. How Kitty and Peter had made what he called a "gimmick," a square board with lights, buzzers, fuses and switches, and a tangle of wiring. Peter was to play with it for two years. (And how once, when Robert sat down to play with it, Peter had asked his mother if it was okay to let his daddy work with the gimmick.)[381] But more often, the children were pushed to the background, turned over to a maid. When Peter was six or seven, Kitty's relationship with him changed dramatically. He seemed to disappoint his mother and she reacted by nagging and goading him—and they fought. According to several who were close to the family in those years, Kitty made life miserable for Peter, and Robert did not come to his son's defense.[382] If Kitty bore little resemblance to the gentle, very proper Ella Oppenheimer, Robert also never offered the unabashed affection and attention that Julius lavished on his sons. Robert's friends had declared his parents "well suited" to each other, but few would say that about Robert and Kitty.[383]

⤳

ON THE NIGHT OF AUGUST 14, a Saturday, Val was helping Ruth prepare for a dinner party at the Tolmans. Suddenly, Richard began to suffer violent symptoms. "Cheyne-Stokes breathing; muscle spasms and gross motor activity," Val would write Robert, at Ruth's request. Stewart Harrison came at once and had Richard admitted to the hospital. Val explained, "By 3 o'clock Sunday morning [Richard] had quieted ... Now [he] seems to be reasonably comfortable."[384] The stroke was serious. In the morning, Val said, Richard had recognized Ruth and Stewart, but wasn't able to speak.

Val wrote: "Ruth, of course, is superb. Last night our united efforts succeeded in getting her to be 'sensible' so Charlie and Sigrid brought her home about 11:30, she took a Seconal and got a good 6 hours sleep. I am either with her at the hospital or here doing chores for her and all the good friends are being helpful and supporting." Val signed off, "I have cancelled my plans and am standing by."[385] She did not leave to meet Ruth Benedict in New York, as planned.

For two weeks after his stroke, Ruth stayed by Richard's side. He died on September 5. Ruth was stunned—inconsolable.

VAL'S LETTER WOULD HAVE ARRIVED just before Robert had to leave for conferences in Paris, Copenhagen, London and Brussels; he was in Belgium lecturing on electron theory when Richard died. Val found herself in a quandary; she had been ready to return to New York and her life with Benedict, but her oldest friend needed her. The day after Richard's death, Val called on Benedict's sister Margery in her Pasadena home. Margery wondered how Val would resolve her conflict between her lover and her best friend, and worried that her "inordinate sense of duty might make her feel she should stay with Ruth." In fact, while Val was close to Ruth Tolman, their relationship did not go beyond that. Ruth simply accepted Val's lesbian relationships, but she knew that neither herself nor Val "would be happy in such a constant and intimate relationship" with one another. Though they would remain close friends, see each other often, and continue to work together, Ruth and Val's friendship required space."[386]

SIX DAYS LATER, ON SEPTEMBER 12, Ruth Benedict, Val's partner, had a heart attack in New York. Found in Benedict's purse at the time was Margery's letter reporting that Val had decided to return to "the old gal—the famous anthropologist."[387] Benedict now needed her even more. Val boarded a train for New York, and was with her in her last hours.

26

Ruth learns to live a different life and Robert hopes they can have time togeth-

er

"How am I?" Ruth wrote in answer to a letter of sympathy from one of her colleagues, "Only part of me seems to be here. This would be inevitable, I think, after 24 years of such a close relationship as Richard and I have had and richness in talking about everything together. I shall have to learn to live this different life. And I am inexpressibly grateful to have a job that needs doing and that is exigent and that provides some kind of continuity with the past."[388]

Robert's return to Europe was his first in almost twenty years. The war had changed not only the landscape, but the mindset. Robert would write Frank that at the important centers of physics where both had studied, the scientists said they felt somewhat out of things. Robert concluded, "It is in America largely that it will be decided what manner of world we are to live in."[389]

Except that in America, the world of physics was being jolted by the House Un-American Activities Committee—HUAC—which was laying waste to political liberals and left-wingers who had any connection with the Communist Party. Frank and Jackie were at risk. Even though *Time* magazine splashed Robert's image on their November 1948 issue and called him "an authentic American Hero," he too was at risk. The main purpose of the letter Robert wrote to Frank from Europe was to urge him to seek "the comfort, the strength and the advice of a good lawyer" for the upcoming committee interrogation. He recommended Herb Marks.

When Robert returned, he paused in Princeton before heading west. He was the one person who would understand the magnitude of Ruth's loss and could comfort her. She wrote to him after the visit, "The precious times with you last week and the week before keep going through my mind, over and over, making me thankful but wistful, wishing for more. I was grateful for them, Dear, and as you knew, hungry for them, too." In response, Robert wrote, "Ruth, dear heart, even if there were not a few practical things, I should want to write in celebration of the good day we had together which meant so very much to me. I knew that I should find you full of courage and wisdom, but it is one thing to know it, and another to be so close. I hope our excursion to the sea did not leave any of our friends cross, either with you or with me. It seemed to me so wonderful."[390]

In the same letter, he returned to her the first chapter of a textbook Richard had been working on at the time of his death. Wanting to keep Richard's memory alive, Ruth had asked Robert to read the manuscript to see if it could be published. Robert saw that it was only an introduction to what Richard had planned to write. He told Ruth, very gently, why it could not be.

After another trip to Berkeley, he went south to see Ruth again. Robert had too many friends and colleagues in Pasadena to keep his visit a secret, so he and Ruth agreed on a subterfuge to be able to spend a day together. She wrote, "How would it be if I said you had to see someone at UCLA and we'd be away for the day, but back for a party at night? Let's think about this."[391]

Soon after Robert became the director of the Institute, Ruth had suggested he include psychology in the scholarly mix. To give himself room to maneuver, Robert had requested a "Director's Fund" to bring in visiting fellows from new disciplines. Robert established the psychology advisory committee including Ruth and her brother-law Edward, along with Jerry Bruner and Ed Boring, Ruth's good friends from wartime Washington. The group would meet once or twice a year at Princeton.

Ruth and Robert also began to arrange to meet in other cities at other times, usually around conferences. "If you are coming East and we must be in Washington near to the same time," he would write, "we just hope that we can have a little time together."[392] It was a refrain that was to be repeated, time and again, in the years to come, as they tried to carve "a little time together" out of their increasingly complicated lives. Another time, Ruth would write in answer to Robert's suggestion they meet the following weekend, that they could go to the sea together "for the day, until the afternoon." She was also planning a dinner party for him and a number of their physicist friends, and asked him, "Anybody else you think would be fun to see?" She ended the letter telling him about a trip with Val: "We saw the long stretch of beach where the sandpipers and gulls played. Oh Robert, Robert. Soon I shall see you. You and I both know how it will be."[393]

⤳

THE COCKTAIL HOUR WAS A ritual for the Oppenheimers, as it was for many of this hard-working generation: Manhattans, Old Fashioneds and Highballs—a mix of whisky and ginger ale. In Berkeley, Kitty had remarked that their liquor bill was often larger than their food bill. Robert was known for his martinis—cold, a hint of vermouth, and powerful. At Olden Manor the liquor cabinet was well stocked, Robert was able to pace his drinking, Kitty was not. Nor did Robert drink during the day. It was also the age of smoking. Robert was seldom without a cigarette—his students used to joke about the day when he would confuse his omnipresent cigarette with the chalk he was using to write on the blackboard.

ROBERT, NOW DETERMINED TO INTRODUCE a strong humanities strain to the Institute, brought in poet and soon-to-be Nobel Laureate T. S. Eliot, historian Arnold Toynbee, theologian Reinhold Niebuhr, social philosopher Isaiah Berlin, among others. For Kitty, an even more impressive group that showed up at the Manor was the Washington Establishment: James Conant was president of Harvard, David Lilienthal was chairman of the Atomic Energy Commission, and Vannevar Bush, president of the Carnegie Institution. George Kennan, a diplomat at the State Department, would become Robert's close friend. Though Kitty seldom went to Washington with Robert, or to New York when it involved government business, he often asked her opinions and sometimes took her advice.

To entertain so many important guests, Kitty requested that the Institute employ a French couple to prepare meals, hoping to raise the culinary level of the Manor. Both Oppenheimers loved good food (though some guests complained there was never enough of it), and they worked together on recipes. In the spring Kitty filled the house with masses of daffodils; in the summer she planned picnics with champagne and caviar. In all seasons she lavished the house with orchids from her greenhouse. Even when she had had too much to drink, she could pull herself together and be a charming, witty, if acerbic, hostess.

Kitty was thirty-nine in 1949 and Robert, forty-five. Their children—Peter, eight, and Toni, four—seemed always on the periphery.[394]

⤳

ON JUNE 7, 1949, ROBERT testified before HUAC about potential spying at Berkeley's Radiation Lab. He was told it was a closed session and, in a stunning display of naivete, he believed that meant anything he said would be held in confidence. He talked freely about former graduate students and his friends. He said one had "committed an incredible indiscretion," another he called a "dangerous man and quite red."[395] The names Robert mentioned, including once good friend Bernard Peters, quickly showed up in the newspapers. Just as quickly, the men lost their teaching positions. Some of the physicists Robert most admired, including Hans Bethe, were angry. And Frank was furious with his brother.

A week after Robert's ignominious appearance, Frank and Jackie were called to testify under oath. The couple decided they would have to admit they had been members of the Communist Party USA but unlike Robert, they would refuse to name others. Frank had given the dean at the University of Minnesota a letter of resignation. The dean assured him that it would not be accepted. But when it became obvious that Frank had lied to the university when he'd denied being a Communist, his resignation was accepted.

At Berkeley, Lawrence let it be known that Frank wasn't welcome back. As was the case for the graduate students Robert had named, there was no place in America where Frank could teach physics or do research. What stung him most was that, after helping him get counsel, Robert had backed away, perhaps because he was now worried about his own fate. For the FBI's Hoover, it was one Oppenheimer brother down, one to go.

AFTER THE BROTHERS' BRUISING APPEARANCES before the House committee, Katherine Page wrote to Robert: "I wish you were on the Pecos. I want to talk with you about so many things." She went on to list them in her usual blunt way. "How can I reach Frank?" she wanted to know, then went on reveal that when Frank "found that he was not going to be at Perro Caliente, I tried to persuade him to buy the Allen place ... He looked at it and loved it but decided he couldn't bear to be so near Perro Caliente."[396] After the war, when the ranch was finally offered for sale, Robert had bought Perro Caliente for himself and inflicted another cut in the bond with his brother. Did Robert remember Proust's words which had triggered his epiphany on Corsica, that the "indifference to the sufferings one causes ... is the terrible and permanent form of cruelty"?

When Frank was offered positions to teach abroad, the State Department refused to issue him a passport. Finally, Frank and Jackie moved to the 800-acre ranch they had bought in the Blanco Basin in Colorado as their own summer retreat, and planned to work it as a cattle ranch. The pair knew nothing about raising cattle, of surviving the deep cold and snow of a Colorado winter, or how they could rear two young children in pioneering conditions twenty miles from the nearest town. But Jackie had never shied away from hard work and all his life Frank had welcomed an adventure. He sold one of the Van Goghs he had inherited from Julius for $40,000, and settled in for years of cattle ranching.[397] Their father's dream of America had become ugly and the Oppenheimer brothers had become object lessons in the imperfections of democracy.

⤴

IN JUNE, ROBERT WAS CALLED to Capitol Hill again, this time to testify in what should have been a routine matter before the Congressional Joint Committee on Atomic Energy. The Atomic Energy Commission had, as a goodwill gesture, suggested that the U.S. offer friendly foreign countries small amounts of radioisotopes to be used for basic research. The General Advisory Committee had agreed that the isotopes posed no threat. One of the four Atomic Energy commissioners insisted the isotopes *could* have a military application. Robert, seeming to forget he was in Washington, responded in the voice laced with sarcasm he usually reserved for students: "You can use a bottle of beer for atomic energy." He went on, comparing isotopes to vitamins and drawing laughter, making a fool of the dissenting commissioner.

That dissenting commissioner was Admiral Lewis Strauss. David Lilienthal noticed that a look of hatred came over his face.[398] The Admiral was not a man who would tolerate being humiliated.

⤴

VAL HAD MOVED BACK TO Pasadena and—her house not immediately available– had moved in with Ruth. By the spring after the deaths of Richard and Benedict, Ruth would write Robert: "Val seems better, with the bad days less frequent and more energy and enterprise than she had for a time. She is settled in her own house, has guests often, comes over here often, and we do many things together when there is time. She no longer tries to run me, though, and is generous and helpful without being demanding. I think that as more time has passed our relationship has become just about right."[399]

WITH RICHARD GONE, RUTH CONCENTRATED on her work. Her articles on criminal psychology and on women psychologists, written during the war, had appeared in a number of professional journals. At one point, Ruth and Val persuaded Linus Pauling and others at Caltech to include the scientific basis of psychoanalyis as a topic in their lecture series[400]. Ruth had spent many hours with Richard and Robert discussing human behavior as a science; comparing the theoretical and the experimental physicists to psychiatrist and the psychologist seemed an obvious step.

This new interest—suggested by her intimacy with physics and its "rigor and austerity and depth"—stimulated her to focus on the differences in language used by psychologists and psychiatrists. With colleague Harry Grayson, a psychiatrist at the VA's Neuropsychiatric Hospital in Los Angeles, she studied the hospital's staff and intern psychologists as well as its resident psychiatrists, analyzing the language used in their reports on their patients. Ruth and Grayson discovered that while psychologists and psychiatrists may have used the same terms, they did not define them the same way.

One example: *aggressive*. The psychologists: *An attitudinal set which is characterized by readiness to react to stimulation with destructive behavior, directed toward self, objects, and/or other persons.* The psychiatrists: *A destructive drive, primarily id in its origin.*[401]

The psychologists' penchant for verbosity, for abstraction and ambiguous definitions, was the result of their academic training, the researchers decided. Ruth hoped that by clarifying the language of observation, making the descriptions more precise and thus the perceptions of clinical data more reliable, results would be more constant, more *scientific.* Later, when it became clear that psychology as a science based on proven theories had far to go, she would admit that perhaps she had "wanted too clear and orderly and rich a body of theory to emerge."[402]

At Cambridge, Robert had once found his way into the right science clubs in his quest to move into the top ranks in physics. Ruth now continued her climb into the upper echelons of her profession. She would become president of the Western Psychological Association and was active in the national American Psychological Association. She said yes to the Governor's Committee on Mental Health. For the national office of the Veterans Administration she traveled to San Diego to inspect a new site for an additional Mental Hygiene Clinic. At the clinic on Broadway in Los Angeles, she worked with Ed Pye, who would always remember her as a wonderful friend to the staff. He was fond of her, he said, "emotionally and professionally." Most of her colleagues felt the same way.[403]

Ruth's letters to Robert were filled with her research, her work on the committee to bring psychologists to the Institute, and reports of their old mutual friends who were coming to Pasadena. Always she added some personal notes: that she was sending him a gift of wine for his birthday and that she had "come to have respect for expendable gifts." That she had "rented the little guest house to a geneticist . . . whom I have seen only twice since he has moved in . . . It means that there is someone on the premises and that I do not have the guilt I mentioned at occupying so many square feet all by myself."[404]

"These last few weeks I have been in a torrent of conflict," Ruth wrote. The psychology department at the University of Michigan had written asking her to consider several faculty positions. "I have needed terribly your help over these days of trying to decide. It is ironic to say that I have missed Richard's wisdom just excruciatingly, for if he were here there could be no such conflict and no such invitation. And just the occurrence of the issue, of course, has made so sharp and vivid my present unwanted 'freedom' and rudderlessness." Ruth said the thought of leaving Pasadena filled her with sadness. She ended with, "Remember how we have always, both of us, been miserable when we had to look more than a week ahead?"[405]

They did, though, have to think ahead.

The growing intensity of their relationship is captured in the few letters from Ruth saved by Robert. "I look back on your wonderful week here with all my heart grateful, Dear. It was unforgettable. I'd give great rewards even for another day. In the meantime, you know the love and tenderness I send."[406]

꙳

ON AUGUST 29, 1949, THE Soviets exploded an atomic bomb in Kazakhstan; nine days later an American reconnaissance plane confirmed it had been a nuclear explosion. President Truman was staggered; he did not want to believe it, not even when the Defense Department brought advisors, including Robert, who verified that it was a close copy of the bomb developed at Los Alamos. Truman took three more days before he admitted to the American people that the U.S. had lost its monopoly on atomic power—as the scientists had tried to convince him it would. In *Time* magazine, Oppenheimer warned that the U.S. monopoly of the science was "like a cake of ice melting in the sun."

The Oppenheimers discover the Virgin Islands, Robert comforts Ruth, and Kitty and Robert have a miserable Christmas

In the early 1950s, after the Soviets tested their own atomic bomb and destroyed the monopoly America thought it had, the scene was set: the race for bigger bombs was on and the anti-Communists in the U.S. were out in force, with Wisconsin Senator Joe McCarthy leading the pack.[407]

The House Un-American Activities Committee (HUAC) began unearthing potential spies everywhere—in universities, Hollywood, the State Department, even in the Army. Anyone who had anything in their pasts suggesting sympathy to Communism was suspect. In the chaos, other powerful people used the opportunity to destroy their own adversaries.

After Joe-1, the "Super bomb" was promoted as insuring American atomic superiority. At the end of January 1950, President Truman announced that the U.S. would pursue a crash program for the Super. The nuclear arms race began. Teller, Lawrence and a powerful combination of military brass and politicians would not forgive Robert for opposing them and even began to question his loyalty. Admiral Strauss began scrutinizing Robert's well-worn FBI record.

⟿

"IN THE EARLY '50S, UNDER Robert Oppenheimer, the Institute had become the finishing school for the best and the brightest young theorists," said Nobel Laureate Murray Gell-Mann, then one of those elite young theorists. One of the great men of physics, Hans Bethe, was to write, "Even more than Berkeley in the 1930s, the Princeton Institute became the centre for physics. Nearly everybody who was anybody passed through its stimulating atmosphere."[408]

Seventeen years into their marriage, physics remained the part of Robert's life that Kitty could not share. Nor could she be part of, or understand, the deepening nature of her husband's friendship with Ruth. Most certainly she sensed it; she always resented any other woman whose company Robert enjoyed. According to Jerry Bruner, Ruth seemed easy and comfortable around Kitty and had no intention of making Robert's home life any more difficult that it obviously already was. What Robert did share with his wife was the convoluted, and sometimes contentious, role he played in government. Kitty was positive that she was his greatest advocate; it gave her a sense of purpose and power—a chance to show the steel in her character.

THE INSTITUTE WAS SIXTY MILES from Kitty's parents' home in Riegelsville, Pennsyvania, near enough for frequent visits. Kitty knew her mother was lonely and wanted to become part of her daughter's family life. After all, Kitty had run for home each time she had found herself unable to cope, and her parents had always accepted her. It was not unreasonable to expect it was time for their daughter to open her life to them.

There is a photograph of Kitty's parents sitting on the terrace at Olden Manor, her father staunch in coat and tie, looking uncomfortable. Chances are the Puenings didn't see their daughter and grandchildren often. Within the decade, Kitty and her mother would become estranged. While the Puenings would have been encouraged by their daughter's marriage to an accomplished and famous man whom she worshipped (though it might have been more to their liking had he not been a Jew) and by their two young grandchildren and the fine house at Princeton, they might also have wondered if Kitty would someday turn up on their doorstep again.

Soon after the war, Kaethe and Franz returned to Germany to visit family members; they saw the terrible toll the war had taken and mourned the deaths of Kaethe's sister by suicide, and of several nephews on the Eastern Front. Kaethe's cousin and one-time suitor, Field Marshal Keitel, had been found guilty at the Nuremberg trials and hanged as a war criminal in 1946.

∽

THE FOUR OPPENHEIMERS SPENT PART of the summer of 1950 at Perro Caliente, playing poker and searching for four-leaf clovers, a favorite pastime of Kitty's, as the magazines pointed out. Kitty began to paint watercolors. Peter was nine and Toni six, both now old enough to ride. Ruth visited, and later sent a note thanking them for "our sweet visits." But the era of high spirits had evaporated. Kitty was now troubled with colitis, and Robert was distracted by nearby Los Alamos, where the H-bomb was underway. And Frank—always so lively and interested in everything—no longer felt welcome.

Even though the raw truths of marriage and politics and circumstances pulled them apart, Robert and Frank longed for their old camaraderie, for the closeness that had been an important part of their younger and more innocent lives. In the early 1950s, Robert began taking another personal trip each year to Colorado. The brothers were working on making amends, but there remained some roadblocks. Frank believed he had become a cattle rancher; Robert was certain his brother was a physicist, and needed to be at a university. Frank believed that Robert had been seduced by the power and glamour of Washington. But it was a given that the affection between the two had not eroded completely.

∽

IN THE SPRING OF 1952, the FBI asked to interview Kitty. Robert insisted on being there, probably to protect both of them from her acid tongue and perhaps to make sure their stories of certain incidents were the same. For two days in March, and another two in April, the agents asked Kitty the same questions she had been asked before. She gave all the same answers. About Joe Dallet, about her membership in the Communist Party, how she had given up the Party but not all of her old friends, at least not right away. It was a rehearsal and she was proving to have talent as a witness.

That spring eight-year-old Toni came down with what doctors said was a brush with polio, and suggested she be taken to a warm climate. The family flew to the West Indies and rented a seventy-two-foot ketch. Robert recovered his old pleasure in sailing. Kitty, who prided herself in her proficiency in almost everything, soon was taking the helm and acting as navigator. Toni recovered quickly. Now, part of each summer would be spent sailing the warm waters of the Caribbean. Eventually the family built a beach house on a strip of white sand on tiny St. John in the Virgin Islands.

∽

ON THE EVENING OF SEPTEMBER 5, 1952, having left Robert in New York, Ruth returned to Washington and promptly wrote: "A line before the plane goes

West to thank you again for the sweet times together," adding, "The good lunch and dinner, the tiny breakfast, the brief calls with the familiar and reassuring sounds on the other end. Thank you for it all, Dear. It was great good luck. I shall always remember the two magic chairs on the dock with the water and the lights and the planes swooping around overhead. I suppose you realized what I did not have to mention—that it was the anniversary—four years—of Richard's death, and the memories of those dreadful days of 1948, and then of many earlier sweet ones were very overwhelming to me. I feel very grateful that I could be with you that night. My love Robert, and again my thanks. Ruth"[409]

After four years, the pain of Richard's death was still vivid. Ruth continued to need Robert's comfort and Robert, who had also loved Richard, could understand.

ONE OF THE FIRST PSYCHOLOGISTS INVITED to the Institute was Harvard's George Miller, who worked on the linguistic side of decision theory. Robert thought Miller a good match for Johnny Von Neumann, the Institute's mathematical genius, who was delving into psychological issues in his own work. Ruth knew Edward Tolman had been invited to the Institute. He was leading the fight against a new "loyalty oath" at Berkeley which essentially required all employees to swear that they did not belong to the Communist Party. The California State Supreme Court eventually ruled for Tolman and the professors who had refused to sign the oath. After that was resolved, Edward could go to the Institute.

In February of 1953, the members of the Psychology Committee were meeting at the Institute, and were to have dinner and drinks at Olden Manor. Robert was in Washington, standing by as a possible witness in the perjury trial of one of his former graduate students at Berkeley, Joe Weinberg. (Like Frank, Joe had been dismissed from the University of Minnesota two years before, another HUAC victim.) Kitty was in Washington with Robert. It was obvious to their friends that no matter how difficult she could be, Robert had come to depend on her in the turmoil created by a frightened and irrational nation.

When the trial ran late, Robert sent a message to the psychologists waiting for him to say he was sorry, and told them to make themselves at home and have a drink. He wrote another memo to Ruth, explaining his delay and saying, "I have, as you know, no choice; but it breaks my heart to be away. Please be, as you so often have, a pinch hit hostess, and have people over to the house for cocktails. Jerry knows where we keep things, and I hope he will tend bar."[410]

On the plane back to California Ruth wrote, careful to include "you both" in the context: "Your sweet, warm hospitality lingers with me happily . . . if [only] you both could have been completely untroubled by all the miseries of subpoenas and the like. It was especially generous of you both to make the visit so warm and good at a time when you felt so worn and worried and frazzled." Robert had confided to her his growing concern that he was being drawn into the vortex that had already consumed Frank. He must have written that he wished she were closer, because Ruth answered: "I too wish that you needed my advice and often I wish I had a book in my guts so that I could ask to work at the Institute with all the incoming hordes of psychologists." As always, she signed it "Robert, my love, Dear."[411]

IN HER APRIL LETTERS, RUTH SEEMED unusually stressed. She complained, something she rarely did, about being tired. She had some "frightfully busy weeks ahead ... with a couple of other papers to prepare and give and one oral examination for the Board of Examiners to arrange for and conduct. I wish it were the end of June, with all this strenuousness over."[412] She nudged him, again, to send his suggestions on the draft of the President's address she was to deliver at the Western Psychology Association conference in June.

Ruth wanted to talk about psychology as both a "pure" and an "applied" science, describing how the theoretician and the practitioner should work together. Since she was comparing physics and psychology, she had asked both Charlie Lauritsen and Robert to read her speech. It is easy to see Robert's hand in it. She quotes one "well-known theoretical physicist," describing a theory as "a picture of the universe that opens up all kinds of new possibilities, just as Freud did in psychology with his theory of the unconscious." It was a serious paper, carefully researched and thought-provoking. And it was a great success; a few months later, it was published in *American Psychologist*.[413]

ON JULY 3, 1953, ADMIRAL Strauss again became the chairman of the Atomic Energy Commission. He had been in the office only a short time when he asked Hoover to send him the latest FBI file on Oppenheimer. A friend of Herb Marks who was with the Commission called to say, "You'd better tell your friend Oppie to batten down the hatches and prepare for some stormy weather."[414]

That same summer, a few weeks after Ruth's success in Seattle, she suffered a heart attack. As she was recuperating, she was struck by another. She was in the hospital in mid-August when all four Oppenheimers returned from a six-week trip to Brazil where Robert had delivered a series of lectures. He wanted to leave at once to be with Ruth, but Lillie sent a telegram asking him to wait. No visitors were allowed, she said, and they didn't know how long it would be before she was well enough to go home.

Charlie Lauritsen—knowing how much Ruth meant to Robert, wrote to him: "Since I am fairly sure that she cannot write you, I thought that I would bring you up to date. By now you know she continued to have a good deal of pain but in the whole she seemed to be improving slowly. Then about two weeks ago she had a second attack. Her doctor was not too alarmed about it, but in my opinion the second attack was considerably more severe than the first. She will certainly remain in the hospital for several weeks more. She has been limited to one 15-minute visit a day . . . she is certainly much more reconciled and willing to accept the consequences of her condition. Unfortunately, I am afraid that this is to a large extent due to the fact that she is much more tired now."[415]

By August 21, Ruth was writing her warm and considerate letters again. To Robert, she wrote: "It was so wonderful to hear your voice yesterday, sounding so near and warm, not only thermally. I got to thinking later, though, that if you are so pressed and busy . . . you ought not to try to crowd in a trip West unless there are other things you have to do here besides seeing me. I don't need to tell you how much I love to have you here (or in Berkeley if I am there). But I also feel a great desire to protect you against doing too much and adding things to your crowded life unless they are really essential. I have made excellent progress . . . though this second coronary was rather worse than the first, both clinically and in severity of pain. But now all the clinical findings are good. I'm soft from so many weeks in bed . . . but I want to reassure you completely, Robert dear, so that no anxiety about my health will influence you to do anything that is strenuous for you. Always my love to you, and to the family."[416]

BY FALL, RUTH WAS GAINING strength, but Robert's calendar had no room for a trip West. He was to deliver the influential BBC Reith lectures in England that November, four talks on the impact of quantum and atomic theory on society, to be broadcast to millions of people around the world. He and Kitty went to London for three weeks, then to Copenhagen for three days to visit Bohr, and finally to Paris to have dinner with Haakon Chavalier and his new wife at their apartment at the foot of Sacre-Coeur. It had been three years since the friends had seen each other; the meeting was, Chevalier would report, as warm as ever, and he opened a bottle of champagne so they could make a series of toasts: "to the health and well-being of all of us, to our long friendship, to the future." Kitty suggested she and Robert sign their names on the cork, as a remembrance. So ended what Chevalier would remember as "a happy reunion and for me a rather fabulous one."[417] He made no comment when Robert indicated, as he said good-bye, that he thought the coming months would be stormy.

Strauss had inserted himself into the happy reunion by ensuring someone from the American Embassy would copy all the phone calls the Oppenheimers made from their room in the elegant George V Hotel, and that Robert would be followed wherever he went. The agents reported that the couple had seen Chevalier, whom French intelligence had on a watch list, suspected of being a Soviet agent.[418]

The two old friends from Berkeley had managed to tangle each other in a Gordian knot so complicated it would become impossible to know which had done the most damage to the other.

ROBERT DIDN'T KNOW THAT HE now had yet another enemy—a former bomber pilot and top Yale Law School graduate named William Borden had become obsessed by national security. He saw rocket-powered nuclear warheads as the weapons of the future, and opposed anyone who could not see the necessity for a hydrogen bomb. As executive director of the Congressional Joint Committee on Atomic Energy, Borden had access to the Atomic Energy Commission's security files. His reading of Robert's file convinced him that the Father of the Atomic bomb could be an espionage agent. Having a top security clearance himself, Borden used his editing talents to selectively reorganize the voluminous files, presenting all the old information in new and dramatic form.[419] He wrote a letter to J. Edgar Hoover about his findings. And while Hoover knew there was nothing new in the letter except Robert's skepticism about nuclear-powered aircraft and hydrogen bombs, he had to send it to President Eisenhower and forwarded a copy to Admiral Strauss, who had become Chairman of the AEC in July. Eisenhower told his press secretary, "We have got to handle this so that all of our scientists are not made out to be Reds. That goddam McCarthy is just likely to try such a thing." With that the president ordered a "blank wall" placed between Oppenheimer and all classified materials.[420]

Borden had provided the Admiral with his next move.

⟿

KITTY AND ROBERT RETURNED FROM Paris on December 13th. The next day Strauss called him to say it "might be a good idea" to come see him in Washington, D.C. Oppenheimer appeared a week later at 3 P.M. Waiting with Strauss was Kenneth Nichols, a former aide to General Groves, and now general manager of the Atomic Energy Commission. Strauss wasted no time. Robert needed to know

that the Commission had "a very difficult problem" relating to his top-secret security clearance. In April, President Eisenhower had issued an executive order for
anyone whose files contained any derogatory information. Strauss built to the big
news: a former government official had questioned Robert's security clearance
and President Eisenhower had ordered an investigation. Strauss went on, there
was going to be a "review," which meant an immediate suspension of his security clearance.[421] Robert listened, quietly asked pertinent questions. Nichols took
notes. Strauss continued, the Commission had prepared a draft of the charges
against Robert, but it had not yet been signed. He could read the charges right
there, right then, but he could not take the draft with him. Robert noted that it
was the same mix of charges brought before, some true but others clearly skewed
to make him look guilty. Still others simply wrong.

Robert was to be given a choice. His tenure as a General Advisory Committee
consultant was about to expire; he could walk away, as Strauss would prefer.[422] Or
he could challenge the government and then go before a special panel and undergo an administrative review. And it was Strauss who would choose the three
members of the panel. The Admiral demanded a response that night; he would be
at home by 8 P.M., he said, so Robert was to answer anytime after that.

Robert went directly to the law office of Joe Volpe, a former counsel to the
Atomic Energy Commission. Herb Marks would join them. The three men talked
for an hour—none of them realizing that the office was bugged; Strauss had convinced Hoover that he needed to be privy to anything said in Volpe's office, client-
lawyer privilege be damned. From this source, Strauss quickly learned that Robert
didn't know what he was going to do—walk away or fight.

Anne Marks came to pick up Robert. "I can't believe what is happening to
me," he said. But what he needed to do, he told them, was get back to Princeton
right away to talk to Kitty. Anne drove him to Union Station. Kitty was waiting,
eager to hear all that had happened and ready to do battle. Robert ignored Strauss'
deadline. The next morning he phoned to say he would give his answer in person,
and that he would be at Strauss' office at nine the following morning. Robert and
Kitty boarded a train that would put them in Washington late in the afternoon,
and went directly to the Marks' house. "He was still in the same almost despairing
state of mind," Anne remembered.[423]

Robert had made his decision. A one-page letter was crafted. Addressed to
"Dear Lewis," Robert explained that he had considered resigning his position, as
Strauss had seemed to suggest, but decided "this course of action would mean that
I accept and concur in the view that I am not fit to serve this government, that I
have now served for some twelve years. This I cannot do. If I were thus unworthy
I could hardly have served our country as I have tried, or been the Director of our

Institute in Princeton, or have spoken, as on more than one occasion I have found myself speaking, in the name of our science and our country."[424]

That settled, Robert excused himself and went to the guestroom. Kitty, Anne and Herb were still in the living room, having a nightcap, when they heard what Anne called "a terrible crash." Robert was in the bathroom, the door shut, and did not respond. It took all three of them to push the door open to find Robert on he floor, unconscious. They got him to a couch; when he came to, he admitted he had taken some of Kitty's prescription sleeping pills. Following orders, the trio kept him walking and made him drink coffee until the doctor arrived.[425]

Robert understood that his reputation was at risk. They were going to fight.

ON CHRISTMAS EVE 1953, AS temperatures dipped into the 20s, two representatives from the Atomic Energy Commission arrived at Olden Manor with orders to remove the classified documents in Robert's possession, to tell him he would no longer have access to the vault, and to relieve the soldier who stood guard.

VIII
IN THE MATTER OF
J. ROBERT OPPENHEIMER
AND AFTERMATH

28

The AEC looks for fundamental defects in Robert's character, Jean haunts the Hearing, Kitty becomes an Accidental Communist and Ruth is "deeply troubled" by Robert's silence

1953: A day or two before Christmas, Robert's secretary Verna Hobson had been in the office at the Institute when Robert and Kitty walked in and, with scarcely a nod, went into his office and closed the door. When they finally emerged, Hobson could see they were in "some kind of trouble." The mood was intense, she remembered; the next day Robert called her into his office, told her about the charges, and explained the larger implications of having his Q clearance denied. Then he spent an hour and a half telling his story—all the way to his childhood—to put his actions in the context of his life. He told her what he would soon write in answer to the Atomic Energy Commission charges. Hobson later explained that she presumed he was likely rehearsing.[426]

Robert poured himself into the task of writing and re-writing what would become a forty-two-page autobiography, with Kitty doing some editing. She drank too much, and could be contentious and embarrassing, but she supported him without question.* As Hobson saw it, "Kitty was Robert's greatest confidant and advisor and so he told her everything and she would get involved in making deci-

---

*Rudolf Peierls once commented that, "Kitty was a person of great courage, both in the saddle and when facing an enemy."

sions."[427] As his defense attorney, Robert settled on Lloyd Garrison, an old-school gentleman and champion of civil rights (like his great-grandfather, the abolitionist William Lloyd Garrison).[428]

IN THE WEEKS BEFORE THE Hearing, Robert would sit in his big leather swivel chair by his office window, Kitty curled up in one of the upholstered armchairs. Garrison was there, sometimes with others from his law firm. At five in the evening, the group would remove to the house. Secretary Kay Russell was there to take notes. Hobson let Robert know she thought he should "push back, kick back, attack his accusers," until one night he walked out with her to say goodnight, and on the front steps told her, gently, that he was fighting as hard as he knew how, and in what seemed to him to be the best way. After that, she stopped pressing.[429]

To most of Robert's friends and a majority of the scientific community, the suspension of his security clearance seemed absurd. They had no idea of the lengths to which Strauss—with Hoover's help—would go to destroy Robert, and his supporters had no idea of the extent of Robert's pre-war connections to Communism. In the political climate of the day, that information could easily be used against him.

Even though Kitty was one of those Communist links, her husband now needed her. "I wish now I could observe Kitty again in those days," Hobson was to say. The situation "called on all her faculties, it was probably the only time in her life she ever really felt that she ... used her capabilities."[430] On January 2, Kitty telephoned Dean Acheson to find out what he knew. When she saw General Groves at a party in New York, she didn't hesitate to ask what he intended to say on the witness stand.[431]

Robert's secretaries were bright, educated women with young families of their own, but they were devoted to Robert. Kay Russell had been his secretary for seven years. "The Oppenheimers *became* her life," Hobson explained, "He expected you to be around and willing to work all kinds of funny hours but it was not that he said now you must be here, it was just the atmosphere ... you wanted to because you could see it was important."[432] Hobson and Russell were part of a long line of secretaries who became mesmerized by their boss, but it was Kitty who became dependent on them. They did most of the planning for the social functions Kitty was expected to host. And sometimes they drank with her late in the afternoon. They also rescued her more than a few times from her accidents. Hobson would say, "What a strange person she was: all that fury and soreness and intelligence and wit. She had a constant state of the hives."[433]

THE EMOTIONAL UPHEAVAL CREATED BY the Hearing spilled onto Kitty's parents. On March 16, when Kaethe and Franz Puening arrived in New York from Bremerhaven, customs agents had been ordered to search the elderly couple's luggage, carefully noting what books and written material they carried. Franz, a bespectacled, gentle figure, was now in a wheelchair. Kitty's parents were so traumatized that they had to be hospitalized.[434] Kitty was soon to make her own trip to the emergency room, to tend to the ankle she broke when she fell down a flight of stairs.

BY THE SPRING OF 1954, Ruth had not seen Robert since the previous summer, after her heart attacks. Now that he was embroiled in crisis, she had to find out what was happening from Bob Bacher and Charlie Lauritsen—both were consulted about testifying for him—when they returned from Washington. She was frantic to hear from Robert. In the first days of April, he finally phoned. Afterward, Ruth wrote to him with palpable relief, "It was incredibly good to hear your voice this morning. I think there has never been a time when so long a period has elapsed without letters or visits or some kind of communication for us." She was, she wrote, "deeply troubled" by his silence: "I suppose you have felt too harassed and confused to write . . . and I was a little confused, too because I did not know how much I was 'supposed' to know—though surely I could have assumed that you were willing for me to know anything which Bob and Charlie told me. You have been constantly in my thoughts Dear, and with, of course, much concern . . . Oh Robert, Robert, how often has it been this way for us! That we have felt powerless to help when we wanted to so deeply."[435]

JEAN HAD BEEN DEAD NOW for ten years, but Robert knew their relationship would be exposed in the Hearing. It would have seemed obscene to betray her memory with explanations, but he had no choice. In an attempt to describe the impact Jean had on his life he wrote (and Kitty read):

"In the spring of 1936, I had been introduced by friends to Jean Tatlock, the daughter of a noted professor of English at the university; and in the autumn, I began to court her, and we grew close to each other. We were at least twice close enough to marriage to think of ourselves as engaged. Between 1939 and her death in 1944 I saw her very rarely. She told me about her Communist Party memberships; they were on again, off again affairs, and never seemed to provide for her what she was seeking. I do not believe that her interests were really political. She loved this country and its people and its life. She was, as it turned out, a friend of many fellow travelers and Communists, with a number of whom I was later to become acquainted. I should not give the impression that it was wholly because of Jean Tatlock that I made leftwing friends, or felt sympathy for causes which hitherto would have seemed so remote from me, like the Loyalist cause in Spain, and the organization of migratory workers. I have mentioned some of the other contributing causes. I liked the new sense of companionship, and at the time felt that I was coming to be part of the life of my time and country."[436]

⤸

ON APRIL 5, THE OPPENHEIMER children were sent to stay with friends for two weeks. Robert wanted Peter and Toni to be protected should the Security Clearance Hearing become public. On the morning of April 12, Robert, Kitty, Lloyd Garrison and two of his staff made their way—slowed because Kitty was on crutches—to one of the temporary buildings assembled on the National Mall during the war. The group was ushered into a bare room, number 2022, which was about to become a Star Chamber. The three Strauss-appointed members of the panel sat at the head of a T-shaped table for the "administrative review." Lawyers and aides sat on either side. A single chair for the witness was placed at the bottom of the T. Not an auspicious venue in which to defrock an American icon.

The Oppenheimer contingent was an hour late and entered looking bedraggled. Kitty was clumsy, her face blotched from a recent outbreak of measles. In the confusion, Garrison offered his apologies to the irritated panel members. Kitty was told she could stay for that first morning session. After, she could appear only when called as a witness. No spectators or press were allowed. The Hearing, the Oppenheimer team was promised, was to be confidential.

The *New York Times* broke the story the next day.[437]

As attorney for the panel, Strauss had chosen Roger Robb, an assistant U.S. attorney with a reputation as a ruthless and skillful prosecutor who excelled in twisting witnesses' words. That the Hearing was presented as a procedural inquiry did not restrict Robb from using "prosecutorial tricks to catch (and confuse) witnesses." David Lilienthal, testifying for Robert, would walk out of Room 2022 and write that he was "so steamed up over the entrapment tactics," he felt "sadness and nausea at the whole spectacle."[438]

On that first day, Robb and each of the three panel members had before them a stack of large green folders. Inside were the "new" FBI files packed with ten years of information gleaned from wiretaps, mail, the family trash and various unsubstantiated accusations from both named and unnamed informants—a mélange of random facts, suspicions and accusatory letters. All of it was available to Robb, who had been granted a fast security clearance, and the panel members. But Robert's lawyers were denied access. What's more, for many months, the FBI had been listening, through wiretaps, to conversations in the lawyers' offices and in the house where Kitty and Robert were staying in Washington, where his defense team met to discuss strategy. Garrison would describe Robert as being "in the most overwrought state imaginable—so was Kitty—but Robert even more so."[439]

Hoover did not want the Hearing to be a trial because the wiretap information would be ruled illegal, not admitted in a court of law.[440] There was no proof that Robert had been a member of the Communist Party. At a time when the country was panicked about the Communist threat, the accusations alone were enough to create doubts about the wisdom of allowing Robert access to any national security secrets.

One by one over the following weeks, some of the most stellar scientists of the twentieth century entered the shabby building to testify "In the Matter of J. Robert Oppenheimer," as the published testimony would later be called: Rabi, Fermi, Bethe, Bacher, Alvarez, Lauritsen, Teller. Also Bush, Conant, Compton, Groves.* Most had come to stand witness for Robert, with a few important exceptions, the most significant being Edward Teller. Ernest Lawrence would have had the most damning influence, had he not avoided testifying.

Although Lawrence had been a close friend since their early days in Berkeley, he had cooled on Robert. One of his reasons was that he had heard whispers at a cocktail party in Pasadena that Robert had seduced Ruth Tolman, while Richard was still alive. Lawrence had deduced that "poor" Richard had died of a broken heart, reason enough for him to declare Robert morally untrustworthy.[441] But Lawrence was shrewd in a way that Teller was not; he understood that testifying against Robert would mean painful repercussions in the scientific community. The lineup of important physicists who would sing Robert's praises was an indication. Illness gave Lawrence an excuse not to testify at the Hearing. Strauss phoned to call him a coward.

Lawrence did tell Strauss the story of Robert's supposed seduction of Ruth. Incensed, Strauss spread the gossip when it served his purposes. ("Did Ernest ever tell you what [Robert] did in the Tolman household?" he would ask Teller.)[442]

⌐

RUTH HAD NO IDEA LAWRENCE was spreading dangerous gossip. The Lawrences had been friends of the Tolmans for many years, had been their houseguests when they came to Pasadena. It was probably because of Ruth that Lawrence had been invited to the cocktail party. After the event, he returned home to his wife Molly, furious because of what he thought he had learned. The woman who had told him was Gloria Gartz, a wealthy and well-regarded civic leader in Pasadena who was deeply involved with women's issues—a psychologist and, as it happened, Val's new love interest. As one of the small band of women psychologists in Pasadena, Gloria would almost certainly have known Ruth. What seems likely is that Gloria engaged Lawrence in conversation and said something about how close Robert and Ruth had been for many years. Perhaps she even offered "how much they loved each other." Or that they had "loved each other for a very long time." It would not be hard for Lawrence to add his own interpretation at a time when he needed to find reason to fault his old friend, to justify turning against him in the Hearing.

～

WITH THE BENEFIT OF TIME and distance, the Oppenheimer Security Clearance Hearing seems more an inquisition than a review; important voices declared it so even at the time. What made the Hearing possible was the fear and the anti-Communist fervor that engulfed the nation. Almost as soon as Robert entered the tawdry room in which his fate was to be decided, the man who could convince anybody of anything, who could captivate men and women alike, his language eloquent and precise, his voice pitch perfect—had vanished.

When Robert left the leather sofa to take the witness chair, he suffered through four weeks of testimony from friends and critics and six days of direct questions from the panel, interspersed with vicious courtroom hammering from Robb, who made Robert seem evasive and equivocal and, worse, embarrassed and humiliated. Robert would say he felt "The way a soldier does in combat, I suppose. So much is happening or maybe about to happen that there is no time to be aware of anything but the next move like someone in a fight and this was a fight. I had very little sense of self."[443]

As Robert suspected, Jean was a vulnerable spot. Robb began the grilling: *Between 1939 and 1944, as I understand it, your acquaintance with Miss Tatlock was fairly casual; is that right?*[444]

> Robert: *Our meetings were rare. I do not think it would be right to say that our acquaintance was casual. We had been very much involved with one another and there was still very deep feeling when we saw each other.*
> Robb: *What were the occasions for your seeing her?*
> Robert: *Of course, sometimes we saw each other socially with other people. I remember visiting her around New Year's of 1941.*

Robb: *Where?*

Oppenheimer: *I went to her home or to the hospital. I don't know which, and we went out for a drink at the Top of the Mark. I remember that she came more than once to visit our home in Berkeley.*

Robb: *You and Mrs. Oppenheimer?*

Robert: *Right. Her father lived around the corner not far from us in Berkeley. I visited her there once. I visited her, as I think I said earlier, in June or July of 1943.*

Robb: *I believe you said in connection with that that you had to see her.*

Robert: *Yes.*

Robb: *Why did you have to see her?*

Robert: *She had indicated a great desire to see me before we left. At that time I couldn't go. For one thing, I wasn't supposed to say where we were going or anything. I felt that she had to see me. She was undergoing psychiatric treatment. She was extremely unhappy.*

Robb was building to the moment when he would take Robert's confession: *Did you find out why she had to see you?*

Robert: *Because she was still in love with me.*

Robb did not ask if Robert was still in love with her; he didn't need to, because the FBI files on their desks described the scene when Robert had met Jean that fateful day ten years before: "He rushed to meet a young lady . . . long dark hair, slim, attractive . . . whom he kissed and they walked away arm in arm." Not unhappy, not that day.

The questions flew back and forth:

Where did you see her? At her home.

Where was that? On Telegraph Hill.

When did you see her after that? She took me to the airport, and I never saw her again.

That was in 1943? Yes.

Was she a Communist at that time? We didn't even talk about it. I doubt it.

You have said in your answer that you knew she had been a Communist? Yes. I knew that in the fall of 1937.

Was there any reason for you to believe that she wasn't still a Communist in 1943? No.

Pardon? There wasn't, except that I have stated in general terms what I thought and think of her relations with the Communist Party. I do not know what she was doing in 1943.

You have no reason to believe she wasn't a Communist, do you? No.

And then at last:

> *You spent the night with her, didn't you?*
> *Yes.*
> With that, Robb attacked: *That is when you were working on a secret war project? Did you think that consistent with good security?*
> Robert stumbled: *It was, as a matter of fact. Not a word . . . it was as if he wanted to stop himself, to say no more—not a word—*He recovered and finished with a curt: *It was not good practice.*
> Robb paused: *Didn't you think that put you in a rather difficult position had she been the kind of Communist that you have described her?*
> Robert wouldn't go that far. He answered: *Oh, but she wasn't.*
> *How did you know?*
> *I knew her.*

John Lansdale, the officer in charge of wartime security for General Groves, took the stand as a friendly witness. Garrison anticipated that Lansdale would give a positive answer to his somewhat innocuous question about Robert's ability to be discreet. *Yes; I believed him to be discreet.* Lansdale answered, then added, *I thought it was indiscreet of him to visit Miss Tatlock.*

> Robb seized on Lansdale's response: *You said that you thought Oppenheimer's discretion was very good, is that correct?*
> Lansdale: *Yes sir.*
> Robb: *You had no doubt, did you, that Jean Tatlock was a Communist?*
> Lansdale: *She was certainly on our suspect list. I know now that she was a Communist. I cannot recall at the moment whether we were sure she was a Communist at that time.*
> Robb: *Did your definition of very good discretion include spending the night with a known Communist woman?*
> Lansdale: *No, it didn't. Our impression was that the interest was more romantic than otherwise, and that is the sole instance that I know . . .*[445]

Robb changed the subject abruptly, cutting Lansdale off before he could add anything positive about Robert.

ON APRIL 15, THE THIRD day of the Hearing, the *Pittsburg Sun-Telegraph*[446] ran a front-page story, "Oppenheimer's Wife Bright Student." Kitty was identified as formerly from Aspinwall, and "an intellectual girl with an inclination to leftist views." The article concluded, "Kitty is one of the reasons her husband has been barred from atomic work." Her parents might have clipped the story from their local paper. Kitty was called to the witness chair two times. Dressed in a dark tailored suit with a white blouse, she sat up straight with her hands folded, (as a child she had been taught to sit still and not fidget, she would explain.) She answered in a clear and sometimes feisty voice. A lawyer from Garrison's firm guided Kitty though her carefully rehearsed testimony. He asked about her relationship with Joe Dallet and let her explain why she had joined the Party—and how she had drifted from it.[447]

Her joining the party was because, Kitty said, *Joe very much wanted me to, and I didn't mind.* The work she did was mostly office work, she typed and mimeographed leaflets and letters. And she had paid dues. *Yes,* she offered, *10 cents a week.* Working to establish that Kitty had been an accidental Communist, the lawyer asked her to define her devotion to the Party. *I don't think I could ever describe it as a devotion or even attachment. What interest I had in it decreased.* She had become a Communist because she was in love with Joe. Her lack of commitment caused her to leave him. She said, *I felt I didn't want to attend party meetings or do the kind of work that I was doing in the office. That made him unhappy. We agreed that we couldn't go on that way.* Anyone who knew Kitty as the director's wife—at Los Alamos and the Institute—would recognize in her words the woman who did what she wanted to do.

Her association with Steve Nelson was certain to come up. At that moment, he was in jail charged with attempting to overthrow the government and was awaiting trial. The plan was to describe Nelson as a kind friend who took care of Kitty in the difficult weeks after Joe was killed in Spain. When asked why Nelson was invited to their home in Berkeley Kitty explained: *We had a picnic lunch . . . We talked about the old days, family matters.*

On the delicate matter of her own membership, Kitty was asked when she left the Party. In 1936, she answered, when she left Youngstown. She conveniently left out her plans to join Joe in Spain. Had she paid any dues since? *No.* How would she describe her current views on Communism? *Very strongly against.*

The chairman of the panel, Gordon Gray, then posed another version of the same question: *Mrs. Oppenheimer, how did you leave the Communist Party?*

Kitty: *By walking away.*

Gray became literal. The phrase "card-carrying Communist" was an epithet in common usage, and he wanted to know if she had a card. *While I was in Youngstown,* yes. What she had done with the card? Kitty brushed him off with: *I have no idea.*

The chairman shifted his attention to the matter of Steve Nelson, and whether or not he had discussed the Communist Party with Kitty. Her response was almost defiant: *I would like to make it clear that I have always felt very friendly to Steve*

Nelson after he returned from Spain and spent the week with me in Paris. He helped me a great deal and the much later meeting with him was something that was simply friendship and nothing else.

ON MAY 4, KITTY RETURNED to the witness chair to be questioned by Gray and Robb. They wanted to know if Robert contributed to the Communist Party. Kitty said she knew that he did from time to time give money. But when Gray pressed her, and asked if money was given on a regular or periodic basis, Kitty retorted: *Do you mean regular, or do you mean periodic?*[448]

When Gray said he really meant "regular," Kitty observed: *I think he did not.*

Gray had a point to make. He asked if it was fair to say that Robert had made contributions to the Communist Party as late as 1942, which would mean that he had not stopped having anything to do with the Party, as Kitty had testified. Gray added: *I don't insist that you answer yes or no. You can answer that any way you wish.*

Kitty shot back: *I know that. Thank you.* Then she said: *I don't think that question is properly phrased.*

Probably with more than a hint of exasperation, Gray asked: *Do you understand what I am trying to get at?* When Kitty said simply *yes,* he urged, *Why don't you answer it that way?* Kitty took her time: *The reason I didn't like the phrase 'stopped having anything to do with the Communist Party' was because I don't think that Robert ever did—*

Gray persisted in trying to pinpoint a date, until Kitty told him: *Mr. Gray, Robert and I don't agree about everything. He sometimes remembers something different than the way I remember it.*

Kitty was not losing her temper; she was contemptuous of the men she saw attempting to destroy her husband, but she managed to control her inclination to slash at them. When she gave a simple answer—*That is right*—and was then asked if she could be mistaken, she replied: *I could be mistaken about almost anything, but I do not think I am.*

Robert, however, did not react with as much poise during his long days of interrogation. He was especially distraught when the Hearings turned to the time when Haakon Chevalier had passed a request to Robert, from another scientist, to share information with the Soviets. Robert had concocted several different answers. All the old questions were asked and all the same answers repeated, except for one moment when Robert seemed exhausted by it all. He answered rashly when Robb demanded, yet again, if he had once said that "X"—meaning Chevalier—had approached three people. Robert answered *probably.* Robb came right back with, *Why did you do that, Doctor?* That was when Robert said: *Because I was an idiot.*[449]

Robb continued the rapid-fire questioning about "X," making Robert seem confused and evasive. Then, after Robert had said that he had not wanted to implicate Chevalier, Robb asked, *Did you know Chevalier as a fellow traveler?*

Robert: *I so told the FBI in 1946 . . .*

Robb: *You knew he was quite a "red," didn't you?*

Robert: *Yes, I would say quite pink.*

When Kitty was on the stand and Gray mentioned the friendship with Chevalier and asked how one "disassociated" oneself from Communism, Kitty answered with defiance: *I think it varies from person to person, Mr. Gray. Some people do the bump, like that, and even write an article about it. Other people do it quite slowly. I left the Communist Party. I did not leave my past, the friendships, just like that.*[450]

BY A VOTE OF TWO to one, the Security Board panel recommended to the Atomic Energy Commission that Robert should be denied a security clearance. The one surprising dissenting vote came from the professor of chemistry, a conservative who concluded that the only new charge he had heard was Robert's lack of enthusiasm for the "Super."

Robert's trial by fire came in two stages. Kenneth Nichols, the general manager of the Atomic Energy Commission, was pleased with the outcome of the Hearing. He had called Robert "a slippery sonuvabitch" and said, "We're going to get him this time."[451] They did. On June 12, the four Atomic Energy Commissioners accepted the Hearing panel's decision and voted (again with one dissenting voice, physicist Henry Smyth) to deny Robert Oppenheimer a top-secret clearance, effectively expelling him from government service. Strauss crowed: "We find Dr. Oppenheimer is not entitled to the continued confidence of the Government . . . because of the proof of fundamental defects in his character."[452]

29

In the summer season Ruth subconsciously expects disaster, Kitty sets fire to the bedroom, and some Harvard alums question Robert's moral qualifications

"Dear Robert and Kitty," Edward Tolman wrote during the Hearing, "All my love, sympathy and understanding and (if I believed in God) my prayers. You are fighting the most important fight in the world today."[453] But the fight had been lost and a formidable voice in the struggle for international control of atomic energy was now compromised. Robert's reputation had been battered. He wasn't certain how the decision would affect his position at the Institute, especially with Lewis Strauss on the Board of Trustees.

Robert needn't have worried; everyone at the Institute was stunned and all of the permanent faculty including emeriti, Einstein among them, made a strong statement of support for Robert.[454] Even the mathematicians who so often tried Robert's patience were with him. With such overwhelming support, the trustees could make no move to replace Robert without creating a firestorm. Strauss was left to scheme from the sidelines.

In July, the Oppenheimer family went to nurse their wounds on St. John in the Virgin Islands, "that place of warm water, bright fish, and soft trade winds," as Robert once described it to Ruth.[455] Kitty, stung by the defeat, treated the pain with alcohol, and exploded at times in angry tantrums. When Robert wrote to Anne Marks, he as usual glossed over the difficulties with Kitty. Anne would write to her, "Robert tells us that your sailing summer was a great success, & that you are restored in mind, body & spirit." [456] The FBI could not follow them to this remote island—there were no paved roads on St. John, no telephone service—but the reprieve was brief. When the family returned to the U.S. at the end of August, FBI agents were waiting at the airport in New York to question Robert.

SOME WHO SAW ROBERT IN the weeks following the Hearing found him changed, aged, tragic. Many who saw him every day found him to switch from worn and tired one day to his old, energetic self the next. Jeremy Bernstein, a young physicist new to the Institute at about this time, wondered how Robert could have been any more captivating. He moved in and out of lectures and discussions—always, as physicist Hans Bethe said, "adding an electric charge to any room he entered."[457] Robert also began to spend more time traveling, lecturing and teaching. Kitty sometimes traveled with him, often leaving Peter and Toni in the care of the secretaries.

Robert's Harvard friend John Edsall visited Olden Manor a few months after the Hearing. His sense was that Robert "had survived this grim ordeal remarkably well and his spirit did not seem to be broken or even particularly depressed." At the time, Edsall said, it seemed as if the Oppenheimers were most worried about the children; Peter's classmates were calling his father a Communist. About Kitty, Edsall would comment: "There was a certain mixture of courage and frankness in talking about this ordeal they'd been through, with a certain kind of flightiness, as if she were trying to escape from painful memories, and yet trying to keep them in focus and face them at the same time."[458] Edsall felt that Kitty acted as if the effects of the Hearing were harder on her than on Robert. He assumed she was feeling guilty for her part in Robert's fall from grace.

More likely Kitty was distressed to be cut off from a role she had wanted to play. She was still openly ambitious, as much for herself as for him, and she preferred the halls of power to the green meadows of the Institute. Now all that was gone, Robert had returned to academia, and once again, she was the odd woman out. There were a few light moments: at a Christmas Eve party at the house of the editor of *Foreign Affairs,* David Lilienthal would report that Kitty looked radiant and Robert looked happy (something Lilienthal said he couldn't remember ever thinking about him).[459] But those moments for Kitty were becoming more elusive.

RUTH HAD SPENT MUCH OF 1953 recuperating from her heart attacks; Robert had been preoccupied through June of 1954 with the Hearing. The two had scarcely been in touch. But with Ruth regaining her energy, they resumed contact by telephone, letter and, whenever they could manage, in person. It required complicated planning. In one letter Ruth sent Robert an elaborate itinerary of her movements throughout the summer, including a trip to Europe. But then she wrote that she doubted she would go. She said she didn't know why "except perhaps that the summer season has become conditioned for me in such a way that subconsciously I expect disaster."[460]

With the Hearing, the nation was told the man who took the world into the Atomic Age was not to be trusted with national secrets. But at the Institute, Robert was in the perfect place to heal. Nothing excited him more than discovering an exceptionally bright young scientist who was intrigued by the unlimited questions that nature, and society, posed. For the next twelve years he would cultivate the persona of public intellectual. He would become the Institute for Advanced Study's longest-lasting director.

⁓

PHYSICIST FREEMAN DYSON ARRIVED AT the Institute in 1953; he was twenty-nine, with a wife and two young children, and he encountered a Kitty others seemed to have missed. Sixty years later, his memory of her was largely compassionate. He remembered that Kitty helped to start the Crossroads Nursery School, which today remains an important community center for the young academic families that energize the Institute.[461] Dyson recounted a painful time in his life; soon after he and his wife had decided to divorce, they were invited to a large dinner party at Olden Manor. It was to be their last public appearance as a couple, he wrote to his parents in England. Dyson took Robert aside and told him about the impending breakup. "This was the first time we told anybody here outside the family. Afterwards when we were leaving Mrs. Oppenheimer came with us to the door and kissed Verena, and tears were streaming down her face. Before I had always found Mrs. Oppenheimer tiresome, but I am grateful to her for those tears." Dyson went on to say that he knew Kitty had a drinking problem, but that he had seen her regularly at social events, and never saw her noticeably drunk.[462]

David Lilienthal, who came to live near the Institute in the mid-1950s, idolized Robert and enjoyed Kitty's company—he liked her barbed wit and unconventional manners, even though he did not see her frequently in the seven years they were neighbors. Others who saw Kitty offered glimpses, moments frozen in memory: Kitty staggering across the lawn; Kitty knocking over a drink and breaking the glass (with Robert instantly pouring her another and leaving the broken glass for the maid to clean up the next day). Kitty humiliating a young woman with a few harsh words. Kitty running to help a neighbor in an emergency with dirt from the garden still on her hands. Kitty entertaining through endless cocktail hours surrounded by academics discussing arcane subjects that too often shut her out of the conversation. A glass of gin with a splash of vermouth would have blunted the disappointment.

THAT KITTY'S BEHAVIOR WAS BECOMING increasingly dangerous was clear to those who saw her every day. Cigarette burns scarred the bedsheets; once she set the bedroom on fire, resulting in minor damage and a small mention in the *New York Times*. (Robert and his family were still considered newsworthy.) Along with boredom and loneliness, Kitty suffered from pancreatitis, most often caused by excessive drinking over a period of time. The intense abdominal pain she endured would help explain her increasingly frequent bursts of anger.

Robert's two secretaries became part of what could only be called Robert's management plan for Kitty's problems. When she took too many pills by accident, he called on the secretaries to help him control Kitty's medications. Once, early on, he confided in Hobson that others had suggested he send Kitty to a treatment center for her alcoholism, but he refused. "He would be her doctor, nurse and psychiatrist," Robert told Hobson, adding that he had made the decision "with his eyes open and he would take the consequences."[463] That is, when he was in town.

In an attempt to explain Kitty, Robert looked for answers in the psychoanalytic theory that had so fascinated him. He told Hobson, "Kitty had some confusions about her own sex and perhaps . . .[had] some resentment toward a male." Her confusions were not about her sexuality, but rather her view of herself as superior to some of the men around her, when she was consistently treated as inferior. Francis Fergusson, Robert's old friend who would spend two terms at the Institute, agreed that as much as Kitty worried about Robert, she "had this repressed hostility toward him."[464]

Others confirmed that Kitty was intensely jealous of Robert, so much so that she could stand neither to see him praised or blamed. It was as if she were caught up in the need to *be* Robert—to live, as ever, through a man.

⁓

IN SEPTEMBER OF THAT YEAR—1954—Ruth's "subconscious fear of disaster" would prove prescient. Her plan to visit Robert and Kitty in Princeton after the American Psychological Association's annual meeting in New York was canceled abruptly when her sister Lillie Margaret fell seriously ill and Ruth rushed back to Berkeley to be with her. This was not the first time Lillie Margaret's illnesses had altered Ruth and Robert's plans: "I felt so disappointed not to have our precious visit," Ruth had written to Robert from the hospital in California several years earlier. "I had been counting on it so happily and with great desire to see all of you."[465] This time, Lillie Margaret was to be diagnosed with inoperable cancer.

⤳

ON JANUARY 4, 1955, ROBERT appeared on the influential CBS television show *See It Now*, hosted by Edward R. Murrow, who had been one of the few reporters to challenge Joe McCarthy. Robert agreed to appear on the condition that the show be about the Institute, not about him, and the Hearing be out of bounds. CBS agreed. The interview proved so compelling that the full half-hour of the broadcast was given over to Robert, with only one mention of the Institute. An hour-long version was made available to colleges and schools. Robert hadn't lost his ability to engage and delight, and through Murrow he reached a wider audience than ever before. The success of the program, linked with the enigma—the father of the atom bomb renounced by his government as a possible traitor—created a swarm of invitations for Robert to speak all over the country.

The controversy, though, was still alive. When the president of the University of Washington canceled a speaking invitation, students and faculty rebelled and the scientific community threatened a boycott. Adding to the annoyances, Lewis Strauss, his obsession unabated, became convinced that Robert was about to defect to the Soviet Union. (In fact, Strauss had been obsessed with this idea since 1953.[466]) At his request, Hoover ordered another series of wiretaps and sent agents to follow the Oppenheimers on a February trip to the Caribbean. Their movements in St. Croix were reported by three FBI informants ("T-4, T-5 and T-6 . . . of known reliability" the FBI memo noted). "Mrs. Oppenheimer was drinking heavily and other guests were horrified at her conduct," T-6 reported, and, "On one occasion she was so intoxicated that she fell into the hotel swimming pool." The informant offered the opinion that "the subject conducted himself soberly and at times had his hands full keeping Mrs. Oppenheimer in check."[467] The islands seemed to be Kitty's place to do as she pleased, even if it meant demolishing hotel rooms and making a public spectacle of herself.

⤳

LILLIE MARGARET AND RUTH SPENT Christmas together in Pasadena, but on February 22, 1955, Ruth was back in Berkeley, anguishing over her older sister's illness. Val wrote to Margaret Mead that she was on her way to Berkeley. "Ruth

Tolman's sister is dying ... and I belong to the rescue squad."⁴⁶⁸ Robert and Kitty left St. Croix the same day. Five days later, Lillie Margaret died. Once again, Ruth needed comforting, and Robert would find his way west to her.

At the University of Oregon, Robert delivered a series of lectures on physics; 2,500 people showed up to hear a talk that only a few in the audience could understand; it didn't matter. When the auditorium filled, spectators spilled into other rooms. Two years later, 1,200 people would crowd into Harvard's largest lecture hall, with an additional 800 listening in an adjacent room. Robert became a scientific superstar, and his legend grew.

⤸

DURING SPRING BREAK IN 1955, Lynn Alexander, a sixteen-year-old junior at the University of Chicago, joined her boyfriend, fellow student Carl Sagan, for the drive to his New Jersey hometown.* Worried that his mother would not approve of them traveling together, he dropped his girlfriend off at an inn in Princeton. Lynn, who had enrolled at the university at the age of fourteen, had seen the Murrow interview so she decided to pay a visit—unannounced—to Dr. Oppenheimer. Soon after, she would write an account of her Sunday afternoon encounter with the Oppenheimer family.⁴⁶⁹ How she, with dark eyes, dark hair and a wide, engaging smile like a young Kitty Oppenheimer, had walked up Olden Lane and was approaching the front door when she ran into the family on their way into town. How she introduced herself to Robert, told him she was a science student from Chicago. How he invited her to come with them, and she had piled into the Cadillac convertible with Peter and Toni in the backseat.

At some point, Peter—almost fourteen himself—had said to her, "You must be smart." She would write that she didn't know how to answer, so she said nothing. But Kitty spoke up "speaking slowly, too distinctly" and told her that Peter had just published his first article, a television column in the university paper. "With his byline," Kitty added. Lynn wondered "if Dr O felt as oppressed by his wife as I did." By the time they arrived in downtown Princeton, it was clear that Kitty objected to this bright young stranger joining their outing. And yet, when Lynn had a chance to speak with Robert about the Murrow interview, he had smiled and "those eyes looking directly at me, he asked warmly if I would like to come back to their home again." Kitty overheard and grimaced.

"Would I be disturbing you?" Lynn said she asked. Kitty answered sharply, "a

*Lynn Alexander would marry Carl Sagan three years later; after eight years they would divorce and she would marry Thomas Margulis (divorced in 1980). She became an important evolutionary biologist and professor at University of Massachusetts, Amherst. She was presented the National Medal of Science in 1999 by President Clinton.

purposefully unmistakable tension in her voice. 'Quite frankly, you'd be welcome only if you stayed just a *little*. This is the only chance we have to be with the children, isn't it, Robert dear?'"

Robert said, so softly his wife didn't hear, "Come, do come home with us. I have something to show you." Lynn described Peter as being "sheepishly buried in the Sunday papers, hunkering down in the back seat with sullen Toni, the 10-year-old daughter."

Lynn did go back to Olden Manor with them and Robert showed her the famous Van Gogh in the living room, then settled down with the Sunday papers: one with an article on the Oppenheimers (in which Kitty was described as "petite, chic, witty, tense and vivacious") and the other containing Peter's first column. When Robert handed this paper to the girl to read, Kitty muttered, "Unfair," and asked "rather fiercely" to see it first.

Robert, Lynn wrote, chided Kitty for "not being very entertaining."

The girl said: "You'd rather entertain your children, I'm sure." And Kitty answered bluntly, "We will, after you leave." In Lynn's account, Robert said to her, "'Oh no. Do stay and eat with us.' He invited me with real feeling in his voice. He seemed sincerely to want me to stay."

She was flattered and it was hard to say no, she admitted, but when she rose to leave, "Mrs. O flashed him a triumphant smile." And then: "Furtively glancing at his tight-lipped wife ... he checked that she wasn't looking and smiled, warmly, deeply. He meant it; I tingled with pleasure. He shook my hand, gazed affectionately at me, then blankly at the street, with melancholy gleaming blue eyes."

Robert, caught in the act of intellectual seduction.

After that, Alexander wrote that she wandered back down Olden Lane, "drunk with Dr. O and scents of spring," on her way to the Inn, "in a dream, wondering about my foray into the Oppenheimer family, I was certain that although Ms. O still resided with him, she had long since deserted him. . . . He had wanted me to stay. I had been permitted to catch a glimpse of, to feel the 'intellectual sex appeal' that had attracted physicists to Los Alamos in 1943. He seemed like an aging stallion staggering from a broken spirit."

With that, the bright sixteen-year-old wondered if he ever thought of Jean Tatlock (her memory resurrected by the Hearing). "Or if he had ever enjoyed a relationship of higher quality, a special plane of intimacy?" Lynn wrote with the same emotional hyperbole of the adolescent Jean, yearning for a depth of love she had not yet experienced.

Lynn Alexander's account of the afternoon was no doubt factually true, yet she was not mature enough to read the other possibilities: that Robert was taunting his wife, and ignoring his children, that he was encouraging her in spite of his wife's clear notice that she considered the girl to be an interloper. The episode offers a disturbing glimpse into the dynamics of the Oppenheimer ménage in the wake of the Hearing. Alexander follows a familiar script about Kitty: rude, a bitch. She does not fault Robert as an intellectual seducer. But it was a role he had, time and again, assumed with both women and men. *His mere physical appearance, his voice, and his manners made people fall in love with him—male, female, almost everybody.*

⤸

AFTER LILLIE MARGARET DIED, RUTH returned to Pasadena and her job at the Mental Hygiene Clinic in Los Angeles. Val moved back to Pasadena after Ruth Benedict's death, established a private practice as a therapist, and was now living with Gloria Gartz. Ruth was on the planning committee for the American Psychological Association's 1955 meeting in San Francisco, and had asked Robert to be the keynote speaker. He rearranged his schedule to accommodate her; it was a coup for Ruth.

On September 1, Robert telegraphed Ruth at the Sheraton Palace in San Francisco, an elegant old hotel from the city's glory days. "Will arrive Saturday morning United flight 717. Shall come straight to the hotel and try to find you or word of you before lunch."[470] She was a major participant and he was the famous speaker, but they were staying in the same hotel, and with luck could find a little private time together.

That fall, while Robert was in San Francisco with Ruth, Kitty sent fourteen-year-old Peter to board at the Quakers' George School in Pennsylvania. At the same time Kitty's parents were in need of support. Franz was increasingly frail and Kaethe wanted her help. But Kaethe—who sometimes called herself "Kate"—criticized her daughter's drinking.[471] The Puenings lived only an hour's drive from Princeton; Kitty rarely saw them. Kaethe was stung by the neglect and she and Kitty became estranged.* When Franz Puening died in the fall of 1955, Kitty sent Verna Hobson in her place. Kate Puening's loneliness was now complete. All she could think to do was to return to Germany to live with her younger sister Hilde.

⤸

RUTH WAS STILL GLOWING FROM her time with Robert in San Francisco, where she was able to introduce her good friend to her colleagues. When Robert sent her a copy of the speech he had given, she wrote, "I have just finished reading

*Anne Wilson once referred to Kitty's mother as a "real dragon."

it again. Really, it is even more wonderful than I had remembered—just beautiful in word and in idea and in feeling." She added wistfully that she had felt "more than ordinarily in need of communication with you these days." It had been a year since Lillie's death, and Ruth was tormented that she had not done enough for her sister at the end of her life. She wrote to Robert, "It seems as if I go through life with that feeling, and so surely much of it must be in *me* rather than in the reality."[472] But understanding didn't make things better, she said. What she needed was to talk to Robert, who could help her assuage not just her grief, but her guilt.

⌒

ON APRIL 26, 1956, THE American Foreign Service office in Genoa, Italy, filed a "Report of the Death of an American Citizen." The name on the passport was Kate Puening; she had disappeared from the Norwegian freighter *Concordia Fjord,* on April 23 or 24. Kitty's mother went missing "under circumstances indicating that passenger had crawled through a window and dropped into the sea. Body was not recovered." The Department of State sent a memo saying all the evidence pointed to suicide. International newspapers ran stories about the mysterious disappearance of Robert Oppenheimer's mother-in-law. The ship's log catalogued the facts: the door had been locked from the inside, no sign of violence, a chair was placed under a high window which was open. Cash had been left behind to cover her account with the ship. Underclothes were lying over a chair. She was naked when she crawled through the window. No note found.[473]

Kaethe's sister Hilde rushed from Stuttgart to the American Consulate in Genoa. She was certain that Kaethe would have left her a message; she wanted to see—to search—her sister's luggage. She found a will and traveler's cheques, but there was no message. Desperate for information, Hilde wrote to one of the passengers known to have talked to her sister on the voyage. In touching English Hilde explained: "I would be very please to you, if you could tell me the impression you got of my sister.... Perhaps we never will know what happened that night to my poor sister. I loved her all my life, she was my mother always and so good to me and I hoped that I could give a new possibility to her to support her life without her husband and without her daughter. And now, I was in Genoa, and my loved sister was not coming and will never come to me anymore. Excuse me all my feelings saying to you—but I would be so fortunate if you could understand me and help me a little bit to get light in this darkness of tragedy. Excuse please the English in the same manner. Yours faithfully, Hilde Vissering de Blonay."[474]

The gentleman sent a kindly reply, speaking of how strongly Mrs. Puening had spoken about her attachment to her husband, how lonely she was, and how her life seemed quite meaningless. He added, in light of the news articles, that, "Personally, I am convinced that her death had nothing to do with professor Robert Oppenheimer. She mentioned once that she was his mother-in-law and added that he was now rehabilitated, a fact that she was very glad about."[475]

The American Foreign Service memo noted that Hilde Vissering had said that in addition to suffering grief over her husband's death, Mrs. Puening had had a "misunderstanding"—Hilde's word—with her daughter, and was consequently feeling very much alone. Hilde was also adamant that Kitty not be told that Hilde had said this.[476]

Two weeks later, on May 15, Kitty sent a cable to her Aunt from Princeton: "Thanks for two loving letters, especially one I got yesterday about the sad events. The State Department telephoned . . . I believe you are correct that it was an accident. You've done everything you could do and you shouldn't let it torment you. Mutti gives you everything that is left, about $9,000 and her clothes. I had hoped in the end that you would get everything and now its true. . . . Kitty."[477]

⁓

ROBERT'S ALMA MATER, HARVARD, INVITED him to give the prestigious William James Lectures in the spring of 1957. The topic would be ethics and philosophy. A small group of alumni questioned Robert's moral qualifications to lecture on the subject. A graduate of the class of 1918 wrote: "Why must Harvard insult a large body of loyal alumni by inviting so dubious a character to lecture?"[478] But Harvard held firm, and the lectures were given. In the audience one night was the physicist Jeremy Bernstein, who had been accepted for a term at the Institute. As soon as Bernstein said he would be coming to the Institute that fall, Robert's face broke into a wide smile, which Bernstein said was like a sunrise. Robert then said, "We're going to have a ball!"[479]

EARLIER THAT YEAR, ROBERT HAD written his Aunt Hedwig in Berkeley: "For no v. good reason I am going to be in SF between the 6th and 9th of March, judging of all things, architecture."[480] One v. good reason to go to California would be to see Ruth.

⁓

WHENEVER ROBERT AGREED TO AN interview with the news media, it was with the proviso that the Hearing was taboo. But midway through 1957, he relented and agreed to talk to a *Minneapolis Sunday Tribune* reporter—explicitly about the Hearing.[481] The timing and the newspaper were curious choices; major papers had been clamoring for three years for such an interview. He clearly wanted to address all those who insisted the Hearing had destroyed him and that he was a shadow of his former self. The substance of the *Tribune* article has Ruth's imprimatur all over it.

The article began with Robert's quote: "I have tried to prove that a security risk can survive." The only way he could do that, Robert said, was to "establish by other means that what was put out as a final judgment about me wasn't the final judgment." The story was nothing new, but because it was about Robert Oppenheimer, other papers picked it up. Robert made clear that he neither intended for the security hearing to define the rest of his life, nor was he comfortable in the role of professional martyr. Alongside his survival story was a sidebar about Frank, explaining how he had lost his teaching position at the University of Minnesota, and that he had been banished to the high mountains of Colorado. Robert's choice of newspapers was a not so subtle reminder that it was the University of Minnesota which had taken part in the travesty that had cost so many good men their careers, Frank included.

Robert ached for his brother; it was time for him to come out of the wilderness and back to the life they both loved: physics. In fact, the mood of the country was beginning to change; Frank was allowed to teach science in the local rural high school. It was a start, and Robert hoped that his brother would soon be back teaching at a university.

Ruth adored Frank, and worried about the strains on the brothers' relationship. The year before Robert's "survival" article appeared, Ruth had visited with Frank and Jackie. The plainspoken Jackie had always caused tension, Ruth knew. She wrote to tell Robert "how much Jackie has grown. I thought she was quiet and poised and thoughtful and understanding. . . . It seemed to me that her attitudes toward people were generous and compassionate and wise."[482] Robert might have thought the description a better fit for Ruth than for his brother's wife, but he would have understood what she was telling him.

⤳

ROBERT'S AUNT HEDWIG WROTE: "The shock what I got today from Pasadena means very much to me. Everyone who knew Ruth Tolman will miss her very hard. I feel deeply with you the big loss of your best true friend. My thoughts are with you like always."[483]

The heavens had opened and a tropical storm drenched Pasadena on September 18, 1957, the day that Ruth Tolman died. She was at home at the end of the season she had come to dread, and her heart had shuddered to a full stop.

Ruth was sixty-four; she was born in the Midwest and had grown up in California, but she would be buried next to her husband in the place he loved best, Woods Hole on Cape Cod. It is not known if Robert visited her grave, or how or where he said goodbye. That he did grieve is without question; Robert's love for Ruth had endured for almost thirty years. Aunt Hedwig understood how deeply the loss of his true best friend would hurt.

After her death, Edward Tolman wrote to Robert: "It isn't much good to try to put one's feelings about death into words. Ruth herself probably could have but I can't. It leaves a tremendous hole for all of us which aches." Robert wrote him back: "I have felt close to you in these weeks since Ruth's death, because you loved each other."[484]

Psychologist Ted Newcomb, who was on the psychology committee at the Institute with Ruth, wrote to say, "Somehow I can hardly face the prospect of attending next year's meeting without Ruth Tolman . . . You were one of the first persons I thought of when Jean Bacher wired me about her death. Though I knew her much less well than you, she was still one of a very very select few in my life whose departure has been hard to take. I don't expect any answer to this. It just did not seem right . . . not to tell you how deeply I share what I know is your own sense of loss."[485]

Jerry Bruner was surprised at the level of desolate grief he felt at Ruth's death. He called her his confidante, his friend, his goad, his confessor. She, he wrote, surely changed the lives of those she touched. And almost plaintively concluded: "How curious that we never fully appreciate that there are some people who make us more civilized with each other."[486*]

The men who loved Ruth wrote to each other; the women—especially Val and Nat and Jean Bacher—sought each other out for consolation. Perhaps with Val in mind, Ruth had willed the Pasadena house, with its adjoining garden gate, to Bob and Jean Bacher for their lifetimes. The three to carry on the old stammtisch.

At the beginning of that winter, David Lilienthal had written a description of the neighborhood at the Institute that he shared with the Oppenheimers: "On this quiet street under the great trees, trees that seem almost more inspiring now that their leaves are gone than when they were heavy and dark with leaves. Yesterday afternoon it snowed, huge fluffy feathers filled the air, and soon the trees were lined with this whiteness, a whiteness so pure it seems like something from Heaven."[487] It is easy to imagine Robert walking those winter woods, his heart heavy at the loss of Ruth, as he had once mourned Jean in the snow-covered mountains rising above Los Alamos.

*In Ruth's honor, her colleagues planned a series of lectures in Berkeley. The speaker at the first Ruth Tolman Memorial Lecture was psychologist Rollo May. More than 1,500 attended.

The poison apple revisited: "He was wonderfully intelligent, charming, fun to be with, dignified and handsome"

John Edsall, a friend from student days at Harvard, seemed to appear at critical junctures in Robert's life. Most important, he had been on Corsica when Robert left abruptly to return to England because of the mysterious poison apple left on his tutor's desk. It would be fourteen years before Edsall saw Robert again, in Berkeley at the Eagle Hill house on a stormy, windblown night not long before the Oppenheimers left for Los Alamos. At that time, Edsall was astonished at the changes that had taken place in his college friend. The awkward, frantic young man he remembered from Cambridge had been transformed. "I felt that he obviously was a far stronger person," Edsall said, describing how Robert had achieved "a great deal of inner resolution." This was an altogether new Robert, confident and authoritative, who radiated "a feeling of such an extraordinarily brilliant and rapidly moving and scintillating mind that was beyond the power of most of us to follow: that he could reach and see intuitively things that most people would be able to follow only very slowly and hesitatingly, if at all."[488] This new Robert had risen, phoenix-like, from the near disaster of the phantom apple left on the desk of his tutor, Patrick M.S. Blackett, experimental physicist at the Cavendish Laboratory at Cambridge and just seven years older than Robert. And also the object, Edsall would say, of Robert's "tremendous admiration, combined perhaps with an intense jealousy—jealously because of his feeling that Blackett was brilliant and handsome and a man of great social charm, and combining all of this with a great brilliance as a scientist—and I think he had a sense of his own comparative social awkwardness and perhaps a personal sense of being physically unattractive compared to Blackett."[490]

One more thing Edsall would remember: Only a month after returning to Cambridge from Corsica, Robert had introduced him to Blackett at King's College. The two had a private conversation and Edsall came away tremendously impressed with Blackett. He would say, "I felt [him] to be an extraordinary person . . . . immediately, just after talking to him for five minutes."[490]

Edsall wasn't the only one impressed with Blackett; Teddy Bullard, another outstanding British physicist and a friend of Blackett's, would describe him as "The most versatile and best loved physicist of his generation and his achievement was without rival . . . he was wonderfully intelligent, charming, fun to be with, dignified and handsome." Another admirer said Blackett was "Tall, slim, beautifully balanced and looking always better dressed than anyone . . . that mysterious intense and haunted visage . . . alive indeed with intelligence, modesty and friendliness."[491] In short, Patrick Blackett was everything Robert Oppenheimer wanted to be. Wherein lies at least part of the poison apple Robert said he left on Blackett's desk.

Some things seem obvious: Robert would not have been so quickly allowed back into the good graces of the Cavendish, and of Blackett himself, if the "apple" had been real and laced with some deadly chemical, say strychnine.[492] Robert's lifelong weapons of choice were a sharp tongue or a poison pen, sarcasm his firepower. Those in command at the Cavendish would have been more inclined to make an exception for a nasty broadside or even an impetuous love letter or poem (the apple here as a symbol of temptation, seduction, an implied homosexuality). It is definitely hard to imagine that attempted murder would have been excused or that Blackett would then be so forgiving as to allow Robert casually to introduce his friend Edsall not long after.

To complicate matters, the explanation that Robert gave when he rushed back to England from Corsica was his second confession of a "poison apple" left on Blackett's desk. The first had occurred six months earlier at the height of Robert's emotional breakdown. He had calmed down considerably since then, and actually was doing some good work. It has been suggested that when Robert hurried back from Corsica, he might have been racing to make changes on a paper he had written and left for Blackett. It was one of Robert's first papers to have a profound effect on his career. So "poison," in this case, could well have meant that while on Corsica he realized a mistake—poison in his own paper—and he hoped to return in time to make a correction.[493] Then again, it could simply have been a metaphor for his erratic behavior.

THE REVELATION ON CORSICA—AN awakening, really—that sent Robert back to Cambridge to attempt to right whatever wrong he had committed, he would later attribute to Proust. His explanation would be purposefully vague, the only hint being a passage he committed to memory, about evil being a rare and estranging state, and that an indifference to the suffering one causes is a "terrible and permanent form of cruelty." Suddenly, Robert felt he had a choice: He could reject the impulses that threatened him—or he could try to remake himself using those attributes of Patrick M.S. Blackett he so admired.[494] He had done this once before when, as a sickly New York City boy, he was sent to New Mexico suffering from colitis and possibly tuberculosis, and met the young Katherine Page, who introduced him to a rugged new way of life which he translated into a cowboy-physicist persona. He went home with a determination to enter Harvard and a new life.

Having survived the emotional turmoil that overwhelmed him in Cambridge, Robert went on to Germany to complete his doctorate and then stayed in Europe for a year of postgraduate work, time enough to burnish his new Blackett image—alive with intelligence, sometimes modesty and friendliness, and always with the mysterious, intense and haunted visage. Fourteen years after Corsica, the conversion was obvious to Edsall, down to the voice that was to mesmerize American audiences, "He spoke in a curious clipped way—an accent that was not quite British but not exactly American either."[495]

IN THE WEEKS WHEN HE was clinging to some kind of sanity in Paris, Robert's sexuality had been tested and he had survived. By the time he married Kitty, he had an established reputation as a ladies' man. There had been a succession of mostly young women in the 1930s, with Jean as the only serious attachment before Kitty. And always there were a few quiet murmurs about the possibility of homosexual tendencies. Robert was seen as an aesthete and, as Wyman had noted after Corsica, "a little precious." But that affect was easily balanced by stories about him challenging the mountain wilderness on a horse named Crisis.

⟋

EDSALL APPEARED AGAIN AT OLDEN Manor in 1954 only a few weeks after the Hearing. By then, in the rarefied world of nuclear physics, Blackett's career had paralleled Robert's in several important ways. The British physicist had spent his post-war years speaking and writing unambiguously against the spread of nuclear weapons, using many of the same arguments as Oppenheimer. Blackett had been cautioned for his leftist politics, but would go on to win the Nobel Prize in physics in 1948. In the 1960s, he would become president of the Royal Society, receive a life peerage as Baron Blackett, and have a crater on the moon named for him. Blackett belonged in a way Robert never had.[496] Robert's America was much less forgiving than Blackett's England. "In the Matter of J. Robert Oppenheimer," the government transcript of the Hearing, would give rise to stage dramas which portrayed Robert as a tragic figure. He angrily dismissed the theatrical productions as "travesties," and was determined to reject this role. Though Blackett and Oppenheimer would have limited contact during their lifetimes, both were described as unrivaled achievers, versatile physicists, *wonderfully intelligent, fun to be with, dignified, and handsome.* Thus, the poison apple—as the symbol for the second of Robert's re-creations—can be understood.

⌒

ROBERT WORKED HARD TO ERASE the image of his martyrdom though it would linger in the American mindset into the next century. Under Robert's directorship, the Institute became an international center of intellectual achievement. Young academics saw it as a kind of Camelot,[497] where they had the luxury of pure thought, or time to write a book or immerse themselves in esoteric research.

Robert gathered in his woodsy corner of New Jersey an astonishingly vibrant collection of some of the world's most inventive men and women (though mostly men, still). He used his special director's fund to bring in old friends, including Francis Fergusson on two occasions (keeping his promise that he would one day make up to Francis for the time in Paris when he'd tried to strangle him), and others from government whom he admired, such as George Kennan, who would become Robert's close friend. The two were born the same year, each spoke multiple languages and the trajectories of their careers seemed destined to bring them together at the Institute. Kennan was a diplomat trained in the Foreign Service who became an advisor to presidents and an authority on the Soviet Union. Known as one of the "wise men" of foreign policy, Kennan was the intellectual architect of the Marshall Plan. But it was his attitude on the Soviet Union, forged in his years in Moscow before the war and then continuing to evolve after, that would make him controversial. Kennan helped to shape the U.S. policy which resulted in the Cold War. He was called "the father of containment," a policy intended to keep the Soviets in check. Both Robert and Kennan were patriots who found themselves at odds with their government. When the

'50s gave way to the 1960s and the Americans raced the Soviets to build ever larger weapons of mass destruction, both men pondered the fallout from their individual actions.

Robert's loves played a larger part in his public life than was true for most figures of the time; he had felt compelled to describe Jean as a "sensitive, yearning creature" to a government panel weighing charges that she (thus he) was wanting in moral character. His deep friendship with Ruth made her the object of gossip meant to smear him. Kitty's early years as an Accidental Communist brought her to the witness stand in an effort to damage him, in a political climate that could not tolerate any shade of red. While Robert was preaching to the world the need for an open exchange of information, he was also excruciatingly frank in his observations about Kitty's psychological problems. He was not a saint, as some observers commented, but he did not betray his wife.

Ruth Tolman had been Robert's lodestar, their friendship deep and lasting. Close friends grew angry when rumors of a sexual affair were even mentioned, as if it besmirched the rare intimacy Robert and Ruth had achieved. Those rumors tracked back to Ernest Lawrence's questionable repetition of something Ruth Valentine's partner was supposed to have told him. So the only tangible evidence that suggests there might have been something more to their relationship can be found in Ruth's own words in her letters to Robert. A year after Richard's death she wrote: "The precious times with you last week and the week before keep going through my mind, over and over, making me thankful but wistful, wishing for more. I was grateful for them, Dear, and as you knew, hungry for them too." And again: "Oh Robert, Robert. Soon I shall see you. You and I both know how it will be."

But in fact *no one* other than Ruth and Robert can ever know how it was between them. Ruth wrote in an effusive style to many of her friends. *Thankful, grateful* can connote offering comfort as well as sex. Yet "even hungry for" does give one pause. Ruth might have destroyed Robert's letters because they would affirm an affair, but it is just as likely it was because he wrote in confidence about people they knew, and the letters, if made public, could hurt feelings or damage reputations.

In quickness of mind and breadth of interests, Robert and Richard had been alike. Robert was forty-four when Richard died, Ruth was fifty-five, and vulnerable; the tone of her letters changed, becoming more emotional and needier. If an affair happened, it would have been at this time, not when Richard was alive.[498] Yet Ruth was also worldly wise and too deeply devoted to Robert as a friend, as he was to her, to want what they had to be damaged. A continent separated Ruth and Robert, they saw each other only a few times a year, and were seldom alone when they did. That they loved each other was obvious to everyone who knew them well. Jerry Bruner was one of these; he came to know Ruth and Robert during and after the war. "Robert did not get close to many people," he offered, then attempted to explain what made Ruth so exceptional. She had, he says, the ability to "think inside your head" which, combined with an exceptional degree of empathy, made her an extraordinary confidante. "She had a wonderful sense of what life was like," Bruner says, smiling at the memory of a Ruth who could raise an eyebrow and tease him out of his doubts. He is certain that Ruth and Robert were emotionally very close, had a deep intellectual connection. "But she also had a sort of steadiness and soundness," he adds, something Robert surely found comforting.[499] In the end, the strength of their emotional connection, and their enduring loyalty, makes the subject of sex seem irrelevant.

~

LIFE IN OLDEN MANOR MOVED with the seasons, the light subtly altering Van Gogh's *Enclosed Field with Rising Sun* in the formal sitting room, as it had in Julius' apartment in New York. (Like his father before him, Robert would bring people in to observe the painting in the changing light.) David Lilienthal was now their next-door neighbor, and settled happily into the pastoral pleasures of the Institute. "I can hear," he wrote, "Toni's horses snorting as they graze, in their paddock just beyond our back fence and shrubs ... Last night, before turning in, I walked round to the paddock and just stood there, watching the two horses grazing."[500] When asked how the children were doing, Robert always said, "Fine." It wasn't true. Peter had been sent away to boarding school, and while Robert would drive the aging Cadillac over to see him, there were always others who were allowed to usurp his time. Toni fulfilled the role of dutiful daughter, doing what was expected of her; she found freedom by galloping her sorrel mare across the Institute's common, and on the trails of its woods. "My sister's regard for horses was similar to her father's," Peter has said, "Sober and appreciative, deep and simple; warm, essentially dignified, I think."[501]

Peter was unwilling to fit into the intellectual mode expected of a child of the Institute director. In May of 1958, the tension between mother and son seemed to reach a turning point when Robert was invited to teach at the Sorbonne in Paris, then go on to lecture in Israel, Greece and Belgium. Kitty took Toni out of her private school for the trip, but she balked at allowing Peter to come with them, using his grades as an excuse. According to Verna Hobson, who would watch over Peter while they were away, "There came a time when Robert had to choose between Peter—of whom he was very fond—and Kitty. She made it so that it had to be one or the other, and because of the compact he had made with God or with himself, he chose Kitty."[502] Hobson would not forgive Robert for leaving his son behind. Eventually, Peter would do what his father had done to find himself: he went west, to his Uncle Frank. He would return to Olden Manor, and to the family, but his future would be in the high wild country of New Mexico.

ᗖ

ON JUNE 19, 1959, VAL wrote to Margaret Mead, "My (noncommunist) physicist friends here are delighted that Admiral Strauss got the axe. So am I."[503] The U.S. Senate voted against confirming Lewis Strauss' nomination to be Eisenhower's Secretary of Commerce because they remained unconvinced of his "character and integrity."[504]

ᗖ

IN NOVEMBER OF 1960, KITTY and Robert traveled to Japan. ("A tragic pair," their neighbor David Lilienthal was to write of them, "The trail from Los Alamos and Alamogordo is a long and terrible one, a Golgotha indeed."[505]) The Japanese greeted him with an excess of civility, and Robert did not speak of evil or of blood on his hands. His message was clear: minds and nations must be open in their sharing of knowledge. Secrecy, he would say, denies governments the wisdom and resources of the whole community. That would also be his message the following year, when he made a lecture tour in Latin America, and then in Europe. Earlier, at Rheinfelden, West Germany, he had sharply criticized his country's inability to discuss the reality of a nuclear war: "What are we to make of a civilization which has always regarded ethics as an essential part of human life" but which "has not been able to talk about the prospect of killing almost everybody except in prudential and game-theoretical terms?"[506]

ᗖ

LILIENTHAL WATCHED THE OLD CADILLAC come up the hill, and raised his walking stick in salute: "The door opened," he wrote, and there was "Kitty, her eyes larger than ever, against the ravages that time and trouble, poor dear, have committed against her."[507] Kitty wanted what she felt time and trouble had taken from her to be returned; Robert knew it wasn't possible. He also knew that it wasn't his life that Kitty wanted restored so much as her own—a life that had been consumed by children and wifely duties, by the stifling rituals of academia, by a war that interrupted the education she believed would have led to equality and a place for her in a man's world. Alongside Jean, alongside Ruth. But Kitty, the risk taker, could not risk being without a man. That need was her primary ambition, as well as her lasting burden.

THE ELECTION OF JOHN F. KENNEDY in 1960 brought a new mood to the country. Finally, Frank was able to move to the University of Colorado at Boulder, and once again taught physics. Some of Kennedy's close advisors were friends of Robert's, and they talked of bringing him back into government, to right a wrong. Robert flinched at the idea; he had no desire to revisit his days as a martyr, to endure another security clearance. Early in the fall of 1963, Robert learned that he was to receive the prestigious Fermi Award and that President Kennedy would be presenting it himself. The date, time, and place were set: December 2, 1963, at 5:00 P.M. in the Cabinet Room of the White House. Ten days earlier, on November 22, the President was scheduled to be in Dallas.

When December 2 arrived, the sorrow of John Kennedy's assassination weighed heavily on the nation. Robert himself was described as "a figure of stone, grey, rigid, almost lifeless." The group of physicists and friends, including Lilienthal, and the new President, Lyndon Johnson, gathered with the Oppenheimers in the Cabinet Room. Kitty was "a study in joy, in exultation almost," Lilienthal would report, while he found "the two Oppenheimer children were embarrassed, particularly Peter, a shy and tender-looking teenager. I think it was more painful than happy for them."[508]

Lilienthal had misread Kitty. Later, when they were all back in Princeton, she would tell him about the day in the White House, her eyes smouldering, burning with resentment: "That was awful; there were some awful things about it." At that, Robert bowed his head "in that kindly, almost rabbinical posture which I have seen so often when Kitty was blazing and saying violent things." He countered that there were some "very sweet things" about the day.[509] Probably he was thinking about the private visit Jacqueline Kennedy had requested after the ceremony. Or even Lyndon Johnson's blustery Texas talk about how "behind every great man there must be two great women—a great mother and a great wife. All of you men in the room know what we would be without either, so Dr. Oppenheimer, although I have never met your mother, I have met your wife, and I want this group to meet this lady who shares honor with you today—Mrs. Oppenheimer." And then the President added, "You may observe she got hold of the check."[510]

It was supposed to have been a joyful step toward rehabilitation. Lilienthal and others saw it differently: "It all seemed to me a ceremony of expiation for the sins of hatred and ugliness visited on Oppenheimer, now, belatedly, being given a gold medal, a plaque, and a check for $50,000 from the Government of the U.S."[511] However smouldering Kitty's resentment, it did not keep her from spending $10,000 on a new mink coat. And later, she would make a trip into New York City to a foreign car dealership to buy Robert a new luxury Peugeot as a surprise for his birthday.[512]

⤳

By 1966, Robert had been smoking for at least forty-two of his sixty-two years. That January he had a persistent sore throat; when finally he saw a doctor, a small cancerous lump was found in his throat. Surgery followed, then cobalt radiation treatments and an awful exhaustion. Lilienthal would stop in to check on Robert. On one of these visits, Kitty took him outside. "I asked her how Robert was getting on," he said, " and she uttered such a moan, began to cry, caught herself, blaming me for making her weep. Then shook it off, looked at me with that little-girl look and asked me if she looked all right now, could we go back and join the others?"[513]

On January 6, 1967, the doctors told Robert that his cancer had returned and was inoperable.

Near the end, old friends began to make regular pilgrimages. Frank came. He lay on the bed alongside his brother and thought, perhaps, of the days of Vienna sausages and whiskey in their saddlebags as they ranged the Pecos. Now they watched an episode of *Perry Mason* on the television, waiting together. Kitty, in agony, could not bring herself to enter the room where Robert lay curled into himself. He died at home on February 18, 1967.

⤳

On a bitterly cold and clear February 25, a Saturday, more than 600 gathered in Princeton University's Alexander Hall for a memorial service. The Julliard String quartet played Robert's choice, Beethoven's Quartet in C-sharp Minor. Hans Bethe spoke about how Robert had done more than any man to make American theoretical physics great. In the long years after the Hearing, George Kennan had become for Robert a source of warmth and respect, of common sense and civility. Like Ruth, Kennan had seen behind the carefully configured persona of Robert Oppenheimer. When Kennan rose to speak, it was of a Robert few in the audience knew, "A man who had a deep yearning for friendship, for companionship, for the warmth and richness of human communication. The arrogance which to many appeared to be a part of his personality masked in reality an overpowering desire to bestow and receive affection."[514]

JEAN, RUTH AND KITTY—ROBERT'S trinity—had understood and returned, each in her own way and in her own time, Robert's deep yearnings, his desire to bestow and receive affection. Jean and Robert had been seekers together when they were young, at a time when he was establishing his place in physics, and was searching for the more intensely moral life, the *engaged* and committed life, that she offered. They shared, too, a fascination with psychology and what seemed the mystical connections between the human psyche and science. Jean looked to him for empathy and the continual search for an answer to the depressions that devastated her. She had loved the brilliant young physicist, but career and depression and war had interrupted, and in the end she could not promise him anything, except to love him.

It did not happen right away; it was to take time, over a period of years, for Ruth to come to adore the compassionate Robert who could listen to the needs, fears and hopes of others. Robert had singled her out early in his California life; like Jean, Ruth was a seeker, open to experiences and challenges. Ruth embraced tradition, but was tolerant enough to push against its boundaries in a way that didn't threaten men. She became a refuge, the wise woman who knew him well.

Kitty loved the dramatic and ambitious Robert who walked the paths of power, and whose success and reputation reflected onto her. She was also the one who challenged him sexually and physically, who loved risk and excitement and had a barbed, witty sense of humor that matched his own. In the realm of the physical, she could do anything he could do, sometimes better: galloping horses, sailing close to the wind, sex without inhibitions, a fierce competitiveness.

Robert loved yet another woman, one who at times had made demands that overwhelmed all the others. She was the one Albert Einstein was referring to when, after the Hearing, he said that Robert "loves a woman who doesn't love him." That woman was the U.S. government.[515]

For Robert's memorial ceremony, Kitty selected a poem that she knew had been one of Robert's favorites and she felt it would reveal how "Robert had appeared to himself." But in the end she decided the poem "The Collar"—written by the seventeenth-century poet and priest George Herbert—was simply too personal, too revealing. She said she did not want to bare Robert's soul in public.[516] She could not have known that this last stanza is an eerie echo of the passion of a young Jean Tatlock.

Away! Take heed;
I will abroad.
Call in thy death's head there, tie up thy fears;
He that forbears
To suit and serve his need
Deserves his load.
But as I rav'd and grew more fierce and wilde
At every word,
Methought I heard one calling, "Childe";
And I reply'd, "My Lord."

"Robert is not only her husband, he is her past, the happy past and the tortured one, and he is her hero and now her great 'problem'"

At 16, Robert had sailed his twenty-eight-foot sloop in summer storms off Long Island's Great South Bay, racing the wind and pushing the boat to its limits. He had tested himself on horseback in the Sangre de Cristos and again at Perro Caliente as the cowboy physicist. When he had met Kitty, she had taken on the challenge and raised the ante and their early days together had been exhilarating. In the last dozen years of his life, Robert and Kitty built the beach house on St. John and discovered the thrill of sailing together in the near-perfect conditions around the Virgin Islands, with trade winds that blow steady from the northeast, transparent waters filled with bright flashes of fish, and a treasure of cays and islands with deserted white sand beaches.

On St. John, the Oppenheimers had thrived. Robert could drop his world statesman-physicist persona and move into an artless life, made simple by the surroundings. Sea and sandy beach on an isolated tropical island. No suits or formal dress. Only bathing suits, open shirts, bare feet. It was a warmer, gentler Perro Caliente. When they grew restless and required adventure, they sailed; when they wanted company, there was a cluster of residents who would eat with them, usually the bounty of the fish traps they set, and drink with them. "It was a life apart—offbeat, expat, a self-selected community that had gone to some lengths to get there," according to Fiona St. Clair, whose family had settled on the island and became friends of the Oppenheimers.[517]

In the month or more each year that the family spent on St. John over a decade, including every Christmas, Kitty again accumulated women friends who drank and gossiped with her as the sun lowered and the light ebbed. Fiona St. Clair's mother remarked about Kitty: "She was not a particularly sweet lady and I am not a particularly sweet lady, so we got along fairly well." Kitty remained bitter about the Hearing, but for the most part, according to the elder St. Clair, "We didn't discuss all the unhappiness of the past."[518] St. John was a reprieve, and after Robert's death, Kitty needed a reprieve. And something more.

Kitty did what she had always done when she found herself without a man. She looked around and saw that another was available, this time Robert Serber. Charlotte had attended Robert's memorial service with him; they sat behind Kitty and Toni. But Charlotte had been diagnosed with Parkinson's disease and had become depressed. Three months after Robert's death, Charlotte took an overdose of sleeping pills. Serber found her body in their apartment the following morning. Not long after, he answered Kitty's call for help. She wanted to arrange a conference in Robert's honor at the Institute to bring together twenty-five top physicists to discuss the current state of theoretical physics. Serber, as always where the Oppenheimers were concerned, obliged.[519] He was on the faculty at Columbia, he had been at Robert's elbow for all of the Los Alamos years, and he knew who should be invited. After the conference, Kitty served French champagne and unlimited caviar at her house. In 1968, Kitty was fifty-eight; Serber, fifty-nine.

Kitty divided her time between Princeton and St. John, an island so undeveloped it did not have a grocery store. She knew that Serber was a skilled sailor; like Robert, he had learned as a boy on Long Island Sound, and he and Charlotte had a thirty-foot sloop. During the Christmas holidays of 1959, the Serbers had sailed in the Virgin Islands as guests of Kitty's former husband, Stewart Harrison, and his wife Helen, on their new fifty-foot ketch. By chance, the Harrisons and Serbers had run into the Oppenheimers while buying provisions on St. Thomas. "It was a little embarrassing all around," Serber would say, no doubt remembering that he was the one who had driven Kitty to Perro Caliente that fateful summer before the war.[520]

By the beginning of 1969, Serber was, as he said, "under the influence of Kitty Oppenheimer." When Serber was asked to be the vice-president of the prestigious American Physical Society, he knew that Charlotte would have told him to refuse, that the position "was not my cup of tea." But Kitty had very different ideas and pushed Serber as she had Robert: he became the APS vice-president.[521]

In the spring of the same year, Kitty also talked Serber into buying a forty-two-foot Rhodes yawl in New York to sail to St. John. Toni christened it the *Undique.*

For the next three years, Serber and Kitty sailed down the Leeward Islands, as far as Granada. Kitty never doubted her abilities as a navigator, he would comment, adding that it sometimes got them in trouble. "When Kitty wanted to do something," Serber would say, "it was difficult not to go along with it."[522] Her daughter had discovered this as well; according to Serber, while Kitty was solicitous toward Toni, she also wanted to control her. She had pushed her daughter to go to graduate school, to complete the doctorate she herself had never accomplished. Toni wasn't interested. She had Kitty's wide smile and dark brown eyes, but not the steel to stand up to her domineering mother. Instead, Toni married an older man, an expert sailor, and the two made plans to sail around the world.

That year, Kitty and Serber were on St. Croix, staying at a club owned by friends (they stayed in separate rooms there, even though the gossip in the physics community had them married). The next morning, the people in the room next to Kitty's told Serber that she had been up all night, breaking furniture and making a terrible scene.[523] Three days later, she was driving back to her place on St. John in a jeep, when she drove off a mountain road and crashed down a hillside. "She'd been a beautiful girl," Serber said, but "then that terrible auto accident . . . her face was all bashed up." He had rushed her back to New York and there had been plastic surgery, but after that, he said, "she looked her age."[524] She was fifty-nine.

Kitty's next project, she said, was to write a biography of Robert and she began to contact some of the physicists who knew him, asking for letters or papers. But drinking kept getting in her way. On a trip back to Santa Fe and Los Alamos, where Robert was to be honored, she managed to miss her plane, disrupting all the plans that had been made by their old friends, and was up again all night, drinking heavily. Another time she went to London to visit Verna Hobson, now working for an architectural firm and living on a houseboat. For the duration, Hobson said, "We'd stay up all night with two or three bottles of vodka, smoke a carton of cigarettes . . . and then she'd sleep all day while I went to my office and then I'd come back and do it again. I didn't sleep for three days and nights."[525] The biography, if started, was never finished.

SERBER TOOK A SABBATICAL FROM Columbia starting in 1972, and Kitty was determined to cruise to the South Pacific and Japanese islands and then meet Toni and her husband in the eastern Pacific. She bought a beautiful fifty-two-foot ketch named *Moonraker*—built in Hong Kong of teak with elegant fittings, fine wicker work, and her own stateroom with bath. Three years earlier she had undergone surgery for severe internal bleeding.[526] Her liver was failing and she had been warned to live a quiet life and to give up alcohol. That was not, Serber reported, Kitty's style. Life on a sailboat is active and exhausting and she had no intention of giving it up. Nor would she tolerate a dry ship. She did not, Serber would offer, fear death.

Kitty had been experiencing bouts of diarrhea in the weeks before departing St. John; she consulted a local doctor, who supplied her with pills. Then, with Serber as captain, Kitty as navigator, and four young men as crew, they set sail. The route took them to Martinique, Grenada, Bonaire, and on to South America. From Cartagena in Columbia, they sailed to the San Blas Islands where they planned to spend two weeks. Kitty was not doing well, though she tried to hide it. Soon her stomach pain became so intense that Serber made for Cristobal in the Panama Canal Zone where he knew she could get good medical care. Once there, they had a grueling hour-long train ride to Panama City where she was admitted to the Gorgas Hospital. Mrs. Robert Oppenheimer was well cared for; the hospital director paid special attention to her and the Governor of the Canal Zone sent flowers. The diagnosis was "a severe intestinal infection." It was as likely to have been an acute attack of pancreatitis or liver failure.

Knowing Kitty was dangerously ill, Serber cabled Toni in French Polynesia. The message took time to reach her; she sailed for Bora Bora and began the long journey back. Air connections between Pacific islands were sporadic and difficult with frustrating delays. For ten days Kitty lay in the hospital becoming steadily weaker, sleeping most of the time.

On October 17, 1972, Kitty Oppenheimer died of an embolism. She was sixty-two. Toni arrived the following day. Serber and Toni scattered her ashes near Robert's in the warm waters within sight of what is now called Oppenheimer Beach on St. John.

EPILOGUE

EPILOGUE

We were seduced by Robert Oppenheimer. Intellectually, historically, even emotionally.

Neither of us can remember exactly when this happened. We had never met him; he was long dead by the time we met. We do know that we began discussing an Oppenheimer book early in our friendship, and we have been friends now for more than three decades. We watched our own children grow up as Oppenheimer biographies began to be published, and we continued to read and talk about Robert and his role in what certainly was one of the most seminal events of our lifetimes. At some point we began to call him by his first name, figuring he had been in our lives long enough for us to take that liberty, though we never went so far as to call him "Oppie." That seemed presumptuous.

We cannot pinpoint the exact date when the subject of a book veered from Robert to his wife Kitty. The biographies continued to be published, we continued to read them and Kitty continued to be maligned. But as we read all the hundreds of thousands of words, we found ourselves tantalized by other repeating, exuberant words or phrases. A name, a hint, a neural flash shimmering out of the pages of all those scores of books and interviews about Robert Oppenheimer.

About his wife Kitty—she could be very bewitching, but . . . fascinating, but not very nice . . .

About Jean Tatlock—a lyrical, sensitive, yearning creature . . . the one person in the room you would always remember.

And Ruth Tolman, the woman Robert's Aunt Hedwig called his best true friend—one of those people who make us more civilized with each other.

We became convinced that these three women who occupied Robert's heart, his mind and great swaths of his adult life had a story worth telling. We felt they were key to his life, lost in the ever-growing shadow of the man who has come to symbolize the world's entry into the Atomic Age. One day we simply knew that we wanted to rescue them from what seemed like historical oblivion. They took us on a voyage of discovery, these three: Kitty and Ruth and Jean.

We must have constructed dozens of timelines during the writing of this book, tracing the chronologies of our four main subjects in increasing detail, keeping track of Jean, Ruth, Kitty and Robert, all born before the First World War, as each moved through the minefields—both public and private—of the twentieth century. We started out by charting the decades and then, as our research brought the four principals together and we began to see how their lives meshed, we plotted single years and at times, even months. We wanted to re-create the impact each of the four had on the others in time and space, played out against some of the most difficult periods in American history. All of this we worked into the pages of this book. What you won't find are some of what were, to us, illuminating stories which fell outside of the timeline, but are too compelling not to mention.

Robert would have been proud of his brother Frank's contribution to the world of science. He and Jackie moved back to San Francisco and started the Exploratorium, a unique science museum that has become the model for others around the world.

From Perro Caliente, Katy Page—"the reigning princess of the House of Chaves"—wrote to Robert at Princeton in his time of trouble, "It makes my heart ache to sit on your porch having tea when you are in the heat and confusion of man's world. I suppose, however, that one of the main functions of a heart is to ache."[527] Katy had her share of sorrow. She married again, moved into Santa Fe. In 1961, she was murdered in her home during a burglary; a neighborhood youth was found guilty.

Anne Wilson Marks, Robert's secretary at Los Alamos and good friend during the Hearing, had her life jolted in 1960 when her husband, Herb, died suddenly of a heart attack, leaving her a widow for forty-six years. Until her death in 2006, she worked for international arms control.

Had this book been fiction, we would have left Herb and Anne together longer, and we would not have allowed so many suicides. We would have saved Jean (perhaps by setting the story in the twenty-first century, when science has found some of the answers to the depression from which she suffered), and bright and funny Charlotte Serber, who couldn't face the ravages of Parkinson's disease. We would have wished an easier death for Kitty's mother. And for Kitty. Toni Oppenheimer deserved a longer life; she hanged herself in the family beach house on St. John in January of 1977. By then, she had been twice married and twice divorced. As her friend Fiona St. Clair said, Toni "could not find her path." The girl her mother had once described as "one of those girls who is so unfortunate as to want to do good,"[528] left a note offering the beach house to the people of St. John as a community center.

After Kitty's death, Toni had returned to live on St. John, and since Fiona was about her age, they became friends. After Toni's death, Fiona married Robert Serber, then seventy. She had a son, Zach, from a previous marriage, and she and Serber had another son, Will. Serber died in 1997 at the age of eighty-eight. We interviewed both Robert Serber and Fiona St. Clair Serber (he in 1994, she in 2012) at their Riverside Drive apartment in New York City.

The journeys we took through cyberspace turned up some of our most exciting discoveries. One of us would call the other and ask, "Are you sitting down?" That happened the day we found Martin Vissering, whose mother was a cousin of Kitty's, in Bremen, Germany. Martin in turn contacted his great-aunt and his brother Ulrich, who gave us the information on the Visserings' family background.

We spent months trying to track down Kitty's first husband, knowing only his name, Frank Ramseyer, that he was a musician Kitty had met in Paris, and that their marriage was annulled after Kitty discovered a journal he kept (in mirror writing) that divulged, she said, that he was homosexual and a drug addict. And that the Court papers had been sealed on the grounds of "obscenity." This is the story reported in Oppenheimer biographies. Online, though, we discovered that Frank was a good deal more than a musician wandering around Paris romancing Kitty Puening. He had graduated from Harvard College and worked in the music department there. In the bulletin of the Maine Coast Heritage Trust, we discovered that the daughters of Frank Ramseyer had donated family land to the Trust. We found one daughter listed in a church bulletin, and sent an e-mail to the church, asking that the message be passed to her. We were thrilled to receive an e-mail from Lin Ramseyer Clayberg. She and her sister, Helene Ramseyer Dickel—Lanie—an emerita research professor of astronomy at the University of Illinois, were delighted to talk about their father; they told us he spent his career teaching in the music department at Wheaton College in Norton, Massachusetts. Lanie wrote: "He was a true Renaissance man, knew the names of birds, ferns, trees ... studied classical Chinese on his own, and first pointed out the summer constellations to me."[529]

Lin said their father was a sweet and humble man, a fine musician, and that he never spoke to them about his first marriage. It was their mother who told them about Kitty, and that Frank had been saddened by the abortion of his son. Their father could do mirror-reading, the sisters told us. They said he may have been bisexual and it is possible that he experimented with drugs at one time in his early life, but certainly he was not an addict. They did know that he and their mother, Linda, were devoted to each other. Frank Ramseyer, clearly, had a long and happy life with his music and his family.[530] Lanie would go on to get a Ph.D. and study the birth of stars, a topic of early interest to both Robert Oppenheimer and Richard Tolman. In 1985, she spent a year doing research at Los Alamos.

Frank was a handsome man; in fact, three of Kitty's husbands looked curiously alike. Joe Dallet was the rugged exception. When one of the wives from Los Alamos met Stewart Harrison after the war, she was startled by how much he resembled Robert.

Jean Tatlock's brother, Hugh, and his wife, Anne Fisher Tatlock, had four children. Their eldest child and only daughter, named Marjorie for her grandmother, was clinically depressed throughout her short life. We located Jean's nephew, John Tatlock (named for his grandfather), in New York City, and he and his brother David searched out family photographs and papers for us. John told us that his sister had been in and out of private institutions; as the youngest child, John would often go with his parents to visit her. She would come home for periods, he said, and during one of these on a New England winter's night, she walked out of their house in her nightgown, through a woods and across the frozen river. She fell through the ice and drowned. She was twenty-six.[531] For Hugh Tatlock, it would have been a reprise of the earlier tragedy.

Hugh never spoke of Jean to his sons. In fact, his son John told us how, as an undergraduate, he was walking across Harvard Yard with a friend who, the night before, had seen the Kipphardt play, *In the Matter of J. Robert Oppenheimer.* The friend asked if he was related to the Jean Tatlock in the play, and John answered that he didn't know.

After Jean's death, it had been Hugh who questioned the coroner's report, but it was not until 1991 that he was contacted by someone who was fascinated by the world of spies and government surveillance and had been investigating Jean's death. The name Boris Pash had raised a red flag. The investigator had eagerly reported, "I knew of him from work I had done earlier on CIA assassination activities...I believe Pash will prove a pivotal character in this story."[532]

The coroner's report on Jean's death prompted the investigator to write: "[Jean] Tatlock's death is suspicious in the extreme....As a doctor, she had access to ample and effective means for suicide. That she would choose such a painful, bizarre and unlikely method as drugging and drowning herself strikes me as questionable.... The autopsy found a trace of chloral hydrate in her system. Chloral hydrate is commonly known as knockout drops or a Mickey Finn. This may or may not be suggestive."[533]

The investigator took the postmortem reports to a clinical pathologist in a reputable big city hospital, who concluded that they were consistent with death by drowning. "Could it have been murder?" the investigator probed. Not likely, the pathologist answered, since there were no signs of trauma to the body. But wasn't drowning "a strange way for a doctor/psychiatrist to commit suicide?" The pathologist responded that he had seen many "weird" suicides, and some of the most bizarre were psychiatrists. But what about the chloral hydrate—the Mickey Finn? The pathologist explained that the chloral hydrate has to be combined with alcohol to be effective, and there had been no alcohol in Jean Tatlock's body."[534]

In his preliminary report to Hugh, the investigator went into detail on plans for "what we should do next." It was a long list, including compiling a list of names and addresses of surviving relatives and close friends to interview. Travel to San Francisco to visit Jean's apartment. Obtain copies of the 1976 hearings of the U.S. Senate Select Committee, chaired by Senator Frank Church, to study intelligence abuses and revealing illegal and immoral—including assassination attempts—practices within the CIA and FBI.

And what about Boris Pash? Was he one of the "rogue elephants" Senator Church inveighed against? And did he have anything to do with Jean's death? The question was to go unanswered; Hugh Tatlock, a medical doctor himself, seems to have accepted the pathologist's explanation.

How to measure how well a life has been lived is the biographer's dilemma, especially when trying to reconstruct the lives of women who are ancillary to the main attraction: Kitty, Ruth and Jean. Much depends on the paper trail, and in the beginning for these women, the paper trail was remarkably thin. We tried to remind ourselves that often, in researching, one or two vehement voices can overwhelm or misconstrue a subject. Kitty Oppenheimer had two main detractors who had the time and the access to know her well: her sister-in-law Jackie, and a sometime friend at both Los Alamos and Princeton, Pat Sherr. Both left a voluble and negative record of Kitty's behavior. Physicist Abraham Pais clearly detested Kitty. Even Verna Hobson's recollections appear at times to have another agenda. In an attempt at balance, we made a concerted effort to find people who actually knew Kitty and could give us a more tempered view. Over the long gestation period of this book, we spoke to a number of the wives (and husbands) who were at Los Alamos and the Institute, to the nieces and co-workers of Ruth and Jean, and to anybody, in fact, who could shed light on that time, that place, those three women.

We met Ruth's nieces, Mary Tolman Kent and Deborah Tolman Whitney (she became the daughter-in-law of psychiatrist Elizabeth Whitney, who was briefly married to Jean's father late in life). It was especially exciting when we located Jerome Bruner, now ninety-eight, who had been Ruth's good friend "Jerry," and a close friend of Robert's as well. Dr. Bruner is referred to as "one of the best known and influential psychologists of the 20th century" as well as the key figure in the "cognitive revolution." He spent time with the Tolmans both in Pasadena and in Washington, D.C., during the war, and after at Princeton. He had ample time to observe Robert with both Ruth and Kitty, and to confirm our own conclusions about both women.

"Ruth had . . . intellectual qualities of the first order and a capacity for reflection," he said. "Kitty was good at conversation, but not at the counter-punctual word play that Ruth and Robert enjoyed." Kitty was, he offered, someone who never seemed able "to get her act together." Bruner was puzzled by the relationship between Robert and Kitty, explaining that she ran the house, was adoring toward Robert and seemed to have dedicated her life to keeping him human and happy and not too conflicted. And he was always respectful of her. Robert and Kitty could work together, he said, but he did not know how emotionally close they were.

It had never occurred to Bruner that there had been an "affair" between Ruth and Robert; when the idea was first mentioned to him, he wondered if he could have been naive. Upon further reflection he was adamant: he never saw an indication that theirs was more than a deep and loving friendship.[535]

JEAN'S PASSIONATE, PRECOCIOUS ADOLESCENT LETTERS allowed us to watch her grow and flower and to feel, almost seventy years after her death, the loss of such talent and promise. Although Ruth lived a full life, when she died our feelings mirrored those of her friends; even from the distance of decades, her empathy and grace endeared her to us. Kitty remained for us, as for most of the people who knew her, an enigma: Bright, frustrated, capable of erratic kindnesses and frequent cruelties, she was the epitome of a life unfulfilled.

UNTIL THE END OF HIS life, Robert remained loyal to these women. He steadfastly treated the memory of Jean and Ruth with respect. For the duration of his marriage, he remained, in some profound way, deeply committed to his wife. Each of the three in her turn helped shape his character, read poetry with him, opened doors to new worlds for him, took risks and laughed and entertained with him, encouraged and comforted him. They gave companionship and friendship and, most of all, the love that Robert Oppenheimer, aloof and arrogant though he could be, needed as much as any man.

Acknowledgments

We live forty miles from each other in Northern California and for a number of years have been meeting halfway, to plot our research and travels. Our first stop was Washington, D.C., and the home of Martin Sherwin, who with Kai Bird produced the Pulitzer-prize winning *American Prometheus: The Triumph and Tragedy of J. Robert Oppenheimer.* Both were wonderfully generous, allowing us to work with their extensive files.

Charles Weiner, the editor (with Alice Smith) of the excellent and oft-cited *Robert Oppenheimer: Letters and Recollections,* shared his knowledge of Oppenheimer along with his interview files. We would also like to thank Nora Murphy at the Massachusetts Institute of Technology for help with the Alice Kimball Smith Papers; Jeff Flannery of the Library of Congress Manuscript Division; Eric Vanslander of the National Archives for locating the Ruth Tolman letters and her OSS file. Also on the East Coast, Christine DiBella guided us to useful letters at the Institute for Advanced Study in Princeton and Rebecca Filner, archivist at Berg Collection, NYPL, alerted us to the treasure of letters between Jean Tatlock and May Sarton. Archivists at the Tamiment Library (part of New York University's Special Collections) were most helpful in finding and copying Joseph Dallet's letters. Dean Rogers at the Vassar College Archives kindly located materials and answered numerous questions. In New York we also met John Tatlock, Jean's nephew. Over brunch and several coffees, he shared his memories of his Aunt Jean and family photographs, adding a poignant dimension to Jean's story.

On the West Coast, we spent hours with the Frank Oppenheimer Papers and Joe Dallet's *Letters from Spain* at the University of California's Bancroft Library. The Boris Pash Papers and Robert J. Norris' interviews for his *Racing for the Bomb* at the Hoover Institute Archives at Stanford University added context to our study. In Southern California, Occidental College holds the papers of Ruth Benedict. At the Archives and Special Collections at the California Institute of

Technology in Pasadena Charlotte (Shelley) Erwin was our guide to the Richard C. Tolman Papers and photographs.

In New Mexico and Los Alamos, Heather McClenahan, Executive Director of the Los Alamos Historical Society, was extremely helpful, as was John Gustafson of the J. Robert Oppenheimer Committee. Alan Carr, the Los Alamos National Laboratory historian, generously provided us with photographs of the Oppenheimer family. Patricia stayed at Los Pinos, where Robert Oppenheimer first fell in love with the Southwest, and rode the trails to Perro Caliente on Grass Mountain, in the Sangre de Cristo Range.

By tracing an address for Karl Ludwig Vissering (Kitty's uncle) on Kaethe Puening's death certificate, we located his grandsons Martin and Ulrich Vissering. They provided us letters, photographs, and little-known information about the family. A clue online led us to Frank Ramseyer's daughters, Lin Ramseyer Clayberg and Lanie Ramseyer Dickel, who shared memories, ideas, photographs of the father they obviously adored.

Barton Bernstein, professor of history at Stanford University and an authority on the politics surrounding the atomic bomb helped us cover an extremely complicated period in American history. Patricia would also like to thank Peter Stansky, emeritus professor of history at Stanford, who read an early draft of the book and offered unceasing encouragement. Patricia also spent many hours with Joe Kanon, the author of the novel *Los Alamos,* talking about the relationships between Kitty and Robert and Jean and Robert.

A special thank you is owed to Peter Oppenheimer, Robert's and Kitty's son. Witness to so much of their story, he answered our notes with unfailing courtesy.

We would also like to thank Mary Jo Nye, professor emerita at the University of Oregon, John Keeler, Dean of the Graduate School of Public and International Affairs at the University of Pittsburgh, Lizette Royer at the Archives of the History of American Psychology, University of Akron, and Chloe Pitard for sharing with us her father's (John Lansdale) unpublished memoir.

We received firsthand information from several remarkable nonagenarians. The physicist Freeman Dyson was at the Institute during most of Robert's directorship, and shared his recollections of Kitty. Saying he didn't trust his then sixty-year-old memories, he referred instead to letters he had written to his parents in England. Ed Lofgren was at Los Alamos and knew a great many of the physicists mentioned in this book. Over a period of several years, he answered our questions patiently and carefully. Lofgren remembered his first interview with "Oppie," at their house in Los Alamos, with Kitty curled up in a corner of the sofa, her legs tucked under her.

We want to thank our families: Mark Streshinsky read and commented helpfully on the manuscript.

Robin and Ian Klaus encouraged writing about the "Oppenheimer women" from the beginning; Laurie Richardson, Elizabeth Mitchell, and Ruth Freeman listened patiently to innumerable stories about "our women."

This book has been a long time coming; we are certain we are forgetting others who helped us. Just know that one day we will remember, and when we do will thank them.

We could not possibly forget the people who saw us through all this: our crackerjack literary agent, Dana Newman, our patient editor, Christina Roth, and all the folks at Turner Publishing who helped us bring Jean Tatlock, Ruth Tolman and Kitty Oppenheimer out from the shadows to give them their proper place in atomic history.

Shirley Streshinsky & Patricia Klaus
Kensington and Petaluma, California

FOOTNOTES

CHAPTER 1

1. Anne Cabot Wyman, *Kipling's Cat: A Memoir of My Father* (Rockport, MA: Protean Press, 2010), 4.

2. Jerome Karabel, *The Chosen: The Hidden History of Admission and Exclusion at Harvard, Yale, and Princeton* (Boston: Houghton Mifflin, 2005), 105–09.

3. See S.S. Schweber, *In the Shadow of the Bomb: Oppenheimer, Bethe, and the Moral Responsibility of the Scientist* (Princeton, NJ: Princeton University Press, 2000), 54; Alice Kimball Smith and Charles Weiner, *Letters,* 9; and Herbert Smith, interview by CW, August 8, 1974 (CWF).

4. See William Tatlock, *The Sin of Drunkenness and its Remedy: Sermons Preached in St. John's Church, Stamford, February 12 and March 19, 1882* (Stamford, CT: W. W. Gillespie, 1882). The Rev. Tatlock may also have been attracted to the reforming message of the famous Harvard President, Charles W. Eliot. Tatlock himself was a temperance advocate and used his pulpit to preach the importance of temperance as well as faith.

5. Mrs. Marjorie Fenton DAR ID Number: 42790. The National Society of the Daughters of the American Revolution, www.dar.org.

6. Elizabeth C. Stevens, *Elizabeth Buffum Chace and Lillie Chace Wyman: A Century of Abolitionist, Suffragist, and Workers' Rights Activism* (Jefferson, NC: McFarland, 2003); Benbow F. Ritchie, *Edward Chace Tolman, 1886–1959: A Biographical Memoir,* Washington, D.C.,: National Academy of Sciences, 1964.

7. Frank Dempster Sherman, *The Ancestry of John Taylor Sherman and his Descendants* (NYPL, privately printed, 1915), www.Archives.org. Roger Sherman was one of only two men to sign all four of the most important documents establishing the United States: the Articles of Confederation, the Declaration of Independence, the Articles of Association and the Constitution.

8. *Daviess County Democrat* (Washington, IN, March 3, 1883). Courtesy of the Indiana County Historical Society.

9. See S.S. Schweber, *In the Shadow of the Bomb* and Ray Monk, *Inside the Centre: The Life of J. Robert Oppenheimer* (London: Jonathan Cape, 2013) on Robert as the outsider.

10. Kai Bird and Martin Sherwin in *American Prometheus: The Triumph and Tragedy of J. Robert Oppenheimer* (New York: Alfred A. Knopf, 2005) provide the conventional interpretation of the impoverished Julius (p. 10), but Monk in his new biography, *Inside The Centre,* argues Julius was not so much a rag-to-riches story as one of the immigrants who joined an already prosperous family (p. 17).

11. K.C. Kelley in *Something Incredibly Wonderful Happens: Frank Oppenheimer and the World He Made Up* (Boston: Houghton Mifflin Harcourt, 2009) says that Ella's family immigrated in the 1880s (p. 27); KB and MS in *Prometheus* state that the family immigrated in the 1840s (p. 11).

12. Martin Vissering to Patricia Klaus, May 23, 2012, personal communication.

13. Robert Serber, interview by Jon Else, 12/15/79, in *The Day After Trinity: J. Robert Oppenheimer and the Atomic Bomb* (documentary film, 1980), Serber File, Martin Sherwin Files Washington, D.C. (This interview and others, conducted by MS and KB, except where stated otherwise, are from the files in Sherwin's personal collection read in 2008. In 2009, these files were donated to the Manuscript Division, LOC, Washington, D.C., as the Martin J. Sherwin Collection Relating to JRO.

14. Robert Serber, interview by Martin Sherwin, 3/11/82. See also Serber interview by Else, 12/15/70, and KB and MS, *Prometheus,* 154–55.

Chapter 2

15. Ella Friedman to Julius Oppenheimer, January 1903, Frank Oppenheimer Papers, 1902–1985, Folder 10, Box 4, Bancroft Library, University of California, Berkeley.

16. Donald Glassman, Barnard College Archivist, wrote that it is not likely that woman would have been teaching at a college at that time; more likely that Ella Friedman would have taught art at Barnard School for Girls. Communication with Patricia Klaus, January 2007.

17. Paul Horgan, interview by AKS, December 21, 1975, MC369, Box 2, Paul Horgan Folder, AKS Papers, Institute Archives and Special Collections, MIT, Cambridge, MA.

18. Ella Friedman to Julius Oppenheimer, March 10, 1903, FO Papers, UCB.

19. Ella Oppenheimer to Julius Oppenheimer, August 27, 1903, FO Papers, UCB.

20. KB and MS note in *Prometheus* that Robert's birth certificate reads "Julius Robert Oppenheimer" (p. 11).

21. Julius began serving on the Board of the Ethical Culture Society in 1907.

22. As quoted in KB and MS, *Prometheus,* 15.

23. Jane Didisheim Kayser, interview by CW, June 4, 1975, CWF.

24. KB and MS, *Prometheus,* 21.

25. Horgan, interview by AKS.

26. Ibid.; Francis Fergusson, interview by Martin Sherwin, 6/8/79, MSF.

27. Peter Michelmore, *The Swift Years: The Robert Oppenheimer Story* (New York: Dodd, Mead, 1969), 9.

Chapter 3

28. Paula Fass, *The Damned and the Beautiful: American Youth in the 1920s* (Oxford: Oxford University Press, 1977), 261.

29. John D. D'Emilio and Estelle B. Freedman, *Intimate Matters: A History*

of Sexuality in America (New York: Harper & Row, 1988), 191-93.

30. Ibid. 224–25.
31. *Blue and Gold,* University of California Yearbook, 1917.
32. Dorothy T. Clemens, *Standing Ground and Starting Point: 120 Years with the YWCA in Berkeley* (Berkeley, CA: Big Hat Press, 1990), 36.
33. Mary Tolman Kent, interview by Shirley Streshinsky, November 28, 2005; Deborah Tolman Whitney, interview by Shirley Streshinsky, November 28, 2005.
34. W.B. Carnochan, "English at Stanford 1891–2000: A Brief History," *Sandstone and Tile,* Stanford Historical Society, 26, no. 1 (Winter/Spring, 2002), 6.
35. Priscilla Smith Robertson to Jean Tatlock, "Promise," ca. January 1944, (written to Jean after her death), courtesy of Charlotte Robertson. There are copies of this letter in the AKS Papers, MIT and PSR Papers, Vassar.
36. Chronology (lecture, Vassar, October 5, 1931), www.Vassar.edu/records/1931.
37. Robertson, "Promise."
38. Vassar Encyclopedia. http://vcencyclopedia.vassar.edu/faculty/prominent-faculty/winifred-smith.html.
39. AKS/CW, *Letters,* 10.
40. AKS/CW, *Letters,* 10.
41. See Walter Görlitz, ed., *The Memoirs of Field-Marshal Wilhelm Keitel.,* trans. David Irving (New York: Cooper Square Press, 2000), originally published in Germany as: *Mein Leben: Pflichterfüllung bis zum Untergang: Hitlers Feldmarschall und Chef des Oberkommandos der Wehrmacht in Selbstzeugnissen* (Gottigen: Germany: Musterschmnidt-Verlag, 1961); Walter Gorlitz, "Keitel, Jodl and Warlimont," in Correlli Barnett, ed., *Hitler's Generals* (London: Weidenfeld and Nicolson, 1989), 139–171.

42. Kitty to Hilda Dallet, August 11, 1937, Joseph Dallet, Jr. Papers, Series I, Correspondence. Box 1, Folder 12, Tamiment Library/Robert F. Wagner Labor Archives, NYU. All letters from Kitty to Hilda Dallet are from this collection unless otherwise stated.

CHAPTER 4

43. Wyman, *Kipling's Cat,* 25.
44. AKS/CW, *Letters,* 70, 90.
45. In *Outliers: The Story of Success* (New York: Little, Brown, 2008), Malcolm Gladwell describes Robert's "lofty perch," the advantages he had which facilitated his success and allowed him to escape the usual sanctions that Cambridge would normally imposed on him for the poison apple incident, whatever it actually was (pp. 98–100).
46. Years later, Robert would say in an interview for *Time* magazine that he was "on the point of bumping myself off." *Time,* November 8, 1948: 71.
47. Robert Oppenheimer to Francis Fergusson, March 7, 1976, in AKS/CW, *Letters,* 92.
48. Francis Fergusson, interview by AKS, April, 21, 1976, AKS Papers, MIT; Francis Fergusson, interview by MS, 6/18/79. Fergusson also wrote about this in his "Account of the Adventures of Robert Oppenheimer in Europe," Fergusson Folder, MSF.
49. Edsall, interview by CW, MC369, June 16, 1975, AKS Papers, MIT.
50. Michelmore, *The Swift Years,* 18.
51. Marcel Proust, *In Remembrance of Things Past.* Vol. 1, *Swann's Way,* Pleiade edition, trans. by C. K. Moncrieff and Terence Kilmartin (New York: Random House/Vintage, 1982) 32.
52. Ibid, 180.
53. William C. Carter, *Proust in Love*

(New Haven CT: Yale University Press, 2006), 193.

54. Edsall, interview by CW.

55. Jeffries Wyman, interview by CW, May 28, 1975. See also AKS/CW, *Letters*, 93.

56. Denise Royal, *The Story of J. Robert Oppenheimer* (New York: St. Martin's Press,1969) 36; Robert Oppenheimer to Frank Oppenheimer, ca. late spring 1926, AKS/CW, *Letters*, 95.

57. Nuel Pharr Davis, *Lawrence and Oppenheimer* (Greenwich, CT: Fawcett Books, 1968), Biographer Peter Michelmore to Frank Oppenheimer, September 16, 1968, FO Papers, Box 4, Folder 23–24. "…the love your brother spoke about was surely not love for a woman but love for humanity—a love that came to him during the weeks he and his two buddies tramped the hills of Corsica, sleeping under the stars, listening to the cries of shepherds, dashing through rainstorms to the comfort of an inn. . . . Wyman and Edsall were good friends, sensitive and intelligent, and their companionship could have helped trigger what was perhaps a kind of spiritual renaissance in your brother." Both Frank Oppenheimer and Michelmore are highly critical of Davis' book. See Frank Oppenheimer, "In Defense of Titular Heroes," *Physics Today* (February 1969), 77–80.

CHAPTER 5

58. Ruth Tolman to Richard Tolman, April 20, 1930, Series X: Ruth Tolman, Box 11, Folder 3, Richard Chace Tolman Papers, Archives and Special Collections, Caltech, Pasadena, CA. All letters from Ruth Tolman to Richard Tolman are from this collection unless otherwise cited.

59. Ruth S. Tolman, "Qualifications Statement for Promotion and/or Reassignment," October 16, 1944, U.S. Civil Service Commission. General Case File 1788–1967, Box 72, Ruth Tolman 1943–1958, J. Robert Oppenheimer Papers, LOC, 1799–1980.

60. Ruth Tolman to Richard Tolman, April 21, 1930.

61. Ibid, April 20, 1930.

62. Frank Oppenheimer, "The Trip West," FO Papers, UCB. The story and the quotations following are from this manuscript.

63. Robert Oppenheimer, interview by Thomas S. Kuhn, November 20, 1963, as quoted in AKS/CW, *Letters*, 114; interview with Frank Oppenheimer by AKS, April 14, 1976, in AKS/CW, *Letters and Recollections*, 134.

64. Jean Tatlock to May Sarton, August 21, 1928, Box 149, Folder 1, May Sarton Papers, Henry W. and Albert A. Berg Collection of English and American Literature, NYPL. All letters from Jean Tatlock to May Sarton are from this collection unless otherwise noted.

65. May's mother was English and her father was an eminent Belgian chemist and historian renowned as the founder of discipline history of science. He came to the United States in 1915, and was a full professor from 1918 until 1940. Of Quaker ancestry, Henry Haviland Field received his B.A., M.A. and Ph.D. in zoology at Harvard and went on to direct an international scientific institute in Zurich. When he died in 1921, the family returned to Cambridge, Massachusetts, so that his sons could attend Harvard. Noel would later achieve notoriety as a Soviet spy; Hermann would marry Jean Clark; he became an architect and one of the pioneers in environmental planning.

66. Jean Tatlock to May Sarton, July 28, 1928.

67. At some point, possibly when John Tatlock was at Stanford, Marjorie became friends with Dr. Elizabeth Whitney, Dr. James Whitney, Jean Macfarlane and Flora (Fergie) Jacobi Arnstein (mother of Edith Arnstein, later to be Jean's good friend), all of whom would be instrumental in the development of the fields of psychiatry and child guidance in the Bay Area.

68. Jean Tatlock to May Sarton, France, October 1, 1928.

69. Ibid., August 21, 1928.

70. Ibid.

71. Ibid.

72. Pat Sherr, who knew Kitty at Los Alamos and Princeton, would offer to an interviewer that Kitty had told her that she "was a wild as hell" in high school.

73. "Oppenheimer's Wife Bright Student." *Pittsburgh Sun-Telegraph,* April 13, 1954.

CHAPTER 6

74. Jean Tatlock to May Sarton, August 21, 1928.

75. Ibid., August 1928.

76. Ibid., France, August 28, 1928.

77. Ibid., Summer 1928.

78. Ibid., France, September 21, 1928.

79. Ibid.

80. Ibid., France, September 28 and 31, 1928.

81. Ibid.

82. Ibid., France, Fall 1928.

83. Ibid.

84. Ibid., October 29, 1928.

85. Ibid., France, November 7, 1928.

86. Ibid., France, October 1, 1928.

87. "Jessie Tatlock Memoir" (unpublished, n.d.), courtesy of John Tatlock.

88. Jean Tatlock to May Sarton, New York, end of December, 1928.

89. Ibid.

90. Ibid.

CHAPTER 7

91. May would describe them "all furiously writing and dash[ing] over to each others homes laden like bees with our honey." May Sarton to Anne Thorpe, April 4, 1929, Susan Sherman, ed., *May Sarton: Selected Letters, 1916–1954* (New York: W.W. Norton, 1997), 42.

92. See D'Emilio and Freedman, *Intimate Matters,* 190–194.

93. Radclyffe Hall's *The Well of Loneliness* (London: Jonathan Cape, 1928) was the lesbian novel published in England and the subject of an obscenity trial (the novel was ruled obscene and corrupting). Published at the same time in the United States by Alfred A. Knopf, it was confiscated by police and was the object of another obscenity trial; however, this time the ruling was favorable to Hall and Knopf. In the 1960s, it was still selling over 100,000 copies a year.

94. May Sarton to Eleanor Mabel Sarton, June 25, 1929, in Sherman, *Selected Letters,* 44–45.

95. Jean Tatlock to May Sarton, June 17, 1929.

96. Ibid.

97. Ibid.

98. Frank Oppenheimer, "The Drive West."

CHAPTER 8

99. Jean Tatlock to May Sarton, June 17, 1929.

100. Ibid., October 1929. Jean's experiences often appeared in her adolescent poetry: *Once*

When I lay down
Naked
In a path of moonlight
Someone
Thought I was crazy
And another envied me
For my frankness,
The moon
Only wept....

101. Ibid., June 27, 1929.
102. Ibid., Summer 1929.
103. Ibid.
104. Ibid.
105. Ibid.
106. Jean Tatlock to May Sarton, November 13, 1929.
107. Thomas Hager, *Force of Nature: The Life of Linus Pauling* (New York: Simon & Schuster, 1995), 101.
108. Hager, *Force of Nature*, 152.
109. Ibid.
110. Ibid.
111. Jean Tatlock to May Sarton, Summer 1929.
112. Ibid., January 1930.

Chapter 9

113. Ruth Tolman to Richard Tolman, April 20, 1930.
114. Frank Oppenheimer, interview by AKS.
115. Frank Oppenheimer, interview by CW, February 9, 1974, Niels Bohr Library & Archives, AIP, College Park, MD, 44.
116. Jean Tatlock to May Sarton, middle of January, 1930.
117. Ibid.
118. Ibid., February 1930.
119. Daniel Benveniste, "The Early History of Psychoanalysis in San Francisco," *Psychoanalysis and History* 8, no. 2, 2006: 195–233.
120. Jean Tatlock to May Sarton, Summer 1929.
121. Frank Oppenheimer would describe Richard as someone who "commanded respect, very much. And he loved the subject [physics] and the beauty of it, and the logical coherence of it." Frank Oppenheimer, interview by Judith R. Goodstein, November 16, 1984, Archives, Caltech, 28.
122. In 1922, when Val applied for a passport, Ruth served as her witness.
123. Helen Campbell Allison, interview by AKS, December 7, 1976, Helen Campbell Folder, AKS Papers, MC369, Box 2, MIT.
124. Quoted in AKS/CW, *Letters*, 137.
125. Robert Oppenheimer to Frank Oppenheimer, January 11, 1935, quoted in AKS/CW, *Letters*, 191.
126. Ruth Benedict to Margaret Mead, July 31, 1931, Special Correspondence, Box 1: Ruth Benedict, Margaret Mead Papers and South Pacific Ethnography Archives, LOC, Washington, D.C. All letters from Ruth Benedict to Margaret Mead are from this collection unless otherwise cited.
127. Ibid., August 10, 1931.
128. Ibid.
129. Robert Oppenheimer to Frank Oppenheimer, Berkeley, August 10, 1931, quoted in AKS/CW, *Letters*, 143.

Chapter 10

130. Jean Tatlock to May Sarton, [Spring] 1930.
131. Ibid., [June] 1930.
132. Ibid., [Before June] 1931.
133. Ibid., [June 1930, after Letty's death].
134. Ibid., June 1930.
135. Ibid., [June 1930, after Letty's death].
136. Ibid., Spring 1931.
137. Ibid., February 1930.
138. Ibid., [June 1930].
139. Joe Dallet to Hilda Dallet, July [1934?], Series 1: Box 1, Folder 13, Joseph Dal-

let Jr. Papers, NYU.

140. Dates of enrollment courtesy of the Office of the Registrar, University of Pittsburgh.

141. Peter Goodchild, *JRO: Shatterer of Worlds* (London: BBC, 1980), 37.

142. Lin Ramseyer Clayberg and Helene (Lanie) Ramseyer Dickel, interviews by Patricia Klaus, April–May 2012.

143. "Ramseyer Family," U.S. Census 1910; U.S. Census 1930. www.Ancestry.com.

144. Michelmore, *The Swift Years,* 33.

145. The Perro Caliente stories are legend and nearly every one of Robert's friends who went there had a story to tell: George and Else Uhlenbecks, Serber, Ruth Valentine, Frank Oppenheimer.

146. May Sarton Diary, copy of letter to Katherine Taylor, July 29, 1931, quoted in Peters, *May Sarton,* 66.

147. Jean Tatlock to May Sarton, Geneva, October 19, 1930.

148. Ibid. [Fall 1930, third letter].

149. Frank W. Ramseyer and Katherine Puening, Application for a Marriage License, December 24, 1932, Department of Court Records, Allegheny County, Pittsburgh PA. They were married on December 26, 1932. Information on the silver provided by Lanie Dickel; Kitty and Frank's address was 1000 Memorial Drive, Cambridge, Massachusetts.

150. Although Kitty stated in her testimony at the Security Clearance Hearing in 1954 that she was a student at Wisconsin, the University of Wisconsin Registrar has no record of her completing any courses there.

151. There is no record on file at the Wisconsin Vital Records Office, Madison, Wisconsin for Kitty and Frank's annulment, although his daughters confirm that their father said the marriage had been annulled; *Harvard Crimson,*

December 9, 1933.

152. Pat Sherr, interview by MS, February 20, 1979, MSF.

153. Lin Ramseyer Clayberg, personal communication with Patricia Klaus, April 29, 2012.

CHAPTER 11

154. Ruth Tolman to Richard Tolman, April 20 [1930], RCT Papers, Caltech.

155. Ruth Tolman, "Qualifications Statement for Promotion or Reassignment," OSS Personnel File, RG226, Box 781, NARA.

156. Ibid.

157. Martin Plessett, interview by MS, March 28, 1983, MSF.

158. Robert Serber, interview by Shirley Streshinsky, 1994.

159. Robertson, "Promise." Jean was also on the editorial board of the *Vassar Miscellany* for three years.

160. Jean Tatlock to May Sarton, Maine, September 9, 1931.

161. Ibid., September 9, 1931.

162. Katherine Taylor, the director of the school where May and the Clarks had been students in 1929, wrote to May asking whether Jean T. needed something, a cause, an urgency, so that she would give up her preoccupation with Letty's death, May Sarton Papers.

163. Vassar Encyclopedia. http://vcencyclopedia.vassar.edu/faculty/prominent-faculty/winifred-smith.html; Another faculty member, Susan J. Turner, said of Winifred, "Miss Smith has been recognized as one of Vassar's great teachers; she was also one of its greatest rebels"; Robertson, "Promise."

164. See reference below.

165. Jean Tatlock, "Account of the General Strike." *Vassar Miscellany,* XIX: 5, October 17, 1934 (1); While at Vas-

sar (regarded as a "hotbed of an extremely active Socialist and Communist movement," Jean also supported a hunger march of unemployed men and women. *Vassar Miscellany,* XIX: 11, November 7, 1934: 1, 4.

166. Robert Oppenheimer to Frank Oppenheimer, July 3 [1934], in AKS/CW, *Letters,* 185.

167. Ibid. 184.

168. Serber, interview by Else.

169. Robert Oppenheimer to Frank Oppenheimer, January 7 [1934], in AKS/CW, *Letters,* 172.

170. Ibid., 169.

171. "Kitty Oppenheimer Testimony," in United States AEC, *In the Matter of JRO: Transcript of Hearing before Personnel Security Board and Texts of Principal Documents and Letters* (Cambridge, MA: MIT Press, 1970), 571. Hereafter referred to as *ITMJRO: Transcript.*

172. Steve Nelson, interview by Martin Sherwin, July 17, 1981, MSE.

173. Steve Nelson, James Barrett and Rob Ruck, *Steve Nelson, American Radical* (Pittsburgh, PA: University of Pittsburgh Press, 1981), 81–85.

174. Goodchild, *JRO,* 38.

CHAPTER 12

175. Jean Tatlock to May Sarton, Spring 1931.

176. Deborah Tolman Whitney and Mary Tolman Kent, interview by Streshinsky. Ruth also had married women friends, among them Sigrid Lauritsen, Jean Bacher and Else Uhlenbeck.

177. John and Mary Ellen Washburn, California Voter Registration, Alameda County, 1926, 1928, 1932, 1934. www.Ancestry.com.

178. Joe Dallet to Kitty Dallet (his sister),

July 13, 1930, Box 1, Folder 12, Joseph Dallet Jr. Papers, NYU.

179. Joe Dallet to Hilda Dallet, [July 1934?]

180. Goodchild, *JRO,* 38.

181. Jean Tatlock to Priscilla Smith [Robertson], March 1935, Box 25.1, Priscilla Smith Robertson Papers, Virginia B. Smith Memorial Manuscript Collection, Archives and Special Collections, Vassar Libraries, Vassar, Poughkeepsie, NY.

182. Ibid.

183. Ibid.

184. Edith Arnstein Jenkins, one of Jean's close friends and a Communist, wrote that she felt that she and Jean had drifted apart because "she was now a Freudian analyst and we considered Freud and Marx unreconcilable, though she claimed she was still a Marxist." Edith Jenkins, *Against a Field Sinister: Memoirs and Stories* (San Francisco, CA: City Lights, 1991), 31.

185. KB and MS, *Prometheus,* 157. Based in part on one of Joe Dallet's letters to Kitty.

186. Steve Nelson, interview by MS; Goodchild, *JRO,* 38.

187. Priscilla Smith would comment that it was Jean's social conscience as well as her earlier contact with Jung that made her want to be a doctor. "Promise."

188. Jenkins, *Against a Field Sinister,* 28.

CHAPTER 13

189. Michelmore, *The Swift Years,* 49

190. Jenkins, *Against a Field Sinister,* 27–28.

191. Jean Tatlock to Priscilla Smith Robertson, July 15, 1936, PSR Papers, Vassar.

192. Serber, interview by MS.

193. Jean Tatlock to May Sarton, September 9, 1939.

194. Michelmore, *The Swift Years,* 49.

195. Kitty to Hilda Dallet, April 2, 1937.

196. Nelson, Barrett, and Ruck, *American Radical,* 188.

197. Kitty to Hilda Dallet, April 2, 1937.

198. Ibid., April, 1937.

199. Ruth Tolman, "Some Differences in Attitudes Between Groups of Repeating Criminals and of First Offenders," *Journal of Criminal Law and Criminology* 30, no. 2 (July–August 1939): 196–203. Based on her dissertation at University of California, Berkeley.

200. Marjorie Tatlock to Priscilla Smith Robertson, May 1937, Box 25.1, PSR Papers.

201. Information courtesy of John Tatlock.

202. Joe Dallet to Kitty, March 30, 1937, in *Letters from Spain* (New York: Workers Library, 1938) 14. The letters quoted here are from www.Archives.org. There are also copies at the Bancroft Library, UCB; and the Taniment Library, NYU.

203. Ibid., April 9, 1937, 21.

204. Ibid., April 19, 1937, 27.

205. Jean Tatlock to Priscilla Smith Robertson, July 11, 1937, Box 25.1, PSR Papers.

206. Ruth Schorr (friend of the Tatlocks), interview by Shirley Streshinsky, 2005. Edith Jenkins, a friend of Jean's, was explicit: "The summer of her mother's dying, Jean grieved for her and burned with rage against her father, who, out of his own need and weakness, would not let her die." *Against a Field Sinister,* 28; Jean Tatlock to Priscilla Smith Robertson, July 11, 1937, PSR Papers.

CHAPTER 14

207. Joe Dallet to Kitty, April 27, 1937, in *Letters from Spain,* 28–29.

208. Ibid., May 17, 1937, 40; June 21–25, 49.

209. Steve Nelson, interview by Peter Carroll, quoted in Peter Carroll, *The Odyssey of the Abraham Lincoln Brigade: Americans in the Spanish Civil War* (Stanford, CA: Stanford University Press, 1994), 161.

210. Richard Polenberg, ed., *In the Matter of JRO: The Security Clearance* (Ithaca, NY: Cornell University Press, 2002), 12. Hereafter cited as Polenberg, *ITMJRO.*

211. Robert Oppenheimer to George Uhlenbeck, June 29 [1937], quoted in AKS/CW, *Letters,* 201.

212. Benveniste, "Early History of Psychoalysis in San Francisco."

213. Kitty to Hilda Dallett, June 13, 1937.

214. Ibid., July 11, 1937. In some of the letters Kitty would forego capitalization.

215. Joe Dallet to Kitty, July 19, 1937, in *Letters from Spain,* 53.

216. FAECT was the controversial union, Federation of Architects, Engineers, Chemists, and Technicians. Army intelligence began watching it, concerned that there were active Communists in the union. Oppenheimer held an organizing meeting for FAECT in the summer of 1941. Lawrence was incensed that the union was trying to organize people in his laboratory.

217. Joe Dallet to Kitty, August 1, 1937, in *Letters from Spain,* 60.

218. Ibid., July 25, 1937, 57.

219. Kitty to Hilda Dallet, September 11, 1937.

220. Ibid.

221. Joe Dallet to Kitty, September 15, 1937, *Letters from Spain,* 62.

222. Carroll, *Abraham Lincoln Brigade,* 161.

CHAPTER 15

223. Kitty to Hilda Dallet, October 18, 1937.

224. Ibid.

225. Ibid.

226. Kitty to Dallet family, Telegram, Box 1, Folder 12, Joseph Dallet Jr. Papers, NYU.

227. Kitty to Hilda Dallet, November 10, 1937.

228. Nelson, interview by MS.

229. Kitty to Hilda Dallet, November 10, 1937.

230. Jenkins, *Against a Field Sinister,* 26.

231. Ibid., 21–22.

232. Ibid.

233. Jean Tatlock to May Sarton, 1930.

234. In a 2002 interview with Gregg Herken, Edith would say that although Jean claimed that she was not homosexual, Edith did not believe her and referred to a comment Jean had made to a mutual friend that she "had slept with every boy she could find to get over it." When Edith asked her later if she regretted not marrying Robert, Jean replied yes; she "would have done so had she not been "so mixed up." Edith offered that Jean didn't love Robert because "she perceived him as essentially nonsexual."*Against a Field Sinister,* 30–31. Serber, who admits he never met Jean, would tell of the arguments Robert and Jean would have and how she would taunt him about her affairs, accounts he would either have heard from Robert, or Kitty later.

235. According to most accounts (Gregg Herken, Ray Monk, Kai Bird and Martin Sherwin) Stewart Harrison was a British doctor, a family friend, whom Kitty had known as a teenager and met again when she was vacationing with her parents in England after Joe Dallet had died. Herken bases this on Army intelligence records in his work *Brotherhood of the Bomb: The Tangled Lives and Loyalties of Robert Oppenheimer, Ernest Lawrence, and Edward Teller* (New York: Henry Holt, 2002). Harrison most likely had not known Kitty when she was a teenager as she was living in Pittsburgh and he was in England, attending Oxford University and then medical school. She probably met him through her friend Zelma Baker who was working on tumors in lung tissue; Harrison had spent some time at Pennsylvania's medical school and his speciality was radiation therapy in cancer.

236. Harold Cherniss, interview by Martin Sherwin, May 23, 1979.

CHAPTER 16

237. Elizabeth Whitney to Hugh Tatlock undated [ca. 1939–1940], letter courtesy of John Tatlock and David Tatlock.

238. Ruth Benedict to Margaret Mead, September 10, 1939.

239. Ibid. October 11, 1939.

240. Helen Campbell Allison, interview by AKS. See Helen Cambpell correspondence with AKS, 1976.

241. Verna Hobson, interview by Martin Sherwin, July 31, 1979. Verna Hobson would meet Wilder Hobson (editor for *Time, Fortune* and *Harper's Bazaar,* a musician and historian of jazz) while working at *Time.* She would be Robert's secretary from 1954 to 1966, when she retired and moved to London, before becoming a writer.

242. Haakon Chevalier, *Oppenheimer: The Story of a Friendship* (New York: Braziller, 1965), 31–32.

243. Serber, interview by Streshinsky.

244. Frank Oppenheimer to Denise Royal, Feb. 25, 1967, Box 4, Frank Oppenheimer Papers.

245. Natalie Raymond to Ruth Benedict, August 1940, Special Correspondence, Box 1: Ruth Benedict, Margaret Mead Papers, LOC.

246. Robert Serber, *Peace and War: Reminiscences of a Life on the Frontiers of*

Science, with Robert P. Crease (New York: Columbia University Press, 1998), 59.

247. Serber, interview by MS.
248. Ibid.
249. Jean Tatlock to Winifred Smith, "Dear Winifred," Box 25.1, PSR Papers, Vassar.
250. Ibid.
251. Peters, *May Sarton,* 130–131.
252. Robert Oppenheimer FBI File, Series I: Correspondence. Folder 15.16, Doc. 154, Archives & Special Collections, Vassar College Library, Vassar. Quoted in KB/MS, *Prometheus,* 162.
253. Nelson, Barrett, and Ruck, *American Radical,* 268.
254. Serber, interview by Jon Else.
255. Chevalier, *Story of a Friendship,* 3.

CHAPTER 17

256. Ruth was chosen as chairman in part because she was not a feminist; it was thought that her "moderate stance" would enable her to deal with the issues facing the use of women psychologists in war work in a most diplomatic manner. See James H. Capshew, *Psychologists on the March: Science, Practice, and Professional Identity in America, 1929–1969* (Cambridge, UK: Cambridge University Press: 1999), 78. For the articles she would write on wartime women psychologists, see the Bibliography.
257. The debate over whether or not Robert was a Communist Party member or joined the Party (semantics are very important in this discussion) surfaced at the Oppenheimer Centennial conference held at University of California, Berkeley in 1904, as well as being a topic of many books and reviews. Some historians, Gregg Herken for example, ar-

gue that Robert was not a CPUSA member; Barton Bernstein believes he was; Martin Sherwin hedges but leans in the direction of Robert being a member. They all agree that Robert, whether he joined secretly or not, was sympathetic during the 1930s to Communism.
258. As quoted in Goodchild, *JRO,* 39–40.
259. Chevalier, *Story of a Friendship,* 42.
260. Ibid.
261. Kitty would flaunt her aristocratic connections, Jackie her working-class origin.
262. Zerka Moreno, interview by Tian Dayton, quoted in Toni Hovartin and Edward Schreiber, eds., Zerka Moreno, *The Quintessential Zerka: Writings by Zerka Toeman Moreno on Psychodrama, Sociometry and Group Therapy* (New York: Routledge, 2006). Accessed at www.Tiandayton.com.

CHAPTER 18

263. Military Application of Uranium Detonation
264. Robert S. Norris, *Racing for the Bomb: General Leslie R. Groves, The Manhattan Project's Indispensable Man* (South Royalton, VT: Steerforth Press, 2002), 239; see also, Barton J. Bernstein, "Reconsidering the 'Atomic General': Leslie R. Groves," *Journal of Military History* 67 (July 2003): 883–920.
265. James G. Hershberg, *James B. Conant: Harvard to Hiroshima and the Making of the Nuclear Age* (New York: Alfred A. Knopf, 1993), 166.
266. Serber, *Peace and War,* 67.
267. Dr. Lewis Hempelmann, interview by Martin Sherwin, August 10, 1979. Hempelmann was working with Ernest Lawrence's brother in the cancer radiation lab at the university and would become one of the medical

doctors at Los Alamos.

268. For an engrossing story of how a psychologist could battle severe manic depression and yet be a member of the psychiatry faculty at UCLA, see Kay Redfield Jamison, *An Unquiet Mind: A Memoir of Moods and Madness* (New York: Alfred A. Knopf/Vintage Books, 1995).

269. Robert Bacher, Robert's second in command, described in an interview later that "I just disappeared into thin air. Lee DuBridge knew where we were going, because he was the director of the laboratory. But nobody else, except Jean, knew where I was going; we just disappeared for two weeks." Robert F. Bacher, interview by Mary Terrall, Oral History Project, June–August 1981, Archives, Caltech, February 1983, Tape 4, Side 1, p. 63.

270. In reality, many of the American scientists, and almost all of the European, would confide in their wives.

271. Hilda Kresch, interview by Shirley Streshinsky, November 28, 2005.

272. Lois Banner, *Intertwined Lives: Margaret Mead, Ruth Benedict, and Their Circle* (New York: Vintage Books, 2004), 422.

273. Natalie Raymond to Ruth Benedict, August 11 [ca. 1943], Series I: Correspondence, Folder 35.1, Ruth Benedict Papers, Archives and Special Collections, Vassar Libraries.

274. Ruth Tolman to Dr. Franklin Fearing, Dept. of Psychology, UCLA, February 27, 1943, Letter from Congressional Files, Courtesy of Eric Vanslander, NA.

275. Norris in *Racing for the Bomb* describes the Manhattan Project as "among other things, a gigantic industrial and engineering effort, run by the military under great security, rapidly accomplished, using unorthodox means, and dealing in uncertain

technologies," 187. Brookings Institute, "The Costs of the Manhattan Project," http://www.brookings.edu/about/projects/archive/nucweapons/manhattan. The complete Manhattan Project, including plants at Oak Ridge and Hanford, would come in at more than $1 billion 1940s dollars.

276. Nelson, Barrett, and Ruck, *American Radical,* 269.

277. This is the account Chevalier wrote in *The Story of a Friendship,* 53–56; Robert's version is from his Security Hearing Testimony, Polenberg, *ITMJRO,* 62; Kitty's version is from a conversation that Hobson related to Sherwin in her July 31, 1979 interview.

Chapter 19

278. Ruth Tolman, "Some Work of Women Psychologists in the War," *Journal of Consulting Psychology* 7 (1943):127.

279. Ruth Marshak, "Secret City," in Jane S. Wilson and Charlotte Serber, eds., *Standing By and Making Do: Women of Wartime Los Alamos* (Los Alamos, NM: Los Alamos Historical Society, 1997), 9.

280. Ibid., 10.

281. John Lansdale, *John Lansdale, Jr.— Military Service* (privately printed), 35. Courtesy of Chloe Lansdale Pitard.

282. Bacher, interview by Terrall, February 1983, Tape 4, Side 1, p. 70, Caltech.

283. Memorandum for the Special Agent in Charge, San Francisco, CA, June 23, 1943, FBI: SF 100-18382, in the Martin Sherwin Collection, LOC, MSF.

284. Ibid.

285. Ibid.

286. Ibid.

287. FBI Confidential Memo, August 23, 1943, MIS (Military Intelligence Service) was requested that the FBI con-

tinue surveillance of Jean Tatlock and "place a microphone" in her apartment. Other FBI memos in August and September 1943 mention an informer and Jean's vacation to the East Coast. See memos in Box 62, Jean Tatlock file, MSC, LOC.

CHAPTER 20

288. Emergency Statement to the People of the U.S., War Production Board, with Conservation Division. See Allan M. Winkler, *Home Front U.S.A.: America During World War II,* 2nd Ed. (Wheeling, IL: Harlan Davidson, 2000).

289. Jerome Bruner, *In Search of Mind: Essays in Autobiography* (New York: Harper & Row, 1983), 44.

290. Priscilla Duffield, quoted in Goodchild, *JRO,* 127.

291. Both Priscilla Greene, Robert's first secretary at Los Alamos, and Dorothy McKibben, who ran the Project office in Santa Fe and who became close friends with Robert, said that Kitty had few friends other than the women with whom she would ride.

292. Thomas Powers, *Heisenberg's War: The Secret History of the German Bomb* (New York: Alfred A. Knopf, 1993), 237.

293. Ibid., 240, 533n17.

294. Bruner, *In Search of Mind,* 44.

295. Powers, *Heisenberg's War,* 238.

296. Jennet Conant, *109 East Palace, Robert Oppenheimer and the Secret City of Los Alamos* (New York: Simon & Schuster, 2005), 200.

297. As quoted in Powers, *Heisenberg's War,* 247.

298. See Robert Oppenheimer, "Niels Bohr and Atomic Weapons," *New York Review of Books,* December 17, 1964.

299. Necropsy Report, CO-44-63, 1/6/44.

9:30 a.m., Coroner's Office, City and County of San Francisco. For additional reports, see KB/MS, *Prometheus,* 637n and Jean Tatlock file, MS, MSF.

300. *San Francisco Examiner,* January 6, 1944, p. 1. Jean's death was also reported in the *San Francisco Chronicle,* January 7, 1944, p. 9, and the *Oakland Tribune,* January 6, 1944, printed the headline, "Woman Psychiatrist of S.F. Drowns Self in Bathtub." p. 12.

301. A poem Jean wrote in 1930 and included in a letter to May Sarton, February 1930.

302. Elizabeth Fenn (John Tatlock's godmother and close friend of his mother) to John Tatlock, ca. 1989. Letty Field's mother thought Jean never recovered from Letty's death. Peters, *May Sarton,* 145. See also Jenkins, *Against a Field Sinister,* 31.

303. FBI Confidential Teletype: "No action will be taken by this Office due possible unfavorable publicity. Direct inquiries will be made discreetly." FBI: 100-20-3581, Jean Tatlock file, MS/LOC.

304. AEC, *ITMJRO: Transcript,* 153. Curiously this phrase is in the statement read by Robb to Oppenheimer on April 14, but not in the prepared statement (p. 8) Robert read before the panel two days earlier.

305. JRO to Maj. Gen. K. D. Nichols, March 4, 1854. This is a draft of the letter that Robert would actually send to the AEC and which was read at the Hearing. Security Hearing Case File, Boxes 198–199, JRO Papers, LOC.

306. This is the final stanza of "Epithalamion" which was among the poems Robert gave to Linus Pauling when they were both at Caltech. Pauling noted the poems as "Poems by JRO 1928." 3. Linus Pauling Safe, Drawer 3, 30186/18.193. Ava Helen and Linus

Pauling Papers, 1873–2011, Special Collections & Archives, OSU Libraries, Oregon State University, Corvallis, OR.

CHAPTER 21

307. J. S. P. Tatlock, "Nostra Maxima Culpa," supplement, *Proceedings of the Modern Language Association,* 53 (1938): 1313. Tatlock was president of the Association in 1938.

308. Edith Jenkins suggested in *Against a Field Sinister* that Jean and Mary Ellen Washburn were lovers; Hilde Stern Hein, Robert's cousin, told KB in an interview on March 4, 2004, that Mary Ellen and Jean were "more than friends." KB/MS, *Prometheus,* 637n.

309. Edith Jenkins thought it was Barbara Chevalier who told her that Jean called Mary Ellen Washburn the night before she died and said she was very depressed.

310. John Tatlock, personal communication to Patricia Klaus, April 20, 2012.

311. Hugh Tatlock, interview by MS, February 2001, MSF.

312. Sherr, interview by MS.

313. Dr. John Whiteclay Chambers II, "Office of Strategic Services Training During World War II," *Studies in Intelligence* 54 no. 2 (June 2010). See also Ruth Tolman Personnel File; Robin Winks comments that in 1944 "the Schools and Training Branch of the OSS was still trying to decide precisely how it should train its people, and a good bit of the program was experimental." Robin Winks, *Cloak & Gown: Scholars in the Secret War,* 1939–1961 (New Haven, CT: Yale University Press, 1987), 128.

314. J.S.P. Tatlock to Winifred Smith, 22 July 1944, Box 25.1, PSR Papers, Vassar.

315. As quoted in Conant, *109 East Palace,*

181.

316. Ibid., 182.

317. On General Groves, see his memoir, *Now It Can Be Told: The Story of the Manhattan Project* (New York: Da Capo Press, 1962); Norris, *Racing for the Bomb,* and Bernstein, "Reconsidering the 'Atomic General': Leslie R. Groves."

318. Sherr, interview by MS. See KB/MS, *Prometheus,* 264.

319. In addition, Theodore Hall, a young physicist who felt that America should not have a monopoly on nuclear discoveries; Harry Gold, a laboratory chemist who helped Fuchs pass information on the bomb project to the Soviets; and David Greenglass, recruited as a spy by his wife, Ruth Rosenberg Greenglass (sister to convicted and executed spy Julius Rosenberg), and passed nuclear secrets via Harry Gold.

CHAPTER 22

320. "The Text of the Day's Communiques on the Fighting in the Various War Zones." *NYT,* October 3, 1944.

321. James MacDonald, "British Battling Inside Muenster," *NYT,* April 3, 1945. MacDonald wrote that "Muenster was done for . . ."; Drew Middleton, "North Reich Cut," *NYT,* April 4, 1945.

322. Information on Kitty's German family courtesy of Martin Vissering.

323. Joseph Shaplen, "Fuehrer 'Bruised.' Bomb Wounds 13 Staff Officers," *New York Times,* July 21, 1944. Hitler dictated to Keitel the letter sent to Field Marshall Rommel in France ordering him to return to Germany if innocent and if not, to commit suicide by swallowing poison (Hitler preferred this method so Rommel's suicide could be attributed to a brain injury). Gorlitz,

ed., *The Memoirs of Field-Marshal Wilhelm Keitel,* 193–95; Peter Hoffman, *Stauffenberg: A Family History, 1905–1944* (first published in Stutgart, 1992; Cambridge: CU Press, 1995), 263–70.

324. Colonel General Alfred Jodl signed the surrender on the Western Front before General Eisenhower on May 7, 1945; Keitel signed the Eastern Front surrender before the Russian's Marshal Zhukov. Official VE Day is celebrated May 8.

325. David McCullough, *Truman* (New York: Simon & Schuster, 1992), 381–82. For the text of Truman's press conference, see www.Presidency.ucsb .edu/ws and for Churchill's speech, http://news.bbc.co.uk/onthisday/hi/dates/stories/may/8/newsid_3580000/3580163.stm. May 8, 1945.

326. See Boris Pash, *The Alsos Mission,* (New York: Award House, 1969); Powers, *Heisenberg's War.*

327. Anne Wilson Marks, interview by KB, March 5, 2002, MSF.

328. Ibid., March 14, 2002.

329. Jackie Oppenheimer, interview by MS, December 3, 1978, MSF; Goodchild, *JRO,* 128.

330. At other times, Robert and Kitty used a commonplace phrase as a type of codeword.

331. Frank Oppenheimer, interview by CW, February 9, 1973, AIP.

332. Jane Wilson, "Not Quite Eden" in Wilson and Serber, *Standing By and Making Do,* 4.

333. Frank Oppenheimer, interview by CW, February 9, 1973, AIP.

334. Frank Oppenheimer, interview by Else, for *The Day After Trinity* (documentary film, 1980). This quotation is from some seven years after the 1973 interview in which Frank told CW that "I don't remember what we said, now."

335. Groves, *Now It Can Be Told,* 298.

Chapter 23

336. Hershberg, *Conant,* 234.

337. Ibid., 233–34.

338. David McCullough, *Truman,* 455.

339. Natalie Raymond to Ruth Tolman, Sunday 1945, Series X: Ruth Tolman, Box 11, RCT Papers, Caltech.

340. Jean Bacher, interview by MS, August 29, 1983.

341. Chevalier, *Story of a Friendship,* ix.

342. Robert Oppenheimer to James Conant, September 9, 1945, quoted in KB/MS, *Prometheus,* 320.

343. See Judith Goodstein, "Tales in and Out of 'Millikan's School,'" The Pauling Symposium, Special Collections, Valley Library, Oregon State University, Corvallis, OR.

344. Bacher, interview by MS.

345. As quoted in KB/MS, *Prometheus,* 323–24.

346. On the twentieth anniversary of Hiroshima, Robert stated in an interview that scientists "had known the sin of pride. We had turned to effect . . . the course of man's history. We had the pride of thinking we knew what was good for man. This is not the natural business of the scientist." As quoted in Charles Thorpe, *Oppenheimer: The Tragic Intellect* (Chicago: University of Chicago Press, 2006), 286.

347. According to Lilienthal, Baruch admitted that "he wasn't much on technical scientific stuff, but he could smell his way through—and that's the way he did things, smell his way." David Lilienthal, *The Journals of David E. Lilienthal,* Vol. 2: *The Atomic Energy Years, 1945–1950* (New York: Harper & Row, 1964), 32.

348. Ibid., 30–31, 72.

349. JFO FBI File 100-17828-79, July 20,

1946. Dated 7/29/46 (Surveillance dates 7/19–7/24), MSF.

350. Wendell McRae to Ruth Tolman, August 7, 1945. Series X: Ruth Tolman, Box 11, Folder 33, RCT Papers, Caltech.

351. James Miller, "Clinical Psychology in the Veterans Administration," *American Psychologist* 1, no. 6 (1946): 181–89; Capshew, *Psychologists on the March*, 172–73.

352. Edwin G. Boring served as director of the Laboratory from 1924 to 1949 during which time he worked, as did Ruth, to establish psychology as a science in its own right.

353. Ruth Tolman to E. G. Boring, January 25, 1946, quoted in Capshew, *Psychologists on the March,* 90. See articles published by Ruth Tolman and E.G. Boring in the Bibliography.

354. Dana L. Moore, "The Veterans Administration and Its Training Program in Psychology," in Donald K. Freedheim, ed., *History of Psychotherapy: A Century of Change* (Washington, D.C.: American Psychological Association, 1992), 776–800; Alice Bryan and Edwin G. Boring, "Women in American Psychology: Statistics from the OPP Questionnaire," *American Psychologist* 1, no. 3 (1946): 75.

355. As Chief Psychologist and Director of Psychological Research at Worcester State Hospital, David Shakow made substantial contributions to the scientific study of schizophrenia and by extension to psychopathology in general. Shakow's schizophrenia work informed his developing ideas on the synergy between clinical practice and research; Ruth Tolman to David Shakow, November 4, 1946, David Shakow Papers, M1358, AHAP, University of Akron, Akron, Ohio.

356. Barton Bernstein interviewed James Douglas, the son of the founder of Douglas Aircraft, who claimed that he visited the Tolman house "one morning during the war" and saw Oppenheimer and Ruth Tolman alone, wearing only dressing gowns." KB/MS, *Prometheus,* 654n.

CHAPTER 24

357. Robert was not opposed to nuclear weapons—it was too late for that—nor was he categorically opposed to the thermonuclear bomb (the GAC with Robert as chairman had approved the quest for the "Super" in 1947). He had opposed it at first because he thought it impossible to build, and later because he did not want the military to be dependent on bombs which would obliterate nations instead of tactical nuclear weapons.

358. May 14, 1946, 4, "To Director, FBI. Compilation of Recent Information Furnished to the SF Office by Confidential Informant." Reports of electronic surveillance of 1 Eagle Hill, most with only date and page number. FBI Microfilms, MSF.

359. Ibid., 5.

360. Ibid.

361. Lilienthal, New Year's Eve, 1946, *Journals,* Vol. 2, 127.

362. FBI electronic surveillance of 1 Eagle Hill report, June 22, 1946, June 31, 1946, MSF.

363. As quoted in Richard West, "Jack B. Tenney, Ex-State Senator, Foe of Communism, Dies at 72," *Los Angeles Times,* November 11, 1970. Tenney (who wrote the hit song "Mexacali Rose") was also an instigator of the Loyalty Oath for University Of California employees that Richard Tolman refused to sign.

364. Kitty and Robert did continue to see

some of their "fellow traveler/Communist" friends: the Chevaliers, the Hawkins, and the Serbers, among others.

365. As quoted in KB/MS, *Prometheus*, 327.

366. Ibid., 360.

367. Throughout the FBI files, there will be recommendations from the San Francisco office from 1946 through the 1950s that the electronic surveillance be discontinued; Hoover would insist otherwise.

CHAPTER 25

368. Ruth Tolman to Robert Oppenheimer, August 24, 1947, Box 72, Ruth Tolman Folder, JRO Papers, LOC. All the Ruth Tolman–Robert Oppenheimer letters are from this collection, Box 72, unless otherwise cited. Ibid., June 31, 1947.

369. Bruner, *In Search of Mind*, 236 and Jerome Bruner, interview by Patricia Klaus, March 27, 2013.

370. Ruth Tolman to Robert Oppenheimer, August 24, 1947.

371. Bruner, *In Search of Mind*, 236.

372. Ruth Tolman to Robert Oppenheimer, August 24, 1947.

373. Kitty, in the midst of an argument with McCutchen over their fence and her privet hedge, wrote: "It is indeed with surprise and with gratitude that I know full well that you have never once complained when one or both of our horses has blundered across your garden." Kitty Oppenheimer to Brunson McCutchen, Olden Farm, June 7, 1960, courtesy of the Institute of Advanced Study, Princeton, NJ.

374. Bruner, interview with Klaus; Bruner, *In Search of Mind*, 236.

375. Ibid.

376. Edward Lofgren, interview by Shirley Streshinsky, 2010; Frank Oppen-

heimer, interview by CW, May 21, 1973, Niels Bohr Institute & Library, AIP, College Park, MD.

377. See Kelly, *Something Incredibly Wonderful*, 86-100.

378. There is voluminous literature on this subject written by historians, among them Barton Bernstein, Gregg Herken, Martin Sherwin and Richard Rhodes, as well as many of the participants in the struggle over American nuclear weapons.

379. Sherr, interview by MS.

380. Ibid.

381. The gimmick story appears in many biographies as was originally observed by David Lilienthal; Dorothy McKibben, interview by AKS, January 1, 1976, Dorothy McKibben Folder, AKS Papers, MIT.

382. See, among others: Serber, interview by MS, March 11, 1982; Verna Hobson, interview by Martin Sherwin, July 31, 1979; Francis Fergusson, interviews by MS/MSF.

383. There were people who thought Robert and Kitty, in their own way, made a good pair: Freeman Dyson, who commented on how they stayed together through better and worse, Robert Serber, and David Lilienthal. Curiously, most of those who made a positive assessment were men. With the exception of Abraham Pais, Kitty's most savage critics were women.

384. Ruth Valentine to Robert Oppenheimer, Monday, August 16, 1948, Ruth Tolman Folder, Box 72, JRO Papers, LOC.

385. Ibid.

386. Margery Freeman to Margaret Mead, September 7, 1948, Series II: Folder 39.8, Ruth Fulton Benedict Papers, Archives and Special Collections, Vassar Libraries.

387. Ibid. This note had been used by at

least two historians to suggest, erroneously, that Ruth Tolman and Val had a lesbian relationship. See Hilary Lapsley, *Margaret Mead and Ruth Benedict: The Kinship of Women* (Amherst, MA: University of Massachusetts Press, 1999) and Lois W. Banner, *Intertwined Lives.*

CHAPTER 26

388. Ruth Tolman to David Shakow, November 16, 1948. David Shakow Papers. Richard left almost a million dollars to Caltech at his death, with the interest to go to Ruth for her life time.
389. As quoted in KB/MS, *Prometheus,* 391.
390. Ruth Tolman to Robert Oppenheimer, undated [Tuesday some time after Richard's death in September 1948]; Robert Oppenheimer to Ruth Tolman, November 18, 1948.
391. Ruth Tolman to Robert Oppenheimer, undated [Tuesday some time after Richard's death].
392. Robert Oppenheimer to Ruth Tolman, November 18, 1948.
393. Ruth Tolman to Robert Oppenheimer, [1949, sometime after July as Ruth referenced Katherine Page's marriage to Charles Kavanaugh in July 1949].
394. Peter was born May 12, 1941; Toni, December 7, 1944.
395. See KB/MS, *Prometheus,* 393–400.
396. Katherine Page to Robert Oppenheimer, July 7, 1949, General Case File, Box 55, JRO Papers, LOC.
397. Frank Oppenheimer, interview by CW, May 21, 1973.
398. David Lilienthal, interview by MS, October 14, 1978, quoted in KB/MS, *Prometheus,* 401.
399. Ruth Tolman to Robert Oppenheimer, April 16, 1949.
400. Ruth and Val worked together on the

symposium, part of the prestigious Hixon Lectures at Caltech, and suggested inviting eminent psychologists and others including Bertrand Russell, Margaret Mead and Robert Oppenheimer.
401. Harry M. Grayson and Ruth S. Tolman, "A Semantic Study of Concepts of Clinical Psychologists and Psychiatrists," *Journal of Abnormal and Social Psychology* 45, no. 2 (April 1950): 216–31.
402. Ruth Tolman to David Shakow, November 16, 1948.
403. Ed Pye, interview by Shirley Streshinsky, 2005.
404. Ruth Tolman to Robert Oppenheimer, April 16, 1949. Ruth had a woman helping her with her house most of the time, something she regarded as a necessity since she entertained often and had many house guests.
405. Ibid.
406. Ibid., August 1, 1953.

CHAPTER 27

407. The detonation of Joe-1 was not the only event that added to America's growing paranoia: in January, Klaus Fuchs, a German scientist who went to Los Alamos with the British, confessed to being a spy for the Soviets; in June, North Korean troops invaded South Korea and by the end of the month, President Truman had committed U.S. troops.
408. Murray Gell-Man, *Physics Today Online;* Hans Bethe, "J. Robert Oppenheimer," *Biographical Memoirs of the Fellows of the Royal Society* 71 (National Academies Press: Washington, D.C., 1997), 202.
409. Ruth Tolman to Robert Oppenheimer, [September 5, 1952].

410. Robert Oppenheimer to Ruth Tolman, February 27, 1953.

411. Ibid., [1953].

412. Ibid., April 18, 1953.

413. Ruth S. Tolman, "Virtue Rewarded and Vice Punished," *American Psychologist* 8, no. 12 (1953): 721–33.

414. As quoted in KB/MS, *Prometheus,* 470.

415. Charles Lauritsen to Robert Oppenheimer, August 7, 1953, Box 45, JRO Papers, LOC.

416. Ruth Tolman to Robert Oppenheimer, [August 1953].

417. Chevalier, *Story of a Friendship,* 86–87.

418. KB/MS, *Prometheus,* 476.

419. KB and MS portray Borden's pursuit of Oppenheimer as almost a personal mania; Barton Bernstein suggests that Borden may have been motivated more by a sincere, if obsessive, concern for national security.

420. Tom Wicker, *Shooting Star: The Brief Arc of Joe McCarthy* (Orlando, FL: Harcourt, 2006).

421. President Eisenhower had signed Executive Order 10450 in April 1953 which specified that anyone deemed a possible security risk should undergo a security hearing, with a three-member panel. Strauss chose the panel members, but not the idea of the panel itself.

422. Strauss wanted to be rid of Robert and had begun an anonymous public campaign to discredit him. *Fortune, Time* and *Life* (all owned by Henry Luce, a friend of Strauss), published articles accusing Robert of undermining the H-Bomb effort and U.S. military preparedness. Strauss, afraid that a public hearing would undermine scientists' confidence on the government, hoped Robert would resign. See, among other, Bernstein, "The Oppenheimer Security-Loyalty Case Reconsidered." *Stanford Law Review* 42 no. 6,

July 1990: 1383-1484

423. Anne Mark, interview by KB, March 14, 2002, MSF.

424. KB/MS, *Prometheus,* 484.

425. Anne Marks, interview by KB.

Chapter 28

426. Hobson, interview by MS.

427. Ibid.

428. Garrison took the case pro bono; had he not, even though Robert was reasonably well off, the trials could well have bankrupted him. Herb Marks offered his support too and probably worked pro-bono as well.

429. Hobson, interview by MS.

430. Ibid. Freeman Dyson would write that Kitty was the rock upon which Robert stood, that he was dependent upon her strength.

431. Priscilla McMillan, *The Ruin of JRO and the Birth of the Modern Arms Race* (New York: Viking, 2005), 199.

432. Hobson, interview by MS.

433. Ibid.

434. KB and MS, *Prometheus,* 491.

435. Ruth Tolman to Robert Oppenheimer, April 3, 1954.

436. AEC, *ITMJRO: Transcript,* 8. Barton Bernstein pointed out that Robert and his lawyers had composed several drafts of the responses. In one of those drafts, Robert gave a slightly different description of his relationship with Jean Tatlock: "It is, indeed, true that Jean Tatlock was one of the immediate occasions of my becoming interested in political questions. I met her at a time when I had suddenly become vulnerable to falling in love . . . I do not, and can not, believe that she was bad—I do know that she was complex and mysterious. Her great interest was in martyrdom, and I can-

not believe that she had the slightest disposition toward conspiracy, or, in reality, politics." Security Clearance File, JRO Papers.

437. In one of the more complicated turns of this saga, one day in January, Robert had been seated next to James Reston, *NYT* bureau chief in Washington, on an airplane; Robert seemed "unaccountably nervous" and Reston began making calls, among them to Robert. Garrison and Robert decide to tell their side of the story with the proviso that Reston not print until the story seemed about to break. Although Robert, the panel and the witnesses had been told the proceedings were secret, Robert and Garrison decided on what they thought of a pre-emptive release and the story broke on the first page of the *NYT* on Tuesday, April 13, the second day of the Hearing, releasing the storm of publicity that Strauss wished to avoid. See KB/MS, *Prometheus*, 502–03.

438. David Lilienthal, *The Journals of David E. Lilienthal*, Vol. 3: *The Venturesome Years, 1950–1955* (New York: Harper & Row, 1966), 505.

439. Goodchild, *JRO*, 249.

440. Bernstein, "The Oppenheimer Loyalty-Security Case Reconsidered," 1445

441. Gregg Herken, in *Brotherhood of the Bomb*, suggests that there was a personal element to Lawrence's animosity and cites an interview with Molly Lawrence, May 20, 1997, 404n81.

442. Lewis Strauss to Edward Teller, December 9, 1957, Strauss to file, Box 1, Lewis Strauss Papers, Herbert Hoover Presidential Library, quoted in Herken, *Brotherhood of the Bomb*, 654n365.

443. "He is normally lightening-quick and intuitive mind seemed partially blocked, and at moments, even para-

lyzed." Robert Coughlan, "The Tangled Drama and Private Hells of Two Famous Scientists," *Life* (12/13/63), 102:

444. April 14, 1954, AEC, *ITMJRO: Transcript*, 153–54. The following quotations in italics from Day Two of the Hearing are from these pages.

445. Ibid., 267.

446. *Pittsburgh Sun-Telegraph*, April 13, 1954.

447. AEC, ITMJRO: Transcript, 572–76. Quotations in italics are from Kitty's testimony on April 26, 1954.

448. Ibid., 916–21. Quotations in italics are from Kitty's testimony on May 4, 1954.

449. Ibid., 137. Quotations in italics are from April 14, 1954.

450. Ibid., 140, May 4, 1954.

451. Bernstein, "Oppenheimer Loyalty-Security Reconsidered," 1449.

452. "Decisions and Opinions of AEC, June 29," in Polenberg, *ITMJRO*, 380.

CHAPTER 29

453. Edward Tolman to Robert Oppenheimer, April 16, 1954, Edward Tolman Folder, Box 72, JRO Papers.

454. KB/MS, *Prometheus*, 553. Robert's old friend Harold Cherniss helped organize the open letter of support that the Institute faculty signed.

455. Ruth Tolman to Robert Oppenheimer, January 15, 1952. Robert must have used these words to describe the Islands to Ruth in an earlier letter.

456. Anne Marks to Kitty Oppenheimer, July 7, 1954, Box 49, JRO Papers.

457. Jeremy Bernstein, *Oppenheimer: Portrait of an Enigma* (Chicago: Ivan R. Dee, 2004), 194.

458. Edsall, interview by CW.

459. David Lilienthal, *Journals of David E. Lilienthal*, Vol. 4: *The Road to Change, 1955–1959* (New York: Harper & Row,

1969), 594.

460. Ruth Tolman to Robert Oppenheimer, May 30, 1952.

461. Freeman Dyson, *Disturbing the Universe* (New York: Basic Books, 1979). Archibald MacLeish, also from the Institute days, would write to Robert how much he had been impressed with "you & Kitty, especially Kitty." July 23, 1948, General Case File, Box 49, JRO Papers.

462. Freeman Dyson to his family, February 11, 1957, in personal communication to Patricia Klaus, February 2, 2012.

463. Hobson, interview by MS. Various friends and colleagues would comment on the fact that Oppenheimer seemed to enable Kitty's drinking and rudeness.

464. Ibid.; Francis Fergusson, interview by Martin Sherwin, June 23, 1979.

465. Ruth Tolman to Robert Oppenheimer, September 5, [early 1950s]; Anne Roe to Robert Oppenheimer, September 2, 1954, Ruth Tolman Folder, Box 72, JRO Papers.

466. Barton Bernstein, "Oppenheimer Loyalty-Security Case," 1451.

467. FBI Memorandum as printed in Mark Wolverton, *A Life in Twilight: The Final Years of JRO* (New York: St. Martin's Press, 2008), 54.

468. Ruth Valentine to Margaret Mead, January 27, 1955, Box C, Margaret Mead Papers, LOC.

469. Lynn Margulis, "Sunday Morning with Robert Oppenheimer," in *Luminous Fish: Tales of Science and Love* (White River Junction, VT: Chelsea Green, 2007), 149–80. All quotations are from this essay.

470. Robert Oppenheimer to Ruth Tolman, Western Union Telegram, September 1, 1955.

471. Information courtesy of Martin Vis-

sering.

472. Ruth Tolman to Robert Oppenheimer, [1956].

473. "Report of the Death of an American Citizen" Form 192, American Consulate in Genoa, Italy, April 26, 1956. The report can be found at www.Ancestry.com, Image 196, from the NARA, Washington, D.C. Later, the *Master of the Concordia Fjord,* Kathe's ship, decided that she had crawled out the porthole, had hit the gangway and was killed instantly before falling into the sea. Her body was never found. See also letters between Hilde Vissering and Captain Kolnes of the Concordia Line, May 31, 1956. Letter courtesy of Martin Vissering, Bremen, Germany.

474. Hilde Vissering de Blonay, Stuttgart, Germany, to Borre Hartvig Sverdrup, Oslo, Norway, June 29, 1956. Letter courtesy of Martin Vissering.

475. Borre Sverdrup to Hilde Vissering de Blonay, July 2, 1956. Letter courtesy of Martin Vissering.

476. Foreign Service Operations Memorandum from the Consulate General, Genoa, Italy, U.S. Department of State, May 4, 1956. Memorandum can be found at www.Ancestry.com, Image 510, NARA.

477. Kitty Oppenheimer to Hilde Vissering de Blonay, *Telegram,* July 2, 1956. Courtesy of Martin Vissering.

478. Wolverton, *A Life in Twilight,* 84.

479. Jeremy Bernstein, *Oppenheimer: Portrait of an Enigma,* 174.

480. Robert Oppenheimer to Hedwig Stern, February 2, 1957, JRO Papers.

481. Victor Cohn, "Can a Security Risk Survive? Oppenheimer Tells for First Time of Fight Against 'Final Judgment.'" *Minneapolis Sunday Tribune,* June 16, 1957, quoted in Wolverton, *A Life in Twilight,* 95–101. Wolverton says that the only other writer with whom Rob-

ert supposedly discussed the Hearing
was John Mason Brown, who wrote in
Through These Men (New York: Harper, 1956). Actually, Brown relied not on
a personal interview with Robert, but
on published articles and interviews.

482. Ruth Tolman to Robert Oppenheimer,
1956.

483. Hedwig Stern to Robert Oppenheimer,
September 30, 1957, General Case File,
Box 69, JRO Papers.

484. Edward Tolman to Robert Oppenheimer, October 1957, General Case
File, Box 72, JRO Papers.

485. Theodore Newcomb to Robert Oppenheimer, October 25, 1957, Ruth Tolman Folder, Box 72, JRO Papers.

486. Bruner, *In Search of Mind,* 237–38.

487. Lilienthal, *Journals,* Vol. 4, 232.

CHAPTER 30

488. Edsall, interview by CW.

489. Ibid., quoted in Thorpe, *Oppenheimer,
The Tragic Intellect,* 39. See also Mary
Jo Nye, *Blackett: Physics, War and Politics in the Twentieth Century* (Cambridge, MA: Harvard UP, 2004). In correspondence with Patricia Klaus, Nye
supported this interpretation: "Nor
is it surprising, given Oppenheimer's
temperament at the time, that he was
envious at Cambridge of the very
skilled and the very handsome Blackett, then in his late 20s," 3/5/13.

490. Edsall, interview by CW.

491. Edward Bullard, "Patrick Blackett . . .
an Appreciation" *Nature* 250 (1974):
370; Sir Edward Crisp "Teddy" Bullard,' geophysicist and close friend to
Patrick Blackett. Stephan Budiansky,
*Blackett's War: The Men Who Defeated
the Nazi U-Boats and Brought Science
to the Art of Warfare* (New York: Alfred
A. Knopf, 2013), 45. The comment was

made by Ivor Richards, a noted literary critic and Cambridge don.

492. KB/MS, *Prometheus,* 50.

493. Monk also suggests this interpretation
in *Inside The Centre,* 111–12.

494. The idea of Robert creating a persona
or re-inventing himself has been commented on by others; I.I. Rabi wrote
in *The New Yorker,* October 1975, that
"You carried on a charade with him.
He lived a charade and you went along
with him." Hans Bethe commented
that Robert had undergone a fundamental adaptation when he became
the administrator at Los Alamos and
then another after the bomb when he
became the public Oppenheimer.

495. Edsall, interview by CW.

496. Unlike Robert, who may have spent a
a good portion of his lifetime trying
to belong, Blackett was by birth and
heritage solidly a member of the English establishment: one grandfather
was a Church of England vicar, the
other a ranking naval officer; his uncle
served in India. His political views remained consistently left wing and, in
the 1950s, became very controversial
with his support of the Soviet Union.
See Patrick Blackett, *Fear, War, and the
Bomb: Military and Political Consequences of Atomic Energy* (New York:
Whittlesey House, 1949).

497. Bernstein, *Oppenheimer: Portrait of an
Enigma,* 173.

498. Ruth's close friends, including Jean
Bacher, Sigrid Lauritsen and her
daughter, denied that there had been
an affair. We began the book assuming
on the basis of most biographers' interpretations (Jeremy Bernstein an exception) that Ruth and Robert had an
affair; after years of reading their letters word by word, we noticed a shift
in intensity that occurs immediately
after Richard's death, but that it only

lasted a year or so. And Ruth would write to others, such as David Shakow, about wanting to find a little time to spend with him. Her friendships with her friends and her words were both warm and affectionate.

499. Bruner, interview by Klaus.
500. Lilienthal, *Journals*, Vol. 4, 260.
501. Peter Oppenheimer to Shirley Streshinsky, May 2013.
502. Hobson, interview by Sherwin.
503. Ruth Valentine to Margaret Mead, June 19, 1959. General correspondence, Margaret Mead Papers.
504. Richard Pfau, *No Sacrifice Too Great: The Life of Lewis L. Strauss* (Charlottesville, VA: U of V Press, 1984), 241.
505. David Lilienthal, *The Journals of David E. Lilienthal, Vol. 5: The Harvest Years, 1959–1963* (New York: Harper & Row, 1971), 440.
506. As quoted in KB/MS, *Prometheus*, 563.
507. Lilienthal, *Journals*, Vol. 5, 439.
508. Ibid., 529–30.
509. David Lilienthal, *The Journals of David E. Lilienthal, Vol. 6: Creativity and Conflict, 1964–1967* (New York: Harper & Row, 1976), 22.
510. Lyndon B. Johnson, "Remarks Upon Presenting the Fermi Award to Dr. JRO," *The American Presidency Project.* www.Presidency.ucsb.edu.
511. Lilienthal, *Journals*, Vol. 6, 439.
512. Lettie Abacassis, interview by Shirley Streshinsky, 2002.
513. Lilienthal, *Journals*, Vol. 6, 255.
514. As quoted in Wolverton, *A Life in Twilight*, 255.
515. As quoted in KB/MS, *Prometheus*, 503.
516. Dyson, *Disturbing the Universe*, 81–82.

CHAPTER 31

517. Fiona St. Clair (Serber), interview by Patricia Klaus, March 12, 2012.
518. Fiona St. Clair, interview by MS, February 17, 1982.
519. Serber, *Peace and War*, 205.
520. Ibid., 197, 208; Serber, interview by Streshinsky.
521. Serber, *Peace and War*, 208.
522. Serber, interview by MS.
523. Serber, interview by Streshinsky.
524. Serber, interview by MS. KB and MS recount many of Kitty's island "adventures" in *Prometheus*, Chapter 31.
525. Hobson, interview by MS.
526. Robert Serber to Hilde Vissering [Fall, 1979, shortly after Kitty's death]. Courtesy of Martin Visscring. The description of the rest of the voyage and Kitty's illness are taken from this letter.

OUTSIDE THE TIMELINE

527. Katherine Page Chaves to Robert Oppenheimer, [ca. 1949], General Case File, Box 55, JRO Papers.
528. Fiona St. Clair, interview by Klaus.
529. Lanie Ramseyer Dickel, personal communication to Klaus, April 2013.
530. Lin Ramseyer Clayberg, personal communication to Klaus, April 2013.
531. John Tatlock, personal communication with Patricia Klaus, 2012.
532. Private investigator, "What we should have done so far," July 15–16, 1991, Thompson Investigations, San Francisco. Box 62, Tatlock File, MS/LOC.
533. Ibid. "What We Should Do Next," and "Surmises and Speculations," July 16, 1991.
534. Patterson letter, "Conversations with Pathologist," July 16, 1991.
535. Bruner, interview by Klaus.

BIBLIOGRAPHY

Acheson, Dean. *Present at the Creation: My Years in the State Department.* New York: Norton, 1969.

Alperovitz, Gar. *The Decision to Use the Atomic Bomb.* New York: Alfred A. Knopf, 1995.

Alsop, Joseph, and Stewart Alsop. *We Accuse!: The Story of the Miscarriage of American Justice in the Case of J. Robert Oppenheimer.* New York: Simon & Schuster, 1954.

Andrews, T. G., and Mitchell Dreese. "Military Utilization of Psychologists During World War II." *American Psychologist* 3, no. 12 (1948): 533–538.

Atomic Energy Commission. *In the Matter of J. Robert Oppenheimer: Transcript of Hearing before Personnel Security Board and Texts of Principal Documents and Letters.* Cambridge, MA: MIT Press, 1971. Text reproduced from the original editions published by Government Printing Office, Washington, D.C., May 27, 1954.

Babington, Anthony. *Shell-Shock: A History of the Changing Attitudes to War Neurosis.* London: Leo Cooper, 1997.

Bacher, Robert F. *Robert Oppenheimer, 1904–1967.* Los Alamos: Los Alamos Historical Society, 1999.

Badash, Lawrence, Joseph O. Hirshfelder, and Herbert P. Broida, eds. *Reminiscences of Los Alamos, 1943–1945.* New York: Springer, 1980.

Baker, Rodney, and Wade E. Pickren. *Psychology and the Department of Veterans Affairs: A Historical Analysis of Training, Research, Practice, and Advocacy.* Washington, D.C.: American Psychological Association, 2007.

Banner, Lois W. *Intertwined Lives: Margaret Mead, Ruth Benedict, and Their Circle.* New York: Vintage Books, 2004.

Barnett, Correlli, ed. *Hitler's Generals.* London: Weidenfeld and Nicolson, 1989.

Baudelaire, Charles. *The Flowers of Evil.* Translated by James McGowan. Oxford: Oxford

University Press, 1993.

Benveniste, Daniel. "The Early History of Psychoanalysis in San Francisco." *Psychoanalysis and History* 8, no. 2 (2006): 195–233.

Bernstein, Barton J., ed. *The Atomic Bomb: The Critical Issues*. Boston: Little, Brown, 1976.

_____. "The Atomic Bombings Reconsidered." *Foreign Affairs* 74, no. 1 (January–February, 1995), 135–152.

_____. "The Oppenheimer Loyalty-Security Case Reconsidered." *Stanford Law Review*, 42, no. 6 (July 1990): 1383–1484.

_____., ed. *Politics and Policies of the Truman Administration*. Chicago: Quadrangle Books, 1970.

_____. "Reconsidering the 'Atomic General': Leslie Groves." *Journal of Military History* 67, no. 3 (July 2003): 883–920.

_____. "Sacrifices and Decisions: Lewis L. Strauss." *The Public Historian* 8, no. 2 (Spring 1986): 105–120.

Bernstein, Jeremy. *Oppenheimer: Portrait of an Enigma*. Chicago: Ivan R. Dee, 2004.

Bethe, Hans. *J. Robert Oppenheimer, April 22, 1904–February 18, 1967*. Biographical Memoirs of the Fellows of the Royal Society, 71. Washington, D.C.: National Academies Press, 1997.

Bird, Kai, and Martin Sherwin. *American Prometheus: The Triumph and Tragedy of J. Robert Oppenheimer*. New York: Alfred A. Knopf, 2005.

Blackett, Patrick. *Fear, War, and the Bomb: Military and Political Consequences of Atomic Energy*. New York: McGraw Hill, 1948.

Blum, John Morton. *V Was For Victory: Politics and American Culture During World War II*. New York: Harcourt Brace Jovanovich, 1976.

Boring, Edwin G. "The Woman Problem." *American Psychologist* 6 (1951): 679–682.

Brode, Bernice. *Tales of Los Alamos: Life on the Mesa, 1943–1945*. Los Alamos, NM: Los Alamos Historical Society, 1997.

Brown, John Mason. *Through These Men: Some Aspects of Our Passing History*. London: Hamish Hamilton, 1952.

Bruner, Jerome. *In Search of Mind: Essays in Autobiography*. New York: Harper & Row, 1983.

Bryan, Alice I., and Edwin G. Boring. "Women in American Psychology: Factors Affecting Their Professional Careers." *American Psychologist* 2, no. 1 (1947): 3–20.

_____. "Women in American Psychology: Prolegomenon." *Psychological Bulletin* 41 (1944): 447–454.

_____. "Women in American Psychology: Statistics from the OPP Questionnaire."

American Psychologist 1, no. 3 (1946): 71–79.

Budiansky, Stephen. *Blackett's War: The Men Who Defeated the Nazi U-Boats and Brought Science to the Art of Warfare.* New York: Alfred A. Knopf, 2013.

Bullard, Edward C. "Patrick Blackett ... an Appreciation." *Nature* 250 (1974).

Burack, Michael L. "Scientists, Security, and Secrecy." *Stanford Law Review* 23, no. 6 (June 1971): 1148–1166.

Capshew, James H. *Psychologists on the March: Science, Practice, and Professional Identity in America, 1929–1969.* Cambridge, UK: Cambridge University Press, 1999.

Carnochan, W. B. "English at Stanford, 1891–2000: A Brief History." *Sandstone and Tile* 26, no. 1 (Winter/Spring 2002).

Carroll, Peter. *The Odyssey of the Abraham Lincoln Brigade: Americans in the Spanish Civil War.* Stanford, CA: Stanford University Press, 1994.

Cassidy, David C. *J. Robert Oppenheimer and the American Century.* New York: Pi Press, 2004.

_____. *Uncertainty: The Life and Science of Werner Heisenberg.* New York: W.H. Freeman, 1992.

Chace, Elizabeth Buffum. Chace Family Papers. Manuscripts Division. Rhode Island Historical Society.

Chambers II, Dr. John Whiteclay. "Office of Strategic Services Training During World War II." *Studies in Intelligence* 54, no. 2 (June 2010).

Chevalier, Haakon. *Oppenheimer: The Story of a Friendship.* (New York: Braziller, 1965), 31–32.

Church, Peggy Pond. *The House at Otowi Bridge: The Story of Edith Warner and Los Alamos.* Albuquerque: University of New Mexico Press, 1959.

Clemens, Dorothy T. *Standing Ground and Starting Point: 120 Years with the YWCA in Berkeley.* Berkeley, CA: Big Hat Press, 1990.

Conant, Jennet. *109 East Palace: Robert Oppenheimer and the Secret City of Los Alamos.* New York: Simon & Schuster, 2005.

Coughlan, Robert. "The Tangled Drama and Private Hells of Two Famous Scientists." *Life* (13 Dec 1963).

Dallet, Joseph. *Letters from Spain.* New York: Workers Library Publishers, 1938.

Daniels, Elizabeth A. *Bridges to the World: Henry Noble MacCracken and Vassar College.* Clinton Corners, NY: College Avenue Press, 1994.

Davis, Nuel Pharr. *Lawrence and Oppenheimer.* Greenwich, CT: Fawcett Books, 1968.

"Education." Victoria County History. *A History of the County of Essex:* Volume 10. Ed. Janet Cooper. Oxford: Oxford University Press, 2001.

Degler, Carl N. *At Odds: Women and the Family in America from the Revolution to the Present*. New York: Oxford University Press, 1980.

D'Emilio, John, and Estelle B. Freedman. *Intimate Matters: A History of Sexuality in America*. New York: Harper & Row: 1988.

Dutton, Samuel W. S. *An Address at the Funeral of Hon. Roger Sherman Baldwin, February 23, 1863*. New Haven, CT: T.J. Stafford), 1863.

Dyson, Freeman. *Disturbing the Universe*. New York: Basic Books, 1979.

Eby, Cecil D. *Comrades and Commissars: The Lincoln Battalion in the Spanish Civil War*. University Park, PA: Pennsylvania State University Press, 2007.

Edsall, John T. "Account of Wyman's Life and Career." *Nature* 33 (1955).

Eisenhower, Dwight D. *The White House Years: Mandate for Change, 1953–1956*. Garden City, NY: Doubleday, 1963.

Ellis, Joseph J. *American Creation: Triumphs and Tragedies at the Founding of the Republic*. New York: Alfred A. Knopf, 2007.

Else, Jon. *The Day After Trinity: J. Robert Oppenheimer and the Atomic Bomb*, documentary film. Santa Monica: Pyramid Films, 1980. Image Entertainment DVD.

Engel, Jonathan. *American Therapy: The Rise of Psychotherapy in the United States*. New York: Gotham Books, 2008.

Evans, Rand B., Virginia Staudt Sexton, and Thomas C. Cadwallader, eds. *The American Psychological Association: A Historical Perspective*. Washington, D.C.: American Psychological Association, 1992.

Fass, Paula. *The Damned and the Beautiful: American Youth in the 1920s*. Oxford: Oxford University Press, 1977.

Fermi, Laura. *Atoms in the Family: My Life with Enrico Fermi*. Chicago: University of Chicago Press, 1954.

Fisher, Phyllis K. *Los Alamos Experience*. Tokyo: Japan Publications, 1985.

Forer, B. R., and Ruth Tolman. "Some Characteristics of Clinical Judgment." *Journal of Consulting Psychology* 16, no. 5 (1952): 347–352.

Freedman, Donald K., ed. *History of Psychotherapy: A Century of Change*. Washington, D.C.: American Psychological Association, 1992.

Gaddis, John Lewis. *George F. Kennan: An American Life*. New York: Penguin Press, 2011.

Gladwell, Malcolm. *Outliers: The Story of Success*. New York: Little, Brown, 2008.

Goldschmidt, Bertrand. *Atomic Rivals: A Candid Memoir Among the Allies Over the Bomb*. New Brunswick: Rutgers University Press, 1990.

Goodchild, Peter. *Edward Teller: The Real Dr. Strangelove*. Cambridge, MA: Harvard University Press, 2004.

Goodchild, Peter. *J. Robert Oppenheimer: Shatterer of Worlds*. London: BBC, 1980.

Goodenough, F. I. "Expanding Opportunities for Women Psychologists in the Post-War Period of Civil and Military Reorganization." *Psychological Bulletin* 41 (1944): 706–712.

Gorlitz, Walter, ed., *The Memoirs of Field-Marshal Wilhelm Keitel: Chief of the German High Command, 1938–1945*. Translated by David Irving. New York: Cooper Square Press, 2000. Originally published in German as Wilhelm Keitel. *Mein Leben: Pflichterfüllung bis zum Untergang: Hitlers Feldmarschall und Chef des Oberkommandos der Wehrmacht in Selbstzeugnissen*. Gottigen, Germany: Musterschmnidt-Verlag, 1961.

Gowing, Margaret. *Britain and Atomic Energy, 1939–1945*. New York: St. Martin's Press, 1964.

Grayson, H. M., and Ruth S. Tolman. "A Semantic Study of Concepts of Clinical Psychologists and Psychiatrists." *The Journal of Abnormal and Social Psychology* 45, no. 2 (1950): 216–231.

Hager, Thomas. *Force of Nature: The Life of Linus Pauling*. New York: Simon & Schuster, 1995.

Herken, Gregg. *Brotherhood of the Bomb: The Tangled Lives and Loyalties of Robert Oppenheimer, Ernest Lawrence, and Edward Teller*. New York: Henry Holt & Co., 2002.

Hershberg, James G. *James B. Conant: Harvard to Hiroshima and the Making of the Nuclear Age*. New York: Alfred A. Knopf, 1993.

Hinsdale, Burke A. *History of the University of Michigan, with Biographical Sketches of Regents and Members of the University Senate from 1837 to 1906*. Edited by Isaac N. Demmon. Ann Arbor: University of Michigan Press, 1906.

Horgan, Paul. *A Certain Climate: Essays in History, Arts, and Letters*. Middletown, CT: Wesleyan University Press, 1988.

Horvatin, Toni, and Edward Schreiber, eds. *The Quintessential Zerka: Writings by Zerka Toeman Moreno on Psychodrama, Sociometry and Group Psychotherapy*. New York: Routledge, 2006.

Howard, Jane. *Margaret Mead: A Life*. New York: Simon & Schuster, 1984.

Howes, Ruth H., and Caroline C. Herzenberg. *Their Day in the Sun: Women of the Manhattan Project*. Philadelphia: Temple University Press, 1999.

Hunner, Jon. *J. Robert Oppenheimer, the Cold War, and the Atomic West*. Norman, OK: University of Oklahoma Press, 2009.

Jamison, Kay Redfield. *Night Falls Fast: Understanding Suicide*. New York: Alfred A. Knopf, 1999.

Jamison, Kay Redfield. *An Unquiet Mind: A Memoir of Moods and Madness*. New York: Vintage, 1995.

Jenkins, Edith A. *Against a Field Sinister: Memoirs and Stories.* San Francisco: City Lights, 1991.

Jette, Eleanor. *Inside Box 1663.* Los Alamos, NM: Los Alamos Historical Society, 1977.

Jones, Ernest. *The Life and Work of Sigmund Freud.* New York: Basic Books, 1957.

Jones, Vincent C. *Manhattan: The Army and the Atomic Bomb.* Washington, D.C.: Center of Military History, United States Army, 1985.

Jungk, Robert. *Brighter than a Thousand Suns: A Personal History of the Atomic Scientists.* New York: Harcourt Brace, 1958.

Kamen, Martin. *Radiant Science, Dark Politics: A Memoir of the Nuclear Age.* Berkeley: University of California Press, 1985.

Karier, Clarence J. *Scientists of the Mind: Intellectual Founders of Modern Psychology.* Urbana, IL: University of Illinois Press, 1986.

Kelly, Cynthia C., ed. *The Manhattan Project: The Birth of the Atomic Bomb in the Words of Its Creators, Eyewitnesses, and Historians.* New York: Black Dog & Leventhal, 2007.

Kipphardt, Heinar. *In the Matter of J. Robert Oppenheimer.* Translated by Ruth Speirs. New York: Hill & Wang, 1968.

Lansdale, John. *John Lansdale, Jr.—Military Service.* Privately printed, 1987.

Lapsley, Hilary. *Margaret Mead and Ruth Benedict: The Kinship of Women.* Amherst: University of Massachusetts Press, 1999.

Lilienthal, David. *The Journals of David E. Lilienthal.* Vol. 2, *The Atomic Energy Years, 1945–1950.* New York: Harper & Row, 1966.

_____. *The Journals of David E. Lilienthal.* Vol. 3, *The Venturesome Years, 1950–1955.* New York: Harper & Row, 1966.

_____. *The Journals of David E. Lilienthal.* Vol. 4, *The Road to Change, 1955–1959.* New York, Harper & Row, 1969.

_____. *The Journals of David E. Lilienthal.* Vol. 5, *The Harvest Years, 1959–1963.* New York: Harper & Row, 1971.

_____. *The Journals of David E. Lilienthal.* Vol. 6, *Creativity and Conflict, 1964–1967.* New York: Harper & Row, 1976.

Makari, George. *Revolution in Mind: The Creation of Psychoanalysis.* New York: Harper Perennial, 2009.

Mattfield, Jaquelyn A., and Carol G. Van Aken, eds. *Women and the Scientific Professions: The M.I.T. Symposium on American Women in Science and Engineering.* Westport, CT: Greenwood Press, 1965.

Margulis, Lynn. "Sunday Morning with J. Robert Oppenheimer." In *Luminous Fish: Tales of Science and Love.* White River Junction, VT: Chelsea Green Publishing, 2007.

Marquis, Donald G. "Social Psychologists in National War Agencies." *Psychological Bulletin* 41, no. 2 (1944): 469–473.

McCullough, David. *Truman.* New York: Simon & Schuster, 1992.

McMillan, Priscilla J. *The Ruin of J. Robert Oppenheimer and the Birth of the Modern Arms Race.* New York: Viking, 2005.

Merriman, Marion, and Warren Lerude. *American Commander in Spain: Robert Hale Merriman and the Abraham Lincoln Brigade.* Reno: University of Nevada Press, 1986.

Michelmore, Peter. *The Swift Years: The Robert Oppenheimer Story.* New York: Dodd, Mead, 1969.

Millier, Brett C. *Elizabeth Bishop: Life and the Memory of It.* Berkeley: University of California Press, 1993.

Miller, James. "Clinical Psychology in the Veterans Administration." *American Psychologist* 1, no. 6 (1946): 181–189.

Miller, Perry. *Errand into the Wilderness.* Cambridge, MA: Belknap Press of Harvard University Press, 1956.

Mitford, Jessica. *A Fine Old Conflict.* New York: Alfred A. Knopf, 1977.

Monk, Ray. *Inside the Centre: The Life of J. Robert Oppenheimer.* London: Jonathan Cape, 2012.

Moore, Dana L. "The Veterans Administration and Its Training Program in Psychology." In *History of Psychotherapy: A Century of Change,* edited by Donald K. Freedheim. Washington, D.C.: American Psychological Association, 1992.

Nelson, Steve, James R. Barrett, and Rob Ruck. *Steve Nelson, American Radical.* Pittsburgh, PA: University of Pittsburgh Press, 1981.

New York Civil War Muster Roll Abstracts, 1861–1900. Archive Collection 13775-83, Box 533; Roll 189. New York State Archives. www.Ancestry.com

Norris, Robert S. *Racing for the Bomb: General Leslie R. Groves, The Manhattan Project's Indispensable Man* (South Royalton, VT: Steerforth Press, 2002).

Nye, Mary Jo. *Blackett: Physics, War, and Politics in the Twentieth Century.* Cambridge, MA: Harvard University Press, 2004.

Oppenheimer, Frank. "In Defense of Titular Heroes." *Physics Today* (February 1969): 77–80.

Oppenheimer, J. Robert. *The Flying Trapeze: Three Crises for Physicists.* London: Oxford University Press, 1964.

_____. "Neils Bohr and Atomic Weapons." *New York Review of Books,* December 17, 1964.

_____. *The Open Mind.* New York: Simon & Schuster, 1955.

_____. *Uncommon Sense*. Boston: Birkhäuser, 1984.

Pais, Abraham. *J. Robert Oppenheimer: A Life*. With supplemental material by Robert P. Crease. Oxford: Oxford University Press, 2006.

_____. *A Tale of Two Continents: A Physicist's Life in a Turbulent World*. Princeton, NJ: Princeton University Press, 1997.

Palevsky, Mary. *Atomic Fragments: A Daughter's Questions*. Berkeley: University of California Press, 2000.

Pash, Boris T. *The Alsos Mission*. New York: Award House, 1969.

Pfau, Richard. *No Sacrifice Too Great: The Life of Lewis L. Strauss*. Charlottesville, VA: University of Virginia Press, 1984.

Polenberg, Richard, ed. *In the Matter of J. Robert Oppenheimer: The Security Clearance Hearing*. Ithaca, NY: Cornell University Press, 2002.

Powers, Thomas. *Heisenberg's War: The Secret History of the German Bomb*. New York: Alfred A. Knopf, 1993.

Proust, Marcel. *In Remembrance of Things Past*. Vol. 1, *Swann's Way and Within a Budding Grove*. Pleiade edition. Translated by C. K. Scott Moncrieff and Terence Kilmartin. Vintage ed. New York: Random House, 1982.

Rabi, I. I., Robert Serber, Victor Weisskopf, Abraham Pais, and Glen T. Seaborg. *Oppenheimer*. New York: Charles Scribner's Sons, 1969.

Regis, Ed. *Who Got Einstein's Office? Eccentricity and Genius at the Institute for Advanced Study*. Cambridge, MA: Perseus, 1987.

Rhodes, Richard. *Dark Sun: The Making of the Hydrogen Bomb*. New York: Simon & Schuster, 1995.

_____. *The Making of the Atomic Bomb*. New York: Simon & Schuster, 1986.

Ritchie, Benbow F. *Edward Chace Tolman, April 14, 1886–November 19, 1959: A Biographical Memoir*. Washington, D.C.: National Academy of Sciences, 1964.

Rosenberg, Rosalind. *Changing the Subject: How the Women of Columbia Shaped the Way We Think About Sex and Politics*. New York: Columbia University Press, 2004.

Rosenstone, Robert A. *Crusade of the Left: The Lincoln Battalion in the Spanish Civil War*. New York: Pegasus, 1969.

Rossiter, Margaret W. *Women Scientists in America: Struggles and Strategies to 1940*. Baltimore, MD: Johns Hopkins University Press, 1982.

Royal, Denise. *The Story of J. Robert Oppenheimer*. New York: St. Martin's Press, 1969.

Saunders, Frances Stonor. *The Cultural Cold War: The CIA and the World of Arts and Letters*. New York: New Press, 2000.

Scarborough, Elizabeth, and Laurel Furumoto. *Untold Lives: The First Generation of American Women Psychologists.* New York: Columbia University Press, 1987.

Schweber, Silvan S. *Einstein and Oppenheimer: The Meaning of Genius.* Cambridge, MA: Harvard University Press, 2008.

_____. *In the Shadow of the Bomb: Bethe, Oppenheimer, and the Moral Responsibility of the Scientist.* Princeton, NJ: Princeton University Press, 2000.

Schwesinger, Gladys C. "Wartime Organizational Activities of Women Psychologists II: The National Council of Women Psychologists." *Journal of Consulting Psychology* 7, no. 6 (1943): 298–299.

Serber, Robert. *Peace and War: Reminiscences of a Life on the Frontiers of Science.* With Robert P. Crease. New York: Columbia University Press, 1998.

Sherman Family. Unpublished family history. Daviess County Indiana Historical Society.

Sherman, Frank Dempster. *The Ancestry of John Taylor Sherman and his Descendants.* New York: privately printed, 1915. www.Archives.org.

Sherman, Susan., ed. *May Sarton: Selected Letters, 1916–1954.* New York: W.W. Norton, 1997.

Sherwin, Martin J. *A World Destroyed: Hiroshima and Its Legacies.* 3rd ed. Stanford, CA: Stanford University Press, 2003.

Simmons, Marc. *The Little Lion of the Southwest: A Life of Manuel Antonio Chaves.* Athens, OH: Swallow Press / Ohio University Press, 1973.

Smith, Alice Kimball, and Charles Weiner, eds. *Robert Oppenheimer: Letters and Recollections.* Stanford, CA: Stanford University Press, 1995. Originally published in 1980 by Harvard University Press.

Snow, C. P. *The Physicists.* Boston: Little, Brown, 1981.

Starr, Kevin. *Endangered Dreams: The Great Depression in California.* New York: Oxford University Press, 1996.

Starr, Walter A. Allen L. Chickering, 1877–1958. *California Historical Society Quarterly* 37, no. 1 (March 1958).

Steeper, Nancy Cook. *Gatekeeper to Los Alamos: Dorothy Scarritt McKibbin.* Los Alamos, NM: Los Alamos Historical Society, 2003.

Stein, Murray, ed. *Jungian Analysis.* 2nd ed. Chicago: Open Court Publishing, 1995.

Stern, Philip M. *The Oppenheimer Case: Security on Trial.* New York: Harper & Row, 1969.

Stevens, Elizabeth C. "Elizabeth Buffum Chace and Lillie Chace Wyman." www.Quahog.org.

_____. *Elizabeth Buffum Chace and Lillie Chace Wyman: A Century of Abolitionist, Suffragist, and Workers' Rights Activism.* Jefferson, NC: McFarland, 2004.

Strauss, Lewis. *Men and Decisions.* New York: Doubleday, 1962.

Tatlock, J. S. P. "Nostra Maxima Culpa." Supplement, *Proceedings of the Modern Language Association* 53 (1938): 1313.

Tatlock, William. *Drunkenness and its Remedy: Sermons Preached in St. John's Church. Stamford, February 12, and March 19, 1882.* Stamford, CT: Wm. W. Gillespie & Co. Undated pamphlet.

Teller, Edward. *Memoirs: A Twentieth-Century Journey in Science and Politics.* With Judith Shoolery. Cambridge, MA: Perseus Publishing, 2001.

Thorpe, Charles. *Oppenheimer: The Tragic Intellect.* Chicago: University of Chicago Press, 2006.

Tolman, Ruth S. "Psychological Services in the War." *Women's Work and Education.* 14, no. 5 (1943): 1–4.

_____. "Some Work of Women Psychologists in the War." *Journal of Consulting Psychology* 7 (1943): 127–131.

_____. "The Subcommittee on the Services of Women Psychologists in the Emergency." *Psychological Bulletin* 40, no. 1 (1943): 50–56.

_____. (1942). "Tentative Suggestions on Undergraduate Psychological Training for Women in the Emergency." *Psychological Bulletin* 39, no. 6 (1942): 406–407.

_____. "Virtue Rewarded and Vice Punished." *American Psychologist* 8, no. 12 (1953): 721–733.

_____. "Wartime Organizational Activities of Women Psychologists I: Subcommittee of the Emergency Committee on the Services of Women Psychologists." *Journal of Consulting Psychology* 7, no. 6 (1943): 296–297.

Tolman, Ruth S. and H. J. Eysenck. "Wisdom Tempered by Prejudice." *Contemporary Psychology* 2, no. 9 (1957): 244–245.

Tolman, Ruth, and Harry M. Grayson. "A Semantic Study of Concepts of Clinical Psychologists and Psychiatrists." *Journal of Abnormal and Social Psychology* 45, no. 2 (1950): 216–231.

Tolman, Ruth S. and M. M. Meyer. "Who Returns to the Clinic for More Therapy?" *Mental Hygiene* 41 (1957): 497–506.

Weisskopf, Victor. *The Joy of Insight: Passions of a Physicist.* New York: Basic Books, 1991.

Wicker, Tom. *Shooting Star: The Brief Arc of Joe McCarthy.* Orlando, FL: Harcourt, 2006.

Winkler, Allan M. *Home Front U.S.A.: America During World War II.* Wheeling, IL: Harlan Davidson, 2000.

_____. *The Politics of Propaganda: The Office of War Information, 1942–1945.* New Haven, CT: Yale University Press, 1974.

Winks, Robin. *Cloak and Gown: Scholars in the Secret War, 1939–1961.* 2nd ed. New Haven, CT: Yale University Press, 1987.

Wolverton, Mark. *A Life in Twilight: The Final Years of J. Robert Oppenheimer.* New York: St. Martin's Press, 2008.

Wyman, Anne Cabot. *Kipling's Cat: A Memoir of My Father.* Rockport, MA: Protean Press, 2010.

York, Herbert F. *The Advisors: Oppenheimer, Teller, and the Superbomb.* San Francisco, CA: W.H. Freeman, 1976.

Photo Credits

The Bancroft Library, University of California, Berkeley (Bancroft)

Courtesy of the Archives, California Institute of Technology (Caltech)

Alfred Eisenstadt/Time & Life Pictures/Getty Images (Eisenstadt)

Getty Images (Getty)

J. Robert Oppenheimer Memorial Committee Photographs (JROMC)

Los Alamos Historical Society (LAHS)

Los Alamos National Laboratory (LANL)

Martin Sherwin Collection at Library of Congress (MSC)

Peuning/Vissering Family Photographs, Courtesy of Martin Vissering (VFP)

Ramseyer Family Photographs, Courtesy of Helene Dickel and Lin Clayberg (RFP)

Taniment Library & Robert F. Wagner Labor Archives, NYU (TL)

Tatlock Family Photographs, Courtesy of John Tatlock (TFP)

Oppenheimer Family Photographs, Courtesy of Peter Oppenheimer (OFP)

page 149: Robert and Ella Oppenheimer (JROMC); page 150: Robert Oppenheimer (JROMC), Kitty Oppenheimer (MSC); page 151: Jean Tatlock (TFP), Ruth Sherman Tolman (Caltech); page 152: Baby Kitty, Kitty and Kaethe Puening (OFP), Robert and Julius Oppenheimer (JROMC), Jean Tatlock (TFP); page 153: Jean Tatlock (TFP); page 154: Jean and Hugh Tatlock (TFP), Robert Oppenheimer (JROMC); page 155: Kitty and grandparents, Kitty and Kaethe Puening, Kitty and Franz Puening (MSC); page 156–157: Kitty and German family (OFP); page 158: Frank Ramscyer (RFP), Joe Dallet (TL); page 159: Kitty Oppenheimer (MSC); page 160: Jean Tatlock, Hugh Tatlock (TFP); page 161: Ruth Tolman, Ruth and Richard Tolman (Caltech); page 162: Jean Tatlock (TFP); page 163: Jean Tatlock

(TFP); page 164: Haakon Chevalier (Bancroft), J. S. P. Tatlock (TFP); page 165: Marjorie, John and Jean Tatlock at Vassar graduation (TFP), Robert and Crisis (JROMC); page 166: Ruth and Richard Tolman at blackboard, Ruth and Richard Tolman at home (Caltech); page 167: Richard Tolman (Bancroft), Ruth Valentine passport (Ancestry.com); page 168: Robert and Peter, Robert feeding Peter (JROMC), Stewart Harrison at Caltech (Caltech), Kitty and Peter (JROMC); page 169: Jean Tatlock (TFP); page 170: Oppenheimer home at Los Alamos (LAHS); page 171: Kitty at laboratory (MSC), Robert at party (MSC) , Kitty smoking on sofa (JROMC), Jean Tatlock (TFP); page 172: Kitty in chair (MSC), Robert with colleagues (JROMC); page 173: Richard Tolman receiving his OBE (Caltech), Ruth Tolman (Caltech), Kitty and her parents at Olden Manor (Getty/Eisenstadt); page 174: Kitty and Robert in Japan (JROMC), Kitty and Robert with Pearl Buck (Getty), Robert receiving the Fermi Award (JROMC); page 175: Oppenheimer family on beach (JROMC), Toni (JROMC); page 177: Kitty sailing (MSC)

INDEX

About the Authors

Shirley Streshinsky is the critically acclaimed author of three works of nonfiction and four historical novels. As a journalist and travel essayist, she has written extensively for *Redbook, Glamour, Preservation, American Heritage, The American Scholar,* and *Condé Nast Traveler* and has been featured on NPR. She is the recipient of the Society of Magazine Writers' Award for Excellence and the National Council for the Advancement of Education Writing Award. She was married to the late photojournalist Ted Streshinsky and has three grown children. She lives in Kensington (Berkeley), California.

Patricia Klaus received her Ph.D. in history from Stanford where she specialized in women's studies, the history of marriage, and the study of war and literature. She has taught at Yale, Stanford, and the University of Virginia and has published scholarly papers on the subject of women. Klaus lives with her husband and two sons on a farm in Sonoma County, California.

Printed in the USA
CPSIA information can be obtained
at www.ICGtesting.com
JSHW021719310723
45679JS00001B/17